PIDGINS AND CREOLES
Volume I
Theory and Structure

CAMBRIDGE LANGUAGE SURVEYS

General Editors: B. Comrie, C. J. Fillmore, R. Lass, R. B. Le Page, J. Lyons, P. H. Matthews, F. R. Palmer, R. Posner, S. Romaine, N. V. Smith, J. L. M. Trim, A. Zwicky

This series offers general accounts of all the major language families of the world. Some volumes are organized on a purely genetic basis, others on a geographical basis, whichever yields the most convenient and intelligible grouping in each case. Sometimes, as with the Australian volume, the two in any case coincide.

Each volume compares and contrasts the typological features of the languages it deals with. It also treats the relevant genetic relationships, historic development, and sociolinguistic issues arising from their role and use in the world today. The intended readership is the student of linguistics or general linguist, but no special knowledge of the languages under consideration is assumed. Some volumes also have a wider appeal, like that on Australia, where the future of the languages and their speakers raises important social and political issues.

Already published:
The languages of Australia *R. M. W. Dixon*
The languages of the Soviet Union *Bernard Comrie*
The Mesoamerican Indian languages *Jorge A. Suárez*
The Papuan languages of New Guinea *William A. Foley*
Chinese *Jerry Norman*
Pidgin and crole languages, Volumes I and II *J. Holm*
The languages of Japan *M. Shibatani*
The Indo-Aryan languages *Colin P. Masica*

Forthcoming titles include:
Korean *Ho-min Sohn*
The languages of South-East Asia *J. A. Matisoff*
Austronesian languages *R. Blust*
Slavonic languages *R. Sussex*
Germanic languages *R. Lass*
Celtic languages *D. MacAulay et al.*
Romance languages *R. Posner*
The languages of Native North America *Marianne Mithun*

PIDGINS AND CREOLES

Volume I
Theory and Structure

JOHN A. HOLM

Hunter College and Graduate Center,
City University of New York

CAMBRIDGE
UNIVERSITY PRESS

Published by the Press Syndicate of the University of Cambridge
The Pitt Building, Trumpington Street, Cambridge CB2 1RP
40 West 20th Street, New York, NY 10011-4211, USA
10 Stamford Road, Oakleigh, Melbourne 3166, Australia

First published 1988
Reprinted 1991, 1993, 1995

British Library cataloguing in publication data
Holm, John
Pidgins and creoles.—
(Cambridge language surveys).
Vol. 1: Theory and Structure
1. Creole dialects   2. Pidgin languages
I. Title
417'.2   PM7802

Library of Congress cataloguing in publication data
Holm, John A.
Pidgins and creoles.
(Cambridge language surveys)
Includes index.
Contents: v. 1. Theory and structure.
1. Pidgin languages.   2. Creole dialects.
I. Title.   II. Series.
PM7802.H65   1988   417'.2   87-22408

ISBN 0 521 24980 5 hard covers
ISBN 0 521 27108 8 paperback

EA

Transferred to digital printing 1999

For Michael

CONTENTS

x *Contents*

PREFACE

The study of those mixed languages called pidgins and creoles has become established as an academic discipline only within the past few decades. Its value has been recognized by a growing number of scholars, not only in general linguistics but also in other fields such as sociology, anthropology, history, and education. Yet both the matter and significance of individuals' research have too often remained unknown even to those within the field. Studying over a hundred language varieties scattered around the globe, researchers have tended to work on particular varieties in relative isolation, missing the more general insights gained by others because of the near impossibility of knowing enough about all the other varieties to be sure to what extent their development and structure were parallel and therefore relevant. This fragmentation of the discipline has been compounded by the frequent inaccessibility of studies published in a great many countries – and in a daunting array of languages.

This work is intended, therefore, as a corrective: a comprehensive survey of the field that will not only serve as an introduction for the general reader with some basic knowledge of linguistics, but also provide a general overview for specialists, making clear the relevance of the work of others. Having this survey in a single work by a single author makes possible the orderly presentation of the most important knowledge gained so far about pidgin and creole languages, their genesis and development, and about the bearing this information has on linguistics in general as well as on related disciplines.

This book has two volumes. The first, which can be used independently, provides an introduction to the discipline, an overview of theory, and studies of the principal linguistic structures that this theory has attempted to account for.

The introductory chapter defines the scope of the discipline and of the present work. Chapter 2 discusses theory, providing a general orientation to the possible frameworks for dealing with the linguistic and sociohistorical material to follow. Because the forms that theories have taken at various periods can be understood better in the context of those times and of what led up to them, the development of theory is presented in approximately chronological order. This also provides a framework for discussing the history of the discipline at these various stages, as well as the contemporary development of pidgin and creole languages. The next three chapters form a unit of comparative studies of various linguistic features of the group of languages that has been a primary focus of research in this field. These features are organized by linguistic level: lexicosemantics (chapter 3), phonology (chapter 4), and syntax (chapter 5).

The second volume is a reference survey of the known pidgin and creole languages. Criteria for inclusion generally follow those in the standard bibliography (Reinecke *et al.* 1975), although in some cases evidence regarding the status of a particular variety has since come to light and led to a reassessment of the appropriateness of its inclusion. In general all of the varieties included fit the definitions of pidgins and creoles discussed in chapter 1 except for several whose distinct or ambiguous identity is clearly indicated. These have been included because of their traditional place in the literature, stemming from their important historical relationship to restructured varieties   (e.g. Réunionnais and other semi-creoles). Sections on individual pidgins or creoles begin with a summary of the sociohistorical events that shaped their development, followed by a description of the current sociolinguistic situation. After a discussion of some of the variety's salient linguistic features, there is a brief text with a morpheme-by-morpheme translation. Whenever possible, these texts have been selected from connected discourse phonemically represented in the international phonetic alphabet. Varieties have been grouped by the language from which they drew their lexicon. Although it has been proposed that this factor is of limited relevance in working out the interrelationship of varieties (e.g. Taylor 1971), it is the conclusion of the present study that there are convincing historical and linguistic reasons to retain these lexical groupings. The varieties within each group were often originally spoken by people who were part of the same political and economic system, so linguistic features were more likely to spread from one variety to another via diffusion. Moreover, the varieties within each group obviously had similar linguistic input from their common source of lexicon, and this has resulted in structural features that are confined to particular lexical groups. Finally, having chapters by lexical groupings provides a more convenient structure for discussing those historical factors and linguistic features common to all varieties within each group. As far as possible, the presentation of sections on particular varieties follows the historical order of their origin, often related to a geographical order; this has been done to make clearer their sociohistorical interrelationship.

While having a single author for such a survey permits greater order and consistency, it also presents a fundamental problem: the scope simply exceeds the competence of any individual. For this reason I am deeply grateful for the help of over 150 colleagues who read the first drafts of those sections that correspond to their areas of specialization, correcting my errors, misinterpretations and omissions: Ralph Adendorff, Robert Allen, Mervyn Alleyne, Philip Baker, Willy Bal, R. K. Barz, Rebecca Bateman, David Bedford, Jorge Bernal, Derek Bickerton, Kenneth Bilby, Annegret Bollée, Lucey Bowen, Maria Luiza Braga, Ingvild Broch, Frank Byrne, Lawrence Carrington, Hazel Carter, Frederic Cassidy, Juan Caudmont, Jean-Michel Charpentier, Robert Chaudenson, Pearly Koh Lye Choo, Pauline Christie, Michael Clyne, J. T. Collins, Vincent Cooper, Chris Corne, Terry Crowley, Dina Dahbany-Miraglia, Charles De Bose, Germán de Granda, K. N. O. Dharmadasa, Marta Dijkhoff, Norbert Dittmar, Nicole Domingue, Emanuel Drechsel, T. E. Dutton, John Edgar, Viv Edwards, Christiaan Eersel, Charlotte Emmerich, Geneviève Escure, Pablo Eyzaguirre, Nicholas Faraclas, Frank Farnum, Bernadette Farquhar, Joan Fayer, Joshua Fishman, Michael Forman, Surendra Gambhir, Glenn Gilbert, Charles Gilman, Naomi Glock, Manfred Görlach, Wilfried Günther, Gwendolyn Hall, Robert A. Hall, Jr., John McG. Harris, John W. Harris, Shirley Harrison, Bernd Heine, Marlis Hellinger, Anita Herzfeld, David Hodges, Maurice Holder, K. J. Hollyman, Annie Huiskamp, Alexander Hull, John Hutchison, Martha Isaac, Kenneth Jackson, Ernst Hakon Jåhr, F. C. Jones, Yamina Kachru, Terrence Kaufman, Alain Kihm, Jan Knappert, Ernst Kotzé, Silvia Kouwenberg, Suzanne Lafage, Roger Lass, William Leap, Ernst Lee, Claire Lefebvre, Gilles Lefebvre, Ilse Lehiste, Nguyen Dang Liem, John Lipski, Pearlette Louisy, Helen McKinney, Merrill McLane, Dennis Makhudu, Rodney Moag, Peggy Mohan, Raleigh Morgan, Peter Mühlhäusler, Rita Munson, Pieter Muysken, Ingrid Neumann, Patricia Nichols, Ricardo Otheguy, Jonathan Owens, James Park, Carlos Patiño Roselli, Matthias Perl, John Platt, Edgar Polomé, Shana Poplack, Richard Price, Edith Raidt, Yves Renard, Richard Rhodes, John Rickford, Ian Robertson, Janina Rubinowitz, Robin Sabino, Hugues St. Fort, William Samarin, John Sandefur, Charlene Sato, Josef Schmied, Carol Scotton, Mark Sebba, Michael Shapiro, Suhnu Sharma, Alison Shilling, Anna Shnukal, Jeff Siegel, Ian Smith, Norval Smith, John Spencer, M. V. Sreedhar, Meena Srithar, Charles Stansifer, Thomas Stolz, Stephanie Stuart, Paul Teyssier, Loreto Todd, Peter Trudgill, Stanley Tsuzaki, Albert Valdman, M. C. J. van Rensburg, Dirk van Schalkwyk, José Vigo, William Washabaugh, Herman Wekker, John Wells, Paul Wexler, Keith Whinnom, Jeffrey Williams, Ruth Williams, John Wilner, Lise Winer, Richard Wood, Hugh Young, Ana Celia Zentella, Douglas Val Ziegler, and Peter Bakker.

I am particularly thankful to those colleagues who offered critical comments, in welcome detail, on a number of chapters or the entire manuscript: Norbert Boretzky, Hans den Besten, Morris Goodman, Ian F. Hancock, George Huttar, Luiz Ivens Ferraz, Philippe Maurer, Salikoko S. Mufwene, John Singler, William A. Stewart, and Sarah Grey Thomason.

I am also grateful to the students in my creoles courses at New York University and University College London whose reactions to my lectures based on the first draft of this book allowed me to make improvements.

I am most indebted to those who bore with me over the five years and numerous deadlines that it took to prepare this book: my editor, Penny Carter; my linguistics (and sociolinguistics!) editor, R. B. Le Page; and my friend and advisor, Michael Pye.

Although this book would have been impossible without the help of these many colleagues, of course I alone remain responsible for its shortcomings.

Finally, I am happy to acknowledge my indebtedness for several awards that supported the preparation of this book: George N. Shuster faculty fellowships from Hunter College of the City University of New York (1982, 1984, 1986); a summer stipend from the National Endowment for the Humanities (1984); sabbatical leave from Hunter College, and a Fulbright award to complete the final draft at University College London (1986–87).

John Holm
New York
September, 1987

ABBREVIATIONS

See also key to maps 1 and 2.

ANT	anterior
ASP	aspect
AUX	auxiliary
C	complement
	consonant
INF	infinitive
LOC	locative
N	nasal
NEG	negative
NP	noun phrase
O	object
p.c.	personal communication
POSS	possessive
PROG	progressive
QW	question word
S	subject
TMA	tense–mode–aspect
V	verb
	vowel
VP	verb phrase

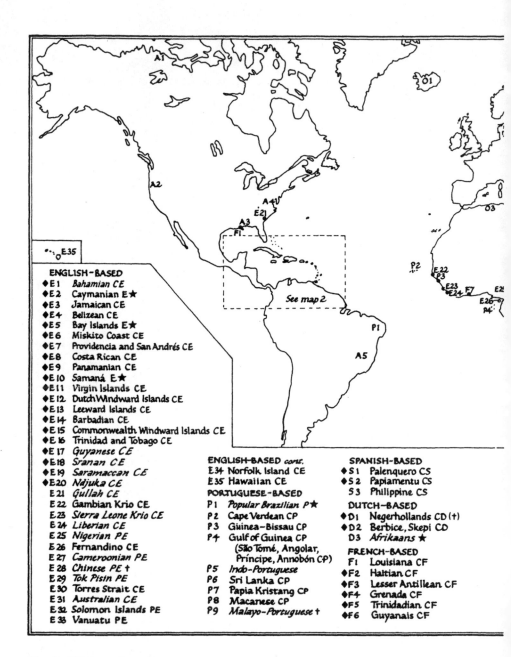

ENGLISH-BASED
- ◆E1 *Bahamian* CE
- ◆E2 *Caymanian* E★
- ◆E3 *Jamaican* CE
- ◆E4 *Belizean* CE
- ◆E5 *Bay Islands* E★
- ◆E6 *Miskito Coast* CE
- ◆E7 *Providencia and San Andrés* CE
- ◆E8 *Costa Rican* CE
- ◆E9 *Panamanian* CE
- ◆E10 *Samaná* E★
- ◆E11 *Virgin Islands* CE
- ◆E12 *Dutch Windward Islands* CE
- ◆E13 *Leeward Islands* CE
- ◆E14 *Barbadian* CE
- ◆E15 *Commonwealth Windward Islands* CE
- ◆E16 *Trinidad and Tobago* CE
- ◆E17 *Guyanese CE*
- ◆E18 *Sranan CE*
- ◆E19 *Saramaccan CE*
- ◆E20 *Ndjuka CE*
- E21 *Gullah CE*
- E22 *Gambian Krio* CE
- E23 *Sierra Leone Krio* CE
- E24 *Liberian* CE
- E25 *Nigerian* PE
- E26 *Fernandino* CE
- E27 *Cameroonian* PE
- E28 *Chinese* PE †
- E29 *Tok Pisin* PE
- E30 *Torres Strait* CE
- E31 *Australian* CE
- E32 *Solomon Islands* PE
- E33 *Vanuatu* PE

ENGLISH-BASED *cont.*
- E34 *Norfolk Island* CE
- E35 *Hawaiian* CE

PORTUGUESE-BASED
- P1 *Popular Brazilian* P★
- P2 *Cape Verdean* CP
- P3 *Güinea–Bissau* CP
- P4 *Gulf of Guinea* CP
  (São Tomé, Angolar, Príncipe, Annobón CP)
- P5 *Indo-Portuguese*
- P6 *Sri Lanka* CP
- P7 *Papia Kristang* CP
- P8 *Macanese* CP
- P9 *Malayo-Portuguese* †

SPANISH-BASED
- ◆S1 Palenquero CS
- ◆S2 Papiamentu CS
- S3 Philippine CS

DUTCH-BASED
- ◆D1 Negerhollands CD (†)
- ◆D2 Berbice, Skepi CD
- D3 *Afrikaans* ★

FRENCH-BASED
- F1 Louisiana CF
- ◆F2 Haitian CF
- ◆F3 Lesser Antillean CF
- ◆F4 Grenada CF
- ◆F5 Trinidadian CF
- ◆F6 Guyanais CF

See map 2

Map 1   Pidgins and creoles

xvi

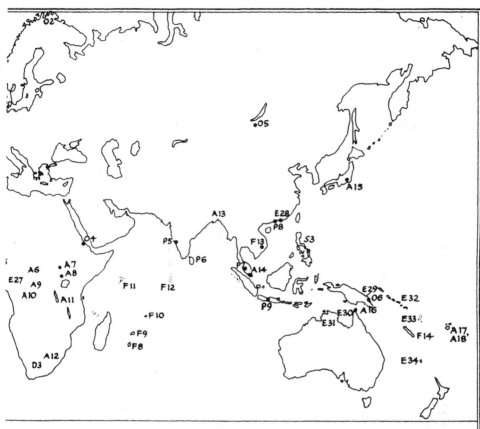

ENGLISH-BASED
E1 *Bahamian CE*
E2 Caymanian E ★
E3 Jamaican CE
E4 *Belizean CE*
E5 Bay Islands E ★
E6 Miskito Coast CE
E7 Providencia and San Andrés CE
E8 Costa Rican CE
E9 Panamanian CE
E10 Samaná E ★
E11 Virgin Islands CE
E12 Dutch Windward Islands CE
E13 Leeward Islands CE
E14 Barbadian CE
E15 Commonwealth Windward Islands CE
E16 Trinidad and Tobago CE

ENGLISH-BASED *cont.*
E17 *Guyanese CE*
E18 *Sranan CE*
E19 *Saramaccan CE*
E20 *Ndjuka CE*
SPANISH-BASED
S1 *Palenquero CS*
S2 *Papiamentu CS*
DUTCH-BASED
D1 Negerhollands CD (†)
D2 Berbice, Skepi CD
FRENCH-BASED
F2 *Haitian CF*
F3 *Lesser Antillean CF*
F4 *Grenada CF*
F5 *Trinidadian CF*
F6 *Guyanais CF*

Map 2 Caribbean creoles

ATLANTIC

OCEAN

VIRGIN
ISLANDS
E11, D1
Anguila
St.Martin
E 12
Saba
St.Kitts
Nevis
E13
Antigua
Montserrat
Guadeloupe — F3
LEEWARD
ISLANDS
Dominica — F3
Martinique
WINDWARD
St.Lucia
St.Vincent
ISLANDS
E15
F4
Grenada
Barbados
E14

HAITI
F2
DOMINICAN
REP.
E10
PUERTO
RICO

SEA

Aruba
S2
Bonaire
Curaçao

Tobago
Trinidad
E 16, F5

VENEZUELA

E 17
D2
GUYANA
E 18
E 19
E20
SURINAME
F6
FRENCH
GUIANA

B I A

| 0 | 500 | 1000 km |
| 0 | 500 miles | |

†   Extinct
★   Semi-creole
Italics   Spoken over a wider area

1

Introduction

1.0 Pidgins and creoles and linguistics

What earlier generations thought of pidgin and creole languages is all too clear from their very names: *broken English, bastard Portuguese, nigger French, kombuistaaltje* ('cookhouse lingo'), *isikula* ('coolie language'). This contempt often stemmed in part from the feeling that pidgins and creoles were corruptions of "higher," usually European languages, and in part from attitudes toward the speakers of such languages, who were often perceived as semi-savages whose partial acquisition of civilized habits was somehow an affront. Those speakers of creole languages who had access to education were duly convinced that their speech was wrong, and they often tried to make it more similar to the standard. With few exceptions, even linguists thought of pidgin and creole languages as "aberrant" (Bloomfield 1933: 471) if they thought of them at all – that is, as defective and therefore inappropriate as objects of serious study. The analogy seemed to be that broken English, for example, was of as little interest to the linguist as a broken diamond would be to a gemologist.

It is only comparatively recently that linguists have realized that pidgins and creoles are not wrong versions of other languages but, rather, *new* languages. Their words were largely taken from an older language during a period of linguistic crisis to fill an urgent need for communication. This makes them appear to be deformed versions of that older language. But if one examines them as linguistic *systems*, analyzing the structure of their phonology, syntax, and word formation, it becomes evident that these systems are quite different from those of the language from which they drew their lexicon (their *lexical source* or *base language*). Their systems are so different, in fact, that they can hardly be considered as even dialects of their base language. They are new languages, shaped by many of the same linguistic forces that shaped English and other "proper" languages.

Pidgins and creoles were largely ignored by earlier linguists not only because of this misunderstanding of their identity, but also because of the prevailing notion of what language was and why it was worth studying. In western Europe this notion had grown out of the Roman tradition of rhetoric: the cultivation and refinement of language for public speaking and writing. During the millennium that western Europeans retained Latin as their medium of writing, it was a foreign language that had to be taught prescriptively, with definite rules as to what was right and wrong. As western European languages came to replace Latin in serious writing, the idea that there could be only one correct form was transferred to them after an initial period of flux. The rise of modern European states reinforced the idea of a language – a relatively uniform variety used by the educated and ruling classes in speaking and writing – as opposed to a dialect – the uncultivated speech of the masses, changing from one locality to another. The appearance of uniformity of written languages was further reinforced by the advent of printing, which hastened the standardization of orthographic conventions.

Written languages were usually studied for a quite practical reason: access to the learning stored in their literature. Languages were regarded as relatively fixed and stable entities, although dialect studies such as Dante's *De vulgari eloquentia* reflected the understanding that languages change over time as well as space. In 1863 the German linguist, August Schleicher, described languages as "natural organisms that come into being, develop, age, and die according to laws that are quite independent of man's will" (cited by Arens 1969: 259). Such a reification of language is at odds with the more current notion of language as an individual's set of habits for communicating that have largely been determined by his or her social experience, guided by an innate ability to decipher and learn the language habits of other humans. These habits for encoding one's thoughts and perceptions into verbal symbols in order to communicate them can shift to some degree with one's social circumstances; similarly, the most frequent language habits of the aggregate of individuals forming the society can also shift (Hudson 1980). Since individuals use language to communicate not only their meaning but also their social identity, they can shift their habits to signal a shift in their social allegiances; similarly, an entire speech community can shift language habits to signal a more focused or cohesive identity (Le Page and Tabouret-Keller 1985). Such an understanding of language as a dynamic part of the interrelationship between the individual and society has allowed linguists to deal with aspects of language that do not fit a static model of artificial homogeneity based on standardized languages. Thus it is only relatively recently that linguists have begun to study language that appears to lack order: the speech of very young children, foreigners, aphasics, and linguistically heterogeneous communities.

The more social view of language began with a nineteenth-century philologist who realized that some western European languages had not only ancestors but also descendants in the form of creoles. This early creolist was Hugo Schuchardt, a student of Schleicher's who rejected his idea of language as a natural organism that followed natural laws such as regular sound change, which the Neo-grammarians held to be without exception. Schuchardt's interest in challenging this theory led him to the creoles, in which sound changes were often irregular because language mixing had disrupted the internally motivated historical sound changes that might be expected in languages in isolation. Schuchardt came to realize that individuals play an important role in the social process leading to language mixture: "Old and new forms are distributed . . . within a single dialect according to sex, education, temperament, in short in the most diverse manner" (1885: 18, cited by Fought 1982: 425). Schuchardt's concern with the social matrix of language change marks him as nearly a century ahead of his time, but his work received only limited attention from his contemporaries. Most linguists continued to consider pidgins and creoles freakish exceptions that were irrelevant to any theory of "normal" language. Yet Reinecke (1937: 6) realized that, because of their very nature, pidgins and creoles could offer important insights into the study of language: "What some Germans have ambitiously called the sociology of language (*Sprachsoziologie*) is still in its infancy . . . Among the localities most suitable for special studies are those in which the marginal languages are spoken. Changes there have been very rapid and pronounced. Languages can be observed taking form within a man's lifetime."

Since the establishment of pidgin and creole studies as an academic discipline in the late 1950s and early 1960s, it has become clear that the linguistic forces that shape pidgins and creoles are exceptional only in that they are indeed "very rapid and pronounced." Moreover, research on the processes of pidginization and creolization has led to important advances in a number of areas of applied and theoretical linguistics. Studies of creole continua (§2.11) led to the development of implicational scaling in linguistics. Labov's work on variation in American Black English (a semi-creole: see §1.3) laid the foundation for modern sociolinguistics, which has in turn cast new light on language change as being socially motivated. Pidginization and creolization have become important to historical linguists as extreme examples of contact-induced language change which challenge the validity of some traditional assumptions about the genetic relatedness of languages, particularly in the family tree model and glottochronology (§2.9). This has brought us closer to a method for establishing whether a language was previously creolized, using both linguistic and sociohistorical data (e.g. Rickford 1977).

A better understanding of pidginization has also contributed to our understanding of the acquisition of second languages (e.g. Andersen 1983), while first-language acquisition theory has been challenged by the concept of the innate bioprogram (§2.12), developed by Bickerton (1981) in the context of creolization theory and having, he claims, implications for the origin of all languages and even language itself. Finally, work on the role that language universals might play in pidginization (Kay and Sankoff 1974) as well as creolization has focused attention on the very nature of universals, thus contributing to grammatical theory.

The practical value of pidgin and creole studies is also considerable. Because these languages were traditionally not written, their speakers have usually had to learn literacy in a foreign or quasi-foreign language, often the lexical source language. Yet because the restructured variety's separate identity or very existence frequently received no official acknowledgment, the (quasi-) foreign language of literacy and instruction was taught as the child's mother tongue – that is, not taught at all. This has caused serious educational problems for the millions who speak creoles in the Caribbean area, and for the scores of millions who speak post-creoles and semi-creoles (§1.3) in such countries as the United States, Brazil, and Australia. Creolists from Caribbean countries have taken the lead in applying the results of their linguistic research to practical problems in education, and they are not alone. However, there is still an enormous amount of work to be done simply to describe these restructured varieties so that educators can understand clearly what the first language of their pupils actually is.

In Papua New Guinea and Vanuatu in the South Pacific area, English-based pidgins have been raised to the status of national languages for the practical reason that they have nationwide currency. Scholars of pidgin and creole languages have taken an active and influential role in language planning in both countries. Several creoles are also being given such status in the Cape Verde Islands, Guinea-Bissau, and the Netherlands Antilles, and creolists from these and other countries are engaged in practical projects from lexicography to the preparation of teaching materials.

1.1 Pidgins

There are problems in defining the most basic concepts in language: *word*, *sentence*, *dialect*, and even *language* itself. Our definitions, like our grammars, often leak: they fail to account for the endless variety of reality. Yet a clear understanding of concepts is important: they are the building blocks we use to construct our theories to account for that reality. The definitions below are presented as straightforwardly as possible in an effort to make them intelligible and useful; their problems and weaknesses will be briefly indicated in the ensuing discussion, and it is hoped that the material that follows in the rest of this volume and the next will make the full implications of their weaknesses clearer. They will be discussed again at the end of volume II.

A *pidgin* is a reduced language that results from extended contact between groups of people with no language in common; it evolves when they need some means of verbal communication, perhaps for trade, but no group learns the native language of any other group for social reasons that may include lack of trust or of close contact. Usually those with less power (speakers of *substrate* languages) are more accommodating and use words from the language of those with more power (the *superstrate*), although the meaning, form, and use of these words may be influenced by the substrate languages. When dealing with the other groups, the superstrate speakers adopt many of these changes to make themselves more readily understood, and no longer try to speak as they do within their own group. They co-operate with the other groups to create a make-shift language to serve their needs, simplifying by dropping unnecessary complications such as inflections (e.g. *two knives* becomes *two knife*) and reducing the number of different words they use, but compensating by extending their meanings or using circumlocutions. By definition the resulting pidgin is restricted to a very limited domain such as trade, and it is no one's native language (Hymes 1971: 43).

Although individuals can simplify and reduce their language on an *ad hoc* basis (for example, New Yorkers buying sunglasses in Lisbon), this results not in a pidgin but a *jargon* with no fixed norms. A pidgin is more stable and has certain norms of meaning, pronunciation, and grammar, although there is still variation resulting from the transfer of features from speakers' first languages. It has been suggested that such stabilization requires *tertiary hybridization*, in which two or more groups of substrate speakers adopt the pidgin for communicating with each other. If superstrate speakers become the least important part of this pidgin triangle and close contact is established and maintained between substrate speakers over an extended period of time, an *expanded pidgin* results: the simpler structure of the earlier pidgin is elaborated to meet more demanding communicative needs (Mühlhäusler 1986: 5).

This description distinguishes pidgins from the imperfect speech of foreigners in other social situations, when native speakers of the target language do not try to follow the foreigners' imperfect version of it, and this does not become established or stabilized. However, two further stipulations are needed to distinguish pidgins from other kinds of language contact. First, social distance must be maintained between speakers of the superstrate and the other languages; otherwise if the substrate speakers so desired, they could eventually acquire enough information about the superstrate language to speak it in a non-pidginized form (Valdman 1978: 9–10). Secondly, it must be assumed that the languages in contact are not closely related, in which case *koineization* or a kind of dialect leveling would result (§1.3). Finally it should be noted that contact languages can evolve between trading partners of approximately equal power, such as Russenorsk (§12.17.1).

Such varieties, if they are indeed stable pidgins rather than jargons, tend to draw their vocabulary more equally from both languages – sometimes even to refer to the same things.

The following is a text of Melanesian Pidgin English, Tok Pisin (cf. 'talk pidgin') used in Papua New Guinea (§10.8.3.1); it is from Hall (1966: 149):

naw mi stap rebawl. mi stap lɔŋ bɪglajn,   mi kətɪm kopra. naw wənfɛlə
Then I   stay Rabaul. I was in work-group, I cut   copra. Then a

mastər   bɪlɔŋ kəmpəni ɛm i-kɪčɪm mi mi kʊk lɔŋ ɛm gɛn. mastər
white man from company he take   me, I cook for him again. Mister

kiŋ. mi stap. naw ɔl mastər   i-kɪk,   i-kɪkɪm
King. I stay.   Then all white men were playing football, they kick

ɛm. naw leg bɪlɔŋ ɛm i-swɛləp.
him. Then leg of   him swell up.

One of the most striking features of this text is the absence of complex phrase-level structures such as embedding. However, this recording was made by Margaret Mead some fifty years ago, when Tok Pisin was not yet widely spoken in an expanded form. Today embedded structures such as relative clauses are found not only in the speech of Tok Pisin's new native speakers, usually children of interethnic marriages growing up in a multi-ethnic urban setting, but also in the speech of adults who are not native speakers (Sankoff and Brown 1976).

1.2 Creoles

A creole has a jargon or pidgin in its ancestry; it is spoken natively by an entire speech community, often one whose ancestors were displaced geographically so that their ties with their original language and sociocultural identity were partly broken. Such social conditions were often the result of slavery. For example, from the seventeenth to the nineteenth centuries Africans of diverse ethnolinguistic groups were brought by Europeans to colonies in the New World to work together on sugar plantations. For the first generation of slaves in such a setting, the conditions were often those that produce a pidgin. Normally the Africans had no language in common except what they could learn of the Europeans' language, and access to this was usually very restricted because of the social conditions of slavery. The children born in the New World were usually exposed more to this pidgin – and found it more useful – than to their parents' native languages. Since the pidgin was a foreign language for the parents, they probably spoke it less fluently; moreover, they had a more limited vocabulary and were more restricted in their syntactic alternatives. Furthermore, each speaker's mother tongue influenced his or her use of the pidgin in different ways, so there was probably massive linguistic variation while the new speech community was being established. Although it appears that the children were given highly variable and possibly chaotic and incomplete linguistic input, they were somehow able to organize it into the creole that was their native language, an ability which may be an innate characteristic of our species. This process of *creolization* or *nativization* (in which a pidgin acquires native speakers) is still not completely understood, but it is thought to be the opposite of pidginization: a process of expansion rather than reduction (although a pidgin can be expanded without being nativized). For example, creoles have phonological rules (e.g. assimilation) not found in early pidgins. Creole speakers need a vocabulary to cover all aspects of their life, not just one domain like trade; where words were missing, they were provided by various means such as innovative combinations (e.g. Jamaican Creole *hand-middle* 'palm'). For many linguists, the most fascinating aspect of this expansion and elaboration was the reorganization of the grammar, ranging from the creation of a coherent verbal system to complex phrase-level structures such as embedding.

There are many questions about the process of creolization that remain unresolved. Is it qualitatively different from the expansion of a pidgin that does not acquire native speakers? How crucial is the uprooting of those who begin the new speech community? There are creoles whose speakers were never uprooted, such as the Portuguese-based varieties in Asia (§§6.4 to 6.6), although in a sense the Portuguese fathers of the first generations were indeed uprooted and their racially mixed progeny formed not only a new speech community but also a new ethnic group. It has been proposed (Gilman 1979) that the significant difference between creoles and extended pidgins is not nativization, since the designation of what is a "first" as opposed to a "primary" language is arbitrary and irrelevant in many multilingual contexts, but rather whether the language is one of ethnic reference. However, this does not decide the issue of whether the differences between creoles and extended pidgins are entirely social rather than linguistic. The restructured Portuguese of Guinea-Bissau (§6.2.2) is an extended pidgin for most of its speakers in that country, but a language of ethnic reference for a group in neighboring Senegal; it is not fully clear whether there are any significant linguistic differences between the two. Singler (1984:68) argues that "The evidence from other West African pidgins and, especially, from Tok Pisin argues for the rejection of the centrality of nativization in the expansion of fledgling pidgins and the recognition of the fundamental commonality of creoles with extended pidgins." Mühlhäusler (1982:452) found that "The structural consequences of creolization of Tok Pisin are less dramatic than in the case of creolization of an unstable jargon. Both Sankoff's and my own findings indicate that, instead of radical restructuring, the trends already present in expanded Tok Pisin are carried further in its creolized varieties."

Some linguists distinguish between the creolization of an extended pidgin, which is both socially and linguistically gradual, and the creolization of an early pidgin or even an unstable jargon, called early (Bickerton in Bickerton *et al.* 1984) or abrupt creolization (Thomason and Kaufman forthcoming). If Caribbean and other creoles did indeed grow out of nativized varieties of unstable pre-pidgin jargons, then the classical definition of a creole as "any language with a pidgin in its ancestry" is technically wrong. The crucial element would seem to be a variety that has been radically reduced (a jargon or a pidgin) rather than one that has stabilized (a pidgin but not a jargon). However, our knowledge of the earlier stages of particular creoles is usually quite sketchy and based on speculation rather than direct evidence. It may be prudent to reserve judgment on this issue.

There are other major issues regarding creolization that remain unresolved. To what extent did adult speakers of the pidgin or jargon help their creole-speaking children organize their speech? To what extent did these adults draw on their native languages to do this? What was the role of universal trends in the acquisition of a first or second language? These issues will be discussed in detail in chapter 2 and then evaluated at the end of volume II in light of the evidence presented in this work.

The following text (Park 1975) is in Ndjuka, an English-based creole spoken in the interior of Suriname in northern South America (§10.2.3):

Mi be go   a onti anga wan dagu fu mi.   A be wan bun onti
I   had gone hunting with a   dog of mine. He was a   good hunting

dagu. Da   fa mi waka so, a tapu   wan he   na a   olo.
dog. Then as I   walked so, he cornered an   armadillo in the hole.

A lon go   so, a tyai   wan he   kon na a   olo
He ran away so, a he brought an   armadillo   into the hole.

Note that unlike the pidgin text in Tok Pisin, the above creole text has an embedded subordinate clause, "fa mi waka so."

Before leaving our discussion of the terms *pidgin* and *creole*, a word about their origin may be of interest. The etymology of *pidgin* is uncertain, and an entire article has been devoted to it (Hancock 1979a). The *Oxford English Dictionary* derives it from the English word *business* as pronounced in Chinese Pidgin English, which was of course used for transacting business (§10.8.1). Other possible sources include the Hebrew-derived *pidjom* 'exchange, trade, redemption'; a Chinese pronunciation of the Portuguese word *ocupação* 'business'; or a South Seas pronunciation of English *beach* as *beachee*, from the location where the language was often used (Mühlhäusler 1986: 1). Lest we run out of alternatives, I will suggest Portuguese *baixo* 'low', used to distinguish pidgin Portuguese (*baixo português*) from standard Portuguese in Portugal's Asian empire during the sixteenth and seventeenth centuries. *Baixo português* was in fact the trade language that preceded pidgin English on the coast of China, and there are no more phonological problems (and certainly fewer semantic ones) in deriving *pidgin* from /baišo/ rather than from /bɪznɪs/.

The origin of the term *creole* is more certain. Latin *creāre* 'to create' became Portuguese *criar* 'to raise (e.g. a child),' whence the past participle *criado* '(a person) raised; a servant born into one's household.' *Crioulo*, with a diminutive suffix, came to mean an African slave born in the New World in Brazilian usage. The word's meaning was then extended to include Europeans born in the New World, now the only meaning of the word in Portugal. The word finally came to refer to the customs and speech of Africans and Europeans born in the New World. It was later borrowed as Spanish *criollo*, French *créole*, Dutch *creol* and English *creole*.

1.3 Other terms

In addition to those terms in italics introduced in the preceding two sections, there are some other terms to be explained here that will recur in the following chapters. They are largely confined to (or have a particular meaning in) pidgin and creole linguistics (sometimes shortened to *creolistics*; cf. French *créolistique* or German *Kreolistik*). Terms having to do with theory (e.g. *relexification, bioprogram*) will be explained in chapter 2 and can be found in the index.

In some areas where the speakers of a creole remain in contact with its lexical donor language (e.g. in Jamaica, where English is the official language), there has been a historical tendency for the creole to drop its most noticeable non-European features, often (but not always) replacing them with European ones – or what are taken to be such. This process of *decreolization* can result in a *continuum* of varieties, from those farthest from the superstrate (the *basilect*) to those closest (the *acrolect*), with *mesolectal* or intermediate varieties between them. After a number of generations some varieties lose all but a few vestiges of their creole features (those not found in the superstrate) through decreolization, resulting in *post-creole* varieties such as (according to some) American Black English (§10.6.4) or vernacular Brazilian Portuguese (§6.7). Others would call these varieties *semi-creoles*, which also means that they have both creole and non-creole features but does not necessarily imply that they were ever basilectal creoles, since both creoles and non-creoles (e.g. Caymanian English, §10.4.6) can become semi-creoles by borrowing features. Thus some believe that Afrikaans (§8.5), particularly the variety spoken by some people of mixed race (§8.5.2), could safely be called a semi-creole but not a post-creole.

The term *creoloid* has been used for so many different kinds of vaguely creole-like languages that its usefulness has become rather limited; here it will be used only to mean languages that superficially resemble creoles in some way (e.g. by being morphologically simpler than a possible source language), but which, on close examination, appear never to have undergone creolization. This may be caused by the language shift of an entire speech community, such as the adoption of Old High German by Romance-speaking Jews, producing Yiddish (§12.16), or the adoption of English by Puerto Ricans in New York, producing Nuyorican. These *xenolects* (slightly foreignized varieties spoken natively) are not creoles because they have not undergone significant restructuring. Nor are *interlanguages* (intermediate varieties of a target language spoken by foreign learners) to be considered pidgins (since they lack shared norms or stability) or even jargons (since they are targeted toward the native speaker's variety and are not confined to a particular domain). As mentioned above, contact of closely related languages can result in *koineization*, in which dialect leveling produces some morphological simplification but leaves intact many fairly complex grammatical features common to both language varieties. This is particularly true in new speech communities overseas, as in the case of the closely related languages of northern India that formed new varieties of Hindustani or Bhojpuri in Trinidad, Guyana, Suriname, Mauritius, and Fiji, spoken by the descendants of contract laborers (Siegel 1983). There is also a tendency toward simplification in isolated overseas *enclave varieties* such as Missouri French (§9.6), particularly when they are used by a dwindling number of speakers who are bilingual in the surrounding language (Maher 1985). However, *language death* or *attrition* can also take place in a language's original location if it gradually loses speakers to an encroaching language and is finally spoken only by bilinguals who lack native-speaker competence in the dying language.

Finally there are *mixed languages* that are none of the above, both in the trivial sense that practically all languages are mixed to some degree by contact with other languages, and also in a miscellaneous category of very mixed languages whose genesis had to be quite different from that of pidgins or creoles. For example there is the strange case of Mbugu or Ma'a in Tanzania, a Cushitic language that acquired Bantu grammar, apparently under duress (Goodman 1971, Thomason 1983). Then there is Anglo-Romani: basically English syntax, phonology and function words holding together Romani or Gypsy lexical items, used principally between English-speaking Gypsies in the presence of English-speaking non-Gypsies in order to maintain secrecy (Hancock 1984). Perhaps the most curious case of language mixing is Mitchif, spoken on the Turtle Mountain Indian reservation in North Dakota in the United States. It appears to consist of perfectly formed Cree verb phrases and perfectly formed French noun phrases, e.g. "Nkii-cihtaan dans la ligne," literally 'I-PAST-go to the-FEMININE state-line' (Richard Rhodes p.c.). Thomason (1984) hypothesizes that Mitchif was created by racially mixed bilinguals (cf. French *métis* 'half-breed,' whence *Mitchif*) in order to assert a social identity distinct from that of speakers of either French or Cree.

This inventory of non-pidgins and non-creoles is by no means exhaustive, but it helps to define the subject at hand by specifying what pidgins and creoles are not.

1.4 Scope of the book

Although the structure of this book is discussed in the preface, a word about its scope is included here since this relates both to theory and some practical matters of research, requiring a more detailed explanation.

As a reference book, the present work attempts to bring together the most important information relating to this field as objectively as possible, avoiding tendentiousness in matters of theory. However, decisions as to which data are important enough to be included, even before any question of their interpretation, always imply a theoretical position. To be explicit, this book reflects the belief that while universal tendencies in pidginization and creolization (§2.12) play some role in shaping creole languages (e.g. the nearly complete reliance on free rather than inflectional morphemes to convey grammatical information), a significant number of the features in a creole language that are not attributable to its superstrate can be traced to parallel features in its substrate languages. Together with creole-internal innovations, borrowings from adstrate languages (those which are neither superstrate nor substrate) and the convergence of all or some of the above, these account for the creole's features. This moderate substratist position (§2.13) has influenced the choice of which languages provide the linguistic features compared in chapters 3 to 5. These are the *Atlantic creoles*, a term first applied to the English-based creoles of the Caribbean area and coastal West Africa (Hancock 1969) and later extended to include the other creoles in these areas, those whose lexicons are based on Portuguese, Spanish, Dutch, and French (e.g. Boretzky 1983). The Atlantic creoles share many structural features on all linguistic levels that are not found in their European lexical source languages, as demonstrated in chapters 3 to 5. Many of these features can be attributed to the substratum of African languages that these creoles share.

Because of their structural affinities, there may be grounds for also including among the Atlantic creoles the Isle de France creoles of the Indian Ocean (§9.8) as well as Hawaiian Creole English (§10.8.2), although there is disagreement on this. For those who favor greater inclusiveness, the term 'Atlantic creole' is no longer appropriate geographically. Some prefer the term 'Afro-creole'; Reinecke (1937: 60) proposed the term 'African creole dialect' for the Caribbean varieties. However, such a term would seem to prejudge the theoretical debate on the origin of these creoles and their common features (chapter 2), so the term 'Atlantic creole' will be used here instead, restricted to those creoles spoken in the Atlantic area.

It might be asked why the comparison of linguistic features is confined to those of the Atlantic creoles rather than those of all creoles and pidgins. The main reason is that it was expected that the Atlantic creoles would form a natural group with comparable features because of shared elements in their genesis and development. However, no claim is being made here that their common features are necessarily traits of all creoles (the fundamental flaw in the work of extreme universalists) – much less traits of all pidgins.

The development of the discipline imposes a logical order in comparative work. Not until individual varieties are adequately described can we start comparing varieties in the same lexical group, and not until comparative studies within lexical groups are completed can we start comparative work for larger groupings. The present work contributes to the cross-lexical-base comparative work on the Atlantic creoles so that, when this is completed, other researchers can go on to compare that group with Asian and Pacific varieties.

The agenda in pidgin and creole studies is still a long and demanding one. The next generations do not need to fear a dearth of important, fascinating research yet to be done.

2

Theory: a historical overview

2.0 Introduction

This chapter traces the rise and sometimes the fall of the major ideas and theoretical perspectives that have shaped the study of pidgin and creole languages. It also provides an overview of the history of the discipline itself, but its primary objective is not to chronicle all important landmarks so much as to provide a better understanding of the climate of ideas in which such advances were made. Reinecke (1981) presents a chronology of major events in the discipline, largely the publication dates of key works. While this list is very useful in any attempt to chart the development of theory within the discipline, it could suggest an unwavering march forward in time toward ever-increasing enlightenment. Of course the movement has actually been quite intermittent, and frequently sideways or backwards, as Reinecke (1977) well knew. The following discussion will therefore use chronology only loosely to order the presentation of ideas, often working forwards or backwards for purposes of comparison in order to avoid becoming too disjointed.

2.1 Before European expansion

Although most of the known pidgin and creole languages arose after western Europeans began establishing overseas colonies in the fifteenth century, there is ample reason to believe that more existed in earlier times than the two that have been documented, i.e. Pidgin Arabic and Lingua Franca (see below). Indeed, language contact seems likely to be nearly as old as language itself. However, languages have not been recorded in writing until the last few millennia, and mixed languages have usually been among the last to be written down. Zyhlarz (1932–33) considered the language of ancient Egypt, first recorded in hieroglyphs in the third millennium BC, to have grown out of a trade language – i.e. a pidgin – that developed among several Hamito-Semitic languages which came together in the Nile valley; if this is the case, it was essentially a creole language (Reinecke *et al.* 1975: 53). In any case the languages of ancient empires from China to Sumer expanded along with their military, commercial, and cultural influence, and it is quite likely that this happened via pidginized varieties, although no known records of such speech remain. In classical Greek drama, foreigners are sometimes represented as speaking broken Greek (Hall 1966: 3); Hesseling (1928) explained the peculiar characteristics of the Tskakonian dialect of Greek by postulating that it had been creolized (Muysken and Meijer 1979: ix). It seems probable that contact varieties – and possibly fairly stable pidgins – accompanied the colonial expansion of not only the Greeks but also the Phoenicians, Carthaginians, and Romans. Hancock (1977) has speculated about the possible restructuring of trade languages such as that used in Britain during Roman times, but these remain undocumented and the few references to them in literature are unclear. There are also reports of a simplified Latin used by Jewish traders (Whinnom 1977: 304), but again there are no extant specimens.

The earliest known record of any pidgin is a brief text of restructured Arabic apparently used along a trade route in central Mauritania during the eleventh century (reproduced in full in section 12.1). In a manuscript completed in AD 1068, the geographer al-Bakrī cites a traveler's complaint that in the town of Maridi "The Blacks have mutilated our beautiful language and spoiled its eloquence with their twisted tongues," followed by a ten-sentence sample of their speech (Thomason and Elgibali 1986). The version of the manuscript containing this passage was uncovered by Elgibali in a library in Egypt only in 1982, so its impact on pidgin and creole studies is very recent.

Lingua Franca (§12.14) may already have been in use at the time the Maridi Arabic text was recorded, but it was not documented until later. Around 1204 a version of the Apostles' Creed in a pidginized Latin resembling later Lingua Franca was recorded in Constantinople (Kahane *et al.* 1958). The first known text of what is clearly Lingua Franca was written in Djerba, Tunisia, in 1353 (Grion 1891, Whinnom 1977: 306).

The question has arisen whether contact-induced restructuring may have played a role in the development of early Germanic languages (Feist 1932) and modern European languages. The Romance languages that grew out of Latin offer no clear evidence of prior creolization: the basic structure of their linguistic systems indicates no abrupt break with that of Latin. Jespersen (1922: 236) found that "no cataclysm such as that through which English has become Beach-la-mar need on any account be invoked to explain the perfectly natural change from Latin to Old French and from Old French to modern French." While there is evidence to suggest language contact and mixture, such as the front rounded vowels found in French and Germanic languages but not in Latin, such innovations may have resulted from language-internal processes rather than borrowing. Such considerations also cast light on the question of the possible role that creolization may have played in the emergence of Middle English, which evolved after the Norman French conquered England's Anglo-Saxon speaking inhabitants in the eleventh century. The massive loss of inflectional endings and other features of Middle English morphosyntax suggest the profound impact of language contact. Adam (1883: 10) compared Middle English to the Caribbean creoles when he suggested that the speakers of African substrate languages "mounted a resistance comparable in some measure to that of the Anglo-Saxons who, after the Norman conquest, made their grammar and phonology prevail over that of their conquerors" despite the massive borrowing of French vocabulary into Middle English. However, most linguists (e.g. Domingue 1977, Thomason and Kaufman forthcoming) stop short of claiming that Middle English resulted from creolization. The similarities of the sociolinguistic situation in England during this period and that in the Caribbean later on would seem to be outweighed by the differences: the English peasants always had a means of communicating among themselves without recourse to a pidgin, although communication between them and their French overlords may well have involved pidginized varieties of both Anglo-Saxon and Norman French during the initial period of contact. Still, the similarity of the linguistic outcome of this situation and that in the Caribbean led an early creolist to observe that English had already been "thoroughly creolized in its grammar" (Van Name 1869–70: 125).

2.2 Early European expansion

The earliest known text of a restructured variety of a European language spoken by sub-Saharan Africans is in a Portuguese poem published in 1516 (Teyssier 1959, reproduced in part in section 6.1). Naro (1978) identifies this Negro Portuguese as a pidgin, although it may have been a less stable variety of foreigners' Portuguese.

The earliest known record of the Spanish word *criollo* (whence *creole*) is in a book published in 1590 (Coromines 1967: 178) and translated into English in 1604: "Some Crollos [*sic*], for so they call the Spaniards borne at the Indies" (*Oxford English Dictionary*). As noted (§1.2), the meaning of the word was extended to both whites and blacks born in the New World or other colonies, and eventually came to refer to their customs and language. The first known use of the word in the latter meaning is in the 1685 diary of the French navigator Le Courbe, who used the term *langue créole* for a restructured variety of Portuguese used by Senegalese traders: "These Senegalese, besides the language of the country, also speak a certain jargon which resembles but little the Portuguese language and which is called the creole language, like the Lingua Franca of the Mediterranean Sea" (cited by Chaudenson 1979: 9). John Barbot, reporting a voyage completed in

1682, referred to Africans' use of "Lingua Franca or broken Portuguese" (cited by Dillard 1979: 264).

This early period of commercial and colonial expansion brought Europeans into contact with a great number of new languages completely unrelated to their own, a fact which had an important impact on the course of philology by the eighteenth century. During the early period of contact, however, these languages were the object of interest and study mostly for their practical use in trade and in establishing outposts and colonies, as well as in spreading Christianity. Lists of words and phrases were collected from the time of the first explorers, and later travelers sometimes noted the contact languages that were emerging around them. In 1640 Jacques Bouton, a Frenchman in Martinique, noted that the Carib Indians there used a jargon of French mixed with Spanish, English, and Dutch, and he recorded a sample (§9.2). Not long afterwards Père Chévillard, a priest on the same island, noted that the Africans were "attentive observers who rapidly familiarized themselves with the language of the European, which was purposely corrupted to facilitate its comprehension" (from a 1659 document cited by Goodman 1964: 104). Pierre Pelleprat, a contemporary, wrote that the changes in the language were initiated by the Africans and then repeated by the Europeans: "We adjust to their way of talking, which is usually with the infinitive of the verb, for example *moi prier Dieu, moi aller à l'église, moi point manger* for 'j'ai prié Dieu' ['I prayed to God'], 'je suis allé à l'Église' ['I went to church'], 'je n'ai point mangé' ['I haven't eaten']. And by adding a word that indicates the future or the past, they say *demain moi manger, hier moi prier Dieu*, and that means 'je mangerai demain' ['I'll eat tomorrow'], 'hier j'ai prié Dieu' ['Yesterday I prayed to God']" (1655, cited by Goodman 1964: 105).

The earliest known creole text is a 33-sentence conversation in Malayo-Portuguese (reproduced in part in section 6.5.2), published in 1692 by Georg Meister, a German who had been in the East Indies with the Dutch. His spelling reflects his Thuringian dialect of German and a smattering of Latin and French, but no knowledge of European Portuguese. As Hancock (1977: 277) has noted, "In the few instances where the early forms of modern creoles have been recorded, it appears to have been by speakers of languages lexically unrelated to them." Such speakers were apparently more willing to deal with the creoles as autonomous systems, and their representation of creole sounds has usually been less obscured by the orthography of the lexical-source language.

The earliest known recordings of a North American pidgin are also from this period. Samples of Delaware Jargon (§12.11) were collected by a Swede, Campanius Holm, in New Sweden in the 1640s, and the Englishman William Penn published some phrases in 1683 (Thomason 1980). The translation of the text published by Thomas (1698) reflects the English of the period: "*Hitah ta-koman* 'Friend, from whence com'st?' "

2.3 The eighteenth century

During the eighteenth century the Caribbean creoles came to be recognized as varieties that were clearly distinguishable from their European lexical-source languages, at least on a practical level by the Europeans who came into regular contact with them. It gradually became clear that somehow foreigners' speech ("broken English," for example) had taken root and become the local language of blacks, influencing the speech of local whites as well.

The first attestation of creole French is found in Père Labat's *Nouveau voyage aux Îles de l'Amérique, 1693–1705,* in which a black woman on Martinique is quoted accusing a certain man of being the father of her child: "Toi papa li" 'You are its father' (quoted by Goodman 1964: 106). This was followed in 1718 by the earliest known text of an English-based creole, Sranan, in J. D. Herlein's *Beschryvinge van de volks-plantinge Zuriname* (reproduced in Rens 1953: 142):

Oudy.	Howdy.
Oe fasje joe tem?	How fashion you stand?
My bon.	Me good.
Jou bon toe?	You good too?
Ay.	Aye.

The spread of Britain's commercial empire during this period led to the emergence of restructured varieties of English in Africa and Asia as well. The first published reference to a local West African variety of English is in Francis Moore's 1734 *Travels into the Inland Parts of Africa*: "The English have in the River Gambia much corrupted the English language, by Words or Literal Translations from the Portuguese or Mundingoes" (p. 294; cited by Hancock 1969: 13, 1977: 282). In his book, *A Voyage to the East Indies in 1747 and 1748,* C. F. Noble gave the first report of a "broken and mixed dialect of English and Portuguese" in China (p. 244, cited by Bauer 1975: 96).

The first serious study of creole languages began in the 1730s when Moravian missionaries were sent to convert the slaves on St. Thomas (1732) and in Suriname (1735). The Church of the United Brethren, often called the Moravian Church because of its origins in Czech Protestantism under Hus, was granted lands in Herrnhut, Saxony, in 1722 under the patronage of Count Nikolaus von Zinzendorf. On attending the coronation of Christian VI of Denmark in 1731, Zinzendorf met an old slave named Andres from St. Thomas in the Danish West Indies. Deeply moved by the slave's account of the miserable existence of his

people and their desire to become Christians, the count organized the Moravian
mission to St. Thomas and visited the island himself in 1739 to reassure the hostile
slave owners regarding the intentions of the missionaries (Stein 1986a). At first the
German-speaking missionaries attempted to use Dutch with the slaves, who spoke
Negerhollands (§8.1). When this proved unsuccessful, they began learning the
slaves' creole Dutch, which they called *carriols* in the early years (cf. Dutch *creol*,
apparently with an epenthetic vowel), one of the earliest known uses of the word
referring to a West Indian language. The Moravians were also among the first to
treat a creole as an autonomous language, to be studied and written as a linguistic
system independent of its lexical donor language. They taught the slaves to read
and write in the creole, leading to a series of remarkable letters such as the count's
farewell address to them and their response (Zinzendorf 1742). The ensuing
literature, including grammars, dictionaries, and translations of the gospels as well
as original sermons and songs (Stein 1986b), has been preserved in the archives in
Herrnhut. Although influenced by the second-language version of the creole
spoken by the missionaries, this literature, particularly the letters written by the
slaves, offers invaluable insights into the structure of the creole as used by the first
generations of its speakers. The earliest letters from the 1740s show no evidence of
the preverbal markers *le* and *ka* (§§5.1.3 and 5.1.5) or the plural marker *sender*
(§5.4.2), and alternation of Dutch *ik* and creole *mi* for 'I,' suggesting that the
creole's structure was not yet stable (Stein 1986a: 9). These letters are now being
prepared for publication (Stein and Beck forthcoming).

The first published grammar of any creole language was Jochum Melchor
Magens' *Grammatica over det Creolske sprog, som bruges paa de trende Danske
Eilande, St. Croix, St. Thomas, og St. Jans i Amerika* (Copenhagen, 1770). Writing
for the competing Danish Lutheran missionaries, Magens was a native speaker of
the acrolectal (§1.3) creole spoken by whites, and he had studied philology in
Denmark. His work contained a 24-page grammar on a Latin model and 43 pages
of dialog translated into Danish, as well as three pages of proverbs.

In 1777 the Moravian missionary Christian Oldendorp published a history of
the mission containing a dozen pages on the creole. However, Stein (1986b) and
Gilbert (1986b) have examined the original manuscript version, which contains 53
pages of grammatical and sociolinguistic information as well as a 189-page
German–Negerhollands dictionary and 13 pages of texts. Oldendorp's comments
on the use of European languages in the West Indies merit quotation in full for the
light they throw on the thinking of this period:

> In the West Indies, the European languages tend to deviate to an
> extreme extent. For the most part, only those people who learned to

speak them in Europe can talk the pure European form of the language. On the other hand, the people who were born here – the Crioles – do not speak the same kind of language. They change it more or less; they employ words taken from elsewhere, arising from the collision of the people of many nations. They have lived together for a long time, or at least have been in constant contact, so that some features of their languages have been passed from one to the other. The children do not hear their mother tongue in a continually pure state as in Europe. In many places they are exposed to a jumble of different tongues, and the people they are most closely associated with generally speak them badly. Furthermore, in the West Indies there are many things that are non-existent in Europe – thus explaining the existence of words and idioms that are in local use only. All of these considerations lead to the customary designation of the Crioles' language as Criole, especially in those cases where it deviates markedly from a European language and is characterized by the admixture of many features foreign to the original national tongue. Hence, there is a criole English, a criole French, and so on. Blacks in these places speak Criole, too. Except for those who have learned the European languages in their youth, from whites for the most part, Blacks generally corrupt the European languages still more, due to their Guinea dialect and to the words which they mix in with their speech. (Oldendorp ms., translated by Gilbert 1986b)

Thus Oldendorp considered all European languages spoken natively by West Indians to have been influenced by the high degree of language contact in the Caribbean area. He attributed the even greater divergence of the speech of blacks from the standard languages to the influence of their African languages. Stolz's (1986: 13) characterization of Oldendorp's view of the creole as simply a reduced form of the lexical source language (apparently based only on Oldendorp 1777) is not borne out by the above quotation from the manuscript. Yet Oldendorp (1777: 424 ff.) considered the creole "a mutilation without plan or rule" of the standard, and his table of contents suggests that he found the creole deficient: "The poverty of the same – granted that it is an apt vehicle for a plain sermon on the gospels. On the necessity of avoiding ambiguities and incorrect syntax in this language. The difficulty of translating verses into the same. On the lack of words for spiritual things, and the introduction of the same" (quoted by Gilbert 1986b). However, Oldendorp was among the first to observe how whites learned the creole spoken by blacks: "Since the white children are taken care of by black women and grow up among black children, they first learn creole, or the language of blacks, and sometimes they never learn another properly. However, this language is spoken better (*feiner*) by the whites than the blacks" (Oldendorp 1777, quoted by Stein 1984: 92).

The Moravians did similar work in Suriname on Sranan (§10.2.1) and Saramaccan (§10.2.2). Besides their translations of the bible from the 1770s onwards, C. L. Schumann wrote a 55-page manuscript dictionary of Saramaccan in 1778 (reproduced in Schuchardt 1914a) and a 135-page manuscript dictionary of Sranan in 1783 (reproduced in Kramp 1983). Like Oldendorp, Schumann distinguished between the creole as spoken by whites and by blacks. In 1778 Pieter van Dyk published a 112-page book on the "Bastert Engels" of Suriname, with parallel columns in Sranan and Dutch – the first book published on a creolized variety of English. As on St. Thomas, the Moravians developed a literary variety of the creole for translating the scriptures. Moreover, the German speakers' errors in phonology and syntax were often not corrected but rather imitated by the native speakers of the creole, laying the foundations for a special variety of Church Creole which is still used on solemn occasions (Voorhoeve 1971).

In 1780 the Dutch published the first grammar and dictionary of Malayo-Portuguese (§6.5) – the earliest such work on any variety of restructured Portuguese (Whinnom 1965: 513). The earliest published text of Haitian Creole French appears in a 1785 book describing the colony, written by a Swiss traveler, Justin Girod-Chantrans (Valdman 1978: 98). It was followed by a guide book to Haiti (Ducoeurjoly 1802) with 24 pages of conversations in creole along with the first French–Creole vocabulary, 72 pages in length, intended for travelers.

It should be remembered that at this time the highly inflected grammars of Greek and Latin were still held up as ideals against which the grammars of other languages were measured – and usually found deficient. The standard varieties of European languages were still being codified: uniformity, logic, and consistency were prized by eighteenth-century neoclassicists, and this was reflected in the increasing rigidity of orthography and the growing authority accorded to dictionaries and grammars. At the same time philosophers of language marveled at the diversity of the languages that Europeans were coming into contact with around the globe, a diversity that challenged the traditional monogenetic theory of the common origin of all languages. The growing British colonial involvement in India spurred an interest in Hindi and the great work of the Sanskrit scholar Pāṇini. As Robins (1967: 134) remarks,

> If any single year can, albeit artificially, be taken to mark the start of
> the contemporary world of linguistic science, it is the year

1786 . . . [when] Sir William Jones of the East India Company read his famous paper to the Royal Asiatic Society in Calcutta, wherein he established beyond doubt the historical kinship of Sanskrit, the classical language of India, with Latin, Greek, and the Germanic languages.

This discovery led to the comparative historical work on the interrelationship of the Indo-European languages which dominated European philology for so much of the following century and finally led to the Neogrammarian school, whose rigidity pushed Schuchardt towards his now famous creole studies in the 1880s (§2.6). Moreover, Jones himself raised the question of the role of language contact in language change: "both the Gothick and the Celtick, though blended with a different idiom, had the same origin with the Sanscrit" (quoted by Hancock 1977: 277).

2.4 The early nineteenth century

While the Moravians continued their work in the Caribbean, other missionaries took up the study of other creole languages. Ceylon became British in 1796, and in 1818 the Wesleyan Mission Press began publishing works in Indo-Portuguese (§6.4.2). In 1825 a short catechism was published in Papiamentu (§7.3), beginning the strongest and longest literary tradition of any creole language. In 1829 the British and Foreign Bible Society in London published the first complete edition of *Da Njoe Testament* in Sranan Creole English for the Moravians in Suriname. The founder of an Edinburgh newspaper attacked the translation and rebuked the Moravians for "putting the broken English of the Negroes . . . into a written and permanent form," which would "embody their barbarous, mixed, imperfect phrase in the pages of schoolbooks" (quoted by Reinecke 1983). While he would approve the translation of the bible into "the spoken [native] language of a district, however defective and uncouth," he opposed its translation into "the blundering phraseology of foreigners when attempting to leave off their original tongue, and to adopt that which is used by the people among whom they have come to dwell . . . Why are not the children taught English?" (ibid.). The philologist William Greenfield replied in a monograph (1830), outlining the history of Sranan (§10.2.1) and emphasizing that it was an established and rule-governed language heavily influenced by Dutch: "it is obvious that it can no longer be denominated 'broken English' or English attempted to be spoken by the Negroes endeavouring to leave off their own tongue" (1830: 17). He went on to argue for the autonomy of Sranan, using the paradigms of traditional grammar to show how English, Sranan, and Dutch handle articles and nouns, pronouns, verbs, and the comparison of

adjectives. He concluded: "From the preceding comparative view of the grammatical inflexion of these languages, I apprehend it will be obvious that in this respect
the Negro-English differs as much from the English and Dutch as these languages
do from each other" (ibid. 32). Since a critic had suggested that a comparison with
creole Dutch would prove that Sranan was in fact English, Greenfield provided
parallel columns of the first chapter of the Gospel of John in Sranan, English,
Dutch, and Negerhollands Creole Dutch – the first published comparison of
creole languages. Greenfield went on to stress that the origin of Sranan was not so
different from that of languages like English, once despised as "a barbarous
jargon, neither good French nor pure Saxon" (ibid. 50–51): "The process by which
they have been framed is precisely that which is presented by the Negro-English,
i.e. by corruption and intermixture, and the subsequent invention of new terms, by
compounding or otherwise changing those already existing" (ibid. 48–49). He
dismissed the idea that Sranan had resulted from the inferior ability of Africans to
learn English: "The human mind is the same in every clime; and accordingly we
find nearly the same process adopted in the formation of language in every
country. The Negroes have been proved to be in no degree inferior to other nations
in solidity of judgment, or fertility of imagination" (ibid. 51).

Unfortunately Greenfield's monograph was soon forgotten, in part because his
ideas on both language and race were much ahead of their time. Despite agitation
for the abolition of slavery in Britain and elsewhere, many clung to the racist belief
that the intelligence of blacks was inferior, and that this justified their "protection"
under that institution. With no understanding of the social factors determining
language acquisition in cases of pidginization and creolization, many white
speakers of the lexical source languages took the divergences they heard in the
creoles as proof of the blacks' incapacity to learn languages properly. This attitude
was reinforced by more general attitudes toward language: "one notices from
Grimm on a definite admiration for flexional morphology" (Robins 1967: 181).
For example, in the nineteenth century declensions were artificially preserved in
written Dutch: "Is not inflection the mark of a civilized language, and its loss a sign
of decadence?" (Brachin 1985: 34). The lack of such inflections in many African
languages, about which European scholars still knew relatively little, was accepted
as evidence of their primitive state of development. Describing Guinean Creole
Portuguese (§6.2.2), the French military officer Bertrand-Bocandé (1849: 73)
remarked:

> It is clear that people used to expressing themselves with a rather
> simple language cannot easily elevate their intelligence to the genius
> of a European language. When they were in contact with the

Portuguese and forced to communicate with them, speaking the same language, it was necessary that the varied expressions acquired during so many centuries of civilization dropped their perfection, to adapt to ideas being born and to barbarous forms of language of half-savage peoples.   (cited in English by Meijer and Muysken 1977: 22)

Regrettably it cannot be claimed that such notions are no longer current, although they are more seldom encountered in print. Western thought has long rested on some basic racist assumptions, and these have shaped the thinking of linguists as well as others. The "thick lips and thick minds" theory of the origin of black speech varieties (Dillard 1972: 11) has a long history, even in the work of creolists who were enlightened for their times. Wullschlägel (1856: viii) explained the phonological differences between Sranan words and their English etyma as the result of "the Negroes ... trying to adapt them to their speech organs." Even Schuchardt (1887: 138) suggested that the preference for labial sounds in Cape Verdean Creole Portuguese "can be explained by the well developed lips of the Negroes," and Saint-Quentin (1872: lviii) referred to their "limited intelligence." As late as 1913 van Ginneken asserted that creoles maintained the "inner form" of African languages because blacks, no matter how acculturated they might appear to be to European ways, "can never give up their Negro way of thinking [negergedachten]" (p. 245).

In the early nineteenth century the Romantic movement placed a high value on everything connected with "the people"; in Europe this helped focus linguistic attention on the dialects of rural peasants (Robins 1967: 176), but overseas it seems to have done little to foster interest in colonial creoles until, possibly, the latter part of the century. It was a French priest, l'Abbé Goux, who published the first systematic treatment of a French-based creole in 1842 (Goodman 1964: 109), a 14-page description of Lesser Antillean Creole (§9.2) attached to a *Catéchisme en langue créole*. Although a fable in Mauritian Creole (§9.8.1) had appeared in an 1818 travelogue, literature in French-based creoles really began in 1846 with *Les Bambous*, a verse adaptation of some of La Fontaine's fables by François Marbot, a native of Martinique (Goodman 1964: 108). The first detailed grammar of a French-based creole was a book on the variety spoken in Trinidad (Thomas 1869), written by a school teacher and clergyman who lived on that island but who may not have been a native speaker (Goodman 1964: 109). Besides the grammar, the book includes a collection of idioms, proverbs, and short texts. The first study of the creole of French Guiana (§9.4) was by a native speaker, Auguste de Saint-Quentin (1872). Goodman (1964: 110) notes that "His treatment of the grammar is concise and almost as lucid and thorough as that of the phonology, describing it in terms of its own structure without gratuitous references to standard French." The 1880s brought a number of works on the creole French dialects, notably those of Mauritius (Baissac 1880) and Louisiana (Mercier 1880, Fortier 1885).

This period also brought the first longer descriptions of two English-based creoles: a 68-page *Kurzgefasste Neger–Englische Grammatik* on Sranan (Anonymous 1854; by H. R. Wullschlägel according to Schuchardt [1980: 102]) and substantial dictionaries of the same language (Focke 1855 and Wullschlägel 1856), as well as a study of Jamaican Creole (Russell 1868) – the first description of any West Indian variety. At this time there also appeared the first dictionary of Papiamentu (van Ewijk 1875), which – like the Sranan dictionaries – was needed for quite practical reasons by Dutch speakers.

2.5 Van Name

Addison Van Name's "Contributions to Creole Grammar" (1869–70) has been said to represent the beginning of the scientific study of creole languages (Stolz 1986: 14). It is the first comparative study of creoles from all four lexical bases found in the Caribbean (French, Spanish, Dutch, English), based on earlier studies (e.g. Oldendorp 1777, Wullschlägel 1856, Thomas 1869) and work with informants. Van Name, a librarian at Yale University, was apparently trained in philology and familiar with a number of European languages. His description of the four lexical groups in some 40 pages is remarkably clear, compact, and well informed. Reinecke (1937: 16) found Van Name's observations "much more sound than many written later"; indeed, one is hard put to think of a single recent article that would serve as a better introduction to comparative creole studies.

Van Name was the first to remark on a number of syntactic features common to many Caribbean creoles, e.g. the use of the third person plural pronoun to indicate plurality (pp. 132, 153, 160; cf. section 5.4.2), the serial use of the verb meaning 'give' (p. 147; cf. §5.3.1), the fact that stative verbs take no progressive marker (p. 157), and the use of the word for 'body' as a quasi-reflexive pronoun (p. 155; cf. §5.4.5). He also noted lexical similarities such as the words for 'it has' meaning 'there is' (p. 156; cf. §5.2.3), or those for 'too much' meaning 'very' (p. 159), as well as phonological similarities such as the regressive nasalization of vowels (p. 129; cf. §4.4). Van Name had a surprisingly good feel for the languages and questioned the authenticity of the passive construction in Negerhollands (p. 163; cf. §3.3.2). Yet in some respects he was rather naive; he thought that the French "Creole has in some cases recovered a final consonant, especially *t*" (p. 131 – actually an archaic or regional feature; cf. §3.2.1) and that Papiamentu Creole Spanish "dipthongs [*sic*] *ie* and *ue* usually return to *e* and *o*, their Latin originals" (p. 150 – actually Portuguese influence, although in certain cases this may have been reinforced by the reduction of *ie* to *e*, possibly via vowel harmony [cf. §4.5], in words like *hèrmèn* 'tool' from Spanish *herramienta* rather than Portuguese *ferramenta* [P. Maurer, p.c.]).

The more general statements that Van Name made about the origin of the creoles (pp. 123–126) are few but provocative, frequently touching on issues that are still being debated. It is clear that he understood creolization to have been preceded by pidginization: "The language spoken by the first generation of blacks was a broken French or Spanish, as the case might be, which, in the course of time, developed into a well defined Creole" (p. 124). Gilbert (1986a: 17) has asserted that the "distinction between pidgins and creoles [was] proposed by Robert Hall in 1966," but it should be borne in mind that the first attested English use of the word *pigeon* in the sense of 'pidgin' was in 1859, only a few years before Van Name's article. Although the word with its current linguistic meaning was apparently not known to him, its referent clearly was, as was its relationship to creolization. Van Name understood the pidginization/creolization process to represent accelerated language change:

> The changes which [creoles] have passed through are not essentially different in kind, and hardly greater in extent than those, for instance, which separate the French from the Latin, but from the greater violence of the forces at work they have been far more rapid . . . here two or three generations have sufficed for a complete transformation.
>
> (Van Name 1869–70: 123)

It is precisely this unresolved relationship of creolization to other kinds of language change that has been attracting historical linguists to creole studies in the 1980s (e.g. Boretzky 1983, Thomason and Kaufman forthcoming). Regarding the actual kinds of changes that creolization causes, "The process has to be sure been mainly, but not altogether, one of decay; the extent of the loss has made some compensation necessary, and we find, if not many new formations, numerous instances of old material put to new uses" (Van Name 1869–70: 123). While Van Name's predecessors saw creoles as the result of the reduction of the lexical source language, Van Name realized that they were also the products of innovation and restructuring. He also grasped the importance of certain social factors in creolization:

> Of the causes which have contributed to the formation of these dialects the chief are: first, the mature age of the slaves, who were brought from Africa at a time of life when the vocal organs are no longer flexible, and when the intellectual effort necessary for the

> mastery of a new language is even under the most favorable
> circumstances very considerable, and here quite out of the question;
> secondly, the fact that they constituted the great body of the
> population, the whites being in a minority seldom as large as one-
> fourth.   (ibid. 124)

Regarding the genetic relationship of the creoles,

> It is scarcely necessary to remark that these languages are not of
> mixed blood, half African and half European, for languages do not
> mingle so readily as races. Even in the Creole vocabularies, the
> proportion of African words is very small . . . Still more remote must
> be the influence of African on Creole grammar. It is rather in the
> phonetic structure of the Creole, in the dislike of an accumulation of
> consonants, the preference, especially marked in the Negro English of
> Surinam, for a final vowel, that such influence may with more
> likelihood be traced.   (ibid. 124)

This appears to be the first salvo in a battle that is not yet over – whether the
Atlantic creoles are European or African languages – the most extreme positions
on which were taken by Faine (1936) and Sylvain (1936) respectively. Van Name's
position is similar to that of Hall *et al.* (1953), who considered Haitian Creole
French to be genetically derived from French rather than African languages,
although Hall did not deny influence from the latter. Moreover, Van Name held the
belief, now shared only by Bickerton (1981:121 ff.), that a creole could differ
genetically on different linguistic levels, e.g. having African traits on the levels of
phonology and lexicon, but not syntax. Van Name's position appears to have been
based on his impressions of what *seemed* African rather than any firm knowledge
of African languages. He also went by logic: "In this tendency to nasalization in
the French creoles we may perhaps recognize an African trait, since it has found its
way into the Spanish, English and Dutch Creole" (Van Name 1869–70:129).
However, he did not extend this logic to identify as African those syntactic features
that are found throughout the creoles but not in their European lexical source
languages (e.g. the third person plural pronoun used to mark plurality). Van
Name repeatedly comments on features without indicating any awareness of
parallels in African languages, such as vowel harmony: "Some Papiamentu sound
changes are apparently due to attraction by an accented vowel in a preceding or
following syllable; thus *aña* (*año*), *caya* (*calle*), *bichi* (*bicho*), *bini* (*venir*)" (p. 150).
Finally, it should be noted that Van Name was probably the first linguist to
quantify variable features: he reported (p. 135) that French creole nouns

agglutinated the final -*s* of French plural articles (e.g. *zami* 'friend' from *les amis*) at a rate varying from creole to creole, e.g. ten to one (40 out of 44 occurrences) in Ducoeurjoly's text of Haitian, but two to one in Trinidadian.

2.6 Schuchardt and his contemporaries

Creole studies blossomed in the 1880s, when there was a surge in the study of individual varieties, e.g. the studies of French creoles mentioned above, and the first studies of American Black English (Harrison 1884) and West African Pidgin English (Grade 1889), as well as of a number of Portuguese-based creoles (Coelho 1880–86). More importantly, there was a surge in thinking about theoretical problems connected with the origin of creole languages, leading to the emergence of two theories which still dominate debate in the field, that of the universalists and that of the substratists.

Adolpho Coelho was a Portuguese philologist who was a member of the Geographical Society of Lisbon, founded in 1878 just before the partitioning of Africa, a time of heightened interest in Portugal's overseas colonies. The society sponsored exploratory expeditions to the colonies and published a Bulletin of its findings. These included Coelho's articles, printed between 1880 and 1886, about the varieties of creole Portuguese spoken in some of the colonies. Although much of the material came from the Cape Verde Islands, it included samples of the folk speech of São Tomé, Goa, Macao, and even independent Brazil, sent to him by correspondents or gleaned from other writings. Coelho's efforts led to a number of further studies of these varieties by other Portuguese philologists over the next fifty years, also done in the traditional manner of European dialectology of the period. However, Coelho is mainly remembered as the first to articulate a theoretical position on the origin of creoles which came to be called the universalist theory:

> The Romance and creole dialects, Indo-Portuguese and all the similar formations represent the first stage or stages in the acquisition of a foreign language by a people that speaks or spoke another ... They owe their origin to the operation of psychological or physiological laws that are everywhere the same, and not to the influence of the former languages of the peoples among whom these dialects are found.   (1880: 193, 195)

In other words, Coelho attributed the present form of the creoles to certain universal tendencies in second-language learning by adults (e.g. simplification) rather than to the influence of substrate languages. He illustrated this with the following:

> For example, one seeks in vain in Indo-Portuguese any influence from
> Tamil or Sinhalese. The formation of the plural by reduplication of
> the singular in the Macao dialect could be attributed to Chinese
> influence, but this process is so basic that little can be established by
> it. In the dialect of the island of Sant' Iago *muito muito* is the
> superlative.   (ibid.)

Coelho supported his hypothesis by pointing to certain widespread features such
as the preverbal progressive marker *ta* and a number of common lexical items like
papia 'speak' and *misté* 'need' (found in Papiamentu and a number of Portuguese-
based creoles) or the preverbal anterior marker *te* (found in both Haitian and
Louisiana Creole French). Meijer and Muysken (1977:25) conclude that "His
analysis was not detailed enough, however, to warrant calling him a major
precursor of modern creole studies" but Gilbert (1986a: 16) sees the ideas "first
hinted at by Coelho . . . appearing in modern form in Bickerton's LBH [language
bioprogram hypothesis]" (section 2.12).

  Coelho's extreme universalist position (allowing for no substrate influence) was
diametrically opposed to the extreme substratist position proposed in 1883 by the
French philologist Lucien Adam (Kihm 1984). Adam wrote *Les Idiomes négro-
aryen et maléo-aryen* after serving as a magistrate for three years in French
Guiana; he compared its creole to that of Trinidad (using Saint-Quentin 1872 and
Thomas 1869) and to several West African languages, and compared Mauritian
Creole French (using Baissac 1880) to the Malagasy language of Madagascar. He
concluded that

> the Guinea Negroes, transported to those [Caribbean] colonies, took
> words from French but retained as far as possible the phonology and
> grammar of their mother tongues . . . Such a formation is surely a
> hybrid . . . The grammar is no other than the general grammar of the
> languages of Guinea . . . I have been able to confirm that the
> phonology of this third colonial language [Mauritian Creole French]
> is of Malagasy provenance and that Mauritian speech constitutes a
> Malayo-Aryan language.   (1883: 4–7)

As Goodman (1964: 113) points out, Adam was the first to bring to light certain
parallels between an Atlantic creole and various African languages, such as the
formation of the plural with the third person plural pronoun, the postposed
definite article *la* (apparently the convergence of French and Ewe function words),
and some phonological features. "A great many of his parallels, however, are of a
much more general nature and thus far less convincing, since they could be true of

any number of languages" (ibid.). For example, Goodman notes that Adam sometimes attributed the same feature (e.g. the lack of grammatical gender) to Malagasy in the case of Mauritian but to West African languages in the case of the American creoles (although there is nothing illogical about this: chance similarities in two unrelated substrata could well have produced the same effect in the resulting creoles). More problematical, some of the Mauritian features which Adam attributed to Malagasy influence are also found in the Caribbean creoles, such as *fin* as a preverbal marker of completive aspect, or the word *corps* 'body' as a quasi-reflexive pronoun.

Tension between the opposing theories of Coelho and Adam – as well as many new ideas – can be found throughout the work of the German linguist Hugo Schuchardt, who published some forty articles and reviews on pidgins and creoles totaling almost 700 printed pages between 1880 and 1914. Widely acknowledged as the father of creole studies, Schuchardt has been described as having "the richest and most complete perception of creoles of any single scholar up to the present" (Meijer and Muysken 1977: 28). Fought (1982: 419) is of the opinion that "By any fair measure . . . Schuchardt must be counted among the major figures in linguistics . . . his work contributed significantly to the emergence of sociolinguistics, both directly and by way of his strong influence within dialectology, particularly in Romance." Schuchardt (1842–1927) studied under August Schleicher, whose *Stammbaum* theory or genealogical tree model for the interrelationship of Indo-European languages made him one of the leading linguists of the mid nineteenth century. Along with Johannes Schmidt, another of Schleicher's students, Schuchardt developed the *Wellentheorie*, or theory of waves of linguistic innovations – such as sound changes – that spread over a given area from dialect to dialect or, in a language contact situation, from language to language (Robins 1967: 179; Fought 1982: 424–427). Schuchardt particularly stressed the role of individuals in the social process leading to language mixture, adumbrating the modern sociolinguistic theories of variation: "Old and new forms are distributed . . . within a single dialect not only according to age, but also according to sex, education, temperament, in short in the most diverse manner" (1885: 18, cited by Fought 1982: 425). As noted above (§1.0), one of the factors that led to Schuchardt's interest in creole languages was his opposition to the Neogrammarians' law of the absolute regularity of sound change. Creoles result from language contact, which disrupts the historical sound changes that might be expected in languages in isolation. Coelho's publications caught Schuchardt's interest and he took on the task of analyzing the material from Coelho's correspondents and later his own. Between 1882 and 1885 Schuchardt wrote to some 343 colonial administrators, missionaries, journalists, and other educated people living in areas he considered likely to have pidgin or creole languages (Gilbert 1984). His records indicate that he received 124 replies to his inquiries about local language varieties, effectively charting – however roughly – the geographical distribution of the major pidgin and creole languages. Reinecke (1937: 21) notes that "At first Schuchardt apparently did not differentiate between the 'creole languages' on sociological or historical grounds. Any more or less broken European language spoken overseas by a whole community was a creole language. However, as his grasp of the field increased and his views matured, he grasped but did not emphasize the difference between the several varieties of 'creole language.'" At the beginning, for example, Schuchardt (1881: 581) suggested including Chinese Pidgin English among the creole languages, and Coelho (1880–86) looked for creoles not only in Curaçao and Cuba, but also Ecuador and Chile, perhaps misled by the Spanish meaning of the word *criollo*: New World white.

Schuchardt's major work was on the Portuguese-based creoles: those of São Tomé (1882a), Annobón (1888a), Senegal (1888b), Cape Verde (1888c), and Príncipe (1889a), as well as Indo-Portuguese (1882b, 1883a, 1889b, 1889c) and Malayo-Portuguese (1890). However, he also published on Philippine Creole Spanish (1883b), Vietnamese Pidgin French (1888d), Melanesian Pidgin English (1883c, 1889d), American Indian English (1889e), Saramaccan Creole English (1914a), Atlantic Creole English (published posthumously by Gilbert 1985), and Lingua Franca (1909), as well as Negerhollands Creole Dutch (1914b).

Schuchardt's position on the origin of creole features lay somewhere between Coelho's extreme universalist theory and Adam's extreme substratist theory; as Gilbert (1980: 6) points out, Schuchardt generally tried to account for particular creole features on a case-by-case basis. Bickerton (1979a: ix) has claimed that there is a "complete absence of any kind of consistent theory in Schuchardt's work. He does not even make a clear distinction – to the modern scholar, the most basic and essential in the field – between native creole and nonnative pidgin." Yet in the very volume that Bickerton was introducing, Schuchardt (1909: 442, translated 1979: 27) does indeed make this distinction, noting that the New World creoles "evolved from communicative languages – both of which certainly have adjacent mother tongues – into mother tongues." If Bickerton did not understand this passage, the problem may lie in Markey's translation of Schuchardt's *Vermittlungssprachen* as 'communicative languages,' which does not correspond to any particular English concept. Reinecke (1937: 22) had translated the term as 'interlanguages' and Gilbert (Schuchardt 1980: 68) as 'go-between' languages. The basic idea of *vermitteln* is to act as an intermediary, and the compound *Vermittlungssprache* is made clear by the following phrase "die ja beiderseits

Muttersprachen neben sich haben," aptly translated by Gilbert as "where both sides retain their mother tongues." Several lines later Schuchardt states that these *Handelssprachen* (Markey's 'commercial languages,' Gilbert's 'trade languages') should not be called creoles, thus making an explicit distinction between *Vermittlungssprache* and *Kreolisch*. If Schuchardt's distinction between pidgins and creoles seems blurred to modern creolists, even those who read him in the original German (e.g. Meijer and Muysken 1977: 42), this is probably partly because he did not always use the modern German terms for these concepts, and partly because, as indicated above, he and his contemporaries did not always have the relevant sociolinguistic information to determine the status of particular varieties, especially at the beginning when they were dealing with quite fragmentary data. Moreover, it was not Schuchardt's style to make explicit pronouncements on theory, although he clearly recognized the importance of theoretical orientation, and his own understanding of the basic issues in the origin and development of pidgin and creole languages deepened and matured throughout his long career. However, much of his thinking has to be inferred from what he did and how he did it.

Schuchardt's first article on a creole language, São Tomé Creole Portuguese (1882a), has not yet been translated into English, but it is an extraordinary piece of work that illustrates the originality of his thinking. As he had remarked in his review of Coelho (Schuchardt 1881), the study of creole languages that he had begun ten years earlier for the light they might cast on the origin of the Romance languages led him to believe that more extensive data which would allow comparisons to be made of the creoles would eventually refute or at least limit Coelho's extreme universalist hypothesis (Schuchardt 1881: 581). Although Schuchardt did not explicitly formulate a substrate theory in the first of his "Kreolische Studien" (1882a), as Adam did the following year, it is clear from his methodology that his working hypothesis was indeed the importance of substrate influence. He cites a number of books on African languages to compare particular forms to those of the creole, concluding that the considerable grammatical differences between São Tomé and Cape Verdean Creole Portuguese may be due to the differences between their substrate languages, which he reckoned to be Bantu and West Atlantic respectively (1882a: 914). He also cites Van Name (1869–70) and remarks on the similarity of São Tomé phonology to that of the Caribbean creoles (Schuchardt 1882a: 895 ff.). He hypothesizes some means of borrowing or diffusion among creoles of different lexical bases: "From Creole Portuguese comes the completely equivalent [progressive marker] *ca* in the Creole French of Trinidad, Martinique, and Cayenne" (p. 911). He hints at the possibility of relexification: considering the phonotactics of Sranan Creole English and São

Tomé Creole Portuguese, he suggests that "one can only think that Negro English was somehow grafted onto [*gepfropft auf*] Negro Portuguese" (p. 901). Such thinking fitted a view of language reflected throughout Schuchardt's work: the Humboldtian concept of a language's inner (grammatical) form as opposed to its outer (lexical) form, with creoles retaining the inner form of their substrate while adopting the outer form of their lexical source language. Finally, Schuchardt introduces the first of his creole studies with what is probably one of the earliest sociolinguistic histories of a creole, relating what he has been able to find out about São Tomé's social history to linguistic features of the creole, such as the derivation of *kitó* 'pocketknife' from the *couteau* of the French corsairs who attacked the island in the sixteenth century.

Meijer and Muysken (1977: 32) consider the influence of substrate languages to have been Schuchardt's main interest. Features of the Atlantic creoles which he attributed to such influence include verb-fronting (section 5.2.4), serial verbs (§5.3), comparative structures (§5.3.3), certain features of the verbal system (§§5.1.1–3), the alternation of /l/ and /r/ (§4.6.4), semantic influence (§3.3.2) and idioms (§3.3.4). However, Schuchardt was always careful to distinguish between such features and those that he considered likely to have arisen from universal processes of creolization. Meijer and Muysken (1977: 34–35) have compiled a very interesting list of such features, which includes various kinds of replacement: of bound grammatical morphemes by free morphemes, of inflected verb forms by infinitives, of unstressed weak forms (e.g. definite articles) by stressed strong forms (e.g. demonstratives), of tense and aspect inflections by preverbal markers – as well as a number of other features such as the deletion or moving of preverbal pronoun clitics. Gilbert (1983) notes that Schuchardt resisted Coelho's universalist explanation of the similarity of the creoles, favoring "cultural, social, and historical explanations. Only when these did not suffice, did he talk about universal processes of simplification." Schuchardt understood the similarities of the Atlantic creoles of all lexical bases to stem not from a single common ancestor (cf. monogenesis, §2.10) but rather from their parallel development: "There exists no common Negro creole from which they could have issued . . . We have no divergence, but rather parallelism. They are fashioned out of the same material according to the same plan, in the same style" (1914a or 1980: 95).

Schuchardt had a clear understanding of the pidgin–creole life cycle:

> Go-between languages, auxiliary languages, languages of exigency are created everywhere and at all times. Most of them disappear again along with the condition that spawned them. Others endure and are stabilized without further substantial development. Some do this by

edging out and replacing the languages which were once also used alongside them. It is in this manner, chiefly, that the Negro creole dialects have come into being, promoted by the rather great variety of languages within the slave populations.   (1914a or 1980: 91)

Schuchardt saw in addition the possibility of decreolization as part of this life cycle in a passage that also adumbrates the creole continuum (§2.11) and the relationship of post-creole varieties like American Black English to their creole origin: "The Negro English that is most widely known is spoken in the southern United States . . . those variants which still show a creole-like character are increasingly falling into disuse by being accommodated to the English of the whites by means of an intermediate speech variety" (published posthumously by Gilbert 1985: 42).

Schuchardt is sometimes credited with (or blamed for) the "baby talk" theory of the origin of pidgins. As elaborated by Bloomfield (1933: 472), this is as follows:

> Speakers of a lower language may make so little progress in learning the dominant speech, that the masters, in communicating with them resort to "baby-talk." This "baby-talk" is the masters' imitation of the subjects' incorrect speech . . . some of its features are based not upon the subjects' mistakes but upon grammatical relations that exist within the upper language itself. The subjects, in turn, deprived of the correct model, can do no better now than to acquire the simplified "baby-talk" version of the upper language. The result may be a conventionalized jargon.

This theory was refuted by DeCamp (1971a: 19) and others as a sole explanation for pidginization and creolization since it did not account for the similarities among the creoles or the mutual intelligibility of the French creoles; that is, it did not allow a role for the Africans, for example, in the creation of the Caribbean creoles. However, Meijer and Muysken (1977: 30) hold that Schuchardt's views on simplification "can certainly not be reduced to the 'baby talk' theory . . . Although this theory constitutes an important element in his work on pidginization, alternative theories receive equal attention." Schuchardt did in fact maintain that creoles are shaped by the "foreigner talk" of the native speakers of the lexical source language: "All mutilation of a language issues from those who have inherited it as their mother tongue, in much the same way as the language of a child depends on the language of its nurse" (1909: 443 or 1980: 69). Elsewhere, however, Schuchardt suggests that restructuring results from a more collaborative effort:

> For the master and the slave it was simply a matter of mutual

comprehension. The master stripped off from the European language everything that was peculiar to it, the slave suppressed everything in it that was distinctive. They met on a middle ground . . . [but] to a lesser extent at the very beginning. The white man was the teacher of the black man. At first the black man mimicked him.

(1914a or 1980:91–92)

The explanation for this apparent contradiction would seem to lie in the different stages in question: at the very beginning of pidginization Europeans initiated the simplification of their language to facilitate comprehension, but later on the Africans introduced changes of their own, e.g. in speaking to Africans of other language backgrounds.

Toward the end of his career Schuchardt engaged in a polemic with the French linguist Antoine Meillet regarding the nature of mixed languages. This lasted throughout the war years (1914–21) and was later taken up again by Hall and Taylor (§2.9) in their debate on the genetic identity of mixed languages. Meillet doubted that any languages were mixed to the degree that this changed their genetic identity despite substrate features that might well be present (e.g. Gaulish features in French). He feared that linguistic theory could not cope with languages having more than one genetic identity:

If we have been able to succeed in reconstructing the history of some languages by comparison, it is because we were sure that each new system had to be explained as coming from a single system. In the case where one would have to take account of two initial systems and of their reactions to each other, the present methods would not be sufficient. For the right that one would have of choosing between two series of original forms would cause such an arbitrariness that every proof would become almost unrealizable. In spite of the hypotheses made in this direction, linguists have, fortunately, never yet been surely in the face of such a difficulty. If the difficulty really happens to occur, linguistics will have to work out new methods more delicate than those which are described here in order to overcome it, and it would remain to test them.   (Meillet 1967:102)

Of course Schuchardt believed that creoles were truly mixed languages that were related to more than one family, so that Meillet's concept of genetic relationship, which could not handle such double identity, had to be untenable (Hall 1958:370).

Schuchardt's work remains a rich source of information and insights in many areas of creole linguistics. He was not only the founder of the discipline but also the first to grasp that "The importance for general linguistics of the creole dialects has not yet been fully appreciated" (1914a or 1980: 91).

2.7 Hesseling and his contemporaries

The Dutch linguist Dirk Christiaan Hesseling published on creole languages and creolization between 1897 and 1934, bridging the work of Schuchardt and Reinecke, the first modern creolist. Hesseling was a Greek scholar whose interest in the development of koine Greek from the older Attic dialects led to his interest in language mixing and creolization. After reading Schuchardt's 1891 study of Malayo-Portuguese, Hesseling developed a theory (1897, 1899) that this creole, which was spoken by slaves that the Dutch took from the East Indies to their colony in South Africa during the seventeenth and eighteenth centuries, had influenced the development of Afrikaans (§8.5). He believed the influence of the indigenous people in South Africa to have been rather limited in comparison to that of the Oriental slaves. He thought that Afrikaans had stopped halfway in the process of creolization because of its particular sociolinguistic conditions. Hesseling's theory, modified and expanded by Valkhoff (1966, 1972), found few supporters in South Africa. Hesseling's interest in Afrikaans led to work on Negerhollands Creole Dutch (1905), Dutch in Ceylon (1910), Papiamentu Creole Spanish (1933a) and a general theory of creolization (1933b, 1934).

DeCamp (1971a: 22) suggested that Hesseling might be viewed as a precursor of the monogeneticists (§2.10). Although Meijer and Muysken (1977: 39) agreed that his view of the origin of Afrikaans might be so interpreted, they felt that the rest of his work did not support such a conclusion. Indeed, Hellinger (1985: 40) points out Hesseling's observation that "Similar causes in Indonesia and on the Cape produced convergent results" (1897 or 1979: 11), a distinctly polygenetic view.

Hesseling was more sympathetic than Schuchardt to the idea of universal processes of creolization akin to adult second-language acquisition. Unlike Schuchardt, he considered the speech of non-native speakers of the lexical source language to be more influential in the pidginization/creolization process than that of the native speakers. Although he often pointed out substrate features in the creoles, he did not believe that the creoles' grammar was simply that of their substrate languages. Moreover, Hesseling did not always agree with Schuchardt as to whether specific creole features should be attributed to universals or to substrate influence (Meijer and Muysken 1977: 39). Muysken and Meijer (1979: xi) point out that Hesseling considered highly idiosyncratic factors to operate in the genesis of creoles, as well as in language change in general – the result of particular sociocultural circumstances, accidental phonetic resemblances between words, or idiosyncratic connotations. Hesseling maintained a distinction between a *gemeng-*

de taal or language that has undergone mixing (i.e. practically any language) and a *mengeltaal* or mixed language (i.e. one whose grammar has been affected, or whose lexicon shows massive borrowing). A creole is a *mengeltaal* that results when there is a clash of languages and these languages are dissimilar. If either of these two conditions does not obtain, then simplification rather than creolization results (1934: 319–321).

The Danish linguist Otto Jespersen dealt with language mixture in an often cited chapter on "Pidgins and Congenors" in his book *Language* (1922). Comparing Melanesian and Chinese Pidgin English with Mauritian Creole French and Chinook Jargon, Jespersen generally agreed with Schuchardt as to the origin and basic nature of pidgins and creoles, although he discounted the role of substrate influence and maintained that more universal processes of language acquisition determined the speech of those who pidginized a language "as if their minds were just as innocent of grammar as those of very small babies" (1922: 228). However, Jespersen also took sociolinguistic factors into account to explain the limited nature of such language acquisition: "My view, then, is that Beach-la-mar as well as Pidgin is English, only English learnt imperfectly, in consequence partly of the difficulties always inherent in learning a totally different foreign language, partly of the obstacles put in the way of learning by the linguistic behaviour of the English-speaking people themselves" (1922: 225). Regarding this last point, Vendryes (1921) had asserted that "Creole ... is the speech ... of a subordinate class whose superiors have never troubled nor desired to make them speak any language correctly."

Hellinger (1985: 43) sees Jespersen's ideas as foreshadowing those of Schumann (1978) and Bickerton (1977b), summed up in his observation that "in all these seemingly so different cases the same mental factor is at work, namely imperfect mastery of a language" (Jespersen 1922: 233 ff.).

2.8   Reinecke and his contemporaries

Hellinger (1985: 45) has suggested that in the 1930s the center of gravity of creole studies shifted from the Old World to the New. Along with this came another shift from armchair creolists, who had almost no direct contact with the object of their study, to creolists who actively pursued fieldwork. A student of Hesseling, Jan de Josselin de Jong, collected texts of Negerhollands in phonemic spelling on St. Thomas and St. John, which he published in 1926. Other early fieldworkers came from the tradition of anthropology, such as Franz Boas, who studied Chinook Jargon (1933), or the folklorist Elsie Clews Parsons, whose massive collection of texts in the English- and French-based creoles of the Caribbean area (1933–43) reflects a keen interest in language. Although Melville and Frances Herskovits were anthropologists, one of their primary concerns was with the pidgin and creole languages of West Africa and the Caribbean as cultural artefacts. The Herskovitses (1936) concluded that from the Sea Islands of South Carolina to Suriname in South America "Negroes have been using words from European languages to render literally the underlying morphological patterns of West African tongues" (p. 131). They were among the first to point out the similarity of idioms (i.e. turns of speech as opposed to purely grammatical constructions) in certain West African languages and the Caribbean creoles. Perhaps most importantly, their anthropological perspective lent a new dimension to their understanding of creolization as a general cultural phenomenon rather than one confined to language.

Substrate influence, for which the Herskovitses adduced considerable linguistic and cultural evidence, had become a perennial point of controversy in creole studies. Lou Lichtveld, a Dutch linguist from Suriname, described Sranan Creole English as having "almost all the outer and inner characteristics of an African language" (1927: 391). L. Göbl's "Problems of Substrate in Creole French" (1933) points not only to substrate influence but also to retentions from archaic and regional French, as well as innovations due to development within the creoles themselves (a source of change apparently not mentioned earlier in the literature). Göbl (1934) also attempted the first comparative structural study of the French-based creoles, or indeed of any lexical base group, which was not superseded until that of Goodman (1964). Hancock did the first comparative studies for subgrouping the English-based creoles, based on lexicon (1969) and syntax (1987), while Alleyne's comparison (1980) included phonology. Such a study of the Portuguese-based creoles has only recently been done by Ivens Ferraz (1987).

After Göbl's careful and balanced approach to the issue of substrate influence, the next two works on creole French took extreme and diametrically opposed positions. The first was by Suzanne Sylvain (1936), a native speaker of Haitian Creole French who was also a linguist trained in African languages. Goodman (1964: 116) describes her study of Haitian morphosyntax as "surely the finest description of any creole dialect up to that time." However, after her thorough and even-handed treatment of what she identified as the French and African features of the creole, she concluded quite surprisingly that "we are in the presence of French which has been cast in the mould of African syntax or, since languages are generally classified according to their syntactic ancestry, an Ewe language with French vocabulary" (1936: 178). Since this sentence is so often cited, it seems only fair to quote a personal communication about it from Robert A. Hall, Jr.: "Suzanne told me, when I discussed the matter with her in Haiti in '49, that this

was not her own opinion, but that of her mentor . . . [who] had required her to put
it in at the end."

The second work, by Jules Faine (1936), was also by a Haitian but an amateur
philologist who claimed that African influence on Haitian was negligible: "at least
three quarters [of the creole] is from the Norman dialect of the sixteenth and
seventeenth centuries, which has been preserved in a very pure state" (1936: 1).
This view is widely held in the Caribbean areas where French creoles are spoken;
indeed, it had been asserted without support in the first doctoral dissertation on a
creole language, written by a Guadeloupean (Poyen-Bellisle 1894: 12). As
Goodman notes (1964: 126 ff.), "Faine could scarcely have chosen a less likely
candidate than Norman among northern French dialects as the source of Creole
phonology" and his evidence on other linguistic levels is equally unconvincing.
Whatever his book's reception, Faine remained undaunted and in 1939 published
Le Créole dans l'univers, a comparison of Haitian and Mauritian Creole French,
claiming that the French creoles came not from a single dialect of French but
rather a composite forming a nautical patois.

The American linguist Leonard Bloomfield devoted several brief but often cited
passages to pidgins and creoles in his popular book, *Language* (1933). Besides
contributing to the theory of baby talk (§2.6), he gave a clear definition of pidgins
and creoles (without using those terms), noting that creolization occurs "especially
when the subject group is made up of persons from different speech-communities,
who can communicate among themselves only by means of the jargon"
(1933: 473). He went on to discuss the speech of American blacks and decreolization (§2.11), concluding with some brief passages illustrating Sranan.

John Reinecke is considered by many to be the father of modern creole studies.
An American mainlander who settled in Hawaii (Sato and A. Reinecke 1987),
John Reinecke's Master's thesis (1935, published 1969) is still the best source of
information on the development of Hawaiian Creole English. His 1937 doctoral
dissertation, done at Yale University's Department of Race Relations, was
entitled *Marginal Languages: a Sociological Survey of the Creole Languages and
Trade Jargons*; it is a remarkably complete guide to what was known about creole
linguistics at that time. Reinecke spent a good part of the rest of his life at the
scholarly tasks that would put the discipline on a solid footing, particularly the
compilation of the comprehensive *Bibliography of Pidgin and Creole Languages*
(Reinecke *et al.* 1975).

It is instructive to consider Reinecke's assessment of the field at the time he
entered it:

many of the problems that concern creolists today had been stated or

at least adumbrated. But if no longer in their infancy, creole studies in
the 1930s had not passed their adolescence either quantitatively or
qualitatively . . . For the most part, creole studies were peripheral to
the main theoretical concerns of linguistics; they were a field
cultivated mainly by amateur or semi-amateur aficionados . . . The
amount of information on any one pidgin or creole ranged from bare
mention to two or three tolerably adequate sketches of it . . . Except
for a few glances at Chinook Jargon, creole studies were Eurocentric,
concerned with languages of European lexicon and especially with
that classic area of plantation creoles, the Caribbean . . . Creole
studies were compartmentalized: Guthrie [1935 on Lingala] and
Jacobs [1932 on Chinook Jargon] and Sawyerr [1940 on Krio], for
instance, might almost have been writing on three different planets for
aught each knew and cared about the others' work. The inaccessibility of much of the writing, unpublished theses in particular,
hindered the development of a wide perspective among creolists.

(1977: vii–viii)

Reinecke interspersed these remarks with observations on how short the current
state of the discipline fell from the ideal, yet one is struck by how much his own
efforts had helped advance the field. His dissertation, which has circulated widely
in its microfilm form since the 1960s although it has never been published as a
book, represents a monumental effort to provide an overview of what he felt
should be the scope of the discipline. The first 150 pages deal with the development
of the theory of restructured languages (surveying the literature up to 1937) and
their classification, as well as sociolinguistic issues regarding their relation to
standard languages, education, and national and ethnic identity. The next 716
pages provide a survey of over 40 pidgin and creole languages, including a number
with non-European-derived lexicons that were brought within the scope of the
discipline for the first time, e.g. pidginized varieties of Eskimo, Mobilian, and
other Amerindian languages, Língua Geral, Pidgin Assamese, Pidgin Japanese,
restructured Arabic, Lingala, and Fanakalo. Each variety is discussed within the
context of its sociolinguistic history (which has since become an integral part of
pidgin and creole studies), followed by an examination of its distinctive linguistic
features and then a full bibliography.

Gilbert's statement (1986a: 19) that "Reinecke . . . never attempted a comprehensive explanation of the problems of linguistic similarity and simplification"
within the creoles rather misses the point of his dissertation, which was to identify
the *socio*linguistic patterns that result in pidginization and creolization. The

German sociologist Ernst Schultze (1933) was the first to identify the value of such an approach, but he lacked Reinecke's background in linguistics, which was necessary to analyze the effects that such sociolinguistic patterns had on language.

Reinecke realized that "A valid classification must be built on a complete and detailed knowledge of all the dialects" (1937: 57), yet he doubted that it would be possible to do this "on a purely linguistic basis – on such points as degree of breakdown of the grammatical structure, size and flexibility of the vocabulary, stability of the dialect, and degree of language mixture . . . [although] such features will be discussed later, to see if it is possible to correlate them with the social characteristics of the marginal languages" (ibid.). Instead, he proposed classifying them "on the basis of the circumstances of their formation, their functions, and their development as fixed and recognized dialects" (ibid.). Thus he arrived at the following categories, each defined in detail and illustrated with a number of examples: (1) plantation creole dialects (e.g. those of the Caribbean area and the islands off West Africa); (2) settlers' creole dialects (e.g. creole Portuguese in Guinea-Bissau and Asia); and (3) trade jargons (i.e. pidgins).

Reinecke's sociological distinction between plantation and settlers' creoles was largely ignored by later creolists since it did not seem to correspond to any discernible linguistic differences between such creoles. However, it is logical to expect both social and linguistic differences between creoles that remain in contact with their substrate languages (Reinecke's settler creoles like Indo-Portuguese) and those that do not (plantation creoles like São Tomé Creole Portuguese). Much recent theorizing about the sociology of creolization has considered only the latter situation, leading to assertions such as the claim that creoles became established as community languages because pidgin speakers had no other means of understanding one another. While this was indeed the case on São Tomé, it was clearly not the case with Indo-Portuguese, whose Indian-born speakers were always bi- or multilingual in the local languages that formed the creole's substrate. The establishment of settlers' creoles as community languages would seem to have much more to do with their association with a particular social identity (e.g. that of Eurasians). This seems likely to have been a key factor in the establishment of plantation creoles as well, which functioned as the badge of a local social identity. Linguistically, creoles that remain in contact with their substrate languages can be expected to be more influenced by them, particularly if the superstrate language is withdrawn and the substrate language is raised in prestige, as happened in the case of the Indo-Portuguese creole of Sri Lanka. This variety now has a great number of morphological and syntactic features with Tamil and Sinhalese counterparts that are not found in earlier texts (Smith 1979a; section 6.4.2). Such linguistic change in the direction of the substrate could not occur in a plantation creole.

Those tracing the nativization of extended pidgins in such places as Papua New Guinea and Nigeria need to bear Reinecke's distinction in mind. Its usefulness has recently been taken up or rediscovered by Chaudenson (1979: 21) and Bickerton (1986), who distinguish between "créoles exogènes" or "plantation creoles" as opposed to "créoles endogènes" or "fort creoles" respectively.

Reinecke, in addition, made a distinction within the plantation creoles (which he also proposed calling "African creole dialects," 1937:60) of "maroon creoles" such as Saramaccan and Ndjuka Creole English, Annobonese Creole Portuguese, and Jamaican Maroon Creole English. He further noted that

> In several instances the slaves were so situated among a majority or a large minority of whites (and there were other reasons as well for the result), that they, or rather their creole children, learned the common language, not a creole dialect; or the plantation creole dialects that had begun to form never crystallized, never got beyond the makeshift stage. This happened in ... Brazil, Cuba and the Spanish-speaking Caribbean countries in general, and in the southern United States in general. (p. 61)

Reinecke further distinguished between settlers' creole dialects and language enclaves of settlers in Europe and North America:

> There are two main differences between these two types of settlement. On the one hand the European and American *Sprachinseln* are either numerous enough usually to keep their language uncorrupted to any great extent, or are so like the surrounding population as to be readily assimilated before their home language has time to break down structurally; while the creole settlements are at the same time small and slowly assimilable by the natives. On the other hand the settlers in Europe and America, set down in a social organization similar to their own, are assimilated rather than assimilators, so that their language remains unsimplified – they have not to speak it in a simplified form with a half-assimilated clientele or native traders. (p. 63)

Reinecke distinguished several other varieties which he considered to lie beyond the scope of pidgin and creole studies: colonial dialects (unrestructured varieties of European languages in the New World, Australia, etc.), foreigners' mixed speech (e.g. the English of foreigners in Hawaii), dying minor languages (e.g. New Jersey Dutch), "babu" language (a school-taught foreign language that becomes a secondary language), and lingua francas that have not been restructured.

Although not all of these distinctions have been accepted, and although Reinecke did not contribute directly to the theoretical debates among those who followed, he was surely a major figure in the founding of modern pidgin and creole studies: he not only staked out the full scope of the discipline but also established its sociological foundations, ensuring that it would be a part of what was to become sociolinguistics.

2.9 Hall and Taylor

Although many of the younger contemporaries of Robert Hall and Douglas Taylor are still publishing and seem very much a part of the current generation of creolists, Hall and Taylor themselves were part of an earlier phase of the discipline's development. Creolist works of the 1930s were not widely read at the time; they had no discernible effect on general linguistics, and they formed no recognized field of study within linguistics. It was in no small measure due to the efforts of Hall and Taylor that there was a revival of interest in pidgin and creole languages after World War II that blossomed into the establishment of a new academic field in the late 1950s.

The war brought Americans suddenly into contact with a number of "exotic" languages in Asia and the Pacific. The challenge they presented to linguistics and language teaching had a profound effect on both and resulted in the description of a number of languages that had never been systematically studied before. One of these was the Pidgin English of Melanesia, described in structuralist terms by Hall and others in a book published for the United States Armed Services Institute in 1943. Hall, who emerged as a leading figure in Romance and general linguistics, pursued his interest in pidgin and creole languages by studying Sranan Creole English (1948) and Haitian Creole French (Hall *et al.* 1953), becoming an authority on the latter. As the first creolist with any extensive first-hand knowledge of a pidgin, he was in a good position to develop a theory of the life cycle of pidgins (1962). Although Hall makes it clear that the distinction between pidgins and creoles regarding native speakers had already been established (1962: 151, fn. 3), his account of creolization made it implicit that creoles *always* have a preceding phase as a pidgin. This position became widely accepted, but Alleyne (1980: 126) objected that "the existence of a prior 'simplified pidgin' remains purely speculative" in the case of the Caribbean creoles, and Mühlhäusler (1986: 8) hypothesizes that creoles may have evolved from pre-pidgin (i.e. unstable) jargons.

Hall and Taylor were the first modern linguists to make their colleagues aware of the theoretical importance of restructured languages. Hall's involvement in more general linguistic theory led him to use data from pidgin and creole languages to test the validity of various hypotheses. In 1959 he cast doubt on the

usefulness of glottochronology, a lexico-statistical technique to establish the number of years that two related languages have been separated, by applying it to the
lexicon of Melanesian Pidgin English: "even from this single instance it would
seem that the 'normal' rate of lexical replacement assumed for glottochronology is
not valid in case pidginization has intervened."

The issue of the importance of substrate languages emerged yet again in the
1950s, the revival of the debate becoming something of a rite of passage for each
succeeding generation of creolists. This time, however, the polemic took a more
sophisticated form, focusing on the validity of the concept of genetic relatedness.
Moreover, the question was no longer whether or not creoles had features that
could be traced to their substrata (it was agreed that they did), but rather how
these features should affect the genetic classification of the creoles. Hall favored
classifying them as dialects of their European lexical source languages, while the
case for classifying them as genetically distinct was advanced by Taylor, an
English linguist who had settled in Dominica and was studying the Lesser
Antillean Creole French spoken there.

Hall noted that creolists were retesting the notion of substratum as developed in
Romance linguistics in his review of Turner's (1949) book on the African features
in Gullah Creole English, a landmark study based on the fieldwork that Turner
had begun in the 1930s under the influence of Herskovits: "The theory of linguistic
substratum, at one time almost wholly discredited by the excesses of its
proponents, is now being reinterpreted and, one might say, rehabilitated in the
light of the more realistic picture of linguistic transfer afforded by pidgin and
creolized languages" (Hall 1950: 54). Hall questioned not the existence but rather
the importance of substrate influence in the creoles and cautioned against extreme
positions on this issue:

> In summary, anyone with some knowledge of pidgin and creole
> languages cannot deny the existence of the influence of the substrata.
> However, our experience with such languages leads us to be rather
> conservative or "eclectic" regarding the possibility of such
> influence . . . Each presumed case for substrate influence should be
> judged independently on its own merits; thus we shall avoid the
> exaggerations of both those who see signs of the substrate every-
> where, as well as those who deny it completely.
>
> (Hall 1955: 9, my translation)

In the same article (p. 2), Hall dubbed these the *sostratomani* ('substratomaniacs')
and *sostratofobi* ('substratophobes') respectively; Bickerton (1981) revived only
the former term.

The following year Taylor published an article which took up the question of the classification of creolized languages. Noting that Hall *et al.* (1953) had classified Haitian as a Romance language (principally on the basis of lexical and phonological correspondences with French) but that one of the coauthors (Sylvain 1936) had also classified Haitian as an African language (principally on the basis of syntactic similarities to Ewe and other Niger-Congo languages), Taylor questioned the suitability of the concept of genetic relatedness when it came to pidgins and creoles, particularly since Meillet had specified that such relatedness implied continuity. Moreover, Taylor asserted that the Caribbean creoles were related to one another across lexical boundaries in ways their lexical source languages were not because of the important role that substrate languages had played in forming the creoles' syntax. Taylor based this assertion on the work of the Dutch linguist Jan Voorhoeve (1953), who had compared the verbal systems of Sranan Creole English and Lesser Antillean Creole French, which he called "a related language" – the first time a relationship had been claimed to exist between two languages without reference to their lexicons. Taylor concluded that "Languages originating in a pidgin or jargon, while genetically 'orphans,' may be said to have two 'foster-parents': one that provides the basic morphological and/or syntactic pattern, and another from which the fundamental vocabulary is taken" (1956: 413). Hall (1958) replied that although traditional historical linguists had assumed that the languages they compared were "pure" and that their change was gradual, neither of these two factors is essential to the validity of the concept of genetic relatedness:

> No linguistic relationship is "pure," whether the change be gradual or brusque . . . no one considers that the basic relationship of the language is changed by the presence of structural borrowings; we do not classify Alsatian German with the Romance languages because it has nasalized vowels. The question now arises: how far can structural borrowings go before they affect our classification of a language?
>
> (1958: 370)

Taylor's (1963) response was one of the earliest affirmations of the monogenetic theory, so it is discussed in the following section.

2.10 Monogenesis

With the emergence of creole studies as a recognized branch of linguistics in the late 1950s and early 1960s, the number of researchers in this area swelled from perhaps a dozen to hundreds in the 1970s (DeCamp 1977: 7). For this reason it becomes more convenient to discuss periods in terms of ideas rather than of the many individuals who advanced them.

The early growth of creole studies was probably related to the movement towards independence in the British West Indies, which helped shift the perspective on language from that of the colonizer to that of the colonized. The participants at the first conference on creole languages, held at the University College of the West Indies in Jamaica in 1959, observed that to "try to deal with people without understanding their native language was bound to be ineffective; to try to form a Federation of the West Indies while ignoring the language problems of the peoples comprising that Federation was to overlook a most important factor" (Le Page 1961: 117).

A growing interest in Caribbean creoles is indicated by the appearance of two pioneering Masters' theses written by English-speaking West Indians: a Jamaican, Beryl Loftman (later Bailey) (1953), and a Guyanese, Richard Allsopp (1958). Both went on to write doctoral dissertations and become leading figures in creole studies. Robert Le Page, an English linguist teaching at the University College of the West Indies (a college in special relationship with the University of London; it became the University of the West Indies after independence), was a major force in establishing academic recognition of creole studies. In 1951 Le Page began a survey of the varieties of English spoken in the British West Indies by sending a questionnaire to local teachers regarding language usage and eliciting the local equivalents of a number of sentences in standard English. Despite a limited response and certain problems with this method, Le Page was able to organize this and other information he had gathered into his ground-breaking "General Outlines of Creole English dialects in the British Caribbean" (1957–58). This was to provide a basis for bringing the teaching of English "into line with the needs of the Caribbean, rather than with the needs of the Home Counties in England" (Le Page 1955: 46).

Le Page also helped make the University College of the West Indies the first center for creole studies through his co-operation with two visiting linguists from the United States, David DeCamp (who was working on dialect geography in Jamaica) and Frederic Cassidy (a lexicographer doing fieldwork for his important 1961 study, *Jamaica Talk*). Cassidy, who was born and partly raised in Jamaica, joined forces with Le Page to compile the *Dictionary of Jamaican English* (1967), the first comprehensive etymological dictionary of any creole, and a model for those that followed.

The conference that Le Page convened in 1959 was small, including only the above scholars and Hall, Taylor, and Voorhoeve, as well as Allsopp and several other graduate students (Morris Goodman and David Lawton) and two American dialectologists (A. H. Marckwardt and E. Bagby Atwood) and an Africanist (Jack Berry). M. Pradel Pompilus of Haiti and R. W. Thompson of Hong Kong University sent papers read in their absence.

> The conference sessions were held in one small room. In spite of the size of the group, never before had so many creolists, representing different continents and different languages, confronted each other face to face. The proceedings of the conference (Le Page 1961) formed the basis of much of the discussion and research of, the following decade. As discussions of the applicability of such concepts as generative grammar, diglossia, continuum, and comparative–historical reconstruction progressed, the participants began to think of themselves more as 'creolists' than just as students of Haitian French or Jamaican English.   (DeCamp 1977: 12).

Among the most consequential ideas to surface at this conference was monogenesis, the idea that many of the world's pidgins and creoles could be traced to a common origin, the Portuguese-based pidgin that arose in the fifteenth century in Africa, perhaps from the Lingua Franca, and that was eventually relexified (or translated word for word) into the pidgins of other European lexical bases that gave rise to the modern creoles. The nub of this idea originated in Whinnom's 1956 book on Philippine Creole Spanish which, he suggested, grew out of the creole Portuguese of the Indonesian island of Ternate which had been transported to the Philippines in the seventeenth century (§7.4):

> The similarities in grammar and syntax, and even of vocabulary, between the Spanish contact vernaculars in the Philippines and Indo-Portuguese, are so many – and they are not attributable to a common substratum – that we can be quite certain that Ternateño did develop out of the common Portuguese pidgin of the Eastern Seas.
>
> (Whinnom 1956: 9, fn. 21)

Whinnom went on to remark that this Portuguese pidgin "may not have been a 'pure' contact vernacular, but a kind of imitation Sabir, the Lingua Franca of the Mediterranean" (1956: 9–10). In a 1957 review of Whinnom's book, Taylor pointed out that many of the features of Philippine Creole Spanish were also found in the Caribbean creoles, e.g. the preposition *na* (§3.4.1), compound prepositions (§5.5.2), completive *cabá* (§5.1.5), and other preverbal markers such as Papiamentu Creole Spanish non-punctual *ta*, anterior *taba*, and future *lo*. Thompson took these up in his 1959 conference paper (published in 1961), concluding that the pidgin Portuguese used by slavers, "much influenced, no doubt, by the West African substratum, may have been the pattern for all the West

Indian Creoles just as, in the Eastern and Pacific worlds Portuguese Creole dialects, well known to Europeans of many nationalities, may have provided the models for the two great branches of pidgin English, China Coast pidgin and Neo-Melanesian" (1961: 113). Responding to an earlier version of Thompson's paper, Taylor (1959: 488) construed this as a suggestion that the Portuguese pidgin had changed "its vocabulary under the pressure of various other national languages, but not – or to a much lesser extent – its grammatical structure." Accepting the possibility of a massive shift from Portuguese to Spanish lexicon in the cases of Philippine Creole Spanish and Papiamentu, Taylor (1960: 156) went on to suggest that it may have been possible that both Sranan and Saramaccan Creole English "began as an Afro-Portuguese pidgin that was later anglicized," an idea subsequently expanded by Voorhoeve (1973) (see below). Stewart (1962: 46) christened this kind of vocabulary shift "relexification," a term taken up by Whinnom (1965: 517) and others as an essential element of what was becoming the formal theory of monogenesis. Yet there was disagreement among proponents of this theory as to how important the African substratum had been in shaping pidgin Portuguese. Taylor (1963: 813) argued that "if there was continuity in the use of a grammatical system, everything points to Africa as the place of that system's origin – probably not in any one African language, but more likely in some Afro-Portuguese pidgin." However, Whinnom (1965: 522) responded that "there is evidence against its originating from the contact of Portuguese with West African languages: Dr. Lopes da Silva [1957: 515] found nothing in the modern Cape Verde dialects that it was necessary to explain by means of the African substrate." Instead Whinnom claimed that the European-based pidgins and creoles showed a much greater degree of simplification than those based on African, Asian or Amerindian lexicons:

> Their simplicity is an Indo-European simplicity, and such simplicity is not achieved simply by "mixing" two languages of different stock. If, then, the European-based creoles are like the alphabet – so simple seeming, but yet in fact very highly sophisticated in this simplicity – I should like to suggest that we do not want to have to suppose that such miraculous simplicity was achieved, independently, twice . . . which brings me back to my original suggestion that Portuguese pidgin may derive from Sabir.   (Whinnom 1965: 522)

Hellinger (1985: 61) interprets the strong version of the monogenetic theory as claiming that *all* pidgin and creole languages can be traced to a single proto-pidgin, which she refutes by pointing to pidgins lexically based on African languages in whose genesis no European language was involved. However, Whinnom (1965: 521) explicitly excluded from his claim pidgins not based on

European languages. Many of the objections of other linguists to the monogenetic theory also hinge on its scope, i.e. whether it is a plausible explanation for the similarity of all European-based pidgins and creoles, or just the Atlantic creoles, or just the creoles of a particular European lexical base. One of the original arguments for a common origin had been the mutual intelligibility of the French-based creoles:

> Speakers from opposite ends of the Caribbean – from Louisiana in the north and French Guiana in the south – are able to converse together with a minimum of misunderstanding . . . Although this mutual intelligibility is in part due to the fact that the various dialects of a Creole derive their vocabularies from the same source language, the fact that Creoles are not mutually intelligible with their lexically related standards shows that vocabulary alone is not a sufficient explanation. What is of equal importance for the Creoles is the fact that their like vocabularies are matched by grammatical structures which are also very much alike. Since it is highly improbable that dialects showing such overall similarities would have developed quite independently of each other, it is difficult to avoid the conclusion that the dialects of at least the French-based Creole must have had some common origin before they became implanted in widely separated parts of the Caribbean.   (Stewart 1962: 45)

Of course the actual mechanism could have been the relexification of a single pidgin in Africa which then spread by diffusion (true monogenesis) or parallel relexification in both Africa and various parts of the New World (actually polygenesis). In a privately circulated sheet of addenda and corrigenda to his 1965 article, Whinnom supported the former:

> Dr. L. P. Harvey of London has in correspondence suggested that, while the theory of polygenesis is untenable, I have applied too rigidly the traditional concepts of linguistic affiliation, and that some of these languages may have arisen by imitation, by "stimulus diffusion," rather than by straight relexification. I am now inclined to believe that this may well be a better explanation of the origin of some of the "awkward" creoles like Melanesian Pidgin, and even, perhaps, Jamaica Talk.

Although Goodman (1964) did not refer to the role of pidgin Portuguese in the formation of the French creoles and later (1987) argued against it, he did support the idea of monogenesis within the lexical base:

Having established both the existence of West African influence in Mauritius and the close historical connection of all the French creoles, one is able to formulate a much clearer idea of how Creole originated and developed. Only by positing a single origin for Creole can one account for this historical connection, and its place of origin can scarcely have been other than West Africa, from which it was transported to the various parts of the world where Creole is now found. It most likely developed out of a slavers' jargon of some sort, whose French element (what up to now has been called pre-Creole) may or may not have been the kind of dialectal mélange which Faine suggests, but which almost certainly incorporated a number of features of the slaves' native languages. It was undoubtedly fairly unstable through time and even at a given time, since only thus can the very real differences between the various creoles and even within single dialects be accounted for ... The West African jargon or pidgin then began to develop independently in the various colonial areas to which it had been transported and to become more stable as it came in increasing measure to supplant the native languages of the Africans. In America early population movement among the various Creole-speaking areas and the presence of stronger West African influence doubtless reinforced certain traits which either were not retained in Mauritius or were never prevalent there ... Geographically proximate areas exerted greater influence upon one another, as would be expected, than upon more distant ones, thereby creating certain dialect areas.

(Goodman 1964: 130)

Stewart (1967) suggested a similar diffusionist model for the origin and spread of restructured English on both sides of the Atlantic:

One possible explanation why this kind of pidginized English was so widespread in the New World, with widely separated varieties resembling each other in so many ways, is that it did not originate in the New World as isolated and accidentally similar instances of random pidginization, but rather originated as a *lingua franca* in the trade centers and slave factories on the West African coast. It is likely that at least some Africans already knew this pidgin English when they came to the New World, and that the common colonial policy of mixing slaves of various tribal origins forced its rapid adoption as a plantation *lingua franca*.

Based on their lexical similarities as opposed to standard English, Hancock (1969) also posited a single origin for the English-based Atlantic creoles, but also hesitated to connect these to pidgin Portuguese via relexification:

> The hypothesis presented in this paper maintains that the English-derived creoles spoken today on the West African coast, and in South, Central, and North America, represent the modern descendants of a single early pidgin spoken probably with local variants along the West African coast from the early sixteenth century. This will be referred to as the "Proto-Pidgin," English-derived unless otherwise stated ... A suggestion that has gained wide currency is the so-called "relexification hypothesis" ... This may well have taken place, but if so it is surprising that so few traces of Portuguese remain in the Atlantic creoles today ... Saramaccan, with 27% of its lexicon traceable to Portuguese, is an exception and may represent the only certain example of large-scale relexification among the languages dealt with here.   (Hancock 1969: 7, 12)

Hancock's paper had been presented at the 1968 Conference on Pidginization and Creolization of Languages held at Mona, Jamaica (Hymes 1971), where there was a considerable amount of theoretical debate regarding monogenesis. The Trinidadian linguist, Mervyn Alleyne (1971: 170), rejected Whinnom's hypothesis that "'pidgins' or 'creoles' are, to a large extent, in their genesis, European phenomena ... I do not think that [the attempt to relate the Portuguese pidgin to Sabir] is necessary for explaining the genesis of 'creole' dialects, nor do I think that a convincing case has been made for it." However, he accepted relexification as the mechanism by which African substrate languages shaped the Atlantic creoles (1980: 109).

Hall was perceived as the leading proponent of polygenesis via spontaneous generation: "A pidgin can arise ... whenever an emergency situation calls for communication on a minimal level of comprehension" and then be "creolized, i.e. [it] becomes the first language of a speech community" (1962: 152–155). DeCamp (1971a: 20) argued against monogenesis as the vehicle of African substrate influence: "No one African language can account for all or even a majority of the 'African' elements in Caribbean creole, nor is any significant 'African' feature in creole shared by all or even a majority of the native languages of the slaves ... Thus there could not have been any significant systematic African 'substratum.'" He found that the theory of monogenesis rested on a number of assumptions without documentary evidence, but still had points to recommend it:

Even if we were to assume that the lexicon and the structure of a language were equally susceptible to change, relexification would still be a better explanation than restructuralization for the development of pidgins and creoles; for the influences which could bring about a wholesale adoption of French vocabulary in French territories, English vocabulary in British territories, etc., are clear and obvious, whereas there is no known sociolinguistic influence which could explain why the structures of five different European languages should have been modified in precisely the same direction . . . The weaknesses in the monogenetic theory are first a very sketchy historical documentation, second the controversial status of Far Eastern pidgin English (which lacks many of the features shared by other pidgins and creoles), and third the problem of certain pidgins and creoles which clearly developed without any direct Portuguese influence.   (DeCamp 1971a: 23–24)

Voorhoeve (1973) proposed that the high percentage of Portuguese-derived words in Saramaccan Creole English provided evidence in favor of the theory of relexification, still closely associated with monogenesis. He rejected the traditional explanation that the Saramaccans' ancestors had fled from the plantations of Portuguese-speaking Jews who had immigrated to Suriname from Brazil (§10.2.2), suggesting instead that slaves arriving directly from Africa spoke a pidgin Portuguese that began relexifying toward English when the colony was held by Britain. While the Saramaccans' ancestors escaped from the coastal plantations before this process had been completed, so that their language retained a considerable amount of lexicon derived from Portuguese, the process of relexification continued on the coast so that Sranan, the creole spoken there today, has a much higher proportion of English-derived lexicon. However, Goodman (1987) has challenged Voorhoeve's interpretation and argued in support of the traditional explanation.

The monogenetic theory has left its mark on creole linguistics, although few creolists today would claim, for example, that Tok Pisin is directly descended from the Lingua Franca via relexification. The concept of relexification itself has a considerable number of adherents in the more restricted sense of calquing on the level of the phrase, frequently accepted as the mechanism by which at least the Atlantic creoles of different lexical bases are related to a common substratum. Indeed, Koopman (1986) has redefined relexification in terms of the Government Binding framework as "the transfer of lexical properties from the native language into the target language" (p. 251). Many still consider massive relexification plausible in the case of closely related lexicons, such as a shift from creole Portuguese to creole Spanish. Robertson (1979) considers the replacement of Berbice Creole Dutch lexical items by words from (Guyanese Creole) English to be a form of decreolization with relexification, and Dalphinis (1986) explains a similar shift from St. Lucian Creole French to (Creole) English lexical items as relexification.

By definition all theories besides monogenesis imply polygenesis, and many believe that pidginization and creolization occurred in different places at different times but under parallel circumstances that produced parallel results. Yet there are still creolists who describe the interrelationship of varieties (at least within Atlantic lexical base groups) in monogenetic terms, i.e. a family tree of creoles with a common origin, a proto variety that spread via normal linguistic diffusion (e.g. Hancock 1987). Although polygenesis and diffusion are often thought of as alternative explanations for the same phenomena – features common to widely separated creoles – they are by no means mutually exclusive.

Finally, there are still frequent references to a possible common West African origin of similar phenomena in Atlantic creoles of different lexical bases. For example, Boretzky (1983: 55), in discussing progressive assimilation of nasalization in the Atlantic creoles (§4.4), notes that vowels that have become nasal after nasal consonants are remnants of an earlier phonological change that no longer occurs: "It should be noted that these are often found in the same etyma, which could almost be an argument in favor of these forms originating on the West African coast." Examples include Portuguese *magro* 'thin' becoming Príncipe Creole Portuguese *mãgu* and Sranan Creole English *mangri* idem, or Portuguese *negro* 'black' becoming Príncipe *nẽgu* and Sranan *nengre* idem. An even more striking parallel is Portuguese *nadar* 'swim' becoming Príncipe *lãdá* and Papiamentu Creole Spanish *landa* idem (Boretzky 1983: 55, 66).

2.11 The creole continuum

Just as the theory of monogenesis could not have evolved without the concept of relexification as a key mechanism, so too the historical connection between creoles and post-creole varieties such as American Black English required the concept of a continuum with decreolization as a mechanism of change. A creole continuum can evolve in situations in which a creole coexists with its lexical source language and there is social motivation for creole speakers to acquire the standard, so that the speech of individuals takes on features of the latter – or avoids features of the former – to varying degrees. These varieties can be seen as forming a continuum from those farthest from the standard to those closest to it. Such a synchronic continuum can also serve as a conceptual model for a diachronic continuum of varieties resulting from a creole progressively dropping its nonstandard features and adding standard ones, or decreolizing.

Decreolization is an areal contact phenomenon, but the diffusion of linguistic features can result not only in creoles acquiring noncreole features, but also in noncreoles acquiring creole features. The fact that diffusion can work in both directions presents a serious problem in historical reconstruction: purely synchronic data might not provide enough evidence to determine whether a particular variety that is mixed (i.e. with both creole and noncreole features) resulted from a creole acquiring noncreole features or vice versa. It is only when seen in a broader historical context that the folk speech of Jamaica, for example, can be identified as a creole that has acquired noncreole features, whereas the folk speech of the Cayman Islands appears to be a noncreole that has acquired creole features (cf. Washabaugh 1983: 174–178). The morphology of the verbal system usually provides a reliable guide as to whether the variety is a creole (with preverbal markers and no inflectional endings for tense) or a noncreole (with such inflections) – at least in the case of the Atlantic varieties – but sometimes even this indication has been obscured by the homogenizing effect of shared geographical (if not social) space of white and black speech varieties, as in Barbados, the Bay Islands of Honduras, and the southern United States.

For a long time linguists were unsure as to how to classify varieties with both creole and noncreole features, particularly the English-based varieties of the West Indies. In 1869–70 Van Name said, "We find in Surinam . . . the only English creole which deserves the name" (p. 125). Schuchardt (in Gilbert 1985: 42, quoted in §2.6) recognized the effect of what Bloomfield (1933: 474) dubbed "decreolizing," but later linguists were unsure of the direction of the change. Reinecke (1937: 274–275) wrote that "The Surinam dialects, like West African Pidgin English, are unmistakably creole dialects in the sense of being simplified to a purely analytic structure. The other West Indian English dialects are not, however, so completely pruned down [. . . and] may be regarded as what Schuchardt called creolizing languages – dialects on the way to complete analytic simplification, but which have for various reasons stopped a little short of it." Reinecke's point is not as naive as it may at first seem. Although simplification is now associated with pidginization rather than creolization, it is also recognized that inflections, for example, can be lost in contact situations that do not involve pidginization (§1.3). There is still disagreement about the nature and sequence of the linguistic forces that shaped such semi-creoles as Afrikaans, Réunionnais, and some varieties of Caribbean Spanish and Brazilian Portuguese – or even Barbadian and American Black English. It is by no means certain what role pidgins or creoles played in

the development of these varieties, although many creolists believe that they
played some role.

As recently as 1962, Stewart restricted the Caribbean English-based creoles to
Sranan and Saramaccan (p. 36), noting that

> There are in addition local varieties of English which are spoken in
> Jamaica, British Honduras, Trinidad, British Guiana, and the Lesser
> Antilles. These, however, are not regarded as Creole languages in this
> survey. The reason is that when all the varieties of English of any one
> of these areas are taken together, the result is a continuum of
> variation, with Standard English at one end and the most deviant
> local form at the other. This is reminiscent of usual dialect variation
> around a standard norm, and contrasts with the situation for the
> Creoles where, no matter how much they may be compromised in the
> direction of their lexically related European standard languages, there
> is always a structural gap between the two at some point, and
> consequently it is always clear just which language is being spoken at
> any particular time. What this means is that there is some constant
> criterion for distinguishing Creoles from related standard languages,
> whereas Jamaican and other regional varieties of English are best
> treated as dialects of English. That such dialects are often referred to
> locally as *creolese* (particularly in the Lesser Antilles) should not be
> allowed to obscure their basic difference from real Creoles.
>
> (Stewart 1962: 50–51)

Stewart (p.c.) has explained that at the time it seemed more prudent to exclude
these varieties from the discussion of creoles since it was unclear whether they were
creoles that had acquired noncreole features or vice versa. By 1967, however, he
felt confident that additional historical sociolinguistic information could clarify
this point regarding what are now widely recognized as post-creole varieties in
both the Caribbean area and the United States. Citing eighteenth-century
examples of restructured English used by American blacks, Stewart concluded
that "After the Civil War, with the abolition of slavery, the breakdown of the
plantation system, and the steady increase in education for poor as well as affluent
Negroes, the older field-hand creole English began to lose many of its creole
characteristics" (1967). Later Alleyne (1980: 194) agreed that something very
similar had happened in the West Indies. In 1965 Stewart applied the idea of the
continuum of American Black English and introduced the terms *acrolect* for the
variety closest to the standard and *basilect* for the variety farthest from it, with
mesolect for those between. In an article published the same year, Bailey (1965)

also asserted that "The American Negro, like the Jamaican, operates in a linguistic continuum" and suggested that the American black dialect be approached from a creolist perspective: "I would like to suggest that the Southern Negro 'dialect' differs from other Southern speech because its deep structure is different, having its origin as it undoubtedly does in some Proto-Creole grammatical structure" (ibid. 43).

Schuchardt had been the first but not the only linguist to suggest that American Black English had evolved from the interaction of a creole and local English. The American George Krapp (1925: 253) suggested that it developed out of a pidgin, and Bloomfield (1933: 474) speculated that a jargon had become nativized

> among Negro slaves in many parts of America. When the jargon has become the only language of the subject group, it is a *creolized language*. The creolized language has the status of an inferior dialect of the masters' speech. It is subject to constant leveling-out and improvement in the direction of the latter. The various types of "Negro dialect" which we observe in the United States show us some of the last stages of this leveling. With the improvement of social conditions, this leveling is accelerated; the result is a caste-dialect . . . It is a question whether during this period the dialect that is being de-creolized may not influence the speech of the community – whether the creolized English of the southern slaves, for instance, may not have influenced local types of sub-standard or even of standard English.

Apparently these analyses, well ahead of their time, fell on largely deaf ears and it was not until the 1960s, with the surge of interest in the culture and history of American blacks that came along with the civil rights movement, that a significant number of people were ready to accept such a reading of American sociolinguistic history. The study of Black English was encouraged not only by the Zeitgeist but also by government grants aimed at improving language-related educational problems of Black English speakers. The growing acceptance of the historical relationship of Black English to pidgin and creole English stimulated greater interest in creole linguistics in the United States, fostering more research and publications aimed at a broader readership than just linguists and educators (e.g. Dillard 1972). In 1966 Hall published the first undergraduate-level textbook on pidgins and creoles, helping to secure a place for the discipline in academia.

Although DeCamp (1961: 82) was the first linguist to apply the word "continuum" to the gradation of varieties between creole and standard English in the Caribbean, the notion (if not the word) had been current among dialectologists of Romance and Germanic languages for at least a century, although they were dealing with a basically different situation in which the gradation was between two varieties that were closely related structurally rather than two quite distinct linguistic systems. The notion of coexisting creole varieties at different distances from the standard goes back to the eighteenth century: Oldendorp (quoted by Gilbert 1986b) first discussed the various creoles and then added, "Blacks generally corrupt the European language still more," implying that another variety, spoken by whites, was closer to the standard. This was also the implication of the 1869 Larousse definition of *creole*: "This language, often unintelligible in the mouth of an old African, is extremely sweet in the mouth of white creole speakers" (quoted by Meijer and Muysken 1977: 22). This is interpreted as suggesting that Europeans knew that "there existed a gradation of speech varieties between a creole and its base language" (ibid. 23). Actually it suggests awareness of no more than two varieties: one used by blacks and another by whites. This would seem to reflect the historical origin of the varieties at each end of the continuum. Cassidy (1964: 267) remarked on "the linguistic spectrum following the social spectrum." M. G. Smith (1972: 258) described Jamaican society as "divided into three social sections . . . the white, the brown, and the black . . . Although these color coefficients are primarily heuristic, they indicate the racial majority and cultural ancestry of each section accurately." While making no claim about the correlation of an individual's race and social group today, this does suggest the historical origin of the various segments of the society, with African and European poles on a continuum of cultural traits that include language.

As early as 1934 Reinecke and Tokimasa referred to a "dialect continuum" between Hawaiian Creole English and the standard (p. 48). In 1961 DeCamp proposed the continuum model for studying Jamaican:

> Nearly all speakers of English in Jamaica could be arranged in a sort of linguistic continuum, ranging from the speech of the most backward peasant or labourer all the way to that of the well-educated urban professional. Each speaker represents not a single point but a span on this continuum, for he is usually able to adjust his speech upward or downward for some distance on it.   (1961: 82)

DeCamp emphasized that despite the apparent social correlates, the continuum should first be described in purely linguistic terms to avoid the circularity of saying that "words characteristic of high-school graduates are commonly used by high-school graduates" (ibid.). His strategy is clearer in his 1964 article proposing a theoretical model for converting the structures of standard English into those of the creole:

Complex as such a set of conversion rules would be, they would be considerably simpler than an entire new grammar developed from scratch. And the result could be a grammar not of one but of all varieties of Jamaican Creole. For it is a characteristic of creoles that the proportions of the component of ingredients never remain constant. One might arrange all the speakers of a given creole in a row, in an order ranging from those whose creole most resembles the relevant standard language to those whose variety is the most deviant. In Jamaica, by the way, these extremes are so different as to be mutually unintelligible. Yet our grammar will serve for all of them. As one moves down the row of speakers, one applies more and more of the conversion rules appended to our grammar. (1964: 231)

In DeCamp's later article (1971b), many more of the actual mechanisms of the continuum model have been worked out. Illustrating it with data from seven informants selected from his survey of 142 Jamaican communities, DeCamp arranged these speakers in a continuum according to their use or non-use of six linguistic features, including lexicon (e.g. English *child* versus Creole *pikni*), phonology (e.g. English /θ/ versus Creole /t/), and syntax (English *didn't* versus Creole *no ben*). These features are numbered and arranged in a hierarchy on the continuum so that "a redundancy convention could be formulated whereby the presence of any index feature implied the presence of all other index features of lower number" (1971b: 353). For example, a speaker who says *nyam* 'eat' (which is very far down the social scale) will also say *pikni* 'child' (which is used much higher up the scale). After these lects were arranged by linguistic criteria only, their speakers were found to fall into a corresponding social hierarchy: the speaker of the variety most like English was a young, well educated business owner from an urban center, whereas the most creole-like variety was used by an elderly and illiterate peasant farmer in an isolated mountain village. DeCamp emphasizes that the linear structure of the continuum is adequate because it is based solely on linguistic features: "Of course the sociological correlates of the linguistic variation are multidimensional: age, education, income bracket, occupation, etc. But the linguistic variation itself is linear if described in linguistic terms rather than in terms of those sociological correlates" (1971b: 354). However, Le Page and Tabouret-Keller (1985) later objected that linguistic variation could also be multidimensional, particularly in multilingual speech communities like Belize and St. Lucia.

DeCamp's efforts to work out a theoretical model that could deal with variation with sufficient rigor was also a reaction to the transformational generative grammar that was coming to dominate American linguistics (DeCamp 1977: 14). Noam Chomsky had stated explicitly that his theory was "concerned primarily with an ideal speaker–listener, in a completely homogeneous speech-community" (1965: 3). William Labov (1969) tried to make this framework more suitable for real speech communities, which are not completely homogeneous, by adding variables to grammatical rules to indicate the likelihood of a variant occurring in a given context. It is relevant that Labov was working with American Black English; although all natural speech has variable features, variation is particularly salient in creole and post-creole continua. Indeed, this variation was what made these varieties so difficult to work with. Bailey tried to overcome this difficulty in writing a transformational grammar of Jamaican creole by "abstracting a hypothetical dialect which could reasonably be regarded as featuring the main elements of the deep structure [of the creole]" (1965: 43). Although few if any Jamaicans actually speak such pure creole, her construct fitted the static theoretical model of transformational grammar. Bailey tried to provide some suggestion of variation by appending a list of morpheme variants such as *de waak*, *da waak*, *waakin* or *iz waakin* – all 'is/are walking' (1966: 139). However, Hellinger (1985: 10) contends that the main impact of Bailey's 1966 book was to demonstrate the limited usefulness of the transformational generative model in dealing with creole languages. Yet DeCamp found Bailey's abstraction of "pure creole" very useful: "It is precisely the idealized extreme variety which had to be accurately described before we could begin on the many varieties intermediate between it and the standard" (1971b: 351).

One of the most fruitful ideas that DeCamp brought to bear on his continuum model was that of the implicational scale, a device first used in psychology (Guttman 1944) and later linguistics (Elliott *et al.* 1969), although DeCamp developed it independently in the late 1950s while working on his Jamaican data (1971b: 369). As noted above, he arranged variable linguistic features along a continuum so that the presence of a particular feature also implied the presence of other variables with lower numbers on the scale (1971b: 353). Derek Bickerton, an English linguist working with data from Guyanese Creole English, devised grids of variable features arranged to show that if a rule was in the process of change, a hierarchy of environments could be established, ranging from least to most favorable, so that "deviances apart, the presence of a basilect index alone in a given column implies the presence of similar indices in all columns to the left; while the presence of a non-basilectal index, alone or otherwise, implies the presence of similar indices, alone or otherwise, in all columns to the right" (Bickerton 1973b: 646). Bickerton's work tended to confirm the wave theory of the American C. J. N. Bailey: "We have seen that, in the history of one rule-change, behavior

followed the sequence categorical–variable–categorical, i.e. that inherent variability may be best regarded as a developmental phase coming between two
categorical phases" (Bickerton 1971: 487). His work with variation in complementizers (1971), the copula (1973a), and pronouns (1973b) indicated that such
polylectal grids could be measured for well-formedness by scalability indices
(percentages representing the sum of non-deviant cells divided by the sum of cells
filled, with 100% indicating a deviance-free grid). The scalability of his tables
ranges from 87.9% (mesolect copula) to 100% (basilect singular pronouns), well
above the chance scalability of 66.6% for a three-place table. However,
Bickerton's book-length discussion of the Guyanese continuum (1975) was
criticized for manipulating data to maximize scalability. Baker (1976a) notes that
although Bickerton was dealing with outputs (i.e. the speech of individuals, which
could vary according to circumstances), he labels these as "speakers" on his tables
and graphs. Thus the same individual could be presented as both a basilect
speaker (e.g. "speaker" 186 on pp. 25 and 64) and a mesolect speaker (p. 115).
Baker concludes that such manipulations "cast very serious doubt on
Bickerton's methodology" and that the "implicational relations do not hold"
(1976a: 22, 31).

Although some scholars are still publishing quantitative analyses of variation
along creole continua (e.g. Rickford 1988), interest in this area has waned, in part
because of the excessive claims as to what such studies could reveal about a wide
range of phenomena from language change to the psychological reality of
grammars. Others, particularly Le Page and Tabouret-Keller (1985), have, as
noted above, objected that the unidimensional model that the continuum offers is
too simplistic to convey the real complexity of actual creole speech communities,
particularly those that are multilingual. Rickford (1988) has responded that it is
the very simplicity of the unidimensional model that makes it usable, unlike
multidimensional models, although the latter "may be decomposable into
combinations of two, three or four unidimensional continua." Whatever the
future of continuum studies, they have helped creole linguistics gain some very
solid ground (as well as some rather boggy terrain), so that many of the aspects of
dealing with decreolizing varieties are much less daunting today than they were
twenty years ago.

Many would disagree that decreolization is only "ordinary contact-induced
language change, akin (for both social and linguistic reasons) to dialect borrowing
from a standard to a nonstandard dialect" (Thomason and Kaufman forthcoming). Unlike the contact between two dialects that are in essence two variants of the
same linguistic system, the contact between a creole and its lexical source language
represents the collision of two very different linguistic systems, and the strategies

for reconciling such irreconcilable differences are a quite extraordinary linguistic phenomenon.

During this period the study of American Black English peaked and then began to decline. Labov, the leading scholar in this field and in sociolinguistics in general, had long rejected the connection between American Black English and the Caribbean creoles: "We must recognize that youth growing up in the inner cities today is not in contact with that Creole continuum" (1972:66). Yet he also encouraged research by young black linguists who often saw that connection as the source of the separate identity of Black English (e.g. Rickford 1977). By 1982 Labov had also come to accept what he called "the creolist hypothesis" of the origin of Black English, in part because of the parallel patterns of copula deletion in Black English, Gullah, and Jamaican Creole (Holm 1976, Baugh 1980).

A number of white American linguists who had come to feel unwelcome in Black English studies turned their energies to creole linguistics, and that field entered a phase of accelerated growth. In 1972 the Society for Caribbean Linguistics was organized at a conference in Trinidad. During the biennial meetings over the next decade at various universities in the West Indies, leadership shifted from North American and British linguists to largely anglophone West Indians, yet tensions within this organization remained largely those between first-world and third-world scholars (e.g. unfair distribution of access to publications and publishing, funding, and the machinery of academic advancement in general) rather than those between blacks and whites. However, there was a definite emphasis on English-based creoles as the focus of common interest. In 1976 the first Colloque International des Créolistes met in France to organize the Comité International des Études Créoles, leading to the publication of the journal *Études Créoles*, which focused on French-based varieties. Meanwhile a newsletter, *The Carrier Pidgin*, had been established in 1973 and work began on *A Bibliography of Pidgin and Creole Languages* (Reinecke *et al.* 1975), both becoming major mainstays of the discipline. A *Journal of Creole Studies* began and ended in 1977, but re-emerged in 1986 as the *Journal of Pidgin and Creole Languages*. A 1973 conference at the University of Papua New Guinea helped focus attention on Pacific pidgins and creoles, a focus that was maintained at the 1975 conference on pidgins and creoles at Honolulu, Hawaii. The University of Hawaii joined a number of other institutions with growing reputations as research centers in creole linguistics, such as the University of the West Indies, City University of New York, Stanford, Pennsylvania, Texas at Austin, Indiana, Montreal, York, Oxford, Amsterdam, Aix-en-Provence, Paris, Bamberg, Bochum, the Australian National University at Canberra, the University of the South Pacific, and the Summer Institute of Linguistics among others. The field was coming of age.

2.12 Universalists again

Although the general usefulness of the continuum model had gained wide
acceptance by the mid 1970s, this model had nothing to do with the origin of the
creoles and thus cast no light on the perennial question of why the Atlantic creoles
in particular should share so many structural features not found in their different
lexical source languages. The position of the monogeneticists – particularly
regarding the genealogical link between pidgin Portuguese and Sabir – remained
unprovable and finally came to be seen as a matter of faith among a dwindling
number of faithful. However, that part of the monogenetic theory linking the
creoles to West African languages via substrate influence (whether or not this
involved the intermediate stage of a pidgin based on Portuguese or another lexical
base language) was not disputed by the competing polygenetic theories and, as
Hall (1968: 365) noted in his summary of the state of creole linguistics, "At present,
the existence of a considerable African element in the various Caribbean creoles,
on all levels of linguistic structure, is recognized by all scholars." Even Bickerton,
who was later to deny such influence altogether, repeatedly referred to it in his
1975 book (e.g. pp. 9, 22, 44, 58 etc.).

As before, language acquisition played a central role in the updated universalist
theory. Chomsky (1965: 27) had proposed that children were born with a
predisposition to recognize certain universal properties of language that facilitated
their acquisition of the language of their particular speech community. These
universals were seen as the general parameters of language, unmarked for the
specific characteristics of particular languages. Ferguson (1971) suggested that
language universals also shaped the simplified registers "that many, perhaps all,
speech communities have . . . for use with people who are regarded for one reason
or another as unable to readily understand the normal speech of the community
(e.g. babies, foreigners, deaf people)" (1971: 143). He noted that baby talk and
foreigner talk resembled the simplified register used in telegrams in omitting the
copula, definite article, and prepositions. He cited an early study of child language
acquisition (Brown and Bellugi 1964) which noted that, without being fully aware
of it, parents tend to simplify their language when speaking to very young children
by avoiding subordination, using simple sentences, and repeating new words.
Ferguson suggested that

> The notion of simplicity in language is important in several ways,
> since it may be related to theories of language universals, language
> acquisition, and language loss . . . it is possible to hazard some
> universal hypotheses. For example, "If a language has an inflectional
> system, this will tend to be replaced in simplified speech such as baby

talk and foreigner talk by uninflected forms (e.g. simple nominative for the noun; infinitive, imperative, or third person singular for the verb)." Several such hypotheses might even be subsumed under a more general hypothesis of the form: "If a language has a grammatical category which clearly involves an unmarked–marked opposition [cf. Greenberg 1966b] the unmarked term tends to be used for both in simplified speech."   (1971: 145–146)

Ferguson concluded that language universals of simplification must play a role in the formation of pidgins since native speakers of the lexical source language followed them in the foreigner talk they used with non-native speakers.

Although they did not refer to Ferguson (1971), Kay and Sankoff (1974) added to the list of possible universal features of pidgins. In addition to the replacement of inflectional morphology by free lexemes (1974: 68), they suggested that pidgins seemed to be universally characterized by a shallowness of phonology or restricted morphophonemics and lack of allophony (p. 62) as well as the occurrence of "propositional qualifiers . . . in surface structure exterior to the propositions they qualify" (p. 64). For example, sentential qualifiers of time, aspect, and manner could be expected to occur outside the predicate, as well as negatives and yes–no question indicators. They concluded that

> contact vernaculars . . . may possibly reveal in a more direct way than do most natural languages the universals of cognitive structure and process that underlie all human language ability and language use . . . pidgin languages are derivationally shallower than natural languages and reflect universal deep (= semantic) structure in their surface structures more directly than do natural languages. Such a generalization would imply in turn that the process of creolization of a pidgin involves the creation of transformational machinery which moves the surface structure progressively further away from universal deep structure.   (1974: 64, 66)

Todd (1974: 42) made the connection between universals in simplification and universals in all languages:

> there are universal patterns of linguistic behaviour appropriate to contact situations . . . pidgins and creoles are alike because, fundamentally, languages are alike and simplification processes are alike . . . human beings are biologically programmed to acquire *Language* rather than any particular language, and . . . the pro-

gramming includes an innate ability to dredge one's linguistic behaviour of superficial redundancies.

Todd went on to note possible parallels in child language acquisition and the formation of pidgins:

> Lamso, in Cameroon, has a vocabulary set, containing several reduplicated forms, which is employed to and by children with whom also tonal contrasts are kept to a minimum. It is a stimulating thought that pidgins may result from such "simple" exchanges. Babies soon discard the simple "idealized dialect" because social pressures put a premium on their acquiring the language of the adult community. But such pressure did not, in the past, prevail in pidgin situations and so the urge to modify towards a more "acceptable" norm was not a factor in the formation of pidgins. (1974: 47)

Although he built on such ideas, Bickerton (1974, republished 1980) departed from them by claiming that it was creoles rather than pidgins that reveal such universals (unstable pidgins remaining essentially chaotic) and that these universals could be characterized not just by general parameters but specific structures: "there is a natural tense–aspect system, rooted in specific neural properties of the brain" (1980: 12). Bickerton claims that this verbal system, with preverbal markers for tense, modality, and aspect occurring in that order in various combinations (§5.1.7), is part of a natural semantax, neurally based, which guides first-language acquisition in its early stages but then is systematically suppressed in natural languages, which have developed their own marked (i.e. non-universal) structures. However, in the earliest stages of creolization, he claims, children use this natural semantax and it is not suppressed by older members of the speech community, who themselves speak an unstable or even chaotic pidgin variety of the language without many norms. Thus Hawaiian Creole English, which he claims arose without any contact with the Caribbean creoles, developed a verbal system identical to theirs. Since there is no historical link between these creoles, he claims, the only other explanation is the innate predisposition to learn this specific structure.

Bickerton (1980: 5) claimed that his predecessors had focused entirely on the pidgin stage in their discussions of universals, but Givón (1979, written in 1973) referred to creoles as well: "once the normal cycle of language acquisition by children is allowed to proceed for a number of generations, normal processes of linguistic change will soon conspire to re-mark the *Creole*, slowly removing it from Universal Grammar and back into the normal range of compromise between universality and markedness" (1979:25, my emphasis). While the positions of Givón and Bickerton are similar in a number of respects, Bickerton rejects Givón's understanding of universals as "a kind of lowest common denominator, what is left when everything that is marked in 'natural languages' has been stripped off" (1980:15) – essentially the view of Greenberg (1966b) – in favor of universals as specific linguistic structures.

In 1976 Bickerton offered additional data to support the above position in a comparative study of the syntax and semantics of the verbal systems of Hawaiian Creole English, a number of Atlantic creoles, and creolized Juba Arabic (§12.1). The last seemed to strengthen his claim for universals considerably since the similarity could not be explained by a common substrate or diffusion, but Thomason and Elgibali (1986:428) later noted that "preverbal particles in the modern [Arabic-based] pidgins and Ki-Nubi cannot be used as evidence for a claim about universals of pidginization, because all forms of Arabic – Cl[assical] A[rabic] as well as Coll[oquial] A[rabic] – have functionally and positionally similar tense/aspect markers in their verbal systems."

In a later article (1977b), Bickerton distinguishes between pidgins and creoles whose speakers have been displaced (which had early and rapid creolization) and those whose speakers have remained in their original environment (often leading to extended pidgins) (cf. §2.8). He then shows that creoles spoken by displaced populations (which somehow include Hawaiians) have a number of features in common beyond their verbal systems: (1) a generic or non-specific Ø article in addition to definite and indefinite articles; (2) fronting of noun phrases for focusing; (3) a distinction between attributive, locative–existential, and sometimes equative copulas (cf. Holm 1976); (4) multiple negation. In a 1979 post script to his 1973 article, Givón also correlated uprooted populations with unstable pidgins, noting that stable pidgins arise

> under conditions where the population was not uprooted, where the original linguistic communities remained intact, viable and vigorous, and where the Pidgin developed slowly, in a non-disruptive situation, over a great number of years as a Lingua-Franca to facilitate inter-communal contact. Further, the indigenous languages – though not mutually intelligible – are within a broad range *typologically similar*. The Pidgin that has evolved under these conditions, according to Bickerton, reflects much less Universal Grammar patterns and is cohesive and stable, relatively speaking. Not surprising, its syntactic patterns are closer to those of the "substratum" languages, to the extent that this has been at all assessed. When children begin to speak

this language natively, the model presented to them is both coherent and sufficiently rich, resembling thus the normal language-acquisition situation. They thus do not introduce Universal Grammar features via acquisition above and beyond what children normally do in acquiring their first "natural" language.

(1979: 30–31; original emphasis)

In 1981 Bickerton published *Roots of Language*, expanding what he now called his language bioprogram hypothesis (LBH). In addition to the five similarities among the creoles mentioned above, he added (6) realized and unrealized complements (§5.1.8), (7) relativization and subject-copying, (8) the use of 'it has' to express both possession and existence (§5.2.3), (9) bimorphemic question words (§3.3.4), and (10) equivalents of passive constructions (§3.3.2), as well as an expanded discussion of the tense–mode–aspect system. To this and a chapter on pidgins (in which he concludes that Hawaiian Pidgin English was not the source of the structure of Hawaiian Creole English, nor are substrate structures in pidgins generally passed on to their ensuing creoles) are added chapters on first-language acquisition and the origin of language in light of his bioprogram hypothesis. The book was widely read, not only by creolists but also by those with a more general interest in linguistics and language acquisition, particularly psychologists. The controversy over this extreme universalist hypothesis heated up, leading to extended debates in a journal of psychology (Bickerton *et al.* 1984) and a special conference in Amsterdam on substrata and universals in creole genesis (Muysken and Smith 1986). Although the exchanges in both forums indicate that few creolists are willing to dismiss substrate influence and diffusion altogether in explaining the structural similarities among the Atlantic creoles, it is clear that the impact of Bickerton (1981) on creole studies has been profound.

2.13 Substratists again

As Hall (1968: 365) noted, there was a consensus of opinion in the 1960s and early 1970s that the African substrate had had a considerable influence on the Atlantic creoles on all linguistic levels. Indeed, substrate influence was a key element in both the monogenetic and polygenetic theories that competed as explanations of these creoles' genesis. Douglas Taylor, whose publications spanned three decades, became increasingly interested in the structural similarities of the Atlantic creoles (1971, 1977), which he attributed to substrate influence: "While African loanwords are relatively few in most West Indian creoles . . . African loan constructions are both common and striking" (1977: 7). Taylor's comparison of ten linguistic features common to Yoruba and six Atlantic creoles (many of which were later presented as universals in Bickerton 1981) led him to conclude that

> Lesser Antillean Creole French in its formative period was in close contact with a language or languages very like Yoruba; and as French-based Haitian and Cayenne creoles, English-based Sranan and Saramaccan, and Iberian-based Papiamentu and Sãotomense (Gulf of Guinea) show very much the same and other resemblances to Yoruba . . . we conclude that these creoles have diverged from what may well have been a common pidgin by lexical replacement from the languages of the slaves' European masters and overseers.
>
> (1977: 9)

Bickerton (1981) objected that Yoruba was a particularly inappropriate language in which to look for substrate features since its speakers were brought to the Caribbean area largely in the late eighteenth and early nineteenth centuries, too late to have influenced the formation of the creoles. However, Taylor's point had been that substrate influence had come from African languages "very *like* Yoruba," and Yoruba is indeed typical of the Kwa group of languages spoken by a significant proportion of the people brought from Africa to the New World during the period in which the creoles emerged. This is demonstrated by a comparison of 20 features in 17 African and 16 creole and post-creole languages (Holm 1976). Alleyne's widely-read *Comparative Afro-American* (1980) also supported a substratist position (e.g. p. 130), taking issue with Bickerton's extreme universalist theory (pp. 133–134). Some creolists who acknowledged the influence of substrate languages (e.g. Baker in Baker and Corne 1982: 254) allowed that "Innate rules as envisaged by Bickerton could be the source of identical grammatical structures in any number of creole languages which developed independently of one another," although the logic of Bickerton's argument allowed for no significant substrate influence on creoles (at least early-creolizing or "radical" – i.e. "true" – creoles), since his original evidence for the bioprogram was that there was no other explanation for the structural similarities of the creoles. Other creolists ignored Bickerton's claim that structural parallels in substrate languages were irrelevant, and continued their research in this area. A German linguist, Norbert Boretzky (1983), provided what Bickerton (1984) claimed was lacking: a "systematic and detailed comparison between substratum structures and the creole structures supposed to have been derived from them." However, Boretzky did not provide a comprehensive theory for the influence of substrate languages in this work, nor did he provide the historical data needed to link the particular African languages he discussed with the particular creole languages he believed they had influenced. Instead, he let the linguistic data speak for itself, showing widespread parallels in the phonology and syntax of certain West African languages and the Atlantic creoles. He also examined a control group of what he considered non-Atlantic creoles with different substrata: Melanesian Pidgin English, Mauritian Creole French, and the Spanish-based creoles of the Philippines. It spoke well for his method that only the Mauritian data yielded affinities with West African structures (particularly in the verb phrase) which he had not expected; this led him to speculate that there was some historical connection that was still not properly understood. This was in fact the thesis of Baker and Corne (1982), to which Boretzky did not have access: Mauritian Creole French evidences "a West African substratal influence" indicating "typological identity with the Atlantic creoles" (Baker and Corne 1982: 122, 127). Boretzky's later work (e.g. 1986) focuses on a more explicit explanation of substrate influence: why some features of substrate languages survive in creoles while others do not. From a comparison of the verbal systems of Fante (an Akan language of the Kwa group) and Jamaican Creole English, he concludes that a grammatical category from the substrate was more readily transferred to the creole if the superstrate had an available morpheme to express it that (a) could be easily isolated and identified, (b) had no allomorphs that differed greatly, (c) was not homophonous with markers of other categories, and (d) was immediately translatable. Since in most cases there was no access to the deep structure rules of the superstrate language, its surface phenomena were identified, analyzed and developed in terms of known (i.e. substrate) categories.

The Zairean linguist Salikoko Mufwene (1986a) points out that the substratist and universalist positions are irreconcilable only in their most extreme forms, i.e. when each excludes the possibility of the other. Most creolists agree that language universals played an important role in the selection of features that were ultimately retained in the creoles, such as the use of free rather than bound morphemes to convey grammatical information. Fewer find the bioprogram a convincing source of specific features, particularly because Bickerton's only proof of the bioprogram is his contention that there is no alternative explanation for the structural features common to the "radical" creoles: "neither substratum influence nor diffusion is adequate to account for the creation of creole languages. In the absence of further alternatives, the LBH or some variant thereof seems inescapable" (in Bickerton *et al.* 1984: 184). However, serious doubts have been cast on the claimed irrelevance of both substrate influence and diffusion in the case of Hawaiian Creole English, which provides Bickerton's crucial evidence for the language bioprogram hypothesis. Goodman (1985) provides evidence that the data on Hawaiian Pidgin English, out of which Bickerton claims Hawaiian Creole English developed, is from too late a period (1900 to 1920) to be relevant to the formation of the creole, which took place in the 1880s. While the later pidgin reflects substrate features from the languages spoken by later immigrants from Japan and the Philippines (features not found in the creole), Goodman asserts that the earlier pidgin that developed into Hawaiian Creole English grew out of an earlier English-based pidgin used between whalers and other seamen and Hawaiians, which spread from the ports to the plantations in the latter part of the nineteenth century (Reinecke 1969). If this pidgin served as the medium by which some of the substrate features of contact English in the Atlantic and Caribbean spread to Hawaii and the rest of the Pacific, there is no need to account for these features by means of a hypothetical bioprogram (Holm 1986).

Among the positive effects of Bickerton's criticism of substratist theory was a renewed effort to sort out which African languages were most relevant to the formation of the various Atlantic creoles (e.g. Singler 1986a). While considerably more research is needed in this area, including more comprehensive descriptions of the grammars and lexicons of the relevant African languages, a growing number of Africanists have begun working with creoles as well, and their research seems promising.

2.14   Other trends in theory

Creole studies have also been strengthened by the contributions of an increasing number of historical linguists such as Thomason and Kaufman (forthcoming), who have discussed theoretical questions regarding pidginization and creolization within the broader context of language contact and genetic linguistics. The work of sociolinguists also continues to be central in shaping the theoretical frameworks guiding creole studies: Le Page and Tabouret-Keller (1985) have proposed a multidimensional model to relate language and social identity in creole communities, viewing "linguistic behaviour as a series of *acts of identity* in which people reveal both their personal identity and their search for social roles" (p. 14). They also propose a conceptual distinction that promises to be very useful in dealing with the sociolinguistics of language change: they contrast communities that are socially and linguistically *focused* ("tightly-knit and closely-interactive communities . . . [in which] the sharing of rules, and the regularity of rules, can be considerable," p. 5) as opposed to those that are *diffuse*, with great variation and seeming irregularity:

> a civilization is a way of life that evolves in response to a particular set of circumstances; it may, like the language which evolves with it, be highly focussed, or it may be diffuse. Most migrations have led to

contact and contests between different groups, to colonization, very often to conquest. The linguistic symptoms of contact initially may be the development of a *lingua franca* or pidgin, accompanied by increased diffuseness in the older linguistic system in use. This can be seen, in the case of Britain, in the effects of both Norse and Norman colonization . . . On the other hand, if the contact is one which appears to threaten a community they may well respond by drawing closer together, identifying more closely with their cultural norms, in which case their linguistic behaviour becomes more highly focussed. This happened in England in the fourteenth century and is happening in Belize today.   (1985: 19)

Although there is a growing body of creolist literature in German, most continues to be written in English or French. This has tended to divide creolists into two camps, each of which is insufficiently aware of the work of the other. While the above broad historical outline is relevant to the development of theory in both, it should be noted that theoretical débates in each camp have followed their own course. The literature on the French-based creoles, written largely in French, has tended to focus more on the influence of the superstrate. The idea of continuity between French and the French-based creoles was stressed in the theory that the creoles grew out of a variety of nautical French that represented a leveling of regional dialects and served as a kind of lingua franca among seamen and in ports (Hull 1968). Although it was later specified that this model included input from substrate languages via relexification (Hull 1979), Chaudenson (1974) minimized such input in his theory that the creoles evolved from a variety of colloquial French (*français avancé*) that was ahead of the standard language in following natural evolutionary tendencies (*tendances évolutives*) such as the loss of inflections. It should be noted that Chaudenson was drawn to these conclusions while working with Réunionnais (§9.7), whose status as creole rather than a regional variety has been disputed. However, his theoretical model has been applied to the genesis of all the French-based creoles despite convincing counterevidence (Baker and Corne 1982) that the genesis of creoles such as Mauritian involved a clear structural break with French due to restructuring under the influence of other languages and universals of creolization. It should be noted that natural evolutionary tendencies of the source language are still invoked to explain the origin of such semi-creoles as popular Brazilian Portuguese (Révah 1963) and Afrikaans (Raidt 1983).

Determining the origin and development of such varieties with both creole and noncreole features poses one of the greatest challenges to creole linguistics in the future. Another challenge, even greater and more basic, is to write comprehensive and exhaustive descriptions of all the extant pidgin and creole languages as well as their sociolinguistic histories. Debates over theoretical models and their implications for general linguistics can only profit from a more adequate and accurate body of knowledge to work from.

3

Lexicosemantics

3.0 Introduction

This and the following chapters on phonology (chapter 4) and syntax (chapter 5) comprise a unit in which a number of Atlantic creoles of various lexical bases are compared by linguistic level. These creoles share many features on all three levels which are not found in their European lexical source languages (Taylor 1971, 1977). These similarities are discussed at some length in this unit because of their importance as evidence for various theories purporting to explain their origin, principally the monogenetic versus polygenetic theories (§2.10), and more recently universalist (§2.12) versus substratist theories (§2.13). Although some of the evidence used in these debates has been from phonology (e.g. Boretzky 1983), the most obvious linguistic level on which to seek features common to creoles of differing lexical bases has been syntax. The level of lexicon, which can be used to establish the similarity of languages in more traditional groupings, is not an obvious area in which to seek similarities among languages which have completely different vocabularies. In the early contact situations, the original pidgins and the creoles that grew out of them had to use vocabulary that came primarily from the Europeans' various languages in order to serve their first function as bridges for communication. In the Atlantic colonies the Europeans spoke the language of political, economic, and social power and the Africans, who had no such power in their state of slavery, had to do most of the linguistic accommodating. The influence of the European languages was further reinforced during the centuries when most of the creoles were used in colonies whose official language of administration was the same as their lexical source. For these reasons the creoles retained relatively few words (usually less than 10% of the lexicon) that were not from the lexical source language, and therefore there are very few words shared by the creoles based on Portuguese, Spanish, Dutch, French, and English which might form the basis of a comparison (except, of course, the Romance or Germanic cognates also found in the European source languages). However, while vocabularies differ from one lexical group to another in *form*, they do share certain traits in the *kinds* of words they retain (e.g. words that are today archaic or regional in Europe) and the *kinds of changes* these words underwent. Some of these changes are at least partly attributable to a common African substratum (e.g. calques, certain semantic shifts, and reduplication) and some to the wholesale restructuring which is characteristic of pidginization and creolization (e.g. the reanalysis of morpheme boundaries). However, all of the kinds of changes described below can be found in noncreole languages as well. The only thing distinctive about pidgin and creole lexicons (for the following discussion is largely applicable to non-Atlantic varieties as well except for certain substrate features) is not the *kind* of changes that words have undergone but rather the *extent* to which the vocabulary has been affected by them (Hancock 1980). For example, while one might with luck find a dozen examples of the reanalysis of morpheme boundaries in English, e.g. *a napron* becoming *an apron*, hundreds of examples of this phenomenon can be found in any French creole.

In order to keep the discussion manageable, each point will normally be illustrated by only one example from each lexical base group: creole English, French, Portuguese, Spanish, and sometimes Dutch (respectively abbreviated CE, CF, CP, CS, and CD after names of particular varieties). Unless otherwise indicated, sources are largely dictionaries or word-lists of creole languages (for CE Cassidy and Le Page 1967, 1980; Bureau Volkslectuur 1961; de Groot 1981, 1984; Fyle and Jones 1980; Hancock 1969, 1970; Holm 1978; Holm with Shilling 1982; Schneider 1960; for CF Bentolila *et al.* 1976; Germain 1980; D'Offay and Lionnet 1982; Valdman *et al.* 1981; for CP Pires and Hutchison 1983; Scantamburlo 1981; Turner 1949; for CS Mario Dijkhoff 1985; for CD de Josselin de Jong 1926; Robertson 1979) or lexical studies (for CE Allsopp 1980; Hancock 1971, 1980; Holm 1981; for CF Valdman 1978; Chaudenson 1974, 1979; for CP Chataigner 1963; Valkhoff 1966; Wilson 1962; Ivens Ferraz 1979, 1987; for CD van Ginneken 1913, Van Name 1869–70).

3.1 Pidginization and the lexicon

While there have been detailed studies of pidgin lexicons (most notably Mühlhäusler 1979), these have been the lexicons of extended pidgins such as Tok Pisin or West African Pidgin English. Regarding the lexicons of such pidgins *vis-à-vis* those of creoles, Hancock (1980) may well be right: "I prefer not to acknowledge a distinction between *pidgin* and *creole*, and to consider *stabilization* more significant than *nativization* in creole language formation" (p. 64; his emphasis). This seems particularly likely in the case of varieties that can be the primary (if not first) language of their speakers, such as Cameroonian English (usually called a pidgin) or Guinea-Bissau Portuguese (usually called a creole).

The size, structure and development of the lexicons of such extended varieties contrast sharply with those of reduced pidgins, and even more with those of pre-pidgin jargons. Regarding the latter, estimates of a total lexicon of several hundred words or less have been given for nineteenth-century South Seas Jargon (Mühlhäusler 1979: 182) and Russenorsk (Broch and Jahr 1984: 47). Regarding pidgins, Bauer (1975: 86) estimates that a knowledge of some 700 to 750 Chinese Pidgin English words were sufficient for most purposes in trade, the pidgin's only real domain. While one may object that such estimations of a pidgin's total lexicon on the basis of written records are as meaningless as saying that the vocabulary of the Beowulf poet was a particular number of words because those are all the words he is recorded to have used (Le Page p.c.), there is still every indication that the lexicons of early (i.e. non-extended) pidgins are very much smaller than those of natural languages. However, certain characteristics of such lexicons partly compensate for their restricted size: multifunctionality (one word having many syntactic uses), polysemy (one word having many meanings), and circumlocution (lexical items consisting of phrases rather than single words). Multifunctionality is discussed in more detail in section 3.7. Polysemy can be illustrated by the broad range of meanings usually found in pidgin prepositions such as Tok Pisin *biloŋ*, Cameroonian *fo*, Russenorsk *på*, or Chinese Pidgin Russian *za*, used to express nearly every locative relationship imaginable. However, this apparently universal tendency in pidgins may also be reinforced by substrate influence in some cases: like West African Pidgin English *fo*, Ibo *na* and Yoruba *ni* "both refer . . . to location in a general way" (Welmers 1973: 453). It seems likely that there is a relationship between polysemy in pidgins and the fairly frequent semantic broadening found in creole words (§3.6.1), e.g. Krio CE *na*, which is also a general locative preposition. Stolz (1986: 236) has pointed to the fact that Afrikaans *vir* can replace almost every other preposition as evidence of an earlier pidgin stage. Polysemy in pidgins naturally leads to circumlocution with modifying phrases to specify the intended meaning, e.g. Tok Pisin *gras biloŋ fes* 'beard' as opposed to *gras biloŋ hɛd* 'hair' (Hall 1966: 91). Finally, the reanalysis of morpheme boundaries as in Cameroonian *æns* 'ant' from the English plural is likely to result from universal processes of restructuring that lead to pidgins and the creoles derived from them (§3.5.1).

The pidgins that led to the Atlantic creoles are largely the constructs of theory, although there is some fragmentary evidence in historical documents that they did in fact exist, e.g. the samples of seventeenth-century pidgin French in Martinique quoted by Goodman (1964: 104; cf. §2.2). The "pidgin" varieties of English, French, and Portuguese spoken in Africa today (sections 10.1.3, 9.1.1 and 6.2.2 respectively) may well share a number of features with the pidgins that led to the

Atlantic creoles, but they probably also differ in many respects for a number of reasons. For example, they may have different – albeit related – substrate languages, they are the product of a different kind of social setting, and they have different domains. For these reasons study of the lexicons of modern African "pidgins" will not necessarily cast unrefracted light on the structure of the lexicons of the pidgins that evolved into the Atlantic creoles. Moreover, efforts to reconstruct the proto-pidgin of a particular lexical base through comparative studies run into serious theoretical problems. In principle comparative reconstruction can be done only once common descent from the same parent language has been demonstrated, but of course it is difficult to establish the genetic relatedness of the English-based Atlantic creoles, for example, except through comparative reconstruction. As Thomason (p.c.) points out, "Comparing the vocabularies of various CE languages is easy; determining that shared words were directly inherited from a common ancestor is something else again: how will you rule out parallel development and borrowing from already crystallized p/c languages? As for syntax . . . the state of comparative syntactic reconstruction even in well-established language families is, to put it mildly, controversial." The only published attempt at such a reconstruction known to the present writer is that of Cassidy (1964). Based on his comparison of Sranan, Jamaican, and Cameroonian, Cassidy made some preliminary conclusions regarding phonology and syntax and then went on to identify some 260 English-derived words common to the three varieties, as well as 27 words derived from African languages and 49 words from Portuguese that are common to Sranan and Jamaican. Hancock's comparative work on the lexicons (1969) and syntax (1987) of the English-based creoles provides extensive data for such reconstruction, but this has not yet been done. There is no comparable work on the proto-forms of the other lexical groups, although Goodman's 1964 comparison of 40 lexical and grammatical items in the French-based creoles led him to the conclusion that such a common pidgin ancestor had existed.

3.2 European lexical sources
The Atlantic creoles drew a considerable part of their lexicons from their European source languages in forms virtually identical to those of the metropolitan standard except for certain fairly regular sound changes (chapter 4) Even these often happened not to affect particular items, leaving words such as Jamaican CE *brij* or Haitian CF *pō* indistinguishable from standard English *bridge* or standard French *pont*. Moreover, those creoles that remained in contact with their lexical-source languages, either through diglossia or a continuum, kept drawing on them for terms needed in modern life, such as French Antillean CF

òganizé, ékonomik, kapitalis, etc. (Stein 1984: 36). In a comparative lexical study Bollée (1981) found that such parallels to contemporary standard French usage constituted over 60% of the Haitian CF lexicon; in Seychellois CF, which has coexisted with standard English rather than French since 1810, such parallels constituted nearly 55% of the lexicon.

3.2.1 Survival of archaic usages

Bollée also found that over 16% of the Haitian CF lexicon and 9% of the Seychellois could be attributed to words considered archaic or regional in France. There is no way to separate the two categories with any precision since the same word may fall into both. For example, *from* is found in a number of English-based Atlantic creoles as a conjunction with the temporal meaning of 'since,' e.g. "*From* I was a child I do that." This usage is part of both archaic and regional English. The last recorded use of *from* with this meaning in the *Oxford English Dictionary* was 1602, suggesting that it was still current – if somewhat old-fashioned – in standard speech when English began spreading throughout the Caribbean in the seventeenth century. However, *from* with this meaning was still current in the regional dialects of Ireland and Scotland when Wright's *English Dialect Dictionary* was compiled around 1900. Thus there is no way of knowing whether *from* meaning 'since' was brought into Caribbean English creoles by speakers of standard (but archaic) English or by speakers of regional British dialects. Of course many other words belong to only one of the two categories. Some examples are current Rama Cay CE *rench* and Sranan CE *wenke*, both 'young woman' from archaic English *wench*. Similarly Negerhollands CD *damsel*, still current around 1900, is from a Dutch (and ultimately French) word meaning 'young woman' which is now archaic in Holland. The word *bay* or *ba* meaning 'give' is current in many of the New World varieties of creole French; it is from *bailler* 'give, deliver' (cf. E *bail*), which was current in standard French until the seventeenth century but which is now archaic (Stein 1984: 45). The word for 'doctor' in Annobonese CP is *babélu* from Portuguese *barbeiro* 'barber,' from days when members of that profession bled clients to cure their ailments (Ivens Ferraz p.c.).

Another kind of archaism found in creoles is the preservation of a pronunciation that is no longer current in the metropolitan variety. For example, Miskito Coast CE retains the /aɪ/ diphthong that was current in polite eighteenth-century British speech in words like *bail* 'boil' and *jain* 'join'; this sound beame /ɔɪ/ in standard English after about 1800. This makes the creole word for 'lawyer' homophonous with standard English *liar* (but there is no confusion since the latter takes the dialectal form *liard* analogous to *criard* 'crier' and *stinkard* 'stinker' – cf. standard *drunkard*). The preservation of archaic pronunciations can be found in the creoles of other lexical bases as well, e.g. Haitian CF *chat* /šat/ 'cat,' the earlier pronunciation of French *chat*, now /ša/. The São Tomé CP word for 'one' is *ũa*, from older Portuguese *ũa* rather than modern *uma*.

Papiamentu CS appears to preserve a sixteenth-century Spanish pronunciation, although this may not be the whole story. Initial /f/ in Latin (e.g. *făcĕre* 'do, make') became /h/ in earlier Spanish *hacer* and then θ in the standard, although the /h/ pronunciation survives in Papiamentu *hasi* idem and in Caribbean Spanish dialects such as the one spoken in Puerto Rico (D. Valenti p.c.). However, the pronunciation *asi* with initial θ is also quite current in Papiamentu, particularly on Curaçao (Maurer p.c.). Moreover, initial /h/ alternates with θ in a great number of Papiamentu words, including many that never had /h/ in Europe, such as Papiamentu *habri* 'to open' (cf. Spanish *abrir* from Latin *aperire*). In fact, this alternation is found in a number of Caribbean creoles, e.g. Miskito Coast CE *ej* and *hej* both mean 'edge' or 'hedge,' while on the island of Abaco in the Bahamas *ear* is what you do with your *hear* (or vice versa). This alternation has often been blamed on Cockney in the anglophone Caribbean, but this would not account for the same phenomenon in Negerhollands CD, in which *hō* can mean either 'hear' (cf. Dutch *horen* idem) or 'ear' (cf. D *oor* idem) (de Josselin de Jong 1926: 84). Stolz (1986: 106) notes that Negerhollands /h/ seems to come not only from Dutch but also "aus dem Nichts" (out of nothingness). Even aspirate French *h* springs back to life in Haitian CF *hey!* (cf. F. *hé!* 'hey!'). Hesseling (1905: 75–76) explained prosthetic /h/ as a general phenomenon in the creoles resulting from the lack of initial vowels in many West African languages, so that /h/ was carried over into this position to conform with substrate phonotactic rules. However, Singler (p.c.) notes that the preponderance of relevant West African languages, including most in the Kwa group, do in fact permit word-initial vowels. Thus Hesseling's hypothesis seems unlikely and we are left with yet another Caribbean mystery, although Cassidy and Le Page (1980: lxii) claim that in Jamaican CE "initial [h] is frequently lost in unemphatic contexts and used as a hypercorrection in emphatic contexts," a pattern that might exist in other creoles as well.

3.2.2 *Survival of regional usages*
The creoles also preserve forms, meanings, and pronunciations that are now found only in regional dialects of their European lexical-source languages. This is a consequence of the fact that the great majority of Europeans who went to live in African or Caribbean colonies from the sixteenth to the eighteenth centuries were uneducated speakers of regional dialects. Studies of British regionalisms in Krio CE (Hancock 1971) and Miskito Coast CE (Holm 1981) suggest that there might

be a relationship between the proportion of regionalisms from various districts in the creole and patterns of actual immigration from these districts to the colony where the creole developed. However, there are a number of factors that complicate such an inference. First, there is the often insoluble problem of determining whether a particular creole word preserves a regional rather than archaic usage, as discussed above. Secondly, the accuracy of European dialect studies in the nineteenth century (when many such words were already falling out of use) was often spotty regarding a word's actual geographic distribution; as Aub-Buscher (1970) remarked, "le jeu de la localisation précise [dans la France] des formes créoles . . . est un jeu dangereux." Finally, it is by no means clear where the particular mix of dialect forms occurred, i.e. whether it was in the colony itself or another colony from which there had been immigration to the colony in question. In the English-based creoles so studied (Krio, Miskito Coast, and Bahamian) the similarity of the proportion of words from the North Country, Scotland, and Ireland suggests that a general colonial variety of English may have formed before being creolized and spread by diffusion.

Examples of such regional forms include Miskito Coast CE *krabit* 'cruel' from Scots *crabbed* or *crabbit* 'ill-tempered.' Isle de France CF *mous* (*a myel*) and Caribbean CF *mouch a myel*, both 'bee,' come from *mouche à miel* (literally 'honey fly') in the northwestern French dialects rather than standard French *abeille* (Stein 1984:46). São Tomé CP *gumitá* 'to vomit' comes from regional and archaic Portuguese *gumitar* rather than standard *vomitar*. Negerhollands CD *kot* 'chicken coop' comes not from standard Dutch *hok* but Zeelandish *kot* (cf. English *dovecot*). Papiamentu CS *wowo* 'eye' seems to come from Leonese *uollo* rather than Castilian *ojo* (Maurer 1986: 7).

European pronunciations that appear to be regional have also been preserved in the creoles, but again it is often impossible to determine if these are in fact regional rather than archaic. Cassidy (1964:272) points out that Sranan words reveal the state of flux of certain vowels and diphthongs in the seventeenth-century English on which Sranan is based. For example, the shift from early Modern English /ʊ/ to /ʌ/ was apparently not yet complete; in some Sranan words /u/ preserves the earlier pronunciation, as in *brudu* 'blood,' while in others /o/ preserves the later pronunciation, as in *djogo* 'jug.' However, this shift has not taken place in many Midlands and North Country dialects of England, where these words are still pronounced /blʊd/ and /jʊg/. Therefore, there is no way of knowing whether Sranan *brudu* or even Bahamian *shoove* /šʊv/ 'shove' preserve an archaic or a regional British pronunciation. Other examples of regional pronunciation include Negerhollands *win* 'wine,' preserving the pronunciation of Zeelandish *wien* /βi:n/

(also found in earlier standard Dutch) rather than modern standard *wijn* /βεɪn/. Finally the vowel in Haitian CF *mwen* 'I' or *bwè* 'drink' preserves the regional and archaic pronunciation of French *moi* or *boire* (Ewert 1933: 61).

It should be noted that regional European dialects appear to have contributed also to the syntax of the creoles through specific lexical items. Examples include French *être après de* (*faire quelque chose*) 'to be (doing something)' (§5.1.3) and Irish English habitual *be* (§5.1.4). These are discussed in the chapter on syntax.

3.2.3   *Nautical usages*
Most creoles arose in maritime colonies whose harbors docked slave ships, cargo ships, warships and countless smaller craft. Because of the mixture of dialects and even languages found among ships' crews, nautical speech has always constituted a distinctive sociolect. A study of the English in log books kept by semi-literate captains and masters in the British navy from 1660 to 1700 (Matthews 1935) reveals that the sailors had a "dialect ... peculiar to themselves" which contemporaries described as "all Heathen-Greek to a Cobler." Hancock (1971: 99–121) analyzed both the phonological and lexical data in Matthews, finding many similarities to Krio CE. This is not surprising, considering the important role that European seafarers played in the founding and maintenance of the colonies where the creoles developed. Today in eastern Nicaragua kitchens or separate cooking huts are called *gyali* in Miskito Coast CE, from nautical English *galley*. In Haitian CF the normal word for 'pull' is *ralé* from nautical French *haler* 'haul' rather than French *tirer*, and 'lift' is *isé* from nautical French *hisser* 'hoist' rather than *lever*. On the Miskito Coast *haal* 'haul' and *hib* 'lift from below' (cf. *heave*) and *hais* 'lift from above' (cf. *hoist*) seem to be used much more frequently than in standard English. The Indo-Portuguese creole term for dismounting (a horse) is *disembarc* (Schuchardt 1883a: 17), and a Bahamian term for returning home is *come 'shore*.

3.2.4   *Slang and vulgar usages*
Europeans brought the dialects of their social class as well as of their region to the colonies. For the urban poor, soldiers, and many others who made up the early settlers, slang was an important part of daily speech. Such words often became a part of the creole and frequently lost their European connotations in the process: if a creole's only word for 'urine' was *piss*, this word became as appropriate as *urine* in any domain, shedding the vulgarity of its etymon, e.g. Krio CE *switpis* 'diabetes,' *pisbag* 'bladder,' *pisol* 'urethra.'

The role of prostitutes in the building of empires has received scant comment from historians, but they were an important factor in settling the Caribbean colonies of Britain and France in the seventeenth century. Prostitutes were brought from France and given as wives to the buccaneers who had been using Haiti as their base in order to encourage them to settle down and farm. An eighteenth-century observer commented that "It is astonishing . . . that their manners, as dissolute as their language, are not perpetuated in their posterity to a greater degree than they appear to be" (quoted by Crouse 1943: 133). In modern Haitian CF the term for 'nonchalant' is *fouben* from French (*je m'en) fous bien*, which today means 'I don't care' but in the seventeenth century was closer in strength to 'I don't give a fuck.'

In the Bahamas one of some twenty precise words for skin color is *dingy*, 'having the complexion of a dark mulatto,' from the eighteenth- and nineteenth-century British slang term *dingy Christian* for a mulatto or anyone with some African ancestry (note that *Christian man* can still be used for 'white man' in South Africa). In Guinea-Bissau CP the normal word for 'breakfast' is *matabiiču*, from Portuguese *matar o bicho* (literally 'kill the bug') meaning 'morning alcoholic drink' from the belief of early settlers that this protected their health. The term survives in Kikongo-Kituba and Lingala *matabisi* 'reward,' in which *ma-* has been reanalyzed as the mass prefix of noun class VI (Mufwene p.c.).

3.3 African lexical influence

Niger-Congo languages were spoken natively by the generations of slaves who used the pidgins that developed into the Atlantic creoles, and they influenced the lexicons of these creoles in a number of ways discussed below. As mentioned above, the portion of non-European words in the pidgin could not exceed a certain level without impairing communication with the Europeans, which was the pidgin's initial function. The first generations of creole speakers were likely to have had some competence in the African languages of their parents. It seems likely that a pidgin-speaking mother often talked to her infant in her own language, but it also seems likely that she would use the pidgin as well, particularly if her spouse did not speak her ethnic language. Although it is difficult to reconstruct the sociolinguistic situation in Caribbean plantations in the seventeenth century with any certainty, Mufwene (p.c.) believes that his own acquisition of an African creole in Zaire may cast some helpful light. He grew up "in a country town where Kikongo-Kituba served as a lingua franca. Even though both of my parents speak the same ethnic language, they often spoke to the children in Kikongo-Kituba too, particularly those that didn't care to speak the ethnic language, Yansi. They usually spoke to me in Yansi, but to my younger brother in Kikongo-Kituba. This practice has been quite common from my generation onward." Like other children in such multilingual situations, or the children of immigrants in other times and places, it seems likely that the children of pidgin speakers in the Caribbean found their parents' first languages to be of limited usefulness with peers and with the larger community, who used the pidgin or its creolized form as a lingua franca. Most children born in the New World probably never achieved full adult competence in an African language, particularly in those areas where slaves were purposely mixed linguistically. There is documentation that this was done in both Africa and the New World to make rebellions more difficult: Dillard (1972: 73) cites the statement by the captain of a slave ship in William Smith's 1744 *A New Voyage to Guinea*: "The safest Way is to trade with the different Nations, on either Side of the River [Gambia], and having some of every sort on board, there will be no more likelihood of their succeeding in a Plot, than of finishing the Tower of Babel." However, there is disagreement as to how widespread or feasible the custom of mixing slaves by language actually was. In the Berbice colony of the Dutch in Guiana, a single African language, Eastern Ijo, appears to have predominated during the early period to judge from the ensuing Dutch creole (Smith *et al.* 1987; cf. §8.2), although this situation was unusual. Moreover, in Brazil "linguistic homogeneity seems to have been valued as it enabled the older generations of slaves to teach the new arrivals" (Le Page and Tabouret-Keller 1985: 33). Even in the West Indies, where mixing by language is claimed to have been widespread, its extent was limited by the planters' preference for certain ethnolinguistic groups that had come to be associated with various traits (Le Page and DeCamp 1960: 79). Still, it seems likely that for most purposes competence in the African ancestral language was not transmitted beyond a generation or two in the West Indies, despite the continuing arrival of newly imported slaves.

However, under some circumstances African languages – or at least extensive parts of their lexicons – did survive. As might be expected, the African component of the lexicon of creoles spoken in Maroon communities (i.e. those established by fugitive slaves) appears to be noticeably greater than that of other creoles, particularly in the domain of secret religious languages (e.g. Cassidy 1961, Daeleman 1972, Bilby 1983). Moreover, the particularly heavy importation of Yoruba speakers from what is today southwestern Nigeria in the nineteenth century led to the survival of their language until this century in Trinidad (Warner 1971) and Guyana (Cruickshank 1916) as well as in Brazil and Cuba (Reinecke 1937).

3.3.1 *African lexical items*

There is a terminological problem regarding words in the Atlantic creoles with etyma that have been traced to Niger-Congo languages. These have been called 'loans' or 'retentions,' but neither term is always satisfactory. Some are retentions in that they were apparently part of the original lexicon of the proto-pidgin reconstructed by Cassidy (1964) for the English-based creoles, suggesting that pidgins of other lexical bases had a similar category of words. Cassidy found that Sranan and Jamaican shared some 27 words whose African source had been identified. This common vocabulary may be attributable to the migration of settlers and slaves from Suriname to Jamaica in the 1670s (§10.4.2): only two of these words were also shared by Cameroonian. Nonetheless it seems likely that some basic items that are today widespread in both African and Caribbean languages were indeed part of an early pidgin lexicon. Such items include *nyam* 'to eat' with cognates with related meanings in scores of Niger-Congo languages (Koelle 1854: 80–81) and *fufu*, a dish made of boiled and mashed starchy vegetables like cassava, plantains, etc. (Turner 1949: 193). If it is likely that such words were part of an early pidgin, they can hardly be called 'loans' into the creole any more than vocabulary derived from European languages. And while 'retentions' may be suitable for these words, it seems possible that other African-derived words were in fact loans, i.e. borrowed well after the establishment of the creoles. These may include the widespread words for Yoruba dishes such as *àkàrà* or cultural phenomena such as *èèsú* 'savings club.' Although it is difficult to date the adoption of such words, some inferences can be made. An *èèsú* presupposes a cash economy, suggesting that this was a nineteenth-century borrowing from Yoruba captives liberated by the British after 1808 (§10.1). On the other hand the variant pronunciation of Bahamian CE *moi-moi* or *mai-mai* from Yoruba *móin-móin* or Ibo *moimoi*, all referring to a dish consisting of mashed black-eyed peas boiled in a leaf, suggests a borrowing into Bahamian CE at a time when there was widespread variation between /oi/ and the earlier /ai/ in English-derived words such as *hais* 'hoist,' although this might well have included the early nineteenth century as well as the eighteenth. Allsopp (1970) suggested an alternative term, 'apport,' to avoid the problems connected with 'loan'; it also avoids those connected with 'retention.'

It is difficult to estimate the proportion of African-derived words in creole lexicons. Bollée (1981) found only 2.7% in her sampling of Haitian CF; later (1984: 57) she noted that the dictionary she had used (Bentolila *et al.* 1976) was not very complete and that she had observed from her own lexicographical work that the proportion of non-French-derived vocabulary grew with the completeness of the lexicon. Cassidy (1961) estimated that general (i.e. non-Maroon) Jamaican CE preserves some 250 words of African origin, but it is difficult to establish a total number of words in the creole lexicon with which these 250 can be compared, since there is no way to determine where the creole lexicon ends and the standard lexicon begins in a continuum. Turner's (1949) study of the Gullah lexicon also lists some 250 words of African origin used in conversation, as opposed to the many more such words claimed to be preserved in personal names and some 90 expressions heard only in stories, songs, and prayers.

Stewart (p.c.) has suggested that words of African origin were often felt to be stigmatized in the New World and were particularly subject to loss during decreolization if they had not already been adopted into the lexicon of the larger society (if the decreolizing speech community coexisted with one). If not replaced outright, such words may be 'masked' or reanalyzed in terms of the European source language. For example, CE *bákra* 'white person' has been traced to Ibo and Efik *mbakara* idem (Turner 1949: 191), which may in turn be related to *beké* 'white man' in Ijo dialects (Smith *et al.* 1987), a likely source of *bɛkɛ* in Berbice CD and *beke* in Lesser Antillean CF with the same meaning. In Belizean CE *bakra* is explained as white people having their "back raw" from sunburn (Donahoe 1946), while in Guyanese CE it is thought to be "a corruption of *back row*, where (in church, etc.) white prisoners and their descendants had to sit" (Yansen 1975). In Sranan the folk etymology is *ba kra*, literally 'brother soul,' possibly influenced by *blue-eyed soul brother* in American Black English (Eersel p.c.). In Trinidadian CE it is believed to be a "term originally used to refer to a Frenchman of low standing. From the French *bas courant*" (Ryan 1985).

Alleyne (1971: 176) has suggested that those African words that did survive in the creoles "belong to a semantic category that can be generally described as *private* in contrast with the broad semantic category of European-derived words that may be termed *public*." In other words, African words often survived for intimate things, such as aspects of sexuality (e.g. Gullah CE *ɲimɪ* 'female breast' from Mende *ɲinɪ* idem; Turner 1949: 199), religion (e.g. some 180 African-derived voodoo terms in Haitian CF; S. and J. Comhaire-Sylvain 1955), or other African cultural survivals with no equivalent in the European language (e.g. dishes such as Papiamentu CS *funchi*, Negerhollands CD *funtji* or Jamaican CE *fungee*, all 'cornmeal mush' from kiMbundu *funʒi* 'cassava mush') – exactly the kind of lexicon likely to survive among immigrants elsewhere.

3.3.2 *African semantic influence*

While the number of actual words in the creole lexicons that can be traced to African languages is relatively small, the influence of these languages is much more extensive in the semantic range of creole words (Huttar 1975). Alleyne (1980: 109) has suggested that this occurred via relexification (§2.10): "the historical development of the lexicon has been in terms of a substitution, massive and rapid in this case, of West African lexemes by English (and Portuguese, Dutch, etc.) lexemes, leaving the former residual in ... the semantic structures which underlie the lexicon." For example, Twi *dua*, Ibo *osisi* and Yoruba *igi* all have a semantic range including 'tree, wood, stick.' In creole English the word *stick* can also mean 'tree' (e.g. Bahamian CE "a stick name pine") or 'wood' (e.g. "a piece o' stick"). The Spanish word *palo* (cf. Latin *pālus* 'stake') had its meaning extended to 'wood' and 'tree' after the sixteenth century, quite possibly under the influence of African languages in the New World. Portuguese *pau* has the meaning 'stick, wood' in Europe but also the meaning of 'tree' in its African-influenced cognates in São Tomé CP, Saramaccan CE, and Brazilian Portuguese. Moreover, Twi *dua* has the additional meaning of 'penis' (S. Obeng p.c.); this is also an extended meaning of Jamaican CE *wood*, Haitian CF *bwa* (cf. French *bois* 'wood'), Papiamentu CS *palu*, and Brazilian Portuguese *pau*, but not of the equivalent words in the European source languages (Holm 1987).

African semantic influence had a far-reaching effect not only on creole lexicon but also on creole syntax; it is particularly noticeable in the semantics of creole preverbal tense and aspect markers (§5.1), which are fundamental to the structure of the Atlantic creoles. The absence of a passive construction on a European model in the basilect of most Atlantic creoles could reflect a feature universally lost in creolization, but a case can also be made for substrate influence in semantics affecting syntax. While Bantu languages have a verbal suffix to mark the passive (generally used in impersonal, agentless sentences), almost all other Niger-Congo languages lack a special passive construction (Welmers 1973: 344; Mufwene p.c.). Instead, they have two kinds of constructions that are also found in the Atlantic creoles: (1) like colloquial English, they can have an active construction with an impersonal 'they' as its subject (cf. Miskito Coast CE "*Dem bil* dat hous laas yiir" 'They built that house last year'); or (2) transitive verbs can take on a passive meaning when their subject could not be the agent ("Dat hous *bil* laas yiir"). Syntactic parallels to both constructions can be found throughout the Atlantic creoles, e.g.

Haitian CF	*Papiamentu CS*	
(1) *Yo réle* li Mari.	*Nan ta yam'* é María.	'*They call* her Mary.'
(2) *Li rélé* Mari.	*E yama* María.	'*She is called* Mary.'

The effect of the second construction in the creoles based on Romance languages is often the omission of the European reflexive pronoun (cf. F "Elle *s*'appelle Marie", S "[Ella] *se* llama María"), with the reflexive (i.e. passive) meaning of the European verb becoming that of a creole stative (Schuchardt 1890: 213). There appear to be two sources for this 'ergative' (Baker 1972) construction, sometimes referred to as 'passivization' of a transitive verb's meaning. First, like some European verbs (e.g. *sell* in "He is selling balloons" and "The balloons are selling well"), transitive verbs in some West African languages can have either an active or a passive meaning, e.g. Efik *ta* and Bambara *dùn* can both mean either 'to eat' or 'to be eaten': "Tò *dùn* Mali la," literally 'Millet-porridge eat Mali in', i.e. 'Millet porridge is eaten in Mali.' Secondly, passive constructions in some European languages lent themselves to reanalysis: since past forms of 'be' could be reinterpreted as markers of tense only (§5.1.2), the locus of passive meaning could be shifted to the verb itself as in West African languages. For example, *was* could be interpreted as only a tense marker in "This house *was* built last year," as could French *été* in "Cette lettre lui a *été* envoyé" 'This letter was sent to him' (cf. Mauritian CF "Sa lèt-la *ti* anvoy li" idem).

Alleyne notes the optional use of the completive marker (§5.1.5) in creole sentences with a passive meaning ('The rice has been cut'):

Jamaican CE	di rais	(don)	kot	
Sranan CE	a alisi		koti	(kaba)
Papiamentu CS	e aros	ta	kortá	(kaba)
Haitian CF	diri-a	(fin)	kupe	

(Alleyne 1980: 12, emended by G. Huttar and Marta Dijkhoff, p.c.)

The completive marker was also used in constructions with passive meaning in Negerhollands CD: "Die hoes *ka* bouw" 'The house is built' (Van Name 1869–70: 163). Although Van Name rejected this construction as artificial, den Besten (p.c.) notes that Magens (1770) had made it clear that a passive construction with *word* was used in the Negerhollands CD acrolect spoken by whites, apparently transferred from Dutch. The attempt of missionaries to replace *word* by *ka* in their writings may have reflected basilectal usage, although there may also have been interference from their own German or Danish in their use of this construction in Negerhollands (§2.3). Papiamentu also has a European passive construction used mainly in writing (Marta Dijkhoff p.c.) which is modeled on Dutch (passive auxiliary *worde*) and Spanish (passive auxiliary *ser*): "E carta ta *worde* skirbí" or "E carta ta *ser* skirbí" 'The letter is written' (Goilo 1972). These constructions may have been introduced by two groups of native speakers of Papiamentu that were traditionally bilingual: Protestant whites, bilingual in Dutch, or Jews bilingual in Spanish or Portuguese (§7.3). It is also conceivable that the passive constructions were introduced into Papiamentu by nineteenth-century Bible translators who felt that its absence represented some kind of impoverishment (although such seeds would have needed to fall on fertile ground). Jules Faine, by all accounts a superstratomaniac, described the absence of a passive construction in Haitian CF as "une grave faiblesse, la plus notable déficience du créole" (quoted by Valdman 1978: 263).

3.3.3   *African syntactic influence on lexicon*

Hancock (1980: 78) quite rightly observes that "Shift of formclass is extremely widespread in all the creoles, and in any language which has little surface morphology." While this is evident in sentences like Nigerian Pidgin English "Dì *bíg* wẹ̀ yù dón *bíg* i *bíg* wẹ̀lwẹ̀l" 'You have really gotten big' (Rotimi and Faraclas forthcoming), it is also true that creoles are not syntactic free-for-alls in which any part of speech can become any other. As Hancock points out, Krio EC *ɔt* can function either as a preposition meaning 'out' or as a verb meaning 'put out; extinguish' (ibid.). However, not all Krio prepositions are multifunctional, and it is worth asking what diachronic factors might have influenced apparent shifts from one syntactic category in the lexical-source language to another in the creole. In this case, standard English *out* could be used as a verb meaning 'extinguish' until the seventeenth century, a usage that has survived in both British and American dialects. This suggests that the Krio "shift" was actually the survival of an archaic or regional usage. Similarly, it is worthwhile asking why so many European adjectives became creole verbs – while relatively few European nouns, for example, underwent this syntactic shift. Examples include the following:

Miskito Coast CE	"If yu wud *sief*, yu wud ron" 'If you want to be safe, you had better run'	(Holm 1978: 264)
Haitian CF	"fãm té *blãš*" 'The woman was white'	(Sylvain 1936: 41)
Palenquero CS	"machete si *bueno* nu" (literally 'machete your good not') 'Your machete is no good'	(Friedemann and Patiño 1983: 130)
Negerhollands CD	"mie *doot* van Honger" 'I'm dying of hunger'	(Hesseling 1905: 261)

In the above examples, the words in italics derived from European adjectives do not need to follow the equivalent of 'to be' as in western European languages (§5.2.2). Moreover, to indicate past (or anterior) tense, these words take the same marker used before verbs; e.g. *té* in "fãm *té* blãš" above is also used to mark verbs as in "li *té* mãžé" 'he had eaten.' In Miskito Coast CE, *did* is an anterior marker for words derived from English adjectives (e.g. "evriting *did* chiip" 'everything was cheap') as well as those derived from verbs ("die *did* gat chilren" 'they had children').

While it is true that adjectives are universally more similar to verbs than nouns are, it is also true that the above pattern is parallel to that in most West African languages. For example in Kru, spoken in Liberia, adjectives are a type of verb and require no copula: "ɔ *kpákà*," literally 'he *old*' (Singler 1981: 20). Similarly in

Yoruba, adjectives function like verbs in that they require no copula (e.g. "ó tóbi" 'he is-big'); they also take a preverbal marker to indicate past or anterior tense (e.g. "ó *ti* tóbi" 'he has become big'; Rowlands 1969). The case for European adjectives having become a type of creole verb under the influence of the African substrate is discussed further in section 5.3.3.

It is possible that in the case of some lexical items the general tendency of the Atlantic creoles to reinterpret European adjectives as verbs may have converged with other factors. In archaic English *sick* was used as a verb meaning 'to become ill' until the end of the sixteenth century, a usage possibly preserved in Bahamian CE "I thought Papa couldn't *sick*." On the other hand, while *red* could be used as a verb meaning 'to redden' (cf. Bahamian "Her eye started to *red*"), this usage was not recorded in standard English after the fifteenth century – well before English came into contact with African languages – although it could have survived in dialects.

3.3.4   *African calques*

Calquing is a process whereby words or idioms in one language are translated word-for-word (or even morpheme-by-morpheme) into another. For example, the English word *foreword* is probably a nineteenth-century translation of the German term *Vorwort*, while German *Wolkenkratzer* (literally 'cloud-scraper') is a partial translation of English *skyscraper*. Whether or not the theory of relexification is accurate in its entirety, there is considerable evidence that the calquing of African words and phrases was a major factor in the genesis of the Atlantic creoles. The semantic evidence for massive calquing is discussed above (§3.3.2) and syntactic evidence can be found both above (§3.3.3) and in chapter 5; this and the following section will deal with lexical evidence.

The calquing of a single morpheme can be traced only if it has affected its semantic range, as discussed above. Two-morpheme calques are more readily identified; in Bahamian CE *big-eye* means 'greedy; wanting the biggest and best for oneself,' as do Haitian CF *gwo že* and Brazilian Portuguese *olho grande* (both literally 'big eye'). This metaphor is widespread in Africa, e.g. Twi *ani bre* or Ibo *aɲa uku*, both literally 'big eye' meaning 'greedy.' Calquing can also affect word-formation rules; in many creoles the sex of animate nouns can be indicated by juxtaposition of the word for 'male' or 'female,' a pattern found in many West African languages:

	'child'	*'male'*	*'son'*	*'female'*	*'daughter'*
Bahamian CE	chil'	boy	boy-chil'	gyal	gyal-chil'
Negerhollands CD	kin	juŋ	juŋ kin	menši	menši kin

	'child'	'male'	'son'	'female'	'daughter'
Papiamentu CS	mucha	homber	mucha homber	muhe	mucha muhe
São Tomé CP	mina	mɔsu	mina mɔsu	mɔsa	mina mɔsa
Bambara	dén	ce	dén-ce	muso	dén-muso
Yoruba	ọmọ	okùnrin	ọmọ okùnrin	obirin	ọmọ obírin

It is possible that the English creole forms may have also been influenced by the parallel Scots forms *lad-bairn* and *lass-bairn*, although it is conceivable that these were themselves calques on Caribbean usages brought home by returning emigrants, much like the semantic extensions of Spanish *palo* and Portuguese *pau* discussed above (§3.3.2). Boretzky (p.c.) has suggested that "The repercussions of creole language phenomena on the respective metropolitan languages should be a new field of investigation."

Taylor (1977:170) points out the two-morpheme parallels in question words in Ibo and a number of Atlantic creoles, corresponding to 'what thing?' (for 'what?'), 'what person?' ('who?'), 'what time?' ('when?'), and 'what place?' ('where?'). Bickerton (1981:71) completes this list by pointing out the parallel form 'what makes?' (for 'why?') in Guyanese CE *wa mek* and Seychellois CF *ki fer*. To these could be added Annobón CP *ja fé* (Schuchardt 1893:407) and Negerhollands CD *watmaak* (de Josselin de Jong 1926:106). Although Bickerton considers the influence of the African substratum on creoles to be insignificant, there are clear parallels in West African languages – e.g. Ibo "gɛ nɛ merɛ" or Yoruba "kíl 'ó ṣe," both literally 'what it makes?' meaning 'why?' – but not in the European lexical-source languages.

A case might be made for creoles having arrived at such terms by a universally logical analysis in which units of meaning are lexicalized, e.g. 'what time?' (for 'when?') or 'male child' (for 'son'). Still others might be attributed to a straightforward description of a widespread culturally-determined practice: the three stones used to support a pot above a fire have a parallel name in Bahamian CE (*t'ree stone*), Haitian CF (*twa pye*), Negerhollands CD (*dri: ste:n*) – and Yoruba (*àrò mɛ̆ta*) (Holm with Shilling 1982). However, many terms seem far too idiosyncratic to be universal. For example, if someone speaks ill of an effort that later fails, he is accused of "putting the mouth on it" in Bahamian CE, i.e. cursing it. There are parallel phrases for this in Haitian CF ("mete bouch nan") and Papiamentu CS ("pone boka riba"). In Africa one simply points at such a person and says "n'ano" in Twi or "ẹnu rẹ" in Yoruba – both 'his mouth.'

Finally it should be noted that sometimes calques on African turns of speech have not created new creole idioms but rather reinforced the choice of one of several possible phrases from the European lexical-source language. While it is possible if somewhat poetic to say "rain is falling" rather than the more idiomatic "it's raining" in western European languages, the former is the normal phrase in a number of Atlantic creoles and African languages:

	Normal creole/African idiom			European idiom	
	'rain' or 'water'	PROG	'fall'		
Jamaican CE	ren	a	faal	E	'It's raining'
Haitian CF	lapli	ap	tonbe	F	'Il pleut'
Papiamentu CS	awa	ta	kai	S	'Está lloviendo'
Annobonese CP	awa	sa ka	se'be	P	'Chove'
Yoruba	òjò	ń –	rò		
Twi	nsuo	re –	tɔ		
Kongo	mvula	yi –	bwa		

Koopman (1986: 246) notes that European "weather verbs" (e.g. F *pleuvoir*) requiring a pleonastic subject pronoun (*il*) do not exist in creoles like Haitian CF or African languages like Vata and Abe. However, their absence cannot be attributed to the absence of pleonastic pronouns, which the latter languages have.

3.3.5 *Reduplication*
While iteration is simply the repetition of a word for emphasis ('a *long, long* walk'), reduplication is a mechanism for forming new words. It involves the repetition of a word (or part of a word) resulting in a distinct lexical item with a slightly different meaning. In European languages reduplication is often associated with hypocorism or baby talk (e.g. *wee-wee*, or French *bonbon*) but this is not the case in the Atlantic creoles and the Niger-Congo languages. It seems likely that reduplication became a productive mechanism for word formation in the creoles via calquing on African models. For example, the Yoruba word *ǹlá* 'big' can be reduplicated to intensify its meaning, i.e. *ǹláǹlá* 'huge'; the same process can be seen not only in Kongo *múpátipáti*, also literally 'big-big,' but also in CE *big-big*, Haitian CF *grã-grã*, and Guinea-Bissau CP *grãndi-grãndi*. Negerhollands CD *vroevroe* 'morning' (cf. Dutch *vroeg* 'early') suggests intensification plus shift of meaning. Cassidy (1961: 69–73) noted some two hundred reduplicated forms in Jamaican CE; he traced 16 of these directly to African sources, such as *putta-putta* 'mud' (cf. Papiamentu CS *pòtòpòtò* 'muddy') from Twi *pɔtɔpɔtɔ* 'muddy' or Yoruba *pòtòpọtò* or Baule *pòtopóto*, both 'mud.' These appear to represent retentions rather than calques. Another ten of the Jamaican reduplications seemed to be from African languages but no etyma could be found, while six seemed to be Jamaican

onomatopoetic creations such as *pooka-pooka* 'sound of a kettle on the boil.' Similar emphatic 'phonaesthetic' reduplications are frequent in African languages, e.g. Mandinka *fitifiti* 'movement of a dog shaking itself' or Kongo *dunta-dunta* 'palpitate.' The largest category in Cassidy's study consisted of reduplications of English words. The productivity of this mechanism in creoles is attested by such forms as Miskito Coast CE *pokpok* 'slow passenger boat with an engine' or Liberian English *holiholi* 'bus,' from "Hold it! Hold it!" (Singler p.c.).

The following illustrate some of the kinds of semantic shifts achieved by reduplication (all CE examples are from Miskito Coast CE). Related to the intensification of meaning discussed above is a superlative meaning, e.g. *las-las* 'the very last' (cf. Mandinka *lábang-labango* 'the very end'). Reduplication can also suggest the accumulation of many small things, e.g. *gravel-gravel* (cf. Kongo *lubwe-lubwe* idem). It can add the idea of distribution, e.g. *wan-wan* 'one by one, gradually'; cf. parallel Yoruba *ọkọ̀kan* and Twi *baako-baako*, as well as Haitian CF *yun-yun* and São Tomé CP *ũa-ũa*, all literally 'one-one' with the same meaning. Sometimes the accumulation implied is that of parts into a mass, e.g. *mod-mod* 'a lot of mud' (cf. Twi *pɔtɔpɔtɔ*). Reduplication can also suggest reiteration, e.g. *krai-krai* 'constantly crying, fretful' (cf. Mandinka *ke* 'do' and *kée-kee* 'keep on doing'). It can also add the idea of familiarity, e.g. *fon-fon* 'done in fun or play' or *lafi-lafi* 'loving fun and laughter.' Such familiarity can also be connected to contempt, e.g. *priichi-priichi* 'continual harping and preaching'; cf. Kongo *bantu-bantu* 'ordinary folk' and Yoruba *hẹbẹhẹbẹ-hẹbẹhẹbẹ* 'waddle along.' Studies of reduplication in creoles (e.g. Ivens Ferraz 1979: 58 ff., Chaudenson 1974: 1051 ff.) and African languages (Rowlands 1959, Carter and Makoondekwa 1976) reveal semantic categories more similar to each other than to those in European languages (Bollée 1978), although there are indeed parallels in all three, suggesting the influence of language universals.

3.4 Other lexical sources

The most important source of lexicon for any of the Atlantic creoles was the European language on which it was based, if only for the sheer proportion of words that the latter contributed to the lexicon of the creole. The influence of African languages was relatively limited in terms of the number of actual words, exceeded by adstrate borrowings in many cases (e.g. in Miskito Coast CE, which has borrowed hundreds of words from Miskito and Spanish), but the impact of the African substrate pervaded the entire lexicon in its effect on semantics, as well as calques on compound words, idioms, and reduplications – and quite likely subcategorizational rules (§3.7), although little research has been done on the last. The remaining lexical sources are Portuguese, which appears to occupy a special position in the history of the Atlantic creoles, and adstrate languages. Since borrowings from the latter closely reflect language contact, which varied greatly from one creole to another, more precise information on any particular creole should be sought in its sociolinguistic history (volume II). The purpose here is simply to summarize.

3.4.1   *Portuguese influence*

Because of the early and prolonged role of the Portuguese in Africa, particularly in the slave trade that led to the formation of the Atlantic creoles, their language played a number of different roles in relation to these creoles. It served as the superstrate for the Portuguese-based pidgin and creoles of West Africa (§6.1), as an adstrate for creoles of other lexical bases in the Guianas and the Caribbean (§§6.7, 10.2), and possibly even as part of the substrate for Papiamentu (§7.3).

The Portuguese-based pidgin that evolved in West Africa from the fifteenth century onwards was well established as the language of the slave trade in the seventeenth century when the Dutch, English, and French began capturing Portuguese forts from the Gambia to the Congo to gain supplies of slaves for their colonies in the New World. It has been claimed that the Portuguese pidgin used around these forts (and possibly by the first generations of Africans brought to the Caribbean) was, according to the monogenetic theory (§2.10), relexified or changed word for word towards the language of the Europeans currently in power. It is possible that the early Martinican contact French which Goodman (1964: 104) quotes from Bouton (1640) and Chévillard (1659) contains words from an earlier Portuguese pidgin, although Goodman (1987) now believes these were from Spanish. They include *magnane* 'tomorrow' (P *amanhã*, S *mañana*), *mouche* 'very, very much' (P *muito*, S *mucho*), *bourache* 'drunk' (cf. *borracho*, P 'drunkard,' S 'drunk'), *capitou* 'captain' (P *capitão*, S *capitán*), and *pequins* 'little ones' (P *pequenos*, S *pequeños*). More convincing evidence of possible remnants of a Portuguese pidgin lies in core vocabulary like *sabi* 'know' (cf. P *saber* idem) or function words such as *ma* 'but' (cf. P *mas* idem) in creoles of non-Iberian lexical bases, e.g. Sranan and Saramaccan CE. Negerhollands CD also has *ma*, although in this case it might be converging with or derived solely from Dutch *maar* 'but' through the regular loss of a postvocalic /r/. There is also a general locative preposition *na* (cf. P *na* 'in the' before singular feminine nouns) in the same languages as well as Papiamentu CS (cf. S *en* 'in') and Krio CE, with possibly related forms in Haitian CF *nã* and Jamaican CE *ina*. Taylor (1971), who drew attention to these similarities, pointed out that the Ibo preposition *na* matched the semantics of the creole forms more closely than Portuguese *na* did, however (§3.1). Hull (1974) pointed out that the Portuguese-based creole of Príncipe and Lesser

Antillean Creole French had the same preverbal markers for the progressive (*ka*) and future (*kɛ*). The future marker *lo* (cf. P *logo* 'immediately') is found not only in some of the Portuguese creoles of Asia but also in Papiamentu CS and Negerhollands CD. The completive marker *kaba* (cf. P *acabar* 'to complete, finish') is found in Portuguese creoles in Asia as well as Philippine CS, Papiamentu CS, and the English-based creoles of Suriname; moreover, there is a possibly related completive marker *ka* in Sri Lanka CP and Negerhollands CD. The Portuguese source may have converged with an African form such as Bambara *ka ban* 'INF finish,' which is also used after verbs to mark the completive aspect (Holm 1986).

Cassidy (1964) points out some fifty words apparently from Portuguese that are shared by Sranan and Jamaican CE. Aside from the uncertainty of some of the etymologies, there are problems in attributing these words to the remnants of an earlier Portuguese-based pidgin, as Voorhoeve (1973) did the considerable Portuguese-derived vocabulary in Saramaccan CE (§2.10). However, the traditional view attributed these words to the Portuguese of the Brazilian Jews and their slaves, who settled in Suriname in 1664 and 1665. Given their arrival during the crucial formative period of the English creole there, it seems plausible that they influenced its lexicon in the decade before most of the English settlers and their slaves left for Jamaica and other British islands after Suriname was transferred to the Dutch (Goodman 1987). Adstrate influence from the Portuguese of other Brazilian refugees during this period seems likely to account for loans in the creoles of French Guiana and the Antilles, e.g. *briga* 'to fight' (cf. P *brigar* idem) or *fala* 'to flirt' (cf. P *falar* 'to speak') (Valdman 1978: 177). It would also seem to account for some of the basic vocabulary of Negerhollands CD, perhaps via Papiamentu CS, e.g. *kabae* 'to finish,' attested since the eighteenth century (Goodman 1987). Still other Brazilian refugees during this period seem likely to have brought their contact-influenced variety of Portuguese to Curaçao, where it contributed to what became Papiamentu (ibid.), although others attribute the Portuguese-derived lexicon in Papiamentu to the remnants of an earlier Portuguese-based pidgin brought directly by slaves from Africa (Megenney 1984).

There seems to be documentary evidence of such influence on Palenquero CS (§7.2): Sandoval (1627) described the slaves coming to Cartagena as speaking "un género de lenguaje muy corrupto y revesado de la portuguesa que llaman lengua de San Thomé" ('a very corrupt, entangled kind of Portuguese called the language of São Tomé'). Moreover, the Portuguese-derived elements in Palenquero cannot be attributed to any other historical source; lexical items include *bae* 'to go' (cf. P *vai* 'he goes' versus S *va* idem), *la* 'there' (cf. P *lá* versus S *allí*), *mɛnino* 'child' (cf. P *menino* versus S *niño*), and others (Megenney 1982).

It should be noted that there is a quite different kind of influence from

Portuguese in the adstrate borrowings of the more peripheral Atlantic creoles. Réunionnais, which may have contributed to the Isle de France creoles of the Indian Ocean, contains over seventy words from Indo-Portuguese, many apparently brought by women speaking that language who married seventeenth-century settlers (Chaudenson 1979). In the Pacific Ocean, Hawaiian CE apparently gained some loans from Portuguese via Chinese Pidgin English in the early nineteenth century and later other loans via the Portuguese-speakers from Madeira and the Azores who came first as crew members on New England whalers and then as agricultural laborers (Carr 1972). Finally, Portuguese-speakers from both island groups were also brought as indentured laborers to some British colonies in the Caribbean area after emancipation in the 1830s; they are the likely source of words like Guyanese CE *preyta* 'person of African descent' (cf. P *preto* 'black') (Yansen 1975: 58).

3.4.2　*Adstrate influence*

Like all but the most isolated languages, the Atlantic creoles have been in contact with a number of neighboring languages from which they have borrowed words. In many respects the Europeans' efforts to impose their political, economic, and social wills on the Caribbean islands – often within an easy sail of one another – were never likely to produce linguistic mirror images of each mother country, each neatly isolated from the next. The realities of trade, war, fugitive slaves, and later labor markets, tourism, and education, have made the Caribbean an area of intense linguistic and cultural contact.

Amerindian languages have contributed a number of words for flora and fauna to the Caribbean creoles, often via Spanish and sometimes via Portuguese. At the time of contact, the two dominant language groups in the Caribbean proper were the Caribs in the Lesser Antilles and the Arawakans elsewhere. Examples of loans include Island Carib *mabí*, a species of tree (*Colubrina reclinata*) whose bitter bark is used in preparing a drink of the same name in Papiamentu CS as well as Puerto Rican and Dominican Spanish; it is called *mabi* in Haitian CF, and *maubi* in Eastern Caribbean CE (suggesting a phonological hypercorrection by analogy of Jamaican *jaa* to standard 'jaw,' or Jamaican *maaga* 'thin' to Eastern Caribbean *mɔːga*). An Arawakan loan is *kenepo*, a tree (*Melicocca bijuga*) bearing small, tart green fruit with a large stone: cf. Caribbean Spanish *quenepo*, Papiamentu CS *kenepa*, Haitian CF *kenèp*, and CE *kinép* or *ginép*. A loan from Tupi in Brazil is *caárurú* 'a thick leaf' via Portuguese *carurú* 'a stew with calalu leaves' via Spanish *calulú* idem. The change from /r/ to /l/ may have been influenced by this alternation in some African and creole languages (§4.6.4). The São Tomé CP term is *kálu*, which may have been borrowed into some West African languages as

Kanuri *kálu* 'leaf, soup' or Ewe or Gẽ *kalalu* via contact Portuguese or English. The CE and Papiamentu form is *kalalu* for a spinach-like vegetable (*Amaranthus gracilis*); in Haitian CF the meaning of *kalalou* has been transferred to okra, another favorite vegetable for stews. Many Arawakan words for flora and fauna were carried via Spanish to Central and South America, whence terms from other languages made the return journey. One of the latter is Nahuatl *ahuacatl* 'avocado' from *ahuaca-cuahuitl*, literally 'testicle tree' from the use of the fruit as an aphrodisiac or perhaps its shape. The standard Spanish form, *aguacate*, is quite close to the Nahuatl, but the local Guatemalan variant, *avocate*, suggests an older variant that led to French *avocat* and Haitian CF *zaboka* (from the French plural, *les avocats*; cf. §3.5.1 below) and Bahamian CE *avogado* and *alvakada*, leading to *alligator pear* by folk etymology. Miskito, a Macro-Chibchan language spoken in eastern Honduras and Nicaragua, has contributed many words to the English creoles of the western Caribbean, including *tahpam* 'a large sea fish' (*Megalops atlanticus*), which was borrowed into standard English as *tarpon* but retains its Miskito form in English creoles from Nicaragua to the Bahamas. Other Miskito words have been calqued in creole English, e.g. *sakanki dusa* (literally 'bat tree') for a shrub (*Saphrantus foetidus*) which is called *rat-bat bush* in CE and the equivalent *palo de murciélago* in local Spanish.

Spanish served not only as the vehicle of a number of Amerindian words borrowed into the creoles, but also as a source of loanwords in its own right. When North European explorers and privateers began coming to the Caribbean in the sixteenth century, Spanish was already well established in many areas and had acquired the vocabulary needed for local natural and cultural phenomena. Spanish influence on early contact French has been referred to above (§3.4.1); loans that became part of the creoles include Lesser Antillean CF (*y*)*iš* 'child' from Spanish *hijo* 'son' or *hija* 'daughter,' in which *j* was pronounced /š/ until its shift to /x/ in the seventeenth century (Goodman 1987) – cf. Island Carib *acoucha* 'needle' borrowed from Spanish *aguja* idem during the same period. Contact between Spanish and creole French was prolonged in several areas: on the island of Hispaniola between what became the Dominican Republic and Haiti (which governed the former from 1822 to 1844); in Louisiana (governed by Spain from 1763 to 1803); and in Trinidad (where the lingua franca shifted from Spanish to French in the late eighteenth century). Contact between Spanish and creole English was relatively slight in the British capture of Spanish Jamaica in 1655, but considerable in Central America from the seventeenth century onward. Refugees from Mexico's Indian Caste War (1847–1853) poured into Belize, so that one-third of its population is Spanish-speaking today. Creole English-speakers along the Caribbean coast of Central America as far south as Panama live in officially

Spanish-speaking countries, and this is reflected in their lexicons. In an incomplete survey (Holm 1978) of some three thousand Central American CE words differing from those in current standard English, over two hundred were found to be from Spanish. British West Indians returning from labor in this area, particularly on the Panama Canal, brought some Spanish words and phrases back to their home islands.

English creole has also contributed many words to other creoles, particularly in areas of close contact such as that with Negerhollands CD in the Virgin Islands (e.g. *bambai* 'by and by') and Berbice and Essequibo CD in Guyana (e.g. the durative marker *dʌz*). English and CE have been influencing Papiamentu CS at least since the British occupation of Curaçao (1800 to 1816, with several years' interruption), and particularly since the immigration of a considerable number of Americans and British West Indians following the establishment of oil refineries on Curaçao and Aruba in the 1920s. Such influence can be seen in a Papiamentu word for 'plunge', *djùmp*, and in *djònikek* 'a delicacy' (cf. CE *johnny-cake*).

English and CE have had an especially strong impact on the varieties of creole French spoken in areas that later became British (i.e. Trinidad and the Commonwealth Windward islands; cf. function words borrowed into St. Lucian CF such as *bikoz*, *rili*) or American (i.e. Louisiana; cf. CF *veille de Chrismice* 'Christmas eve' or *dex* 'desk' influenced by American Black English). The question of whether such borrowings are from an adstrate or a new superstrate language is by no means clear. Where the language of administration differing from a creole's lexical source language remained distant from creole speakers and had little impact on their lexicon (e.g. Danish in the Virgin Islands, which has left only a few words in the creole English like *gade* 'street'), the language can hardly be considered a superstrate. Other adstrate languages of administration might include Swedish on creole-French-speaking St. Barthélemy (1784 to 1877; see §9.2.5) or Dutch on the English (creole)-speaking Dutch Windward Islands (§10.3.3). New languages of administration with a much greater and more intimate impact on creoles (i.e. on their phonology and syntax as well as lexicon) could well be considered new superstrates. Examples might include the relationship of Dutch to the English-based creoles of Suriname, and possibly to Papiamentu CS; English to the French creoles of Trinidad, Grenada and Louisiana – and perhaps St. Lucia and Dominica; and Spanish to the English creoles of Central America (except Belizean).

The final group of languages that had an important impact on the lexicons of some Caribbean creoles was Hindustani/Bhojpuri and other Asian languages such as Javanese and Chinese which were spoken by the immigrants and indentured laborers brought over by the British and Dutch after emancipation in the nineteenth century. People of Indian descent today make up 55% of the population of Guyana, 46% in Trinidad, and 37% in Suriname (as well as 67% in Mauritius; see below). Hindustani/Bhojpuri survives in all of these countries and has contributed many words to the creoles in such semantic domains as food, clothing, and the cultivation of rice (Rickford 1976).

The Indian Ocean varieties of creole French share only some of the adstrate languages of the Caribbean. Besides Indo-Portuguese and Hindustani/Bhojpuri mentioned above, they share some Amerindian and other words in the "vocabulaire des îles" (Chaudenson 1974), the Antillean creole lexicon brought half way around the world by the maritime community that settled both areas. They also have a number of words from the Malagasy language of Madagascar, although its status as a substrate or adstrate language is not clear because of the continuing importation of speakers after the formation of the creole (Baker 1976b) – which is indeed the case of the African languages vis-à-vis the Caribbean creoles. The relationship of the Atlantic creoles in Africa to their neighboring languages is also complex in that some of the indigenous languages have also functioned as both substrate and adstrate. Finally, it should be noted that the lack of agreement on the status of some of the languages contributing to Hawaiian CE (i.e. Hawaiian, Chinese, Portuguese, and Japanese, as well as Philippine and possibly African languages) as substrate or adstrate languages helps make its classification as an Atlantic creole problematic.

3.5 Morphological changes

The above sections discussed lexical influence on the Atlantic creoles from various languages. The remainder of this chapter will deal with internal linguistic processes that led to certain widespread types of changes in creole words vis-à-vis their European etyma. As mentioned above, these processes affect the lexicon of all languages, but the extent to which they are evidenced in the creoles suggests that they are accelerated by pidginization and creolization.

3.5.1 *Morpheme boundary shift*

Pidgins and creoles are sometimes claimed to be languages without any inflectional morphology whatsoever. While this seems to be true of most Atlantic varieties that are not decreolizing, there are some ambiguous cases. The Portuguese-based creoles of West Africa have what appears to be an inflectional marking of the past participle, e.g. Príncipe CP *fá* 'speak', *fádu* 'spoken' corresponding to P *falar* and *falado* respectively (Günther 1973). Forms ending in *-du* can be used actively (e.g. "n táva *fádu*" 'I had spoken') but such constructions are rare; they are primarily used to give the verb a passive meaning (e.g. "ótu *samádu* pédu" 'The other was called Peter'). It is possible that this creole -*du* plays a semantic and syntactic role that is distinct from that of its Portuguese model. According to the analysis of Smith (1979b), etymologically related Sri Lankan CP "-tu, 'perfect participle,' is actually a post-clitic whose preferred position is attached to the verb." In Guinean CP, verbs with -*du* have a passive meaning similar to those of Príncipe CP (Kihm 1980), e.g. *skribi* 'write' versus *skribidu* 'written': "kriol i ka ta *skribidu*" 'Creole is not written.' However, Kihm analyzes -*du* as a derivational rather than an inflectional morpheme, analogous to the suffix -*tu* on intransitive verbs in Mandinka (both a substrate and adstrate language): e.g. *bàng* 'finish (transitive)' versus *bànta* 'finish (intransitive).' The fact that both Guinea-Bissau and Sri Lankan CP coexist with languages with a similar morpheme may explain this as a later borrowing. Although this would not explain the Príncipe CP forms with -*du*, this may well also be a derivational rather than an inflectional morpheme.

Papiamentu CS has a partially similar category of what appears to be a past participle. In verbs of Iberian origin this involves a shift of accent to the final syllable, e.g. *máta* 'kill'/*matá* 'killed' (cf. S or P *máta* 'he kills'/*matádo* 'killed') (Marta Dijkhoff 1985; Maurer 1986a). In many verbs of Dutch origin, the past participle is marked with a prefix, e.g. *fangu* 'catch'/*difangu* 'caught' (cf. D *vangen*/*gevangen*; the prefix has the allomorphs *gi-*, *ge-*, *he*, *i-*, and *e-*). Still other past participles take no marking: "Su plannan a wordù *dòbelkròs*" 'His plans were stymied' (Maurer 1986: 17). While the history of these forms is not known to the present writer, the inflections appear to be relatively recent borrowings akin to decreolization. Wood (1972) points to the importation of Spanish morphology ("E tábata papya*ndo*" 'He was talking') encroaching on older uninflected Papiamentu forms ("E tábata papya").

Perhaps the best case for the existence of inflectional morphology in a basilectal Atlantic creole is that of Berbice Creole Dutch, which has what appear to be verbal endings. For example *draɪ* 'become' takes -*tɛ* to mark the past: "a draɪtɛ gu" 'It became big' (Robertson 1979: 228). The superstrate source of this marker is clearly the Dutch past tense ending, e.g. "ik hoop*te*" 'I hop*ed*'. While this is unambiguously an inflectional ending in Dutch, the status of the Berbice CD morpheme is less certain. Historically the Dutch ending appears to have converged with the Eastern Ijo suffix -*tɛ̝ɛ̝*, which marks perfect aspect (Smith *et al.* 1987). Like other languages with subject–object–verb word order, Ijo has postpositions rather than prepositions and postverbal markers rather than preverbal markers (Robertson 1986). The closeness of the relationship of verbal markers to verbs is somewhat ambiguous in both West African and creole languages. Although verbal markers are often treated as free morphemes and written separately, in some African languages they are written together with the verb like bound morphemes. The

Africanist/creolist Jan Voorhoeve (1970) suggested that the preverbal markers in Sranan CE should be treated as prefixes, i.e. bound morphemes. Except for the atypical Papiamentu future marker *lo* (§5.1.6) and certain completive markers whose status as verbal markers rather than serial verbs is unclear (§5.1.5), most Atlantic creole verbal markers cannot be separated from the verb to which they refer except by the other markers with which they combine (§5.1). They may indeed occupy an intermediate status between bound and free morphemes, somewhat like clitics.

The above shows that the status of morphemes transferred from European to creole lexicons could change from inflectional to derivational, and perhaps from bound to free. European morpheme boundaries also disappeared in the creoles: in creole English one can speak of one *ants* or one *matches* or one *tools*, in which the English word and its plural inflection have become a single creole morpheme with either singular or plural meaning (§5.4.2). A similar morpheme boundary change occurred more frequently in the French-based creoles, e.g. Haitian CF *zié* 'eye' from the French plural "les *yeux*" /lezyë/ rather than the singular "oeil," or *zanj* 'angel' from "les *anges*." In both cases the final sound of the plural definite article (pronounced /lez/ before a noun with an initial vowel, but /le/ elsewhere) has been agglutinated to the creole noun to form a single morpheme, e.g. "youn *zanj*" 'one angel.' The same phenomenon occurs, although much less frequently, in creoles based on other Romance languages, e.g. São Tomé CP *zonda* 'wave' from P *as ondas*, or Papiamentu CS *sanka* 'buttocks' from S *las ancas* or P *as ancas* (Maurer 1986: 8).

Other forms of the article have also become agglutinated, e.g. Haitian CF *légliz* 'church' (cf. F *l'église* 'the church') or *lalin* 'moon' (F *la lune*). In some cases two etymologically related forms both survive, each with a distinct meaning, e.g. Haitian *nonm* 'man (i.e. a male adult)' from F *un homme* 'a man' as opposed to *lèzòm* 'man (i.e. mankind)' from F *les hommes*. Baker (1984) surveyed CF lexicons for count nouns having an initial syllable wholly derived from a French article; he found 112 in Haitian, 337 in Rodrigues, 444 in Seychellois, and 471 in Mauritian – but only 12 in Réunionnais, providing further evidence that it was not as creolized (§9.7). Such reanalyses are much less frequent in creoles of other lexical bases, but they do occur, e.g. São Tomé CP *osé* 'sky' from P *o céu* 'the sky.' Papiamentu CS *lamá* 'sea' is from S *la mar* 'the sea,' while *dehel* 'hepatitis' is from regional or archaic Dutch *de geel*, literally 'the yellow' (cf. standard D *geelzucht* 'hepatitis'). Sranan CE *didibri* 'devil' may come from English 'the devil.' The agglutination of articles has also occurred in loans into non-creole languages, e.g. English *alligator* from Spanish *el lagarto* 'the lizard,' or Spanish *algebra* from Arabic *al jabr*, literally 'the reduction.' Other function words can also be agglutinated, e.g. Negerhollands CD *taventit* 'evening' is from Dutch *te avond tijd* 'at evening time.' Jamaican CE *nej* 'to ache (of teeth)' comes from "on edge" by reanalysis of /mi tiit an ej/ as /mi tiit a nej/, in which *a* is interpreted as the progressive marker (Cassidy and Le Page 1980). Similarly, some New Yorkers speak of "a nurge" (e.g. to kill).

Agglutination of this kind in creoles usually reflects the frequency of the source form in the European language, e.g. some words are more likely to be heard in the plural like CE *shuuz* 'shoe' (made unambiguously singular with a quantifier: "wan *fut* a shuuz") or *brienz* 'brain' (with the derived adjective *brienzi* 'intelligent'). Similarly, some verbs may be more likely to occur in their past or past participle form, which serves as the etymon for the creole verb, e.g. CE *márid* 'to marry.' However, CE *brok* 'break' seems to come from Scots and Irish English *bruck* 'break' rather than from standard *broke*. Similarly, CE *lef* 'leave' and *las* 'lose' appear to come from regional British *leff* and *loss* idem, although these could well have been reinforced by the standard past tense forms losing their final /t/ through a regular phonological rule (§4.2.3). Evidence that *lose* may have occurred more frequently in its past form can be found in the parallel Berbice CD form *flɔrə* 'lose' (cf. D *verliezen* 'to lose' versus *verloren* 'lost') (Robertson 1979: 263). Finally, English creole verbs sometimes agglutinated the *-ing* ending, e.g. Bahamian *to courtin*, *to loadin*, *to fishin*, and could then take the mesolectal progressive marker *-in*, e.g. *go fishinin*.

There is some question about the survival of European morphemes as separate entities when they have been borrowed into creoles in combinations, i.e. French *jugement* 'judgment' consists of two morphemes, but does Haitian CF *jijman*? Taylor (1953: 295) suggested that Hall *et al.* (1953) created a false impression by treating certain morphemes under 'derivation' since the actual derivation had occurred in French but could not occur in Haitian CF, in which morphemes like *de-*, *pro-*, *trãs-*, *-e*, *-ti*, *-asyõ*, etc. could not be used in forming new words, even though they might be recognizable as distinct elements. Similarly, Hancock (1980: 83) claims that "an English incoining such as *destaticize* could not occur in a creole (unless it were a monomorphemic lexical adoption from English)." As a matter of fact, new morpheme combinations are indeed found in creoles, e.g. Haitian CF *sivéyé* 'watch' (cf. F *surveiller*) plus *-man* 'nominal suffix denoting action' yield *sivèyman* 'surveillance' (cf. F *surveillance* idem) (Valdman 1978: 138). Hancock (1980) himself mentions Trinidadian CE *brɔ:tʌpsi* 'a state of being well brought up' from *brought up* plus *-cy*, and *makošʌs* 'prone to gossip' from *mako* 'gossip' plus *-tious*. An explanation for this apparent contradiction could be that in their early stages of development the creoles had lexicons consisting of almost entirely monomorphemic words and although these could combine as free morphemes (§3.5.2), there were no productive derivational affixes. Later, through analogy (e.g. contrasting items like *jij* 'judge' and *jijman* 'judgment') and possibly further contact with the European lexical source language, some (but not all) creole words derived from European morpheme combinations became reanalyzable along the lines of their etyma, and the derivational morphemes thus isolated became available for new combinations. Still, Valdman has remarked that "in creole the productivity of the derivational process seems very weak, especially compared to that of . . . French" (1978: 144). By contrast, Mühlhäusler (1979: vi) notes that in Tok Pisin, which is not an Atlantic creole, the "powerful derivational lexicon distinguishes NGP from virtually all other pidgins and many creoles."

3.5.2 *New morpheme combinations*

Although the number of new combinations of bound morphemes in the Atlantic creoles is quite limited, free morphemes have readily combined to create new compounds, particularly in the English-based creoles. Combinations that were influenced by the African substrate languages were discussed above (§3.3.4). Many more seem to have been creole innovations to meet new communicative needs, some probably with the collaboration of the European colonists. In Miskito Coast CE, for example, two familiar words (*mountain cow*) were combined to refer to the unfamiliar tapir. When the settlers and their slaves came across a fifty-pound rat with webbed feet (*Hydrochoerus capybara*), they christened it *water hog*. A parallel example in Guinea-Bissau CP is *piis-kabalu* 'hippopotamus' from Portuguese *peixe* 'fish' plus *cavalo* 'horse.' Some such terms impose a cultural redefinition on their etyma, such as Miskito Coast CE *fiéri bwai* (cf. *fairy boy*) 'ancestral spirit inhabiting the jungle.'

Some of the English-based creoles have created a number of new phrasal verbs such as Miskito Coast CE *appear up* 'appear, show up,' *dark up* 'turn dark,' *drunk up* 'become intoxicated,' *hug up* 'hug,' *old up* 'become old,' *wet up* 'soak,' *wind up* 'become flatulent.' However, caution is usually advisable before anything is labeled an innovation. Valdman (1978: 131) points out the error of earlier lexicographers who labeled as such some creole morpheme combinations like Haitian CF *betizé* 'to joke' (cf. F *bêtise* 'foolishness' plus *-er*, verb-forming suffix). Although such combinations might seem new to speakers of standard French, they can be found in regional dialects and therefore may not represent innovations in the creoles. It is possible that some of the Miskito Coast CE phrasal verbs mentioned above actually represent survivals of archaic or regional British usages, but since lexicographers have largely ignored the status of phrasal verbs as separate lexical items until recently, such an origin for these terms is difficult to establish. However, when they include verbs based on English adjectives (e.g. *old up*), the case for their being true innovations is much stronger.

Some creole compounds seem redundant, for example Miskito Coast CE *hed skol* 'skull,' *han elbow* 'elbow' (*han* referring to both the arm and hand, like the corresponding term in many West African languages), *mout lip* 'lip,' *rakstuon* 'stone,' etc. These may be vestiges of an earlier stage of the lexicon's development, dating back to non-native-speaking parents (pidgin speakers) and their native-speaking children (creole speakers), and serving as a bridge between the two. Although they were members of the same speech community, their language was in a state of profound upheaval; it seems possible that teenagers and perhaps even older children had, as in other immigrant communities, English-derived vocabularies that far exceeded those of their parents, whose mother tongue was African. The precise English word, more likely to be unknown to the parent, may have come to be accompanied by a more general word of higher frequency of occurrence to serve as a mnemonic device. Similar examples in other creoles include Trinidadian CE *sɔu pɪg* 'sow,' *gɔ:t kɪdi* 'kid,' and Krio *blɛn-yai*, literally 'blind-eye,' meaning 'blind' (Hancock 1980: 72). As Hancock points out, it is also possible that some of these terms represent partial calques on African terms. For example, Yoruba *agbári* 'skull' (from *igbá* 'calabash' plus *orí* 'head'; Abraham 1962) may have influenced the formation of CE *hed skol* via intermediate forms analogous to Ndjuka *kaabási fu éde* (Huttar p.c.) or Negerhollands CD *kalbas fan de kop* (Bradford 1986: 93), both literally 'calabash of the head' meaning 'skull'; i.e. *skull* may have initially been interpreted as 'calabash,' whence the combination *hed skol* to distinguish it from other kinds of calabashes.

3.5.3 *Coining*
Hancock (1980: 68) notes that the spontaneous creation of words with no exterior model does not appear to be very common in any language. However, he lists some creole examples such as Trinidadian CE *bobolops* 'a fat lady,' Krio CE *flɛŋgbɛnšiš* 'smartly dressed,' and Papiamentu CS *kɔŋkəl* 'to knock together' (although Dutch *konkel* has the regional meaning of 'box on the ears'; den Besten p.c.). Bahamian CE examples might be *spokadocious* 'very attractive (of women)' or *pamolly* 'a swelling from a bump on the head' or *wumpers* 'sandals made from the rubber of a car tire' (although this last might be onomatopoeic).

3.6 Semantic changes
In previous sections there were discussions of differences between the meanings of creole words and their European etyma due to the influence of archaic usage (§3.2.1), regional usage (§3.2.2), and usage in substrate languages (§3.3.2). This

section deals with semantic changes resulting not from external influences but rather from internal developments that may have taken place some time after the pidginization of the lexical-source language.

3.6.1 *Semantic shift*

Like any language used in a new geographical setting, when the European languages that provided the creoles' lexicons were first taken to tropical Africa and the Caribbean, they lacked words to refer to local plants, animals, customs, objects, etc. that were unknown in Europe. While some of these gaps in the lexicon were filled by borrowing or creating new words, very often old words were simply used for new referents. On the Miskito Coast, *lion* came to be used for the local cougar, and *tiger* for the jaguar. Similarly, in Guinea-Bissau CP the hyena is called *luubu* from Portuguese *lobo* 'wolf.' Obviously such semantic shifts had to be made by Europeans who knew both referents. A further example is Negerhollands CD *pinapəl* 'pineapple' from Dutch *pijnappel* 'fir cone.' The relationship of English is unclear; until the eighteenth century *pineapple* had the latter meaning, which still survives in British dialects. A 1665 document cited by the *Oxford English Dictionary* in reference to the tropical fruit notes that "To outward view it seems, when it is whole, to resemble our Pine-apple," while a contemporary source refers to "The Ananas or Pine-Apple." Another semantic shift occurred in the French term *l'hivernage*, which in Europe referred to the laying up of ships during winter; in Lesser Antillean CF *livèrnaj* came to mean 'hurricane season.' Other shifts may have resulted from misunderstandings; Guinea-Bissau CP *kaloor* 'sweat' comes from Portuguese *calor* 'heat,' often used in the phrase *faz calor*, literally 'it makes hot,' meaning 'it's hot' in reference to the weather.

3.6.2 *Semantic broadening*

Semantic shift represents an extension of a word's meaning with the loss of its earlier meaning (e.g. *pineapple* no longer means 'fir cone' in standard English). Semantic broadening is such extension without the loss of the original meaning. For example, *tea* in most English creoles refers not only to the infusion made from various leaves, but also to any hot drink. A Bahamian CE speaker can say, "I must have my tea before I go to bed – either coffee or cocoa." *Coffee-tea* is used throughout the Anglophone Caribbean, including Guyana where Berbice CD speakers use the term *kofitei* (Robertson 1979: 265); while this may have been influenced by the CE term, the final vowel suggests its lexical source was Dutch *koffie* and *thee*. In Lesser Antillean CF 'hot cocoa' is *dite kako* (cf. F *du thé* 'some tea'). The semantic source of this extension of the meaning of 'tea' might be the calquing of monomorphemic words in West African languages meaning 'hot

drink,' a meaning apparently transferred to *ti* even as a loan in Twi (S. Obeng p.c.).
Another example of semantic broadening is Papiamentu CS *blat*; while Dutch *blad*
can refer to a blade of grass, a leaf, or a sheet of paper, Papiamentu *blat* can have
the more general meaning of 'one of two sides or parts of an object,' e.g. *blat di
chanchan* 'buttock' (Marta Dijkhoff p.c.).

As mentioned above (§3.1), the extension of meaning is characteristic of pidgins,
which in their reduced form must make do with a much smaller lexicon than
creoles and other native languages. Such polysemy is seen in Cameroonian *bɛli*,
which has not only the meaning of its English etymon *belly* but also 'appetite,
hunger, pregnancy, internal parts, seat of emotions, secret place, secret' (Schneider
1960) – although some of these meanings may have been influenced by African
substrate languages. The large number of extended meanings of the word for
'belly' in a number of English-based creoles (Alleyne 1980: 117) suggests that some
of the polysemy of pidgin lexicons may be retained in certain items of their creole
descendants.

3.6.3   *Semantic narrowing*

The restriction of a word's meaning seems to be less frequent than its extension in
creole languages. One example in Miskito Coast CE is that *stew* has acquired the
specialized meaning of 'boiling meat and vegetables in coconut milk,' while boiling
them in plain water is to *run* them *down*. In Haitian CF, which makes no gender
distinctions in adjectives as French does, *vè* (from the French masculine form of
vert 'green') means only the color while *vèt* (from the feminine *verte*) means
'unripe.'

3.6.4   *Other kinds of semantic change*

Hancock (1980) classifies several other kinds of semantic shifts. One is metaphor.
Bahamians call a machete whose blade is sharp on both sides a *French knife*, which
is also a term of abuse for a two-faced person. Haitian CF *kouto de bò* and
Papiamentu CS *kuchu di dos banda* also have both meanings. Hancock also
identifies playforms such as phonological modifications, intentional puns, and
intentional etymologies. The last might include Bahamian *donkeyfy* 'not caring,
especially about social norms'; there is a slightly different alternate pronunciation,
don't-ca(re)-if-I (do or don't), but the first form carries the extra idea of a donkey's
contrary obstinacy. The final category of semantic change is that caused by a
word's use as a euphemism. In Bahamian *hip* is a euphemism for 'buttocks'; it is
the only part of their anatomy that ladies ever fall on. The Krio euphemism is *wes*
from *waist*.

3.7 Change of syntactic function

External (i.e. substrate) influence on creole words taking on a syntactic function different from that of their European etymon (primarily adjectives becoming verbs) was discussed above in section 3.3.3. This section deals with language-internal factors causing such changes. In the pidgins there was a general lack of morphology to help maintain syntactic categories. In English, for example, words that can take an *-ed* inflection are usually verbs, while those that take *-ly* are usually adverbs. The absence of such bound morphemes makes it easier for words to change their syntactic function, e.g. *jump* can be either a verb or a noun in English but *jumped* can be only a verb (or verbal participle), and it is quite impossible to make a noun out of *easily*. Moreover, the first generations of pidgin speakers had to contend with notional equivalents that did not always correspond to the same syntactic categories in both their mother tongues and the target language. For example, *to be thirsty* and *avoir soif* refer to the same notion, but the English phrase consists of a copula and an adjective while the French phrase consists of a verb and a noun. Yet another language might use a single intransitive verb for the same idea, like archaic English *thirst*. If a native speaker of an African language which had the third construction encountered a Frenchman saying "J'ai soif" and the meaning was clear, he might analyze the words as 'I thirst' or 'X thirst.' In fact Mauritian CF "mo swaf" is a subject and verb meaning literally 'I thirst,' i.e. the French noun *soif* has become a verb in the creole. Given these factors, it is not surprising that multifunctionality was quite widespread and many words took on different or additional syntactic functions. It seems likely that many such changes in the pidgin or early creole lexicon were later changed back in the direction of the European lexical-source language during decreolization. Some evidence for this can be seen in a comparison of Miskito Coast Creole English equivalents with English borrowings into the Amerindian language of the Miskito, which appear to preserve usages in an English-based pidgin documented from the early eighteenth century onwards (Holm 1978). Miskito includes words like *tayad* 'fatigue' and *sari* 'sorrow' that are not found in the modern creole.

Category changes found in Miskito Coast Creole include nouns from adjectives ("He catch *crazy*" 'He became psychotic'), from adverbs (*afterwards* 'leftovers'), and from prepositions ("He come from *out*," i.e. 'from abroad'). Verbs can come from nouns ("He *advantage* her," i.e. 'took advantage of') as well as adjectives ("She *jealousing* him," i.e. 'making him jealous'). In Haitian CF the French noun *peur* 'fear' has become a verb *pè* 'to fear': "Li *pè* lãmo" 'He fears death,' while the F verb *chanter* 'to sing' has become a noun *chanté* 'song' (cf. F *chanson* idem). The F adverb *là-haut* 'up there' has become a creole preposition *lò* 'above, on' (Stein 1984: 40–42).

Changes in subcategorizational rules for specific lexical items represent another kind of syntactic change affecting the lexicon. For example, in Miskito Coast CE some mass nouns have become count nouns so that one can speak of *one bread* 'one loaf of bread.' Some count nouns have also become mass nouns, requiring a count noun for the measurement of units, e.g. "one grain of *beans*" 'one bean.' This parallels the Italian plural count noun *spaghetti* becoming a singular mass noun in English ("a piece of spaghetti"). Changes in subcategorizational rules for verbs have resulted in new sequences of permissible objects and complements: "Guess *me* this riddle"; "I would never do *you* that"; "He beg me *a piece of fish*"; "She curse me *black*"; "I will give *you*." Koopman (1986: 245) found that similar "lexical properties of verbs [i.e. double object constructions, selection of complement type] in Haitian and West African languages are parallel to a great extent, and differ in general from those of French."

While some of the above changes in syntactic function and in subcategorizational rules can be attributed to the influence of substrate languages, others may preserve archaic or regional usages in the European lexical-source language, while still others seem to have resulted from the general restructuring that took place during pidginization and creolization.

4

Phonology

4.0 Introduction

This chapter is a study of some of the phonological features found in a number of
Atlantic creoles but not their standard European lexical-source languages. The
theoretical orientation of this study is that discussed in section 1.4, the position
that creole languages resulted from a number of forces and that their features
reflect the influence of both superstrate and substrate languages, universals of
adult second-language acquisition, borrowing from adstrate languages, creole-
internal innovations, and the convergence of all or some of these. Sorting out
which of these influences may have resulted in particular phonological features is
by no means an easy task. It is particularly difficult to determine the degree of
continuity from the superstrate language ("internal" phonological development –
if this concept is indeed applicable to creolized languages) as opposed to that of
the substrate languages (sound substitution conditioned by systems external to the
language creolized). Not least of the difficulties is the lack of detailed information
about the phonology of the sixteenth- and seventeenth-century varieties of the
particular European dialects involved, to say nothing of the nearly total lack of
documentation of the relevant African languages of this period. Still, the challenge
of reconstructing the phonological development of creole languages has led to
some fascinating linguistic detective work, notably by N. S. H. Smith (1987)
among others.

Superstrate influence is problematical because there is less continuity between
the European languages and their creoles than there is between them and their
overseas regional varieties that have not undergone creolization. The latter are the
products of ordinary language change, and one can speak of their features in the
usual terms of historical linguistics, describing New England vowels, for example,
as the "reflexes" of the early Modern English vowels that preceded them. But if
basilectal Jamaican Creole is a different language from English (and most would
agree that it is at least a different linguistic system), is it still meaningful to speak of
"reflexes" as Le Page did in the *Dictionary of Jamaican English*? He now believes

that "Jamaican Creole vowels are not reflexes of Received Pronunciation or any other modern English vowels in any historical sense; the whole question of what became what is very difficult because there was multiple input from many African languages and many European dialects" (Le Page p.c.). Yet the term "reflex" is convenient for indicating that the vowels in the Sranan CE words *aj*, *baj* and *taj* correspond to those in English *eye*, *buy* and *tie*, so long as it is borne in mind that such correspondence is often irregular in creoles: cf. Sranan *paj* 'pay' or *ten* 'time' (Smith 1987: 450–451).

Substrate influence on creole phonology has been assumed since Van Name (1869–70: 124). Schuchardt (1882a: 895) explicitly states, "In the phonological system of São Tomé [CP] the influence of African languages can be clearly seen; this explains its many correspondences with other creole languages [Negerpatois]." However, Schuchardt's views on African influence can hardly be called an assumption since he goes on to compare specific phonemes in São Tomé CP and Mbundu. Recent objections to the significance of substrate influence have come from universalists who have focused on syntax (primarily Bickerton 1974 ff.) and have not denied substrate influence on creole phonology. The very mechanism of such influence requires some reference to universals, not in the Bickertonian sense of innate linguistic structures (§2.12) but rather the universals of adult second-language acquisition that played a role in pidginization. Valdman (1983), building on the work of Schumann (1978) and others, makes a strong case for the parallels between pidginization and second-language learning, claiming that both processes involve cognitive and linguistic universals at play in the acquisition of another language. The crucial difference is that in the case of pidginization there is a restriction of information about the target language that is determined by the social situation (i.e. trade, slavery, etc.). In creolization, the pidgin-speaking community's restricted version of the target language (with considerable transfer of first-language features) is nativized, perpetuating many such features. Thus later monolingual creole speakers have features of African languages in their speech although they themselves have no knowledge of their forebears' languages.

The kinds of phonological changes that can result from language contact are outlined by Weinreich (1953). Transfer results from a speaker identifying a phoneme in the second language with one in his first language and then subjecting it to the latter's phonetic rules. This can result in underdifferentiation (the merger of two sounds that are distinct in the second language but not in the first), overdifferentiation (the imposition of phonemic distinctions from the first language on allophones of a single phoneme in the second), or outright substitution (using a phoneme from the first language for a similar but distinct phoneme in the second). Moreover, there can be similar transfer in intonation and syllabic structure.

Universals can also be seen to play a role in the pidginization and creolization process in that sounds that are found throughout most of the world's languages (e.g. /d/ or /m/) are more likely to survive pidginization and creolization than sounds that are relatively rare (e.g. /θ/ in English and Greek, or /ð/ in English and Icelandic), if only because of the relative improbability of contact between languages which both have the same latter highly marked (i.e. non-universal) sounds. In general, contact languages are built on those features common to the languages in contact, so the phonemic inventory of a pidgin can be expected to be based on such sounds, although the phonetic realization of particular phonemes may vary to follow the rules of each speaker's first language. Creoles are likely to select those realizations of a pidgin's phonemes that are most common among the group whose children are beginning to speak the language natively – not those of superstrate speakers. However, creoles can also have phonemes (as well as phonetic realizations of phonemes) that are not found in their superstrate languages, particularly if superstrate influence is removed at an early stage of the creole's development or contact is maintained with substrate languages (e.g. the co-articulated stops in Saramaccan and Krio CE, §4.6.1). Language universals can also be seen as including the general patterns of phonological change that are found throughout the world's languages. For example, high front vowels are so often associated with the palatalization of preceding consonants that the change of Portuguese /ti/ to Príncipe /či/ (e.g. *čia* 'aunt') could be attributed to this universal tendency without reference to' any substrate pressure in this direction. However, it is the position of the present study that the likelihood of such change is greater when both substrate influence and universal tendencies converge.

There is such strong evidence to support substrate influence on creole phonology that the validity of this interpretation has never been seriously challenged. Beyond the systematic correspondences discussed in this chapter, some Atlantic creoles have phonological features found in African but not European languages. In addition to the co-articulated stops /kp/ and /gb/ mentioned above, some creoles have word-initial pre-nasalized stops (/mb, nd, ñdj, ŋg/; §4.6.2), as well as phonemic tone (§4.7). The importance of substrate influence is assumed in the studies of creole phonology on which the present study draws (CE: Alleyne 1980, Cassidy and Le Page 1980, Smith 1987, Turner 1949; CF: Stein 1984, Valdman 1978; CP: Ivens Ferraz 1979, 1987, Günther 1973; CS: Mario Dijkhoff 1985; CD: Stolz 1986; Boretzky 1983). The reader should be alerted to the fact that these authors do not always follow the same conventions in notation; some use /j/ for the palatal glide, others for the palatal affricate; some use /y/ for the former and others use it for the high front rounded vowel; some use /ɲ/ whereas others use /ñ/ for the nasal palatal; some use /´/ and /`/ to mark tones, others to mark stress or vowel quality. The present writer will try to use his own notational system consistently and clarify the potentially ambiguous usages of others where this is deemed necessary, but he hesitates to follow the bold rationalization of Alleyne (1980: 58), who uses his own symbols even when quoting others, whereby Turner

> Older Gullah speakers seldom use [tʃ]; they substitute for it the palatal plosive [c] . . . Among the older Gullah speakers [dʒ] is seldom heard; they substitute for it the palatal plosive [ɟ]   (1949: 27)

becomes

> "among older Gullah speakers [dž] and [tš] are seldom heard: they substitute for them the palatal plosives [dj] and [tj]."

(Alleyne 1980)

4.1 Continua

Before discussing creole phonology, it is necessary to consider the fact that the phonological systems of some of the Atlantic creoles vary according to their speakers' socioeconomic status and education. As noted in sections 1.3 and 2.11, there is frequently a continuum of speech varieties ranging from the basilect (which diverges most from the standard) to the acrolect (distinguishable from the standard in only relatively minor ways). Intermediate varieties (the mesolect) share features with both the basilect and acrolect in various combinations. Speakers' phonologies can vary considerably depending on their position on this continuum of lects, as can the phonology of a single speaker who commands a range of lects for different social situations. Although there is a clear gap between many creoles and their superstrate languages for a number of sociohistorical reasons (e.g. São Tomé CP, Sranan CE, Haitian CF), it is important to bear in mind the added complication of sociolinguistic continua in discussing the phonology (as well as syntax and – to a lesser extent – the lexicosemantics) of certain varieties such as the post-creole English of the Caribbean proper. To minimize this difficulty, it should be understood that in the following discussion of such varieties it is always the phonology of the basilect that is being referred to unless otherwise specified.

4.2 Phonotactic rules

With relatively few exceptions (e.g. Ewe, Vai, and Wolof), West African languages have a basic CV syllabic structure, i.e. a single consonant followed by a single vowel. In some cases the consonant can be a co-articulated stop, /kp/ or /gb/, which functions as a single phoneme (§4.6.1). There can be nasalization of the vowel (§4.4) and even of the consonant (§4.6.2), but the basic CV structure remains for all syllables except a limited number of function words consisting of a single vowel. There is abundant evidence of this phonotactic rule having been carried over into a number of Atlantic creoles, particularly those whose structure is least influenced by that of their European lexical-source language such as the Portuguese-based creoles of the Gulf of Guinea or the English-based creoles of interior Suriname (once called the most "conservative" creoles in reference to their African features, but rechristened the "radical" creoles by Bickerton 1981). However, remnants of this phonotactic rule can also be found in decreolizing varieties. Since many words in the creoles' lexical-source languages were incompatible with this rule, they had to undergo the phonological changes discussed below. These often had the effect of breaking up consonant clusters in the European words so that the corresponding creole words conformed to the CV syllabic structure rule.

4.2.1 *Aphesis*

Aphesis is the omission of one or more sounds at the beginning of a word. The omission of the initial member of a consonant cluster can achieve the CV pattern, as in Sranan CE *tan* (from E *stand*) or Negerhollands CD *tomp* 'stump' (D *stomp*). This is stigmatized in decreolizing varieties and leads to hypercorrections in which there is a "replacement" of an initial consonant (usually /s/) which is thought to be missing, e.g. Bahamian CE *scrumbs* 'crumbs' or Papiamentu CS *strena* 'thunder' (cf. S *trueno* idem). The omission of an initial (usually unaccented) vowel can also achieve a CV pattern, e.g. Príncipe CP *bi* 'to open' (P *abrir*), *kupa* 'occupy' (P *ocupar*) or *géza* 'church' (P *igreja*). The fact that verbs never begin with a vowel in many West African languages may have reinforced the phonotactic rule in some cases (Boretzky p.c.), e.g. Trinidadian CF *vale* 'swallow' (F *avaler*), *rive* 'arrive' (F *arriver*) or *coche* 'to hook' (F *accrocher*) (Stein 1984: 39). The widespread effect of aphesis can be seen in the word for 'American' in a number of creoles: Bahamian CE *Merican*, Haitian CF *meriken*, Papiamentu CS *Merikano*, and Negerhollands CD *Merkin*. However, aphesis is probably less typical in later borrowings: Liberian distinguishes between *mɛɛkɛ̃* 'Americo-Liberian' and *amɛɛkɛ̃* 'American' (Singler p.c.).

4.2.2 *Syncope*

Syncope is the omission of one or more sounds from the middle of a word. The omission of an internal consonant in a European word could also reduce a consonant cluster to achieve a CV pattern, e.g. Príncipe CP *gani* 'big' (P *grande*) or *buká* 'to seek' (P *buscar*). Examples from Sranan CE include *kosi* 'curtsy' and *sisa* 'sister' (cf. also §4.2.8).

4.2.3   *Apocope*

Apocope is the omission of one or more sounds from the end of a word. While early creoles tended to add a vowel to a word to prevent a final consonant or consonant cluster (§4.2.6), decreolizing varieties that have developed a phonotactic rule tolerating a single final consonant still omit the second element of a final consonant cluster in the lexical-source language, particularly when the consonants are both voiced or both unvoiced. In the English-based varieties this represents an extension of the colloquial English rule permitting the dropping of a final stop in a cluster before a word beginning with another stop (e.g. *roun' table*) in that creoles and post-creoles also allow final stops to be dropped before a vowel (e.g. *roun' apple*) or θ (*It's roun'*). Examples in American Black English include *roun* 'round' and *des* 'desk' (note like voicing of elements in the final consonant clusters of the etyma). Parallels in Haitian CF include *wonn* 'round (e.g. of surveillance)' (cf. F *ronde*) and *ris* 'risk' (F *risque*). A Negerhollands CD example is *tan* 'tooth' (D *tand*). Since this loss of a final consonant can also be stigmatized, decreolizing varieties sometimes develop hypercorrect forms that "replace" a consonant thought to be missing, e.g. Miskito Coast CE *sinimint* 'cinnamon.'

4.2.4   *Prothesis*

Prothesis is the addition of a sound at the beginning of a word; the addition of a vowel can give each consonant of a word-initial cluster its own vowel. Prothesis is frequently found in Spanish and Portuguese (e.g. *estado* 'state' from Latin *status*), but it is unusual in the Atlantic creoles, in which the tendency is towards a CV rather than a VCV pattern. However, it is found in the creole of French Guiana: *espor* 'sport' (F *sport*), *estatü* 'statue' (F *statue*) – perhaps under the influence of Portuguese (cf. P *esporte* and *estátua* versus Spanish *estatua* but *deporte*).

4.2.5   *Epenthesis*

Epenthesis is the insertion of a sound in the middle of a word; a vowel so inserted can serve to break up a consonant cluster. Such epenthesis is quite widespread in the Atlantic creoles; examples include Príncipe CP *álima* 'soul' (P *alma*), Negerhollands CD *kini* 'knee' (D *knie*), and Cameroonian *sitón* 'stone.' However, other factors can also lead to such vowels besides phonotactic rules. Bahamian CE *worrum* 'worm,' like the corresponding word in most other English-based creoles, has a second vowel that does not correspond to the standard form but does correspond to archaic English *wurem* and the regional British form *worom*. Adam

(1883: 51) noted epenthetic vowels in Mauritian CF, e.g. *carabe* 'crab' (F *crabe*) and *pilime* 'feather' (F *plume*). His observation that this pronunciation was characteristic of "most old people" suggests that it was already dying out.

Epenthetic vowels in Papiamentu CS, like those in other creoles, tend towards vowel harmony (§4.5), e.g. *sukú* 'dark' (S *oscuro*, P *escuro*), *delegá* 'thin' (S, P *delgado*), or *konofló* 'garlic' (D *knoflook*) (Maurer p.c.).

4.2.6 Paragogue

Paragogue is the addition of a sound to the end of a word; words in the most conservative Atlantic creoles often have such a vowel after what was the word-final consonant of their etymon: e.g. Príncipe CP *dósu* 'two' (P *dois*) or *méze* 'month' (P *mês*); Saramaccan CE *láfu* 'laugh' or *dágu* 'dog'; Negerhollands CD *grōtō* 'great' (D *groot*) or *ribi* 'rib' (D *rib*) – although the latter may have evolved from word-final inflectional /ə/ in Dutch and Zeelandic (den Besten p.c.). There are remnants of paragogic vowels (probably once more widespread) in Caribbean CE and Krio; the latter has examples such as *gladi* 'glad' and *dede* 'dead.' The loss of final *-i* in two Krio words (*les* 'lazy' and *fambul* 'family') suggests hypercorrection. A similar pattern of addition and subtraction of paragogic (and a few other) vowels may have taken place in Papiamentu CS as well. Paragogic vowels were added to a number of loanwords from Dutch such as *boto* 'boat' (D *boot*) and *buki* 'book' (D *boek* – but cf. the nonstandard diminutive *boekie*, warns den Besten p.c.). Although most Spanish words already end in a vowel, Papiamentu may have gone through an earlier stage of adding vowels to those that did not, followed by a later stage of decreolization in which such vowels were dropped. Hypercorrection could then have led to such modern Papiamentu forms as *kabes* 'head' (S *cabeza*) or *kas* 'house' (S *casa*) (Boretzky 1983: 74). It should be noted that Nigerian PE has a kind of optional paragogue between words ending and beginning with consonants, which can be seen as a kind of epenthesis: *snék dé* ('There is a snake there') can be pronounced "*sìnékì dê*" (Rotimi and Faraclas forthcoming). Finally, both epenthetic and paragogic vowels are particularly susceptible to vowel harmony (§4.5).

4.2.7 Metathesis

Metathesis is a change in the order in which two sounds occur in a word. In some cases metathesis served to break up consonant clusters, e.g. the Portuguese word *criar* 'to raise, bring up' became Príncipe CP *kiryá*, breaking up the initial Portuguese cluster and leaving each consonant with an adjacent vowel (*kir-ya*). The Virgin Islands CE word *pistarckle* 'person acting in a boisterous manner and otherwise making a spectacle of himself' (Valls 1981: 96) comes from Negerhollands CD *pistá:kǝl* idem, from Dutch *spektakel* via metathesis (Stolz 1986: 98). Some cases of apparent metathesis like Sranan CE *wroko* 'work' may have resulted from epenthesis (*wóroko*) followed by a shift of stress to the epenthetic vowel (*woróko*) and then the elision of the original vowel (*wroko*). Evidence supporting this interpretation can be found in the double vowel of the related Saramaccan equivalent, *wooko*, which followed another course of development in which both the epenthetic and the original vowel were retained and the /r/ was lost through a later rule deleting intervocalic liquids (Alleyne 1980: 47, Boretzky 1983: 76). The development of Sranan *wroko* may explain the metathesis in other creole words such as French Guiana and older Haitian CF *drōmi* and Papiamentu CS *drumi*, both 'to sleep' (cf. French, Spanish and Portuguese *dormir* idem). However, other cases of metathesis may actually represent the survival of archaic or regional forms, e.g. Bahamian CE *aks* 'ask' or *cripsy* 'crispy.'

4.2.8 *Elision of vowels*

Elision is a sandhi rule involving the omission of sounds between syllables or words in connected speech. The loss of one of two vowels at a word boundary (e.g. XV # #VX becoming XVX) is found in all the lexical-source languages of the Atlantic creoles: e.g. English *there's*, French *c'est* (cf. *ce* 'this,' *est* 'is'), Spanish *del* (cf. *de* 'from,' *el* 'the [masculine singular]'), Portuguese *dos* (cf. *de* 'from,' *os* 'the [masculine plural]'), Dutch *thuis* (cf. *te* 'at,' *huis* 'home'). It is also found in many African languages (e.g. Yoruba *n'ilé* from *ní* 'at,' *ilé* 'home') and Atlantic creoles: e.g. Príncipe CP *déli* from *da* 'for' and *éli* 'him'; Papiamentu CS *m'a bai* from *mi* 'I,' *a* PAST, *bai* 'go'; Haitian CF *l'ap vini* from *li* 'he, she,' *ap* PROG, *vini* 'come'; Sranan CE *j e fgiti* from *ju* 'you,' *e* HABITUAL, *fǝgiti* 'forget.' The loss of the vowel in *fgiti* is an example of syncope (§4.2.2), or word-internal vowel elision. Unlike the elision of one of two vowels between words discussed above, the elision of a single vowel between two consonants in a word will lead to a consonant cluster (e.g. CVC at the beginning of *fǝgiti* becomes CC in *fgiti*). Eersel (1976) believes that an earlier CV syllable pattern in Sranan was disturbed by borrowing words from Dutch without making them conform to this pattern, e.g. *skrifi* 'write' (with an initial consonant cluster) from Dutch *schrijven* idem. This development of a phonotactic rule permitting consonant clusters (which may have carried prestige through its association with the official language) led to the creation of new consonant clusters through the elision of earlier epenthetic vowels, e.g. *sikóro* 'school' (now heard only in poems and in Ndjuka) became *skoro*.

To conclude this section on phonotactic rules, it should be noted that there are entire groups within the Atlantic creoles which do not share the tendency toward a

CV syllabic pattern. As Ivens Ferraz (1987) notes, the Upper Guinean varieties of creole Portuguese (i.e. those of the Cape Verde Islands and Guinea-Bissau) do not follow the same phonotactic rules as those spoken on the Gulf of Guinea islands. The Upper Guinean varieties have no constraint against words ending in a consonant, e.g. Cape Verdean *rəpaž* or Guinea-Bissau CP *repas*, both 'boy' (P *rapaz*). This can be attributed to the fact that the two groups of Portuguese creoles have different substrate languages within the Niger-Congo family: the Gulf of Guinea creoles were most influenced by Kwa and Bantu languages, while the Upper Guinean creoles were influenced by Mande and West Atlantic languages. These permit final nasal consonants and final consonants respectively, and vowel elision in Mande languages results in consonant sequences not permitted in many other West African languages (Boretzky 1983: 75). The French-based creoles show very few of the phonotactic constraints discussed above; except for the absence of word-final consonant clusters, there are few if any such constraints in the French-based creoles that are not found in standard French (Goodman p.c.). Except for those spoken in colonies that later became officially anglophone, the French creoles remained in closer contact with their lexical-source language than did the "conservative" creoles of the Gulf of Guinea and Suriname. A further explanation might be that seventeenth-century pidgin French was more influenced by the West Atlantic languages (spoken in Senegal, where the French established their first trading post early in the century) than by the Kwa languages (spoken around Whydah, where they established another post in the late seventeenth century).

4.3 Oral vowels

The predominating vowel pattern in West African languages is the following:

	front	*central*	*back*
high	i		u
high mid	e		o
low mid		ε	ɔ
low		a	

This seven-vowel system is found not only in Kwa languages like Yoruba, Bini, and Ewe, but also in Mande languages like Bambara and Susu. However, it should be noted that there are a number of languages with eight to ten vowels, ranging from Ibo to Dyola (Boretzky 1983: 51, Greenberg 1966a). In many of these [ε] and [ɔ] are sub-phonemic, conditioned by vowel harmony etc. Moreover, Kongo and a number of north-western Bantu languages have a five-vowel system in which [ε] and [ɔ] are allophones of /e/ and /o/ respectively. Given these facts, it might be expected that the original vowel systems of the Atlantic creoles consisted of either seven vowels as above or five vowels with [ɛ] and [ɔ] as allophones. This does, in fact, appear to be the case.

The vowel systems of the European base languages range from five vowels with phonemic status in Spanish to nine in Portuguese to the 12 or 13 vowels of French, Dutch, and English. Thus it is noteworthy that the seven-vowel system found throughout much of West Africa is also the basic system of many of the Atlantic creoles, from the Gulf of Guinea varieties of creole Portuguese to the New World creoles based on French and English (Günther 1973, Valdman 1978, Alleyne 1980). Divergences from this pattern seem to lie largely in decreolizing varieties that have been borrowing vowels from their superstrates. For example, Papiamentu's core vocabulary has the five-vowel system of Spanish, in which [ɛ] and [ɔ] are allophones of /e/ and /o/, but later lexical borrowings from Dutch (perhaps reinforced by African words like *flɛngɛflɛngɛ* 'skinny' and *pɔtɔpɔtɔ* 'muddy'; Maurer p.c.) have resulted in the establishment of nine distinct vowel phonemes, including /ɛ/, /ɔ/, and two front rounded vowels.

The phonemic status of [ɛ] and [ɔ] is unclear in several creoles. Boretzky (1983: 50) notes that in Sranan both vowels were assigned phonemic status by Herskovits and Herskovits (1936) but not by Voorhoeve (1957 ff.) or Hall (1948). However, the Bureau Volkslectuur *Glossary* (1961) lists what seem to be minimal pairs, e.g. *séri* 'sail' and *seri* 'sell' with /e/ and /ɛ/ respectively. Wekker (p.c.) considers /ɛ/ a phoneme in Sranan, however rare, but not [ɔ]. In Ndjuka there is free variation of both sounds, e.g. [dede ~ dɛdɛ ~ dɛde] 'die' or [bo ~ bɔ] 'bow,' although only [ɛ] and [o] occur before nasals (Huttar and Huttar 1972: 3). Such asymmetrical behavior of [ɛ] and [ɔ] in Sranan and Ndjuka is unusual and further research may yield a different analysis. Saramaccan treats /e, ɛ, o, ɔ/ as four distinct phonemes, as in *léi* 'learn,' *lέi* 'ride,' *kóti* 'cut,' and *kɔ́tɔ* 'cold' (Rountree 1972a: 24). Since these Saramaccan phonemes preserve distinctions from English that are not preserved in Sranan, this suggests that Saramaccan developed independently rather than as an offshoot of Sranan. Finally, in Negerhollands CD [ɛ] and [ɔ] are allophones of /e/ and /o/ respectively (Stolz 1986: 61).

The seven-vowel system was probably characteristic of many varieties of creolized English in the eighteenth century, but Lalla (1986) postulates the more reduced five-vowel system for early Jamaican CE. Sierra Leone Krio, which may have been influenced by the speech of Jamaican Maroons and North American blacks at the end of the eighteenth century (§10.1.1), has seven oral vowels (Fyle and Jones 1980: xix), as does West African Pidgin English (Schneider 1966: 14).

In the following discussion of the development of European vowels into their corresponding forms in the creoles, it should be recalled that the starting point was not necessarily the same as the modern vowel of the standard European language, but rather the corresponding vowel of the speech of the fifteenth to seventeenth centuries (for Portuguese and Spanish) or seventeenth to eighteenth centuries (for French, Dutch, and English) (cf. §3.2.1). Moreover, this speech often represented social or regional dialects (cf. §3.2.2). However, since the purpose of this section is only to outline general sound shifts rather than to present a detailed study of each creole, some of these complicating factors will not be dealt with, in order to present a clearer overview.

4.3.1 *High front vowels*

Since /i/ in the seven-vowel system that predominated in the substrate languages corresponded closely to the single high front vowel in Portuguese, Spanish, and French, the creoles that drew their lexicons from those languages adopted this sound without change. However, the opposition of /i/ and /ɪ/ in English and Dutch was less easily accommodated in their related creoles. Negerhollands CD had both /i/ and a variable sound that fluctuated between [ɪ] and [i] (de Josselin de Jong 1926: 9). English /i/ and /ɪ/ fell together in the Surinamese creoles (cf. Sranan *si* 'see' and *bigi* 'big') and Krio (*si*, *big*). Although the English-based creoles of the Caribbean proper have developed a clear opposition (cf. Jamaican *sii*, *big*), this may depend more on vowel length than vowel quality (Alleyne 1980: 41). There are vestiges of an earlier single vowel in variants like Jamaican *asliip* and *aslip*; in the Central American creoles final unstressed /i/ as in *rédi* 'ready' is an intermediate sound, more lax than English /i/ but more tense than English /ɪ/.

4.3.2 *Mid front vowels*

The opposition between /e/ and /ɛ/ in many substrate languages matched that in Portuguese and French, and both sounds were adopted in the creoles related to them in Africa and the New World, e.g. São Tomé CP *zema* 'egg yolk' (P *gema* /ˈžemɐ/ versus *tɛla* 'land' (P *terra* /tɛřɐ/), or Haitian CF *geri* 'heal' (F *guérir*) versus *bɛl* 'beautiful' (F *belle*) – although the French creoles do not always preserve the French distinction when /e/ or /ɛ/ are in word-final position. Moreover, the Isle de France creoles of the Indian Ocean lack the /e/ versus /ɛ/ distinction altogether, e.g. Mauritian CF *met* 'put' (F *mettre* /mɛtr/). This supports the view that the Indian Ocean varieties were influenced by substrate languages different from those influencing the New World varieties of creole French.

Spanish /e/ and Papiamentu /e/ and /ɛ/ were discussed in §4.3, as were these two sounds in Negerhollands and the English-based creoles of Suriname. Krio CE shows a clear contrast, e.g. *get* 'gate' and *gɛt* 'get,' but there is also free variation of

[e] and [ɛ] in words like *lɛg* and *ɛd* 'head,' not only in Krio but in Caribbean CE, although this suggests a phonetic explanation of vowel raising before a voiced consonant (Singler p.c.). Jamaican CE /ɛ/ is described as "more close and more tense" than the corresponding sound in standard English (Cassidy and Le Page 1980: xxxix). Standard English /e/, phonetically [eʸ] with an off-glide, corresponds to /ie/ with an on-glide in the Western Caribbean, apparently owing to the influence of regional dialects in northern England and Scotland (ibid. xlvi).

4.3.3 *Mid central vowels*

The schwa sound [ə], which has varying realizations in Portuguese, French, Dutch, and English, has no equivalent in the seven-vowel system of many substrate African languages. Portuguese /ə/ often became /i/ in the Gulf of Guinea creoles, e.g. São Tomé CP *nglãji* 'large' (P *grande* /grɛndə/), but this tendency was sometimes weaker than that towards vowel harmony (§4.5), e.g. *kustumu* 'custom' (P *costume* /kuštumə/) or *fɛblɛ* 'fever' (P *febre* /fɛbrə/). French /ə/ was replaced by various vowels in the New World creoles, e.g. Haitian CF *bezwɛ̃* 'need' (F *besoin* /bəzwɛ̃/), *vĩnĩ* 'come' (F *venir* /vənir/) or *duvã* 'in front of' (F *devant* /dəvã/). Papiamentu CS has [ə], without phonemic status, probably from Dutch, e.g. /tigər/ 'tiger' (cf. S *tigre*, D *tijger*) or /lamentabəl/ 'lamentable' (S *lamentable*).

In the English-based creoles, English unstressed /ə/ was regularly replaced by /a/ in many varieties, e.g. Sranan, Krio /bita/ 'bitter,' Jamaican /bɪta/, but Gullah and Bahamian /bɪtə/. English stressed /ʌ/ in *cut* became /o/ in some creoles (e.g. Sranan, Ndjuka, and Saramaccan *kóti* 'cut'), but also /ɔ/ (Krio and Liberian CE /kɔt/) and /ɵ/ (Jamaican /kɵt/: the vowel is "short, centralized or mid-back, half-rounded, approximately ɵ" according to Cassidy and Le Page 1980: xxxix). In Gullah and Bahamian, this vowel is the same as that of standard English. The vowel in *first* (/ɝ/ in rhotic varieties of English, /ɜ/ elsewhere) often followed the same path as English /ʌ/ in the creoles, e.g. Sranan *fosi*, Krio *fɔs*, Jamaican /fɵs/, Gullah and Bahamian /fʌs/ or /fʌɪs/ (the latter following usage along the North American coast from Brooklyn to Texas). However, in some cases the English model seems to have been the seventeenth- and eighteenth-century pronunciation /ar/, retained in the British pronunciation of a few words like *clerk*, *Berkeley* and *Derby* (ibid. li). This can be seen in the form for 'hurt' in Sranan and Saramaccan *ati* and Krio and Jamaican *at* (Alleyne 1980: 40).

The English creole equivalents for standard /ʌ/ suggest a time continuum of increasingly closer approximations to the standard vowel, starting with seventeenth-century /o/ (preserved in the Surinamese creoles), eighteenth-century /ɔ/ (preserved in Krio), and the later even closer approximations of /ɵ/ (in Jamaican) and /ʌ/ (in Gullah). Since close contact with English was in fact broken in the seventeenth century for the Surinamese creoles and in the late eighteenth century for Krio, this suggests that the other creoles that have now moved closer to the standard pronunciation may have once used the earlier vowels preserved in the Surinamese creoles and Krio.

4.3.4 Low central vowels

The single low central vowel /a/ of the seven-vowel pattern found in many substrate languages served in the creoles not only for the same vowel in all of the superstrate languages, but also for several others. In the Gulf of Guinea varieties of creole Portuguese, /a/ corresponds not only to Portuguese /a/ (cf. São Tomé CP *tasu* 'pan' and P *tacho* /tašu/ idem) but also to a higher low central vowel in Portuguese, /ɐ/ (cf. São Tomé *kada* 'each' and P *cada* /kɐdɐ/). Since Spanish had only /a/, this was adopted without change in Papiamentu, e.g. *ala* 'wing' (S *ala*). Negerhollands CD appears to have had both the /a/ and low back /ɑ/ of Dutch, but the latter fluctuated and was probably not a stable phoneme. The same distinction in French was lost in most French-based creoles, e.g. Haitian CF *laž* 'age' (F *âge* /ɑž/) and *šat* 'cat' (F *chat* /ša/). However, the /a, ɑ/ distinction is found in Dominican and St. Lucian CF, e.g. /la/ 'there' (F *là* /la/) versus /lɑ/ 'lard' (F *lard* /la:r/) (Valdman 1978: 60, quoting Taylor 1947). The creole French /ɑ/ always corresponds to French /a:r/, and may be related to the Caribbean CE distinction between /hat/ 'hat, hot' and /haat/ 'heart.' There is a problem in determining what the seventeenth-century British English input was for these CE vowels: first, it is unclear whether Middle English /a/ had already undergone the phonemic split that paved the way for the modern standard British distinction between /æ/ and /ɑ:/; secondly, the quality of the long and short reflexes in the seventeenth century was probably not identical to the present-day British sounds, i.e. they are just as likely to have been [a] versus [a:], much like the Caribbean CE sounds (J. Harris p.c.). No distinction between the vowels in *hat* and *heart* (or indeed *hot* and *hurt*) is made in some English creoles, and all four words correspond to Sranan *ati* and Krio *at*. Modern English low front /æ/ also corresponds to /a/ in Jamaican and Gullah *hat* 'hat,' but unlike Jamaican, Gullah distinguishes the vowel in /hɒt/ 'hot' (also /hɒt/ in standard British pronunciation and in some parts of New England, but normally /hat/ in standard American pronunciation). British /ɑ:/ in *father* and r-less *farther* corresponds to /aa/ in most Caribbean varieties, but the vowel in *farther* is /ar/ in Barbados. The /ɔ/ vowel in *fall* (considerably higher in Britain than in North America) became /a/ in Sranan *fadon* 'fall (down)' and /a:/ in Jamaican *faal*, but remained /ɔ/ in Krio and many eastern Caribbean varieties of CE (but cf. Gullah /fɒl/). (See also section 4.3.7 on vowel length.)

4.3.5   *Mid back vowels*

Since distinct phonemes for /o/ and /ɔ/ existed in many of the African substrate languages, both sounds were preserved in a number of creoles (although the phonemic status of [ɔ] is unclear in others; cf. §4.3). The Gulf of Guinea creoles usually maintain the distinction in their Portuguese etyma, e.g. São Tomé CP *oze* 'today' (P *hoje* /ožə/) and *vɔzu* 'voice' (P *voz* /vɔž/), but not always. The New World French creoles have maintained the distinction between French /o/ and /ɔ/ only when the latter preceded /r/ in French, which was omitted in the creoles, e.g. Haitian CF *po* 'skin' (F *peau* /po/) and *pɔ* 'port' (F *port* /pɔːr/). However, the Isle de France creoles have a single phoneme /o/ for both French vowels, e.g. Seychellois CF *so* 'hot' (F *chaud* /šo/) and *sofa* (F /sɔfa/). Negerhollands CD appears to have had a phoneme /o/ with an allophone [ɔ] (Stolz 1986: 61). As noted in §10.3.4, English /ɔ/ and /ɒ/ became /aː/ and /a/ in a number of creoles, perhaps reflecting the contextual merger of these sounds in a number of seventeenth- and eighteenth-century dialects (Cassidy and Le Page 1980: xlix) more than the unavailability of /ɔ/ as a potential creole phoneme from African substrate languages.

4.3.6   *High back vowels*

The phoneme /u/ in many substrate languages matched the single high back vowel in Portuguese, Spanish, Dutch, and French, and this sound in words from the latter languages was carried over unchanged into their creole equivalents. However, the distinction between English /u/ in *pool* and /ʊ/ in *pull* was lost both in the Surinamese creoles (cf. Sranan *lútu* 'root' and *fúru* 'full') and in Krio (cf. *ful* 'full; fool'). This suggests that the opposition between /u/ and /ʊ/ in Jamaican might not have developed until after the end of the eighteenth century. Even today the distinction between Jamaican *ful* 'full' and *fuul* 'fool' may be one more of vowel length than vowel quality (Cassidy and Le Page 1980: liv; see below).

4.3.7   *Vowel length*

In some European languages, vowel length is significant, e.g. Dutch *stal* 'stall' versus *staal* 'steel' (although here there are other differences besides quantity; the quality of the first is closer to /a/ and that of the second to /ɑ/). Boretzky (1983: 52) has suggested that Negerhollands CD was the only Atlantic creole with phonologically relevant long vowels "if one can trust the notation" (i.e. of de Josselin de Jong 1926). The latter's glossary lists pairs like *stal* 'stall' and *stāl* 'steel', but in each case of opposition (i.e. a, ā; e, ē; i, ī; o, ō) the shorter or unbarred vowel is indicated as "variable" in the guide to the notation (1926: 9). Boretzky notes that in the other European base languages vowel length does not carry a high functional load; it is conditioned by stress in Portuguese and Spanish, and is becoming nondistinctive in French (e.g. the difference between *mettre* 'put' /mɛtr/ and *maître* 'master' /mɛ:tr/ is not being maintained). In English, earlier long and short vowels have been kept distinctive not by quantity but quality, i.e. differences in height (and off-glides).

A great number of West African languages have what at first seem to be long vowels, i.e. two identical vowels in succession as in Yoruba *maa* 'preverbal marker of habitual aspect' as opposed to *ma* 'indeed.' However, while the effect of re-articulation is indeed one of length, it is clear that such double vowels actually represent two distinct syllables in that each can take a different tone, e.g. Yoruba *oore* 'kindness' as opposed to *òóré* 'vista.' As Boretzky notes, Saramaccan double vowels can also take different tones, e.g. *dóò* 'door' or *doón* 'drum'.

Alleyne (1980) postulates an absence of distinctive vowel length in all New World English creoles as the first stage in the reinterpretation of English vowels, accompanied by the earliest changes in the quality of the corresponding vowels as discussed above. Each vowel of the output, /i, e, a, o, u/, later acquired a long counterpart in some creoles in the second stage. This may have been a simple doubling of vowels as in substrate languages, with no English difference in vowel quality, to judge from modern opposing pairs like Jamaican /i/ versus /ii/, /a/ versus /aa/, and /u/ versus /uu/. Finally, Alleyne postulates a third stage in which Jamaican /e:/ and /o:/ developed on-glides as /ie/ and /uo/, although Le Page (p.c.) sees these as presumably earlier results of northern English and Scots dialect influence.

4.3.8 *Unrounding of front vowels*

With very few exceptions (e.g. the Bantu language Yansi), Niger-Congo languages lack front rounded vowels. Although these are also absent in English, Spanish, and Portuguese, they are found in French and Dutch, i.e. /y/ as in F *rue* 'street' or D *u* 'you (polite),' /ø/ as in F *feu* 'fire' or D *sleuren* 'to drag,' and /œ/ as in F *sœur* 'sister' or D *fust* 'cask.' Regarding Negerhollands CD, de Josselin de Jong (1926: 9, 10) lists the notational symbols *y* (/y/) and *ö* (/œ/), but no words with these are found in his glossary, suggesting that their status in Negerhollands was marginal. Stolz (1986: 61) considers them to have belonged solely to the acrolect, but den Besten (p.c.) interprets them as optional allophones conditioned by the phonetic environment, e.g. *bök* 'stoop,' although related to D *bukken* idem, is probably /bek/ with some lip rounding conditioned by the preceding /b/. Papiamentu CS has borrowed both front rounded vowels from Dutch along with lexical loans, i.e. /y/ in Papiamentu *hür* 'hire' (D *huren* /hyrə/) and /œ/ in Papiamentu *drùk* 'press' (D *drukken* /drœkə/). Maurer (p.c.) has raised the question as to whether these borrowings are recent or possibly much older, long used by bilingual Papiamentu speakers of Dutch origin.

In the French creoles, Hall (1966: 28) claims that two stages of borrowing from French can be distinguished in Haitian CF according to the way in which front rounded vowels were made to conform to the seven-vowel pattern. In the earlier stage, the vowels remained round but lost their front quality, i.e. /y/ became /u/, a back rounded vowel, e.g. F *brûler* 'burn' became Haitian *bule*. Likewise, the mid front rounded vowel /ø/ became the mid back rounded vowel /o/, e.g. French dialect *yeux* 'they' became *yo*. At a later stage the French vowels remained fronted but lost their rounding, i.e. /y/ became /i/ (e.g. F *coutûme* 'custom' became Haitian *kutim*) and /ø/ became /ɛ/ (e.g. F *l'heure* 'the hour' became Haitian *lè* 'hour, time'). Goodman (p.c.) rejects this interpretation, suggesting that the different equivalents were determined by phonetic factors (e.g. adjacency to /r/ or a palatal).

Valdman (1978: 59) notes that the French front rounded vowels have been reborrowed into the Frenchified varieties of creole French often used by the urban elite. In such speech the French rounded vowel often varies with the creole unrounded equivalent, e.g. /žy/ varies with /ži/ for 'juice' (F *jus*), /zø/ with /ze/ for 'egg' (cf. F *les oeufs* /lez ø/), and /kœ/ with /kɛ/ for 'heart' (F *cœur*). This *refrancisation* or "re-Frenchification" is a sociolinguistic marker in the francophone Caribbean, much as the use of the interdentals /θ/ and /ð/ is in the anglophone Caribbean. Baker (1972: 39) notes that while the ordinary creole French of Mauritius has no front rounded vowels, all three found in French are used in the creole as spoken by Mauritians whose first language is French. A "refined" creole spoken by some Mauritians whose first language is the ordinary creole contains a single front rounded vowel /œ/ which corresponds to all three vowels in French.

4.3.9 *Diphthongs*

As noted in §4.3.7, vowel sequences in many West African substrate languages should be treated as two elements rather than one since they can carry different tones and thus represent distinct syllables. This is also the case in Saramaccan, e.g. *léi* 'teach' or *láu* 'wilted,' in which each vowel constitutes a separate syllable rather than the vowel and glide of a diphthong. European diphthongs were often replaced by single vowels without glides in the early creoles. Some examples from São Tomé CP include the change of Portuguese /ai/ to CP /a/ (e.g. *basu* 'under' from P *debaixo*) or P /oi/ to CP /o/ (e.g. *dodo* 'crazy' from P *doido* or possibly the older form *doudo*). English diphthongs also underwent such a change in the Surinamese creoles, in which /ai/ often became /e/ (e.g. *wefi* 'wife'), /oi/ became /o/ (Sranan *bori* 'boil'), and /au/ became /o/ (e.g. *oso* 'house'). Some of these changes can also be found in Krio (e.g. *wɛf* 'wife,' *os* 'house'), but more recent borrowings have the English diphthong, e.g. *laybri* 'library' or *lawnj* 'lounge'. A number of Caribbean varieties of CE preserve the earlier English pronunciation of the diphthong that is now /oi/, e.g. Miskito Coast CE *jain* 'join'.

Burling (1973: 33) notes monophthongization in American Black English and the more general dialect of the southern United States, in which the glide is reduced or lost in words like *pride* (/aɪ/ becoming /a:/) and *proud* (/aʊ/ becoming /a:/), especially before voiced consonants; /ɔɪ/ also tends to become /ɔ:/ before /l/ and in certain other positions. It is plausible but unproven that there is a historical connection between this and the parallel reduction of diphthongs in some Atlantic creoles.

4.4 Nasal vowels

Normally the air stream producing oral vowels is released through the mouth, but in most languages an oral vowel preceding a nasal consonant (such as the /ɪ/ in /ɪn/) is slightly nasalized: the air stream is partly released through the nose in anticipation of the nasal consonant. This weak nasalization is phonetic since it is conditioned by the environment and does not occur in minimal pairs; thus the phonetic realization of /ɪn/ is [ĩn] in English. However, a great number of West African languages have nasal vowels with the status of phonemes, i.e. ones that contrast with oral vowels in minimal pairs such as Yoruba *dá* 'to be rare' versus *dã́* 'to polish.' Such nasalization is much more noticeable than the assimilation of nasality on the phonetic level, which is also a feature of many West African languages. Thus Yoruba /ɔmɔ/ 'child' is phonetically realized as [ɔ̃mɔ̃], with nasalization that is both regressive (occurring before a nasal phoneme) and progressive (occurring after it). The nasal phoneme triggering the assimilation of the nasality of adjacent sounds can be a nasal vowel as well as a consonant as in the regressive nasalization in Ịjọ /sɔrɔ̃/, which is phonetically [sɔ̃r̃ɔ̃] (Boretzky 1983: 56). Assimilation of nasality over word boundaries is also found in African languages such as Yoruba, in which /wɔ́ á wá/ 'they will come' is phonetically [wɔ̃́ ã̀ wã́] (A. Oyedeji p.c.).

Boretzky (1983) claims that the influence of substrate languages affected the assimilation rules of nasal vowels in creoles derived from European languages that already had such vowels (i.e. Portuguese and French) and led to nasal vowels with phonemic status in creoles derived from languages that did not have them (i.e. English, Dutch, and Spanish). Portuguese has five nasal vowels with phonemic status, /ĩ, ẽ, ã, õ, ũ/; these can combine to form nasal diphthongs. Historically these are derived from the regressive nasalization of a vowel preceding a nasal consonant followed by a stop or word boundary. Even today, the phonetic realization of the nasal in *entro* 'I enter' can vary from [entru] to [ẽntru] to [ẽtru]. Speakers of European Portuguese are struck by the strength of nasalization of vowels preceding a single intervocalic nasal consonant in Brazilian Portuguese, so that *Copacabana* seems to be pronounced *Copacabãna* (Ivens Ferraz p.c.); this may reflect the substrate influence of African languages on Brazilian Portuguese. However, while the assimilation of nasalization is only regressive in Portuguese, it is also progressive in the Portuguese-related creoles, e.g. São Tomé CP *kamĩza* 'shirt' (P *camisa* [kamiza]).

French has four nasal vowels with phonemic status, /ɛ̃, œ̃, ɔ̃, ã/, although the contrast between /ɛ̃/ and /œ̃/ is not maintained by all speakers. Like the Portuguese nasal vowels, they are historically derived from the regressive nasalization of a vowel preceding a nasal consonant followed by a stop or word boundary. This is reflected in the orthographic use of nasal consonants to indicate the nasalization of preceding vowels, and in the usual generative treatment positing an underlying nasal consonant (e.g. /bɔn/ for [bɔ̃] 'good'), justified by the pronunciation of the nasal consonant as such when followed by a word beginning with a vowel, e.g. [bɔn ami] 'good friend.' Until the seventeenth century vowels could also be nasalized before a single nasal consonant belonging to the next syllable, e.g. *jamais* 'never' could be pronounced [žãmɛ] (Stein 1984: 29). Today the French creoles have nasal vowels resulting not only from the latter kind of regressive nasalization but also from progressive nasalization, e.g. Haitian and Lesser Antillean CF *žãmɛ̃* 'never'. This suggests that African substrate languages had a similar effect on nasalization in creoles based on both Portuguese and French; whereas nasalization is only regressive in the two European languages, it is also progressive in their creoles. African influence is especially clear in the case of Haitian CF, which has two nasal vowels not found in French, i.e. [ĩ] in [kašĩmbo] 'clay pipe' (cf. kiMbundu *kišima* 'perforated shaft') and [ũ] in [bũnda] 'buttocks' (cf. kiMbundu *mbunda* idem). These two nasal vowels occur only in words of African origin, but their phonemic status is unclear since there are no minimal pairs: they may have resulted from assimilation on a phonetic level. Valdman (1978: 65) points out that Haitian has two kinds of nasal vowels, which are apparently phonemic and phonetic respectively. The first kind, which produces quite noticeable nasality and is the only kind found in French, is that which occurs before non-nasal consonants (e.g. *dimãš* 'Sunday' from F *dimanche*) and in word-final position (e.g. *šẽ* 'dog' from F *chien*). A second kind of nasality, which is weaker, characterizes nasal vowels near a nasal consonant, e.g. in *mẽnẽ* 'to lead' (F *amener*). The two can apparently contrast – rare among the world's languages (Singler p.c.) – in minimal pairs like /šam/ 'charm' (F *charme*) and /šãm/ 'room' (F *chambre*). However, there appear to be serious problems in determining the phonetic or phonemic status of nasal vowels adjacent to nasal consonants; Boretzky (1983: 55) posits an earlier stage in which progressive nasalization was much more widespread, so that the formulation of a synchronic rule is not possible. Regressive nasalization remains much more frequent; vowels before the nasal consonants /n, ɲ, m/ are often nasalized even over word boundaries as in some West African languages, e.g. /li mɛm/ 'he himself' is phonetically realized as [lĩ mɛ̃m]. The Haitian CF nasal palatal consonant /ɲ/ in gɛ̃ɲɛ̃ 'have' (cf. F gagner 'gain') can be replaced by a nasalized palatal glide [j̃] as in /gɛ̃j̃ɛ̃/. This sound, found in West African languages but not in French, also occurs in Papiamentu CS (Maurer p.c.) and Príncipe CP (Günther 1973: 42).

Although European varieties of English, Dutch, and Spanish have no nasal vowels with phonemic status, nasal vowels of uncertain status are found in the creoles derived from all three. De Josselin de Jong (1926: 13) indicates nasal vowels in Negerhollands CD words corresponding to an oral vowel before a nasal consonant in Dutch, e.g. dãs 'dance' (D dans); others correspond to oral vowels before non-nasal consonants in Dutch, e.g. mɛ̃ši 'girl' (D meisje). Stolz (1986: 61) considers Negerhollands' nasalized vowels [ɛ̃, õ, ã] to be subphonemic variants of the corresponding oral vowels. Nasalized vowels also occur in Papiamentu CS kamĩnda 'road' (S camino) and nɛ̃nga 'deny' (S negar) (Tinelli 1981: 8 ff.).

The nasalization of vowels is found throughout the English-based creoles and post-creoles; indeed, it is one of the features that speakers of British English find most noticeable about American Black English and more general regional varieties that have been in contact with it. However, there is disagreement as to whether nasal vowels have phonemic status in any English-based creole or post-creole. There would seem to be minimal pairs, e.g. Sranan [brõ] 'to burn' and [bro] 'to breathe.' However, Alleyne (1980: 35) points out that this contrast does not exist before nasal consonants, e.g. Ndjuka [santi]~[sãnti] 'sand.' Huttar (p.c.) points out the further variant [sãti] but not *[sati]; in other words the phonetic realization of /VN/ is [VN], [ṼN], or [Ṽ] – as in Portuguese entro discussed above. This suggests that there is a nasal phoneme that is realized phonetically as a nasal vowel, a nasal consonant or both. These may be in free variation, as in Ndjuka santi, or allophones conditioned by the phonetic environment, like American Black English /don/ 'don't,' which is [don] before a vowel ([don ai] 'don't I?') and [dõ] elsewhere, like French bon. Both would seem to be the synchronic result of a similar diachrony: Alleyne (1980: 37) postulates that in the earliest forms of the English-based creoles, English words with a vowel followed by a syllable-final nasal consonant (i.e. one before another consonant or a word boundary, e.g. man) were reinterpreted as ending with either a nasal vowel plus nasal consonant (mãn), or just a nasal vowel (*mã*) or an oral vowel (*ma*). Since /Vn/, /Vŋ/, and /Vm/ could all merge as /Ṽ/, the original form of the nasal consonant could not always be reconstructed later during decreolization. This could account for such hypercorrect forms as Miskito Coast CE *skriim waya* 'screen wire,' and denasalized forms such as Bahamian CE /əbáras/ 'embarrassed'.

4.5   Vowel harmony

A number of West African languages have classic harmony systems, in which vowels are divided into two mutually exclusive harmonic sets (e.g. according to height or laxness) so that all the vowels in a word will belong to either one set or the other. For example in Ịjọ all the vowels will be either lax (ɪ, ɛ, ʊ, ɔ) or tense (i, e, u, o) (Williamson 1965). This and other kinds of vowel harmony are found in other Kwa languages like Ewe, Fante, and Ibo, as well as in Bantu languages like Kongo (Boretzky 1983, Ivens Ferraz 1979). A more restricted kind of vowel harmony is found in Yoruba, in which words can contain either the high mid vowels /e/ and /o/ or else the low mid vowels /ɛ/ and /ɔ/, but not members of both sets (Singler p.c.). Yoruba also has a related but distinct phenomenon called vowel copying; for example, the third person singular object pronoun is simply a repetition of the vowel of the preceding verb, e.g. "mo r*a a*" 'I bought it' versus "mo y*i i*" 'I turned it.' Vowel copying can be seen as the assimilation of adjacent sounds on the phonetic level, while classic harmony systems are something quite different: morpheme structure rules restricting possible sequences of vowels.

Although Alleyne (1980: 40) makes a strong case for the importance of vowel harmony in Saramaccan CE, it is not clear whether the creole has productive harmony rules or just sporadic lexicalizations, local umlaut, or simple vowel copying. The present account will have to leave this question open and restrict itself to summarizing what evidence has been adduced for the importance of vowel harmony in the Atlantic creoles in general.

Vowel harmony or copying appears to have played a role in determining the paragogic vowel (§4.2.6) in the Surinamese creoles, e.g. Sranan *bigi* 'big,' *dede* 'dead,' *ala* 'all,' *mofo* 'mouth,' *brudu* 'blood' (Alleyne 1980: 67). Epenthetic vowels (§4.2.5) also seem likely to have been affected, e.g. Ndjuka *somóko* 'smoke' or *sutuún* 'lemon' (cf. D *citroen* /sitrú:n/) (Huttar p.c.). There may be remnants of vowel harmony or copying in Krio (e.g. *pɛtɛtɛ* 'potato') and Jamaican, particularly in the epenthetic vowels in *simit* 'Smith' and *wɔrɔm* 'worm' (although the latter may actually be a British regionalism).

In the Gulf of Guinea varieties of creole Portuguese, paragogic vowels are also usually the same as the stressed vowel of the etymon, e.g. São Tomé CP *dotolo* 'doctor' (P *doutor*), *mɛlɛ* 'honey' (P *mel*), or *zulu* 'blue' (P *azul*). Harmony or copying may also have affected other vowels, e.g. *kɔdɔ* 'rope' (P *corda*) or *sebe* 'to know' (P *saber*). Such a rule was applied even to words borrowed from other African languages, e.g. São Tomé CP *oko* 'calabash' (cf. Bini *uko* idem) or *lɔlɔ* 'to lick' (Bini *lalɔ* idem).

In Haitian CF the harmony of vowels in particular lexical items is much less widespread, often involving only a tendency toward the same vowel height, e.g. *gwɔsɛ* 'size' from F *grosseur* (with both vowels low mid instead of the expected *gwose*, although Valdman [p.c.] has encountered the latter form as well). However, Haitian also has a synchronic rule of vowel harmony or assimilation involving the personal pronoun *u* 'you, your,' which can assimilate to the height of the vowel in the preceding word, e.g. "pje *u*" 'your foot' becomes "pje *o*" (both vowels high mid) while "avɛ *u*" 'with you' becomes "avɛ *ɔ*" (both low mid) (Valdman 1978: 93).

Vowel harmony or copying in Papiamentu CS can be found not only in epenthetic vowels (§4.2.5) but in other cases as well, e.g. *dede* 'finger' (S *dedo*), *caya* 'street' (S *calle*), *rosponde* 'answer' (S *responde*), *bichi* 'insect' (S *bicho*). In Negerhollands CD epenthetic vowels seem to have been similarly affected (e.g. *kini* 'knee' from D *knie* versus *konop* 'button' from D *knoop*), as do paragogic vowels (e.g. *be:de:* 'bed' from D *bed* versus *duku* 'cloth' from D *doek*) (Stolz 1986: 56).

While it is difficult to find clear evidence for the survival of any Niger-Congo language's vowel harmony *system* in the Atlantic creoles, there is abundant evidence for at least a pattern of vowel copying in the earliest stages of some creoles, particularly in epenthetic and paragogic vowels. Although this suggests substrate influence, a case can also be made for a universal tendency here: such added vowels do not actually come out of nothingness since the mouth is already in the appropriate position to produce the original vowel. However, some specific rules (e.g. the assimilation of the Haitian CF pronoun *u* to *o* or *ɔ*) seem quite likely to have resulted from substrate influence.

4.6 Consonants

In addition to the seven oral and nasal vowels discussed above, Alleyne (1980: 76) has proposed the consonants listed in table 1 as part of the earliest creole English phonological system. The table suggests a more general picture of the consonants of the earliest Atlantic creoles of other lexical bases as well: if we disregard for the moment certain African consonants found mainly in the Surinamese creoles (i.e. the co-articulated and pre-nasalized stops), the system that is left (adjusting the palatal stops to the affricates /tš/ and /dž/, and /sj/ to /š/) is approximately that of the other Atlantic creoles before their acquisition of certain consonants peculiar to their superstrates (e.g. Portuguese /ʌ/ or French /ɥ/) – consonants that today can be found in the acrolect but are marginal to the creole's basic system. Like modern

Table 1. *Consonants in the earliest creole English phonological system*

Manner of articulation	Point of articulation							
	Bi-labial	Labial-dental	Alveolar	Palatal-alveolar	Palatal	Velar	Labial-velar	Glottal
Stop	p b	t d	.		tj dj	k g		
Co-articulated stop							kp gb	
Nasal	m		n		ñ	ŋ		
Pre-nasalized stop	mb		nd		ñdj	ŋg		
Liquid			l~r					
Fricative		f		s~sj				
Glide/con-tinuant	w					j		h

Source: Alleyne 1980: 76.

Yoruba, many of the early creoles apparently had only voiceless fricatives, but most now include the voiced fricatives /v, z, ž/. Symmetry (and Alleyne 1980: 51) suggest the inclusion of /ŋ/; although this sound lacks phonemic status in such creoles as Ndjuka (Huttar p.c.) and Negerhollands (Stolz 1986: 64), it is a phoneme in Haitian and some other French creoles despite its absence in French (Valdman 1978: 51).

4.6.1   *Co-articulated stops*

A number of Niger-Congo languages (largely West African) have voiceless and voiced labial–velar co-articulated stops, represented as /kp/ and /gb/ respectively although each represents a single phoneme. They are articulated with the back of the tongue against the velum and the lips closed; the tongue is lowered and the lips open simultaneously while air is expelled (or drawn in in the case of the labial–velar implosives /kɓ/ and /gɓ/). Each contrasts with the corresponding labial or velar stop (e.g. Yoruba *gbọ* 'to hear' versus *bọ* 'to nourish' versus *gọ* 'to embarrass') and acts as a single consonant in the CV syllabic pattern. They are found in the eastern West Atlantic languages as well as in Mande, Kru, Gur, and Kwa languages and some northern Bantu languages.

The creole Portuguese of Príncipe (but not São Tomé) has /gb/, which Günther (1973: 41, 45) describes as a labial–velar plosive and treats as an integral part of the creole's phonological system. However, Ferraz (1975: 155) treats it as an implosive which "is not a productive unit in the incorporation of borrowings, and is only found in archaic borrowings from African languages," e.g. *igbegbé* 'snail' or *igbé* 'testicles.'

Saramaccan CE has both /kp/ and /gb/, often in words of African origin for flora and fauna, e.g. *kpasi* 'vulture' or *gbono-gbono* 'moss' (Alleyne 1980: 50, who refers to them as implosives). Donicie and Voorhoeve (1963: v) note that Saramaccan /kp/ and /gb/ have the allophones [kw] and [gw] respectively; indeed, /kp/ has replaced /kw/ in some words of European origin such as *kpéi* 'slobber' (cf. Dutch *kwijlen* idem). Boretzky (1983: 62) notes that in some dialects of Ewe /kp/ and /gb/ correspond to /kw/ and /gw/ in other dialects of the same language. Saramaccan /kp/ and /gb/ often correspond to Sranan /kw/ and /gw/, e.g. *kpiñi* versus *kwinsi* 'squeeze' (cf. British dialect *squinch*) or *dagbe* versus *dagwe* 'type of snake.' Ndjuka also generally has /kw/ and /gw/ like Sranan, but while Sranan lacks the co-articulated stops, some Ndjuka speakers have variants of certain words with them, e.g. *kwo-kwo ~ kpo-kpo* 'type of fish soup,' or *gwé ~ gbé* 'leave' (cf. E *go away*) (Huttar p.c.). Alleyne speculates that such pairs resulted from allophones in the earliest Surinamese creole(s), as well as in some of the African languages which were the mother tongues of some pidgin speakers. Boretzky's data on Ewe dialects would support this hypothesis. Alleyne further surmises that the [kw] allophone came to predominate and eventually replace [kp] in those varieties that remained in contact with Dutch, which lacked the co-articulated stops. Although Bickerton (1981: 122) claims that these stops are found in no creole besides Saramaccan, both /kp/ and /gb/ are part of the phonological systems of Krio (Fyle and Jones 1980: xix), Liberian CE (Singler 1981: 25), and Nigerian PE (Rotimi and Faraclas f.c.). Boretzky (1983: 60) suggests that these may represent more recent (i.e. nineteenth-century) borrowings from neighboring African languages; indeed, most words with these phonemes do occur in loan words such as Liberian *gbasa jamba* 'cassava leaf' from Vai, or *kpiti* 'fists' from Klao (Kru). Turner (1949: 241) mentions the occasional use of co-articulated stops in Gullah CE, but of the four words he mentions only one (*wulisâkpakpa* 'woodpecker' from Mende idem) is among words listed as used in conversation rather than as used only in stories, songs, and prayers. The status of the co-articulated stops would therefore appear to be quite marginal in Gullah.

4.6.2 *Pre-nasalized stops*

Among the Niger-Congo languages, Alexandre (1967: 48) notes "la fréquence très grande (presque universelle, en fait) des consonnes prénasalisées," although Singler (p.c.) notes that they are not found in many Mande or Kru languages. Pre-nasalized stops consist of stops preceded by homorganic nasals (e.g. /mb/, /nd/, /ŋk/) functioning as a single phoneme – e.g. as C in languages permitting only CV syllabic structure. Such monophonemic pre-nasalized stops (in which the nasal is part of the segment) are not to be confused with homorganic nasals (in which the nasal is a separate segment which takes on the place of articulation of the following segment). The separate status of homorganic nasals in Yoruba is made clear by the fact that they can take a tone distinct from that of the following segment. For example, a homorganic nasal indicating progressive aspect can precede a verb: *dé* 'arrive,' *ńdé* 'is arriving'; *bọ̀* 'come,' *ḿbọ̀* 'is coming'; *gbọ̀* 'hear,' *ńgbọ̀* 'is hearing' (phonetically [ŋ͡mg͡bɔ́] with a co-articulated nasal) (Ogunbọwale 1970: 197).

Although a number of Atlantic creoles have nasal consonants that are homorganic with a following stop occurring at the beginning of a word or syllable, it is often difficult to determine whether these are monophonemic pre-nasalized stops or biphonemic sequences. In the absence of tones that might distinguish syllabic nasals from a following segment, only the strictness of CV syllabic structure rules can indicate whether it is a case of one consonant or two, but often the phonotactic rules of the original creole have been disturbed by those of the superstrate language so that no solution is possible. That said, both analyses indicate substrate influence on the creoles since neither pre-nasalized stops nor phonotactic rules permitting syllable-initial nasals plus stops can be attributed to the superstrate languages or language universals.

The Gulf of Guinea creoles have word-initial nasals that are homorganic with following stops, e.g. São Tomé CP *nda* 'to walk' (P *andar*), *ŋgana* 'fowl' (P *galinha*), *njanja* 'quickly' (cf. P *já, já!* 'immediately'). Ivens Ferraz (1979: 26) analyzes these as sequences of two consonants, although the language has a predominant CV syllabic structure. His analysis also requires a special rule for CVC syllables ending in a nasal, followed by a homorganic consonant beginning another syllable, e.g. *sum-bu* 'lead' (P *chumbo*), *tam-pa* 'lid' (P idem), *ziŋ-ga* 'to move' (P *gingar*). Treating the nasal-plus-stop sequence as a single phoneme, on the other hand, would yield a CV–CV syllabic structure: *su-mbu, ta-mpa, zi-ŋga*.

Palenquero CS, which may be closely related to the Gulf of Guinea creoles (§7.2), also appears to have pre-nasalized stops. Bickerton and Escalante (1970: 256) noted these in words of African origin such as [ŋguba] 'groundnut', but Patiño also found a number of words of Spanish origin with this feature, e.g. *ngatá* 'spill, waste' (S *gastar*), *nda* 'give' (S *dar*), *mbosa* 'purse' (S *bolsa*) (Friedemann and Patiño 1983: 99 ff.). Because such forms with initial nasals vary with others which do not have them, minimal pairs cannot be obtained to establish the phonemic status of the initial segment; for this reason, Patiño chooses to analyze the difference between the two sets as subphonemic.

Stolz (1986: 76) identifies some nasals plus stops in Negerhollands CD where Dutch has only nasals, e.g. *ha:mbu* 'hammer' (D *hamer*) or *skondu* 'entirely' (Stolz derives this from D *schoon* 'beautiful, clean' in its comparative form *schoner*, but a more likely source semantically is the idiom *schoon op* 'all gone'). Although he calls the nasal clusters "pränasalierte Okklusive," he analyzes them as biphonemic.

In Haitian CF the elision of vowels can yield sequences such as *mpil* 'a lot' (F *en pile*) or *ntirɛlmã* 'naturally' (F *naturellement*), according to Tinelli (1981) – although Valdman (p.c.) claims that the forms are *ãpil* and *natirèlmã* respectively. The Haitian personal pronouns *mwẽ* 'I' and *nũ* 'we, you' can lose their vowels before verbs, but instead of becoming parts of pre-nasalized stops they become syllabic nasals, e.g. *n tunẽ* 'we return' is phonetically [n̩tunẽ] (Valdman 1978: 88). However, in St. Lucian CF when *mwẽ* occurs before certain preverbal particles it fuses with the following stop, producing a homorganic nasal: *mwẽ* 'I' and *ka* PROG become [ŋa], while *mwẽ* and *pa* NEG yield [ma] (ibid. 93).

Rountree (1972a: 22 ff.) assigns phonemic status to the four pre-nasalized stops in Saramaccan, i.e. /mb/, /nd/, /ndj/ (i.e. /ɲɟ/), and /ng/ (i.e. /ŋg/). She justifies this on the grounds that the allophone [i], which occurs only in non-nasal syllables, occurs before pre-nasalized stops (e.g. [vinde] 'throw'), indicating that the division of syllables must be [vi-nde] rather than [vin-de]. Moreover, native speakers indicate a syllable break *before* a pre-nasalized stop but *after* a nasal followed by other consonants (e.g. [vi-nde] 'throw' but [vin-tu] 'wind'). Ndjuka has word-initial nasals that are homorganic with following stops, mostly in words of African origin, e.g. *mboma* 'boa constrictor,' *ndiká* 'fishtrap,' *ŋkólá* 'snail'; however, Huttar (p.c.) analyzes these nasals as syllabic rather than part of pre-nasalized stops. Sranan has simple nasals where Saramaccan has nasals with stops, e.g. *meti* instead of *mbéti* 'meat,' *neti* instead of *ndéti* 'night,' etc. There is similar variation within Saramaccan which, according to Alleyne, suggests that pre-nasalized stops may have once been more widespread, replacing not only simple nasals but also nasals followed by voiceless stops, as in Saramaccan *kandá* 'sing' (cf. P *cantar*), *diingi* 'drink,' *djómbo* 'jump,' *piñdja* 'pinch.' They also preserved (while transmuting) nasal-plus-voiced-consonant sequences that were simplified in Sranan, e.g. Saramaccan *béndi* 'bend' versus Sranan *beni* idem.

Turner (1949) indicates several Gullah words with initial nasals homorganic with following stops that were used in conversation, e.g. *ndɔ* 'to know' (cf. Mende *ndɔ* 'to find out') or *mpuku* 'rat' (cf. Kongo, Tshiluba *mpuku* idem). However, these seem to be marginal, as do those in Krio found in loans from local languages such as *nkɔdɔ* 'my friend' (Temne idem) or *mbolo* 'long dust maggot.' However, Wilson (1962: 14) notes that while Krio's three nasal phonemes are distinct before a pause, they are identical before a following sound, i.e. homorganic with stops and nasals but nasalizing the preceding vowel before all other sounds. Final nasals behave similarly in Mandinka and Guinea-Bissau CP (ibid. 13, Rowlands 1959: 10–11).

4.6.3 *Palatalization*

Palatalization is the raising of the tongue towards the hard palate, often as a secondary feature of articulation, as in the initial sound of the standard British pronunciation of *dew* as opposed to *do*. Such palatalization affects several sounds in a number of the Atlantic creoles. Since the symbols used to indicate palatalization are not always consistent, a chart is provided (table 2) to make clear the notation used in the discussion below.

Table 2. *Palatalization*

	Alveolar	Alveo-palatal	Palatalized alveolar	Palatalized velar	Velar
Plosive: voiceless	t	tš	ty	ky	k
voiced	d	dž	dy	gy	g
Fricative: voiceless	s	š	sy		
voiced	z	ž			

In many languages there tends to be palatalization of consonants articulated before front vowels, especially high ones that bring the tongue near the palate. For example, the Latin phoneme /k/ developed the allophone [tš] before the higher front vowels /i/ and /e/; in Italian /tš/ is now a phoneme, with contrasting pairs such as *ciarpa* /tšarpa/ 'scarf' versus *carpa* 'carp.' Similarly Latin /g/ became palatalized in Italian to /dž/ (originally only before higher front vowels), but retained its velar position elsewhere; today there is a phonemic contrast between the two in *giusto* /džusto/ 'just' and *gusto* 'taste.'

Palatalization is also a feature of many African languages. For example in a southern variety of Kongo the alveolar phonemes /t/, /s/, and /z/ all palatalize before the high front vowel /i/ to their respective alveopalatal allophones [tš] (in the present notational system), [š], and [ž]; e.g. /tobola/ 'to bore a hole' is phonetically [tobola], but /tina/ 'to cut' is phonetically [tšina] (Ivens Ferraz 1979: 51 ff.). It should be noted that the alveo-palatal affricate /tš/ can result from the palatalization of either the alveolar /t/ (as in Kongo, above) or the velar /k/ (as in Italian), just as its voiced counterpart /dž/ can result from the palatalization of either alveolar /d/ or velar /g/ (as in the CF examples below). There can also be correspondences between palatals and palatalized alveolars; for example in some

Twi dialects /ky/ corresponds to /ty/ in other dialects, and a similar correspondence exists between their voiced counterparts /gy/ and /dy/ (Westermann and Bryan 1952: 90). In general, African languages with palatal consonants fall into two broad categories: in the first, palatal and the corresponding non-palatal sounds are allophones of the same phoneme (like late Latin [k] and [tš], or southern Kongo [t] and [tš]); in the second, they constitute separate phonemes (like Italian /k/ and /tš/).

In Portuguese, as in Italian, alveo-palatals are distinct phonemes that contrast with their non-palatal counterparts, e.g. *chapa* 'metal plate' (/šapɐ/, earlier /tšapɐ/) versus *tapa* 'slap.' However, the creole Portuguese of São Tomé has developed a system in which its alveo-palatals are in complementary distribution with their non-palatal counterparts, apparently under the influence of substrate languages like southern Kongo discussed above. According to Ivens Ferraz (1979: 41 ff.), São Tomé CP alveo-palatals [tš], [dž], [š], and [ž] occur only before high front /i, ĩ, y/, while the corresponding non-palatals [t], [d], [s], and [z] occur elsewhere. In words of Portuguese origin, non-palatal alveolars have been palatalized before the high front vowels – e.g. *kĕci* /kĕtši/ 'hot' (P *quente*), *daji* /dadži/ 'age' (P *idade*); *dɔši* 'sweet' (P *doce*), *kwaži* 'almost' (P *quase*) – while Portuguese palatals in this position have remained alveo-palatals. Elsewhere, however, Portuguese palatals have been depalatalized – e.g. *bisu* 'animal' (P *bicho*), *zɛmɛ* 'moan' (P *gemer*) – while non-palatal alveolars have remained the same. There are relatively few exceptions to these rules, although some can be found in words recently borrowed from Portuguese, e.g. *dozi* 'twelve' (P *doze*) replacing the older São Tomé *dɛš ku dosu*, literally 'ten and two.' The parallels between alveo-palatals and non-palatal alveolars in São Tomé CP and southern Kongo are striking, particularly in comparison to Portuguese; it seems clear that substrate languages like southern Kongo imposed this part of their phonological system on São Tomé CP.

In Papiamentu CS, some Spanish consonants followed by a palatal glide have been reinterpreted as alveo-palatals, e.g. *džente* 'tooth' (S *diente*) or *šete* 'seven' (S *siete*). There has also been palatalization before /i/, as in *kušina* 'kitchen' (S *cocina*) or *duši* 'sweet' (S *dulce*). In Negerhollands CD, /s/ and /š/ appear to have merged into a single phoneme tending to have the allophone [š] before /i/ and [s] elsewhere, e.g. [ši] ~ [si] 'his' (D *zijn*) but [pus] 'push' (from the English) (Stolz 1986: 72). Moreover, [t] varies with [ty] and [tš] before /i/, e.g. *biti*, *bitji* (i.e. /bityi/), and *bitši*, all 'a little bit' (D *bitje*) (Bradford 1986: 86).

Caribbean varieties of CF tend to palatalize French /t/ and /d/ before /y/, and /k/ and /g/ before any front vowel (all of which are high or mid in French, whether rounded or not). This can be seen in Goodman (1964) and in the examples below from Stein (1984: 24–25), given in the notation discussed above. The forms are from the creoles of the Lesser Antilles, French Guiana, and Haiti; some are variants within the same dialect.

tiens bien	'hold (on) well'	tšẽbe		kyẽbe	kẽbe
coeur	'heart'	tšɛ	tyɔ	kyɛ	kɛ
diable	'devil'	džab	dyab	gyab	
gueule	'muzzle'	džɔl		gyɔl	

This pattern is partially parallel to Twi dialect variation between /ky/ and /ty/ on the one hand and /gy/ and /dy/ on the other, as discussed above. Moreover, Lesser Antillean CF alveo-palatals can be followed by /w/, e.g. *tšwizin* or *twizin* 'kitchen' (F *cuisine* /kɥizin/), and *zedžwi* or *zedwi* 'needle' (F *les aiguilles* /lez egɥiy/). Although /w/ is back and non-palatal, its lip rounding preserves a feature in the French high front rounded semivowel /ɥ/ and may correspond to similar labialization of certain monophonemic segments in Twi dialects represented as /kw/ (or /tw/) and /gw/ (or /dw/). Before /i/ these palatalize to [tšw] and [džw] respectively, whence the pronunciation of the language's name, [tšwi] (Boretzky 1983: 64, Westermann and Bryan 1952: 90). It should be noted that in Haitian CF /t/ and /d/ become palatalized to [ts] and [dz] before /i/, another feature of Akan/Fante (or Fantsi) dialects.

While New World varieties of creole French have /s/ and /š/ as two distinct phonemes that generally correspond to their French counterparts, there is occasionally some variation as in Haitian [šošɛ] or [sosyɛ] 'witch' (F *sorcière*). Early texts of Louisiana CF show alternation not only between /s/ and /š/ (e.g. *çassé* 'to hunt' from F *chasser* versus *chien* 'dog' from the same French word) but also between /z/ and /ž/ (e.g. *manzé* 'to eat' from F *manger*) (G. Hall forthcoming). The Isle de France varieties of CF in the Indian Ocean ordinarily have no palatals, e.g. Mauritian CF *sɛz* 'chair' (F *chaise*) and *lazã* 'money' (cf. F *l'argent*) (Valdman 1978: 53). Stein (1984: 24) notes that /š/ and /ž/ are not found in the Malagasy language of Madagascar, generally considered an important substrate language of the Isle de France creoles but not of the New World varieties. However, speakers of the former who also speak French tend to vary [s], [š], and [sy] (e.g. [kasɛt] ~ [kašɛt] ~ [kasyɛt] 'hiding place' from F *cachette*) as well as their voiced counterparts (e.g. [menizye] ~ [meniže] 'carpenter' from F *menuisier*) (Papen 1976).

Certainly palatalization, like other aspects of the phonology of the creoles based on French and other languages, has been subject to many influences besides that of substrate languages. In a comparative study of the phonology of French dialects, Canadian French, and the French creoles, Hull (1968, 1979) points to the importance of maritime French in the spread of a number of features. Canadian French has palatalized forms like /tšur/ 'heart' (cf. F *cœur*) and *quienbin* 'catch, hold' (cf. CF *kyɛ̄be*) idem. Moreover, "palatalized /k/ and /g/ are found throughout northern France, and were virtually standard in the 17th century, so obviously would have occurred in MarF" (1968:258). Of course phonological features, like sailors, could travel in all directions, which makes it difficult to establish that any single source of a feature is the only true one.

Alleyne (1980:56 ff.) deals with palatalization in a number of English creoles (his use of /j/ corresponds to /y/ here). He traces the palatal plosives in the Surinamese creoles to two different sources. First, /k/ and /g/ developed palatal allophones before front vowels, e.g. *géi* or *djéi* 'to resemble.' Secondly, the alveo-palatals /tš/ and /dž/ in English and Portuguese were reinterpreted as these palatalized alveolars, e.g. *djombo* 'jump' and *tjuba* 'rain' (P *chuva*). Since these also occurred before back (i.e. non-palatalizing) vowels, a phonemic split took place because the palatalized alveolars now contrasted with velar stops, e.g. Saramaccan *tjubi* 'hide' versus *kúbi* 'kind of fish.' Later influence from English and Dutch established velar [k] before front vowels, particularly in Sranan, leading to variants such as [kina] ~ [tjina] 'leprosy.' It also led to forms such as *waki* 'watch' (via *watji*) and *wégi* 'wedge' (via *wédji*). The Surinamese creoles generally have /s/ where English has /š/ (e.g. Sranan *sipi* 'ship,' *fisi* 'fish') but Ndjuka has the allophone [s] before /i/ and /y/ (e.g. [šípi] 'ship,' [šyɛŋ] 'shame') and even /wi/ (e.g. [šwíti] 'pleasant' from E *sweet*) (Huttar p.c.), suggesting a connection to the palataliz-ation of labialized consonants in Twi and CF discussed above.

Turner (1949:24) notes that "[c] – The voiceless palatal plosive ... usually occurs in Gullah in positions where *ch* would be used [in General American English] . . . [and] before front vowels, including [a], as a subsidiary member of the [k]-phoneme. In this position it is sometimes slightly affricated." Its voiced counterpart [ɟ] is similarly used for English /dž/, especially among older speakers, and as an allophone for /g/ in words like *ɟadn* 'garden' (ibid.). In Gullah palatal [šy] or [š] can also replace /s/ before front vowels, e.g. [šyiəm] ~ [šʌm] 'see them' (ibid. 26, 247), much like allophones of /s/ in Ewe, Ibo, and other West African languages.

Alleyne (1980:58) points out that while the decreolizing shift from palatalized stops to English alveo-palatal affricates is virtually complete in Jamaican CE and other varieties in the Caribbean proper, there are lexical remnants of an earlier variation between velars and alveo-palatals, e.g. *kitibu* or *tšitšibu* 'firefly' and *gaagl* or *džaagl* 'gargle.' As Cassidy and Le Page (1980:238) point out, the intermediate form for the last was probably /gyaagl/. The palatals /ky/ and /gy/ occur in a number of Jamaican CE words (e.g. /kyaad/ 'card,' /gyaadn/ 'garden') in which they would not be expected because of proximity to any high front vowel. Cassidy and Le Page (1980:lviii) note that in seventeenth-century British usage [k] and [g] occurred before back vowels like /ɔ:/ (preserved in Jamaican CE /kaad/ 'cord' and /gaadn/ 'Gordon') while the palatals [ky] and [gy] occurred "before low-front [a] and [a:]." While [a] is a low back vowel in American usage, it is indeed low front in IPA terms. Harris (forthcoming) suggests that Middle English /a/ had varying reflexes in early Modern English, including low front [æ] and mid front [ɛ], which led to the palatalization of adjacent velars. Despite the later backing of the vowel itself, Harris sees the preservation of this palatalization in an on-glide after the velar (e.g. *kyat* 'cat,' *gyas* 'gas') and an off-glide before it (e.g. *bayg* 'bag'). The latter is lexically selective in the Caribbean – e.g. *hayg* 'hag' or *blayk* 'black' (Warantz 1983: 84) – but regular in Ireland, as is the former. Although Irish Gaelic has palatalized velars, this in itself "cannot explain the fact that the distribution of palatalisation [e.g. in contact English in Ireland and the Caribbean] faithfully mirrors historical contrasts in the superstrate" (Harris forthcoming), leading to the conclusion that the relevant palatalization of historical velars took place in England itself and "was well represented in the speech of English colonists in both Ireland and the New World. If the West African and Irish Gaelic substrata did make any contribution to the establishment of the feature in the emergent contact vernaculars, this is likely to have been at best reinforcing or 'preservative' " (ibid.). Surinamese CE words also seem likely to have been based on such palatalized British forms as now archaic or regional *kyabbage* (cf. Saramaccan *tjábisi* 'cabbage'). Jamaican has the word *john-crow* /džáŋkra/ 'buzzard,' which Cassidy and Le Page (1980: 250) derive from *carrion crow* via a shift of the initial sound from /ky/ to /ty/ to /dy/ to /dž/. Part of this process may have occurred in Suriname (cf. Sranan *djankro* and Ndjuka and Saramaccan *djankoo* idem), after which the form with the palatalized alveolar spread to Jamaica and elsewhere via diffusion.

Some Jamaican forms recorded in the nineteenth century (Russell 1868: 17) indicate that palatal [sy] may once have varied with [š] as an allophone of /s/ before a high front vowel or semivowel, e.g. *laša* 'last year,' *diša* 'this (here)'; as Alleyne (1980: 60) points out, a modern remnant of this is *buša* 'overseer' (cf. Sranan *basja*, Ndjuka *basia*).

The voiced alveolar fricative /z/ and the corresponding alveo-palatal /ž/ seem to have been an integral part of the earliest stages of the phonological systems of the Portuguese creoles of the Gulf of Guinea (but not of Guinea-Bissau, where they occur only in recent loans from Portuguese) and of the French creoles of the New World. However, there is evidence that both sounds may have been borrowed relatively recently into the English creoles. Alleyne (1980: 60) notes "[s] in Saramaccan as a reflex of English [z] (as in *núsu* 'nose') . . . [z] has some frequency in Saramaccan in initial and intervocalic positions, and may in some cases be a

Dutch borrowing or may represent an internal phonetic development of [s] since the first formation of the language: *zéi* 'sail,' *zaun* 'elephant' . . ." While D *zeil* is indeed a likely source of *zéi*, D *olifant* is a less satisfactory etymon of *zaun* than Kongo *nzawu* 'elephant' (Daeleman 1972), suggesting that loans from African languages may also have played a role. Berry (1961: 12) notes that in the most basic Krio vocabulary there is no opposition between /s/ and /z/ and concludes that /z/ and /ž/ must be recent innovations. In Jamaican there is little evidence for /z/ not being an integral part of the phonological system (except for rare doublets like *singkuma* and *zingkuma* for a kind of plantain, possibly indicating earlier variation), but English /ž/ normally corresponds to Jamaican /dž/; e.g. *pleja* 'pleasure.' Cassidy and Le Page (1980: lx) note that /ž/ was not naturalized as an English sound until the seventeenth century. Turner (1949: 26) states flatly that /ž/ does not occur in Gullah; Stewart (p.c.) agrees that there is no such phoneme, but notes that /z/ can palatalize to [ž] before /i/ or /y/ as in [ɪžyu:] 'is you.'

4.6.4 *Apicals*

Apical consonants are produced with the tip of the tongue against the upper teeth or the alveolar ridge; they can be a stop (e.g. [d]), a nasal [n], a lateral [l], or a flap [r]. These sounds are related in a number of African languages, either as allophones or as the distinctive parts of allomorphs or as corresponding sounds in different dialects of the same language. For example, in Bambara the perfective marker has the allomorphs *-ra*, *-la*, and *-na*. In Yoruba the contraction of *ní* 'say' is *l*: "nwǫ́n *l'*ó kú" 'they say he died' is the equivalent of "*nwǫn ní ó kú*." Twi /r/ corresponds to /l/ in other Akan/Fanti dialects, and in Ewe [l] and [r] are in partial complementary distribution. Klao (Kru) and some related Liberian languages have various kinds of alternation between [l], [d], and [n], which can all vary with [r] in Liberian English.

In the Portuguese creoles of the Gulf of Guinea, /l/ replaces both Portuguese flapped /r/ (e.g. São Tomé CP *ali* 'air' from P *ar*) and trilled /r̄/ (e.g. *latu* 'rat' from P *rato*). In Príncipe CP /r/ has been retained; Valkhoff (1966: 89) claimed that /d/ and /l/ could vary (e.g. *dosu* or *losu* 'two' from P *dois*) but Ivens Ferraz (p.c.) considers this a misinterpretation.

A number of Papiamentu CS words have apical consonants differing from those of their etyma, e.g. *nanishi* 'nose' (S *narices*), *karson* 'pants' (S *calzón*), *mitar* 'half' (S *mitad*). Maurer (p.c.) suggests that *mitar* resulted from the practice of nineteenth-century Dutch clergymen correcting "missing" *r* in verbs like *mata* 'kill' (S *matar*); the rural variant is *mitá*. Alternation of apical consonants is also widespread in Palenquero CS; Patiño notes *merio* 'half' (S *medio*), *lemedio* 'medicine' (S *remedio*), *selá* 'to close' (S *cerrar*), and *kumina* 'food' (S *comida*) among others (Friedemann and Patiño 1983: 94 ff.). Some such alternation can be found in Negerhollands CD *wolter* 'root' (D *wortel*) or *re:l* 'to bring up' from English *rear* (Stolz 1986: 65).

In Haitian CF /l/ and /n/ can alternate in certain allomorphs as in Yoruba (above); the definite article is *la* after a non-nasal consonant (e.g. *jurnalis-la* 'the journalist') but *nã* after a nasal consonant (e.g. *bɔn-nã* 'the maid'). There is a similar variation of *li* 'his/her/its': *papa-li* 'his father' but *mãmã-ni* 'his mother' (Valdman 1970: 188–189, Boretzky 1983: 66).

In the Surinamese varieties of creole English, /l/ and /r/ merged as /l/ in word-initial position, e.g. *lobi* 'love; rub.' Alleyne (1980: 61) claims that "recent Dutch loans in Sranan with initial [r] have now conferred phonemic status on the Sranan distinction between [l] and [r]," but of the 13 entries with initial /r/ in the Bureau Volkslectuur *Glossary* (1961), over half seem to be from English, e.g. *redi* 'red' (cf. D *rood*). Sranan frequently has /r/ between vowels (e.g. *kaseri* 'kosher'), even when the etymon had /l/ in English (e.g. *furu* 'full') or Dutch (e.g. *eri* 'whole' from D *heel*).

The English creoles of the Caribbean retain only a few remnants of the earlier alternation between /r/ and /l/, e.g. Miskito Coast CE *flitaz* 'fritter' or Bahamian CE *ling* 'ring for playing marbles.'

4.6.5   Labials

Voiced labials include the bilabial stop [b], the bilabial continuant [w], and the labiodental fricative [v]. The last sound is not found in some Atlantic creoles; it is also absent from the phonemic inventory of a number of West African languages from Mandinka to Yoruba, although it is found in other Niger-Congo languages. In Bambara and Malinke, which lack [v], intervocalic /b/ sometimes becomes the bilabial fricative [β], as does intervocalic /w/.

A contrast between /b/, /v/, and /w/ is found in the Gulf of Guinea varieties of creole Portuguese, but Ivens Ferraz (1979: 35) notes that in Portuguese itself /b/ and /v/ alternated until the end of the fifteenth century, when the African colonies were founded. Thus there are cases in which Portuguese /v/ (possibly /b/ at the time of first contact) corresponds to São Tomé CP /b/, e.g. *bo* 'you' from archaic P *vós*. In other cases there is no change (e.g. *vede* 'green' from P *verde*), but in the CP of Guinea-Bissau and Cape Verde /v/ is found only in recent loans from Portuguese and in most cases Portuguese /v/ corresponds to CP /b/, e.g. Cape Verdean CP *baka* 'cow' (P *vaca*).

There are few lexical remnants of a lack of contrast between /b, v, w/ in the French-based creoles, but in a small area of Guadéloupe one finds the forms *bini* for *vini* 'come,' *bje* for *vje* 'old,' etc. (Goodman 1964: 61). Word-initial /v/

sporadically becomes /w/ in CF, e.g. French Guiana CF *wa* is an archaic future marker corresponding to Haitian CF *va* (ibid. 87).

In Negerhollands CD there are also some examples, e.g. *bobo* 'above' (D *boven*) and *o:bn* varying with *o:vn* 'oven' (D *oven*) (Stolz 1986: 69). Moreover, [v] can function as an allophone of /w/, e.g. *huwe:l* or *huve:l* 'how much?' (D *hoeveel*) or *wēstə* or *vēnstə* 'window' (D *venster*) (ibid.). However, it should be noted that Dutch orthographic *w* represents a labiodental continuant with less friction than /v/ rather than English /w/ (except in Flanders), and it is no longer possible to know the exact value of the symbols used to represent sounds in the extinct creole. Although there is no contrast between orthographic *b* and *v* in American Spanish (both /b/ with the allophone [β] between vowels), /b/ and /v/ are separate phonemes in Papiamentu CS, apparently from Dutch influence, e.g. *biaha* 'travel' (S *viajar* /byaxár/) and *vibora* 'snake' (S *vibora* /bibora/).

Alleyne (1980: 60) postulates that there was no /v/ in the earliest English creoles. In the Surinamese creoles /b/ regularly corresponds to English /v/, e.g. *libi* 'live,' but Saramaccan has acquired /v/ in loans from Portuguese and other languages, e.g. *vivo* 'alive' (P *vivo*). Ndjuka has /v/ in some words of African origin, e.g. *vongo-vóngo* 'biting fly' (cf. Mooré *vounouvougou* 'black mud wasp') (Huttar p.c.). There are remnants of /b/ for English /v/ in the CE of the Caribbean proper, in which there is variation in a few words such as *beks* 'to be annoyed' (cf. E *vex*), *nabel* 'navel' or *hib* 'heave.' In Gullah and Bahamian /v/ and /w/ have fallen together as a single phoneme /β/ with [v] and [w] as allophones in apparently free variation. This feature is also found in the speech of whites in coastal South Carolina and the Bahamas (Holm 1980b) as well as in the Caribbean proper, e.g. the Bay Islands of Honduras (Warantz 1983). It may be related to the alternation of /v/ and /w/ in some varieties of eighteenth- and nineteenth-century London speech. Singler (p.c.) notes that /b/ and /v/ frequently become [β] in Liberian English.

4.7 Suprasegmentals

It has long been noted that the intonation of creole and post-creole languages differs markedly from that of their European lexical-source languages. Herskovits (1941: 291) speculated about a possible explanation: "That the peculiarly 'musical' quality of Negro English as spoken in the United States and the same trait found in the speech of white Southerners represent a non-functioning survival of this characteristic of African languages is entirely possible, especially since the same 'musical' quality is prominent in Negro-English and Negro-French everywhere." Megenney (1978: 160) notes that this feature is shared by the Portuguese spoken in the predominantly black areas of Brazil and by the creolized Spanish called Palenquero. However, he adds that "no definite conclusions can be drawn from present data concerning the influence of African tonal languages on Indo-European languages since these data are highly subjective in nature. Only careful studies carried out with the aid of the good ear of a linguist acquainted with a variety of African tone languages will be able to yield positive results in helping to solve this most intriguing problem."

Indeed, little progress was made in this difficult area until it attracted the interest of Africanists – particularly Berry (1959), Voorhoeve (1961), Dwyer (n.d.), and Carter (1979 ff.) – and native speakers of creoles such as Lawton (1963), Allsopp (1972), and Holder (1982). One of the fundamental problems is the difficulty experienced by most speakers of non-tonal languages (e.g. the Indo-European languages) in dealing with tone in tonal languages (e.g. all the Niger-Congo languages except Fula, Wolof, and Swahili), particularly in practice – i.e. recognizing and producing the tone patterns that are crucial to meaning. On an abstract level, however, the basic difference between intonational and tonal languages is easily explained.

Three interrelated features in intonational languages like English are (1) pitch – i.e. high versus low notes, comparable to those on a musical scale; (2) stress – i.e. loudness or intensity; (3) length – i.e. how long the articulation of a syllable is drawn out. These are linked in English in that syllables that receive primary stress also receive greater length and more prominent pitch (usually higher, but sometimes noticeably lower than surrounding syllables) as in the word "univers-ity" or the sentence "I want to *walk*." However, the association of these features is not constant; pitch can vary in English according to factors such as utterance type, attitude, position in the sentence, etc. (Carter 1983). Moreover, English is stress-timed, i.e. there is approximately the same amount of time between syllables receiving primary stress regardless of the number of intervening syllables (although this feature is not linked with English being an intonational language).

Most tone languages are syllable-timed, so there are no reduced syllables with reduced vowels (although there are also intonational languages like Spanish that are syllable-timed – i.e. this feature is not linked with tone). However, the distinguishing feature of tone languages is that each syllable has its own tone or relative pitch, which is not related to stress. In tone languages the relevant pitch pattern is that of each word or segment, while in intonational languages the relevant pitch and stress pattern is that of the whole sentence (e.g. to convey emphasis, a question, an attitude, etc.).

There is also an intermediate type of language which is neither a tone nor an intonational language; this is the pitch-accent language, in which "there cannot be more than one syllable per word which receives the tonal accent". (Hyman 1975: 231).

Yoruba is a tone language with three tones: high ('), low (`), and mid (no mark). Low tone could be thought of as the musical note do, mid as re, and high as mi (although the important thing is their pitch relative to one another). The word for 'school' is *ilé-ìwé* (literally 'house of books'), which basically has the tone pattern mid–high–low–high, or re–mi–do–mi (although this is something of a simplification ignoring low-level phonetic rules of tone sandhi). The word must have this same little tune every time it is said or it may not be understood. Many words are distinguishable only by their tone, e.g. *kí* 'to greet' versus *kì* 'to arrest.' Tone is therefore phonemic; it may seem partly analogous to stress in English, which is the distinguishing feature between the noun *súbject* and the verb *to subjéct*. Here, however, besides the slight difference of vowels, there is a difference in the loudness and length of the syllables as well as the difference of pitch, and all three of these features are variable, as pointed out above.

Besides its function in the lexicon, tone can also play an important role in grammar. For example in Kongo the difference between *engudi* 'mother' (pre-verbal subject) and *éngudi* (post-verbal object) is signaled not only by word order but also by tone (Carter 1979: 3). Of course stress can also disambiguate syntactic relationships in intonational languages, e.g. *Énglish teacher* (noun adjunct: a teacher of English) versus *English téacher* (adjective plus noun: a teacher from England). The point is that tone is an integral part of the *system* of tone languages, just as stress is an integral part of the entire system of English. This point is an important one, because in attempting to demonstrate whether certain Atlantic creoles are tone languages – as were most of their substrate languages – researchers have sometimes focused on ambiguous surface phenomena rather than the system as a whole (Carter 1979).

Finally, it should be pointed out that tone systems can vary considerably from one language to another. For example, one Niger-Congo language may have two tones while another has four; in one, tone may carry a heavy load in distinguishing otherwise identical lexical items, in another this load may be very light. Tone may play an important role in the tense system of one language, but not in another. Carter (1979: 3) notes that "It seems *a priori* unlikely that speakers of such diverse systems would take over into English a coherent and consistent structuring of tonal signalling – though aprioristic reasoning is notoriously subject to error – but in the sense of persistence of surface features, whether or not they retain their original values, I think there is strong evidence for African survivals."

Günther (1973: 48–51) claims that Príncipe CP is a tone language, with high tones (') corresponding to stressed syllables in Portuguese and low tones (unmarked) corresponding to unstressed syllables, e.g. *tóši* 'a cough' (P *tosse*, stressed on the first syllable) versus *tošī* 'to cough' (P *tossir*, stressed on the second syllable). In addition there is a third tone that is rising (ˆ), representing a development from Portuguese words whose final stressed syllable was lost in the creole, e.g. *kwê* 'run' (P *correr* /kuRér/) versus *kwé* 'rabbit' (P *coelho* /kwéλu/). As can be seen from the above examples and monosyllables such as *fá* 'speak' (P *falar*) and *fa* 'negative particle' (origin unknown), minimal pairs present opposition between high and low tones and between high and rising tones, but not between low and rising tones.

Ferraz and Traill (1983), working from recordings of Príncipe CP made by Ferraz, reject Günther's assertion that the creole is a tone language, claiming instead that it is a "free pitch-accent language." Ferraz found that his informant also used a falling pitch (which they symbolize more conventionally as /ˆ/) in opposition to a rising pitch (/ˇ/ in their notation), e.g. *fûːtà* (falling – low) 'steal' (P *furta* 'he steals') versus *fŭːtà* (rising–low) 'breadfruit' (P *fruta* 'fruit'). They deduce that the falling pitch resulted from the deletion of a sonorant *after* the stressed syllable in Portuguese, while the rising pitch resulted from its deletion *before* it. Their logic in concluding that the creole is a free pitch-accent language is based on the distribution of pitch: in polysyllabic words, there is only one "tonal accent" (high, rising, or falling pitch) which must co-occur with a "non-tonal accent" (the less prominent low pitch) on all other syllables. The term "free" comes from the fact that any syllable can be the prominent one, undergoing "increases in loudness, pitch and [vowel] length" (1981: 208), although its prominence is primarily one of pitch.

Kihm (1980: 37 ff.) analyzes the creole Portuguese of Guinea-Bissau as having two tones linked to syllabic structure, therefore resembling the tonal system of Mandinka (widely spoken by creole speakers) rather than that of, say, Yoruba. For example, polysyllabic words beginning with a consonant have a high–low–high pattern, while monosyllabic words usually have a high tone. While high tones correspond to the stressed syllable of the Portuguese etymon, they are not accompanied by an increase in loudness.

In Papiamentu CS, tonal distinctions seem to be important mainly in the domain of verbs (Römer 1977, Marta Dijkhoff 1985). The verb *mata* 'kill' (cf. S *máta* 'he kills') has a low–high pattern with tonal accent on the first syllable, while the passive participle *matá* (cf. S *matádo*) has the same pattern except with the accent on the second syllable. Both are distinct from *mata* 'plant' (S idem), which has a high–low pattern with the tonal accent on the first syllable.

Very little has been done on the suprasegmental features of the French creoles aside from work carried out by Ariza (1980), who focuses largely on pitch patterns on the level of the phrase rather than the word in Haitian CF and draws no conclusions regarding tonality. Sylvain (1936: 42) remarked that there was a difference of tone in Haitian CF reduplications of adjectives: the first, the tone of whose syllables she indicated as "—__," conveys intensity of meaning, e.g. *rō-rō* 'very round'; the second, the tone of which is indicated as "/—," conveys attenuation, e.g. *rō-rō* 'rather round.' Goodman (1964: 114) points out that Baissac (1880: 89) noted that pronunciation indicated a similar difference of meaning in Mauritian CF reduplications, although he did not describe the pitch patterns.

In the English-based creoles, Carter (1987) distinguishes between the Guyanese tone patterns in iteration (conveying intensity) and reduplication (conveying attenuation). Iteration is the simple repetition of a word with no change in pattern, e.g. "táll! táll"; in her notational system, this indicates that both syllables have high tone (´) but there is a downstep (!) at their juncture. (Downsteps are the synchronic result of an earlier high–low–high sequence of tones in which the low tone makes the following high tone phonetically lower than the first high although it remains higher than the low; later the low is lost but the second high still remains lower than the first high.) Reduplication, on the other hand, shows the same tone pattern as compounding: the first element loses its high tone and is incorporated into the tone-group of the second element, whose first syllable has high tone no matter what its uncompounded pattern is, e.g. "tall-táll" 'rather tall.' Carter notes that "compounding and reduplication patterns such as those of Guyanese can certainly be found in Twi, and the dominant Guyanese pattern is very similar to the Twi one; however, both of these are paralleled in the other African languages here discussed" (i.e. Yoruba and Kongo) (ibid.).

Jan Voorhoeve's 1961 "Le Ton et la grammaire dans le saramaccan" was among the first publications identifying a creole as a tone language. He isolated two tones, high (´) and non-high (no mark), in minimal pairs such as *dá* 'to give' and *da* 'to be.' Moreover, he demonstrated that tone plays an important role in Saramaccan not only on the lexical level but also on the grammatical level, marking compound words and other syntactic units. For example, the tones of the words *mí* 'my' and *tatá* 'father' are different in isolation from their tones when they occur as a noun phrase, *mi tata* (1961: 148). Rountree (1972b) furthered research on tone in Saramaccan in relation not only to grammar but also to intonation conveying attitude. Saramaccan words normally have high tone on the syllable corresponding to the stressed syllable in their etyma, e.g. *fája tóngo* 'tongs for a fire' or *fáka* 'knife' (P *faca* /fákɐ/) or *dáka* 'day' (D *dag*). In Sranan, which is not a tone language, such syllables are marked by stress. Alleyne (1980: 73) postulates that tone became distinctive in the earliest English creoles, of which Saramaccan is the best preserved example, when it distinguished otherwise identical words from different sources, such as Saramaccan *kai* (from English *call*, via the intermediate form *káli* plus deletion of the intervocalic liquid) versus *kai* (P *cair* /kaír/). Ndjuka, which is also a tone language (de Groot 1984: 1), also has this minimal pair. It is relevant that such creoles preserved a large number of African words with their tone pattern. In most of the English-based creoles that remained in contact with English, stress took over the role of tone in distinguishing lexical items. However, earlier pitch patterns appear to have remained a characteristic feature of larger segments such as phrases and sentences.

Cassidy (1961: 26 ff.) identified some of the features distinguishing Jamaican intonation from that of English. He noted that 69% of the syllables in the Jamaican speech he studied represented a change in pitch, whereas only 35% of the standard English syllables did. The frequent change of pitch in Jamaican stopped only when a speaker became excited and went to his highest pitch and stayed there. Moreover, declarative sentences in Jamaican ended on rising pitch, making them sound like questions to speakers of standard North American and British English (although a pattern similar to that of Jamaican is found in the regional English of Ireland, Liverpool, Glasgow, and Newcastle).

In her 1979 paper "Evidence for the survival of African prosodies in West Indian creoles" Carter concluded that her data provided "insufficient evidence to permit a judgement on whether or not the Creoles are systematically tonal, in the sense of signalling distinctions of grammar and lexis by pitch differences. The surface features however are entirely consistent with derivation from African tonal systems." She further noted that despite superficial resemblances, creole English pitch patterns did not seem to be derived from English. For example, they did not include the tail, a primary feature of English prosody. The English pitch pattern for sentences has its nucleus on the last accented word, and its tail consists of all following syllables until the end of the sentence. Moreover, creole intonation patterns consistently conveyed unintended connotations to speakers of British English; intonation patterns that conveyed a pleasant attitude in creole English were almost without exception interpreted as unpleasant (e.g. surly, judicial, detached, cold, hostile, etc.). After surveying intonation patterns most common in creole speech, Carter concluded that

> Creoles have more patterns than does the typical African tone-language. Thus, only a portion of Creole features could in any case be directly derived from the latter. If the Africanisms are cases of survival, they have certainly acquired different values from those with which they arrived. The system (or systems) now obtaining have developed into something which is neither African nor English nor French, nor anything else but distinctively Creole.   (1979: 14)

However, in 1982 Carter reversed her position after she and David Sutcliffe studied the speech of a Jamaican student who had moved to Britain at the age of nine; his normal speech was educated Jamaican English rather than British English and he could still speak Jamaican Creole to some extent. She found that his speech showed a pattern of pitch polarity: each syllable was opposite in tone to the preceding one, i.e. it started on a high tone, then low, then high, etc. In other words, tone depended on where a word happened to fall in this alternation, e.g. *Pául Nelsón* but *Kévin Nélson*. Since the classical definition of a tone language is one in which "pitch patterns belong to segments" (Guthrie 1954), Carter concluded that the segment to which the tone-pattern of Jamaican Creole belongs is not the word but the phrase, which she calls the "tone-group" (1987). In light of the Jamaican data, she found the alternating tone pattern which Kihm (1980) had identified in Guinea-Bissau CP to be a valuable contribution (Carter p.c.); indeed, it suggests the need for further comparative studies in creole suprasegmentals across lexical boundaries.

Carter (1987) agrees with Allsopp (1972) and Holder (1982) that tone does indeed distinguish lexis in Guyanese CE in the many minimal pairs displaying pitch-accent such as *turkéy* (the bird) versus *Túrkey* (the country), concluding that Holder "rightly observes that this feature would make Guyanese qualify as a *pitch accent* language" (1987). Lawton (1963) had shown how pitch disambiguates various syntactic structures in Jamaican CE such as *di man háas* 'the man's horse' versus *di mán hás* 'the stallion,' or *mieri bróŋ* 'Mary Brown' versus *miéri broŋ* 'Mary is brown.'

It is less surprising to find creole tone languages in Africa, where many speakers are bilingual or multilingual in other tone languages. Berry identified Sierra Leone's Krio as a tone language as early as 1959; Liberian CE, which has a partly parallel history, appears to be a pitch-accent language (Singler p.c.). In 1966 Schneider established that it was pitch rather than stress that was contrastive in the Cameroonian variety of West African Pidgin English. Dwyer (n.d. – *c.* 1967) and Mafeni (1971) confirmed this for the Nigerian variety also, in which the study of tone is now well advanced (Rotimi and Faraclas forthcoming). Clear minimal pairs are found, such as *tú* 'two' and *tù* 'too' (ibid.).

This chapter has compared a number of phonological features in the Atlantic creoles across lexical boundaries and pointed to parallel features in African languages that seem likely to have been part of the creoles' substrate. While in a number of cases there seems to have been converging influence from the creoles' superstrates (e.g. the palatalization of velars) or language universals (e.g. the alternation of [l] and [r]), it can clearly be concluded that the influence of the substrate languages on the creoles' phonology was both systematic and fundamental.

5

Syntax

5.0 Introduction

This chapter is a study of some syntactic features that are found in a number of Atlantic creoles but not in the standard European languages from which they draw their vocabularies. The number of such features is quite large, and they are so widespread that their existence can hardly be explained by mere coincidence. One of the central issues in creole studies has been the development of a theory of genesis that satisfactorily accounts for these syntactic similarities among the Atlantic creoles based on Portuguese, Spanish, Dutch, French, and English. The syntactic data discussed in this chapter are generally considered to be of primary importance in evaluating the relative merits of these theories, which are discussed in some detail in chapter 2. The orientation of the present study is that these common syntactic features reflect the influence of both superstrate and substrate languages, as well as universals of adult second-language acquisition, creole-internal innovations, and often the convergence of all or some of these.

Language universals – in the Greenbergian or Chomskyan sense of general parameters on possible structures rather than the Bickertonian sense of specific, innate structures – seem likely to have played an important role as a filter in the selection of syntactic features in the pidgins and the creoles that grew out of them. With few exceptions (§3.5.1), the creoles rely on free rather than inflectional morphemes to convey grammatical information; this seems likely to have resulted from a universal tendency in adult second-language acquisition to isolate such information through lexicalization. However, this universal tendency was probably reinforced by a similar tendency in many substrate languages, such as those of the Kwa group.

The importance of the superstrate input is surely not restricted to lexicon; the European auxiliary verbs that provided the etyma of many creole preverbal markers (§5.1), for example, are related to the latter not only on the level of lexical form, but also on the level of syntax and semantics. However, the creole preverbal markers also bear a fundamental and systematic relationship to the preverbal markers in many substrate languages; indeed, this semantic and syntactic similarity is on the whole greater, and often cannot be explained by reference to the properties of the superstrate auxiliary.

Although Bickerton (1974 ff.) has raised no objections to substrate influence on creoles on other linguistic levels, he claims that their influence on creole syntax was insignificant (§2.12). He argues against drawing any conclusions from the similarity of syntactic structures in the Atlantic creoles to those in African languages:

> The immense diversity of the substrata of creoles effectively rules out the possibility of their influence. Even if we limit ourselves to Caribbean creoles, with their West African substrata, this remains true. The belief, widespread among creolists, that the latter have profound and far-reaching similarities is not borne out by general studies of West African languages (see e.g. Manessy 1977).
>
> (Bickerton 1984: 8)

But the evidence from Manessy (1977: 148) is only the observation that verb phrases are not similar in Hausa, Fula, and the Bantu languages. Of course Hausa and (according to some classifications) Fula are not Niger-Congo languages (Greenberg 1966a). While the Niger-Congo languages are certainly not uniform, they do share a significant number of structural features, which is the basis of their classification into a single language family (Koopman 1986). Languages within subgroupings (e.g. Mande, West Atlantic, Kwa or Benue-Congo) show a greater degree of similarity to one another.

Bickerton (1984: 10) also claimed that "No substratum argument has ever supplied . . . historical evidence that speakers of the relevant languages were in the right place at the right time in the right numbers to have had even the possibility of influencing the development of particular creoles." However, the validity of this second objection presupposes the validity of his first objection, i.e. that there was insufficient typological similarity among the Niger-Congo languages to influence the creole in similar ways. When typological studies of African languages (e.g. Heine 1976) indicate that a particular syntactic feature is found in 80% to 95% of the three hundred languages compared, it seems perverse to insist that a parallel structure in a creole must be traced to only one of the hundreds of languages that may have influenced it.

Niger-Congo languages extend along the entire area from which Africans were taken in slavery to the New World, primarily the west coast from Senegal to Angola (Greenberg 1966a, Rawley 1981). Although there are often considerable problems in determining the precise origins of people brought to particular colonies during particular periods, great strides have been made over the past decades in interpreting the relevant historical documents (Le Page and DeCamp 1960, Curtin 1969, Rawley 1981, Singler 1986a). In some cases very precise assertions can now be made, e.g. "The evidence for the period from 1711 through 1740 suggests that the two most important African language groups for the formation of Haitian Creole are Mande and Kwa, particularly Bambara-Malinke-Dyula and Ewe-Fon" (Singler 1986a).

However, there is a larger problem in the insistence that we look for substrate influence only from those African languages whose speakers are historically documented to have been present in large numbers in particular colonies at particular times. Given the problematical nature of much of the documentation (e.g. that colonial terms for slaves' origins often referred to the port where they were purchased rather than their ethnolinguistic group, which was usually farther inland), collaboration is needed between linguists and historians to uncover the missing information. The heuristic value of linguistic data in discovering historical facts should not be underestimated; the African origin of the earliest speakers of Berbice Creole Dutch was identified as the Niger delta through the presence of many Eastern Ijo words in the creole (Smith *et al.* 1987). This was confirmed by the rediscovery of the fact that the Dutch family running the colony in Guiana obtained its slaves from precisely this area during the relevant period.

Creolists looking for parallel structures in substrate languages have generally been guided by known historical patterns and common sense; southern and eastern Bantu languages have not been pursued, and widely spoken languages have usually been preferred to small, obscure ones. Lexical evidence (e.g. Twi words in Jamaican or Fon words in Haitian) has also tended to guide studies in comparative syntax. Some researchers (e.g. Boretzky 1983) have offered no historical justification of their choice of African languages as sources of possible substrate influence, letting the linguistic data speak for itself instead. Unless there are compelling historical reasons for rejecting such data, the method would seem to have considerable heuristic value. Moreover, structures from African languages presented for comparison with parallel structures in creole languages are understood to imply only the general claim that structures of this *type* exerted substrate influence, not that the structure in this particular language was the *source* of the creole structure.

Although there are many syntactic similarities between the Atlantic creoles and their substrate languages, it should also be borne in mind that there are some important similarities between the substrate African languages and the superstrate European languages. For example, in most Niger-Congo languages the usual word order is subject–verb–object (except the Mande and Gur languages, which are SOV; Bantu languages are SVO with noun objects but SOV with object pronoun affixes; Welmers 1973: 382). SVO is also the usual word order in the superstrate languages (except for SOV with object pronouns in the Romance languages, and in Dutch subordinate clauses; see §5.6). During the initial stages of contact it is likely to have been significant (although not crucial) that the Europeans as well as most of the Africans were looking for a basic SVO pattern in one another's attempts to communicate – the pattern now found throughout the Atlantic creoles.

Many of the creole syntactic features discussed below are viewed here as historically linked to similar features in substrate languages, rather than as constituting any kind of typology of creole languages in general. In other words, no claim is being made that languages with these features are likely to be creoles, or that all creole languages will have these particular features. On the contrary, a creole language with a different substrate would seem likely to have different features that could be traced to that substrate. These features might sometimes coincide with those of the Atlantic creoles; they may even represent features that have spread from the Atlantic area by diffusion, such as *save* as a verbal marker of habitual aspect in Tok Pisin PE of Papua New Guinea (Wurm 1977: 522), which may be thus related to *sabi* with the same use in Cameroonian PE (Todd 1984: 143), perhaps via *savvy* in general maritime usage. On the other hand, reduplication is an example of different substrates producing different creole features. In the Atlantic creoles adjectives can be reduplicated to intensify their meaning, as in many African languages: e.g. Bahamian CE *big-big* and Yoruba *ńlàńlá*, both 'huge' (§3.3.5). Although the reduplicated meaning can occasionally be extended to that of many small things in the Atlantic creoles, this is quite distinct from the use of reduplication to indicate plurality in Asian varieties of creole Portuguese and some Asian languages: e.g. Indo-Portuguese *kryãs-kryãs* from P *criança* 'child,' or Malay *budak-budak* 'children' from *budak* 'child' (Ivens Ferraz 1987). The identification of a language variety as a creole requires some knowledge of its sociolinguistic history, rather than its having some set of "features that define creoles as creoles" as Markey asserts (1982: 170). As Singler (1986b) points out, the features that Bickerton (1984) has posited as those typical of "radical creoles" are in fact those common to the Kwa languages.

This chapter began as a comparative study of some twenty syntactic features in the Atlantic creoles and some twenty African languages, undertaken with the help of some faculty members of the University of London's School of Oriental and African Studies (Holm 1976, 1978: 238 ff., 1985). It is also based on the comparative work of Ivens Ferraz (1987), Goodman (1964), Valdman (1978), Baudet (1981), Hancock (1987), Taylor (1971), and Boretzky (1983). To make the data more manageable, syntactic structures will usually be illustrated with sentences from just one of a number of possible languages: one African language and one creole from each lexical-base group.

5.1 The verb phrase

The verb phrase has been of central importance in creole studies. While it is true that no particular set of syntactic features will identify a language as a creole without reference to its sociolinguistic history, it is also true that the structure of the verb phrase has been of primary importance in distinguishing creole varieties (e.g. Jamaican CE) from non-creole varieties (e.g. Caymanian English) of the same lexical base. In the Caribbean, the non-creoles have their European system of tense marking (e.g. auxiliary verbs and verbal inflections) more or less intact, whereas the creoles have a radically different way of dealing with tense and aspect. With few exceptions (§3.5.1), basilectal Atlantic creole verbs have no inflections, although they can include the fossilized remains of European inflections, as in CE *marid* 'to marry.' Instead, they are preceded by particles indicating tense or aspect; these often have the outer form of auxiliary verbs from the lexical-source language (which occupy a similar position and serve a similar function), but semantically and syntactically they are much more like the preverbal tense and aspect markers in many of their substrate languages.

Individual linguists have been noting isolated similarities in the verb phrase – both among creoles and between creoles and African languages – since Adam and Schuchardt in the nineteenth century. However, systematic comparisons across lexical boundaries are relatively recent. Thompson (1961) noted the syntactic, semantic and even partial formal similarity of three preverbal markers in ten creoles of various lexical bases spoken not only in the Caribbean area and Africa but also Asia. Taylor (1971) did comparative work on the semantics of preverbal markers in 13 Atlantic creoles, which he later expanded (1977). Bickerton (1976) noted that the preverbal markers of the Atlantic creoles (as well as those of Juba Arabic and Hawaiian Creole English) combined similarly, which he interpreted as primary evidence for the role of linguistic universals in the formation of the creoles. Holm (1978) noted that this systematic similarity of preverbal markers existed not only among the Atlantic creoles but also between them and certain West African languages that were likely to be structurally similar to those in the creoles' substrate. This study was broadened by Boretzky (1983) within the context of a more general study of substrate influence.

Table 3, *Tense and aspect markers in various creole and African languages*, is intended to provide an overview of what will be discussed in the following sections. It is the expansion of a similar table (Holm 1978:262) and includes data on

Table 3. *Tense and aspect markers in various creole and African languages*

	Unmarked		Progressive		Habitual		Completive		Irrealis	
		Anterior		Anterior		Anterior		Anterior		Anterior
São Tomé CP	θ	ta(va) –	s(a)ka –	tava ka –	ka –	tava ka	za		ka	ka
Cape Verde CP	θ	– ba	ta –	ta – ba	ta –	ta – ba	ja		ta –	ta – ba
Papiamentu CS	θ		ta –	tabata –	ta –	tabata –	– kaba	a – kaba	lo S –	lo S a
Palenquero CS	θ		ta –	taba –	ase –	aseba –	a –	a – ba	tan	tanba
Negerhollands CD	θ	(h)a –	lo –	a lo –	lo~ka(n) –	a ka –	ka –	a ka –	lo~sa(l) –	a sa
Lesser Antillean CF	θ	te –	ka –	te ka –	ka –	te ka –	– fin?		ke –	te ke –
Haitian CF	θ	t(e) –	ap –	t-ap –	θ~ap –	t(e) –	fin –?		(v)a	t-a
Sranan CE	θ	(b)en –	(d)e –	ben e –	θ~(d)e –	(b)en –	– kaba		(g)o~sa	ben o –
Jamaican CE	θ	ben –	(d)a~de –	(b)ena –	θ~a –	doz	don ~ don	don	go~wi	wuda
Gullah CE	θ	bin –	(d)a – ~ – in	bina –	da~doz –		don	don	gwɔi	wuda
Yoruba	θ	ti –	ń –	ti ń –	maa ń –	ti maa ń –	– tán	ti tán	á~yíò	yío ti
Bambara	θ		bɛ –	tun bɛ	bɛ	tun bɛ	ye – ka ban	tun ye ka ban	bɛna	tun bɛna

–, position of verb; S, subject.

preverbal markers from tables in the chapters in volume II on the creoles based on Portuguese, Spanish, Dutch, French, and English. These are compared with the verbal markers in Yoruba (a Kwa language) and Bambara (a Mande language), based on Rowlands (1969), Bird *et al.* (1977) and Singler (p.c.). The creole data come from some sixty works, as indicated in connection with the charts in volume II. As Bickerton (1981: 73 ff.) has noted, there are a number of problems in interpreting accurately so many often contradictory accounts of such varying quality, especially since the tense and aspect systems are so easily misunderstood by native speakers of European languages. Moreover, it should be borne in mind that given the sheer number of languages, tenses, and aspects involved, there are sure to be a substantial number of individual differences of varying importance. Still, the general similarities are indeed remarkable and merit close examination.

5.1.1   *The unmarked verb*

The simple form of the verb without any preverbal markers refers to whatever time is in focus, which is either clear from the context or specified at the beginning of the discourse. For example, in the following passage it is clear that the verbs refer to a permanent state of affairs, corresponding to the simple present tense in English. A speaker of Nicaragua's Miskito Coast CE is discussing how each jungle spirit guides the animals under his protection to hide them from hunters: "Him a di uona. Him *tek* dem an *put* dem an dis wie . . . die *kom* an him *liiv* dem all hiia an *guo* de," i.e. 'He is their owner. He *takes* them and *puts* them on the right path . . . They *come* and he *leaves* them all in that place and *goes* off" (Holm 1978).

On the other hand, unmarked verbs can also refer to past actions which in English would be expressed in the simple past tense. In the following passage, another speaker of the same creole is relating how he and his family moved to town so he could go to school: "Wi *liiv* from der an *kom* doun hiir fo stodi. Ai *staat* to pas mai gried-dem . . .," i.e. 'We *left* that place and *came* down here so I could study. I *started* to pass from one grade to the next . . .' (ibid.).

This is similar to the way tense is handled in a number of languages without verbal inflections. Yoruba is typical of many such West African languages; Rowlands (1969: 18) observes that the "Yoruba verb does not contain any built-in distinction between past and present." For example, *mo j̧eun* could mean either 'I eat' or 'I ate,' depending on the context (ibid. 76).

A good deal has been written about the importance of the creole distinction between stative and non-stative verbs regarding tense (e.g. Bickerton 1975). However, this actually has more to do with the problem of translating unmarked creole verbs into the suitable European tense, rather than any overtly marked distinction made within the creole verbal systems. A stative verb refers to a state of affairs (e.g. "I *have* a sister" or "I *know* the way") rather than a single action ("We *put* it there"). When people talk about actions they are simply more likely to have already occurred (and thus correspond to the English past tense) than are states, which by the very nature of their meaning are more likely to be open-ended and extend into the present. However, it is not the case that unmarked creole stative verbs always correspond to the English present tense, and that unmarked creole non-stative verbs always correspond to the English past tense. Although this is often the case because actions frequently occur at a single point in time whereas states occur over a span of time, examples are by no means difficult to find (e.g. the first passage above) to disprove the rule that the unmarked creole verb "signifies past with nonstatives and nonpast with statives" (Bickerton 1979b: 309).

5.1.2 *Anterior tense*
One of the more useful contributions of Bickerton (1975, 1979b) to creole studies is the notion of the anterior tense in the Atlantic creoles as opposed to the past tense found in Indo-European languages, although the validity of this distinction has often been disputed (e.g. Maurer 1985). The present analysis agrees with that of Bickerton: in basilectal creoles, anterior markers (table 3) indicate that the action of the following verb took place before the time in focus (i.e. the time reference of the unmarked verb). The anterior tense can correspond to the English past or past perfect; unlike these, however, the anterior is relative to the time in focus in the preceding discourse rather than to the time of the utterance. This parallels the use of anterior markers in a number of relevant Niger-Congo languages such as Yoruba, in which "the addition of *ti* represents the state referred to as having come into being some time, however brief, before the actual time of reference, which as usual may be in the present or the past" (Rowlands 1969: 76). For example, while the unmarked verb in *mo jẹun* can be translated as either 'I eat' or 'I ate' depending on context, the verb preceded by the anterior marker *ti* in *mo ti jẹun* can be translated as either 'I have (already) eaten' or 'I had (already) eaten,' again depending on the context. Another example of an anterior marker is *tun* in Bambara, which functions quite similarly, both syntactically and semantically (Bird *et al.* 1977, Singler p.c.).

However, in decreolizing varieties the semantic import of the anterior marker may begin merging with that of the past tense in the superstrate: "It is my impression that wherever an anterior marker is used to express a simple (narrative) past, we are faced with superstrate influence" (Boretzky p.c.). This seems particularly likely in Papiamentu CS, which has long had native speakers who are bilingual in Dutch or Spanish.

While the function of creole anterior markers seems to follow that of parallel markers in West African languages, their lexical form is often derived from the past or past participle of the word for 'be' in the European superstrate. Largely lacking semantic content other than tense, these forms were apparently reinterpreted as markers of tense only, yielding São Tomé CP *tava* (cf. P *estava*), Haitian CF *te* (cf. F *était* or *été*), or Jamaican CE *ben* (cf. E *been*). Decreolizing varieties of CE often have alternate forms derived from *did, had,* or *was*; these are frequently less deviant from standard usage and thus less stigmatized.

While fairly general, the pattern of an anterior marker preceding the verb is not found in all Atlantic creoles. In Cape Verdean CP, for example, the anterior marker *ba* occurs after the verb. Almada (1961:116) suggests that this marker is derived from the Portuguese inflection *-va* for the imperfect indicative of first conjugation verbs, as in *falava* '(he) was talking' from *falar*. Bickerton (1981:81) derives it from the completive marker *kaba* (§5.1.5); Stolz (1986:188) notes that while *ba* cannot be separated from the preceding verb in Cape Verdean (e.g. *êl sintiba êl* 'he felt it'), it can be separated in the closely related CP of Guinea-Bissau (e.g. *el sîti-l-ba*, literally 'he feel it ANT'). Kihm (forthcoming) notes that while Guinea-Bissau CP *ba* usually behaves like a verbal marker in that it occurs with verbs and combines with other such markers, it can also occur with nouns: *i jila ba* 'he was a merchant.' He further notes that in Manjaku, a West Atlantic language spoken in Guinea-Bissau, the verb *ba* 'finish' can be used after another verb to express past tense, e.g. *a tuk ba* 'he fled.' Bambara also has a verb *ban* /bã/ 'finish' used in a similar way (§5.1.5), and there may indeed be a historical connection between these, the completive marker *kaba,* and the anterior marker *ba* in the Upper Guinea varieties of CP. Boretzky (p.c.) prefers to derive *ba* from *kaba* "since we know of no other cases where European inflexional morphemes were abstracted from the word stems and used independently." However, such a case might well be made for the Berbice Dutch postverbal marker *-tɛ*, which seems to be derived from the Dutch inflection for past tense *-te* (e.g. *ik hoopte* 'I hoped'), although it is by no means clear that the creole marker is also a bound morpheme (§3.5.1). Robertson (1979) identifies *-tɛ* as a past marker as opposed to *wa* (cf. D *was* 'was'), which he identifies as a completive marker. However, *wa* appears to be more similar to the anterior markers of the other Atlantic creoles in that it can combine with other markers, unlike *fama* 'finish,' which appears to correspond more closely to completive markers in the other creoles.

There is a similar problem in distinguishing the functions of the markers *(h)a* and *ka* in Negerhollands CD (Sabino 1986b), although *(h)a* appears to correspond more closely to the anterior and *ka* to the completive (cf. Stolz 1986). While *(h)a* could come from D *had* 'had,' early sources give the form as *hab*, suggesting a Dutch dialect source *habben* 'have' (cf. standard D *hebben* idem; den Besten p.c.)

or possibly influence from *haben* in German, the language of many of the early
missionaries who recorded Negerhollands.

Finally, there is a problem in analyzing the verbal system of modern
Papiamentu in the terms that suit the other Atlantic creoles. Maurer (1985: 55)
may well be right in his assertion that "le papiamento possède une opposition
/ ± passé/ plutôt que / ± antérieur/, donc une opposition de temps absolu et non pas
relatif." As mentioned above, there is evidence that Papiamentu's verbal system
has been influenced by that of Spanish and possibly Dutch. Bickerton (1981: 86–
88) argues that Papiamentu "originally . . . had *taba* anterior and *ta* nonpunctual."
The form *taba* would have corresponded quite closely to the anterior marker *tava*
in the Gulf of Guinea varieties of CP, and *ta* to the progressive markers in the
Upper Guinea varieties and Palenquero CS; these may have combined to form
tabata, as anterior and progressive markers combined in that order in the other
creoles. The semantics of *tabata* still fit that of the anterior progressive (e.g. *nos
tabata kome* 'we were eating') or the anterior habitual (e.g. *e tabata landa* 'he used
to swim') (Maurer 1985: 52). However, Bickerton hypothesizes that "*a* has moved
in to fill the 'vacuum' created by zero-marked past-reference nonstatives, thereby
bringing the PP TMA [Papiamentu tense–mode–aspect] system closer to European
models" (1981: 88). Bickerton claims Papiamentu and Palenquero *a* "most
probably derive from Pg. *ja* 'already' " (ibid. 86) (actually written *já*), although its
phonological form /ža/ makes this source seem less likely than the archaic
Portuguese present perfect auxiliary *há* /a/ or its Spanish equivalent *ha*, as in *ha
cantado* '(he) has sung.' Maurer interprets *a* as a perfect marker, apparently in the
Romance sense of marking an action corresponding to the simple past in English.
Bickerton's hypothesis that *a* came to be used as a past marker with unmarked
verbs referring to what corresponded to the past tense in Spanish or Dutch seems
plausible. Similarly, Maurer interprets *ta* as a marker of the present tense, with an
allomorph θ before stative verbs, an interpretation compatible with its evolution
from a progressive marker (§5.1.3). Thus the analysis of Papiamentu verbal
markers suggested in table 3 should be understood as referring to a largely
undocumented stage of its development before decreolization.

Despite these divergences, the overall pattern that can be seen in table 3 is fairly
clear: most of the Atlantic creoles have a preverbal marker indicating anterior
tense that can occur either alone or before another preverbal marker. This led
Bickerton (1980: 6) to claim that "all markers are in preverbal position" and "can
combine, but in an invariant ordering, which is: 1. anterior. 2. irrealis. 3.
nonpunctual." Muysken (1981) and others have noted that this is not always the
case; there are some postverbal markers (§5.1.5), and the Papiamentu irrealis
marker *lo* can occur before the subject – quite outside the verb phrase (§5.1.6). The

overall similarity of the pattern from one creole to another is, however, still remarkable.

5.1.3 *Progressive aspect*

While certain features of the creole verb phrase discussed above may seem unfamiliar to speakers of English, there is nothing alien to us about the notion of progressive aspect, the difference between our 'simple present' (actually habitual) "She sings" and the present progressive "She *is* sing*ing*." When a Miskito Coast CE speaker says, "Mi baan wen hi *waz ruulin*" 'I was born when he was ruling' (Holm 1978), the progressive construction would seem to be straight from English, but its history is probably more complicated.

The progressive in English is not a tense (referring to the time of an action's occurrence) but rather an aspect (referring to its duration, recurrence, completion, etc.). There has been some mystification of aspect in creoles, as if this made their verbal systems totally unlike those of their European source languages, but of course both tense and aspect are dimensions in the semantics of the verbal systems of both groups of languages. While there are some fundamental differences, there is also a fair amount of common ground, as in the case of progressive aspect.

It is interesting to note that the progressive "tenses" of those superstrate languages that have them (i.e. Portuguese, Spanish, and English) did not develop into their present form until around the time of contact. While the progressive constructions in these European languages evolved from language-internal developments and there is no need to postulate their being borrowed from external sources, it is conceivable that their development was reinforced through contact with similar constructions in the New World creoles. Latin had no verbal forms with progressive meaning, but late Vulgar Latin developed a periphrastic construction with a gerundive, e.g. *stat spargendo*, literally '(he) stands scattering' (Mattoso Câmara 1976). This led to the Portuguese construction *está espargindo* idem (first occurring in the sixteenth century; Boretzky p.c.) and the equivalent Spanish *está esparciendo*, in which the auxiliary verb had evolved in meaning from 'stand' to 'be' (in reference to states and location) and was followed by the present participle of the main verb. Today the Spanish construction is in frequent use in both Spain and Spanish America; the Portuguese construction thrives in the received language of Brazil, but in Portugal it has been replaced since the early nineteenth century by an infinitival construction, *está a espargir*, literally '(he) is at scattering.'

English progressive constructions are rare before the sixteenth century and are usually found in translations from Latin (Baugh 1957: 352). However, there is a

Germanic infinitival construction, e.g. German *ich bin am Schreiben* or Dutch *ik ben aan 't schrijven*, both literally 'I am at writing.' Although these are in no way comparable in frequency to modern English *I am writing*, they are similar in structure to early modern English *I am on writing*, which developed into *I am a-writing* and the modern form. The semantic connection of all of these progressive constructions with position or location is striking and suggests a language universal (cf. Mufwene 1984). Indeed, a semantically parallel progressive structure is found in a number of African languages such as Bambara "A bɛ na tobi *la*," literally 'He *is* sauce cook *at*,' i.e. 'He is cooking sauce' (Singler p.c.; Bird *et al.* 1977). The Bambara progressive marker *bɛ* is identical to the form of 'be' indicating location, e.g. "A *bɛ* Bamakɔ" 'He is (in) Bamako'; parallels are found in many other Niger-Congo languages such as Kikongo-Kituba (Mufwene 1984). Welmers (1973: 314) points out the interrelationship between structures indicating location and action in progress in Yoruba, Igbo, Fante, and Kpelle: "the underlying idea of present action appears to be 'be-at . . . -ing.'"

Thomas appears to have been the first to notice the similar function of CE *da* and CF *ka* as progressive markers (Van Name 1869–70: 144), which Schuchardt further identified with São Tomé CP *ka*: "This *cá* is without doubt the locative adverb: *en cá cumê* 'ich (bin) hier (beim) Essen' [i.e. 'I am eating'], just as one says in Sranan: *mi de njamnjam*, where *de* 'there' indicates the durative present" (1882a: 911). Schuchardt later identified this marker with Guinea-Bissau CP *na* (also a locative preposition), Cape Verde CP *ta*, and American Black English *na* or *da* (1914b: 132). He attempted to trace the progressive/locative link to an African source such as Herero *me ri* 'I am eating' from *mu + a + i ri*, literally 'at is I eat' (1882a: 912). Much later Taylor (1963: 812) suggested that Lesser Antillean CF and São Tomé CP "*ka* might have originated in a contraction of Portuguese *ficar* 'stay,' employed by analogy to Delafosse's 'dahoméen *no* "rester, demeurer"'' to form this aspect." Portuguese *ficar* is often used for more or less permanent location, as in "Onde fica a casa?" 'Where is the house?'; moreover, it can be used with the present participle in a durative construction, e.g. *fica olhando* '(he) keeps looking.' This use of *ficar* seems quite likely to have led to the São Tomé CP habitual marker *ka* (§5.1.4), from which the progressive marker is distinguished by a preceding *sa* 'to be' (*sa ka* usually being pronounced /ška/). However, P *cá* 'here' may have also played a role, as Schuchardt suggested; in both cases the etymology of the marker is closely linked to location. There is no reason to rule out the convergence of multiple sources, which may include the Mandinka progressive and habitual marker *ka* (Dalphinis 1985: 108).

Location is linked to the etymology of most of the other progressive markers in table 3 as well. *Ta* in Cape Verdean CP, Papiamentu CS, and Palenquero CS comes from Portuguese or Spanish *está*, often pronounced /ta/ in informal speech in both the Iberian Peninsula and Latin America. Besides its auxiliary use in progressive constructions like *está cantando* '(he) is singing,' *estar* is used as a main verb 'be' before locatives, suggesting less permanence than P *ficar* or S *quedar*. As noted above (§5.1.2), Papiamentu CS *ta* appears to be evolving into a marker of the present tense rather than progressive aspect. Like a progressive marker, it is usually not used with stative verbs like *sa* 'know,' as stative meaning is seldom compatible with the idea of action in progress (cf. the unacceptability of English **I am knowing*). However, some Papiamentu stative verbs like *stima* 'love' can occur either with or without *ta* in the present tense, while a third group of stative verbs like *kere* 'believe' require *ta*, suggesting a change in progress (Maurer 1985: 49). Kouwenberg (p.c.) believes that Aruban Papiamentu is developing toward a system which distinguishes between present tense/general non-punctual (*ta*), progressive aspect (*ta* + verb + -*iendo* or -*ando*), and habitual aspect (*sa*). A similar change seems to be under way in the French Antilles, where there is widespread bilingualism: the progressive marker *ka* is becoming an obligatory present-tense marker (Stein 1984: 80).

Creole English *de* (with variant forms *da* and *a*) is thought to come from English *there*; it also serves as a locative copula (§5.2.3), although in Nigerian PE there is a tone difference between *dè* (the progressive marker) and *dé* (the locative copula) (Rotimi and Faraclas forthcoming). CE *de* could be related to both Twi *da* 'lie, be situated' and the Twi progressive marker "*re* (originally *de* 'to be')" (Christaller 1933: xxiii). The *a* form may have been influenced by archaic and dialectal English *a*, as in "He's *a*-coming," and possibly by *are* as an auxiliary in the present progressive. In decreolizing varieties, *de* can alternate with or be replaced by a more English-like construction with no auxiliary before the verb plus -*in*, as in this Miskito Coast CE passage: "Di gal no *de* briid, man. Di gal, shi *did* fiil laik shi *wa* briid*in*, bot shi no ___ briid*in*" 'The girl wasn't pregnant. She felt as if she was pregnant, but she wasn't pregnant' (Holm 1978: 258). The anterior marker takes the form *did* before *fiil*, but *wa* or θ before the -*in* verb *briidin*. Progressive -*in* is one of the first inflections found in decreolizing varieties of CE, if it is indeed an inflection at that stage. It may be a postverbal aspect marker like Berbice CD -*a*, which marks both progressive and habitual (Robertson 1979: 108).

The Negerhollands CD progressive marker *lo* appears to come from the Dutch verb *lopen* 'run, walk, go.' The creole equivalent *loop* has the alternate form *lo* (Hesseling 1905: 106), and Dutch *lopen* itself has come to be used in durative constructions along with certain other verbs of motion or position. For example, "ik heb een hele tijd *lopen* dubben" means 'I have been worrying for some time,' i.e. *lopen* has become largely desemanticized and for the most part expresses duration (Stolz 1986: 178). According to Brachin (1985: 124), these grew out of earlier coordinate constructions like "ic sta *ende* wachte," literally 'I stand *and* wait,' which became infinitival, e.g. "ik sta *te* wachten," literally 'I stand *to* wait' – i.e. 'I stand waiting.' The complementizer *te* is not used with perfect auxiliaries; the first verb of motion or position may no longer have much literal meaning, so the English equivalent would be 'I am waiting.' This construction, "so frequent that it is virtually impossible to read a page of Dutch without coming across it, nevertheless does not, oddly enough, date back further than the 17th, indeed the 18th century" (Brachin 1985: 124). The eighteenth-century texts of Negerhollands had *le* rather than *lo*. Hesseling (1905: 106) traced this to D *leggen* 'lay,' which – like its English equivalent – has long been confused with its intransitive counterpart *liggen* 'to lie' (den Besten p.c.), used in durative constructions like *liggen te dromen* 'to be dreaming.' Rademeyer (1938: 78–79) reported a particle *lê* in nonstandard Afrikaans which Stolz (1986: 180) interprets as a marker of the progressive, iterative, and future. Makhudu (1984: 88–89) also notes nonstandard Afrikaans *lê* (e.g. "Hy *lê* wag daar" 'He always waits there') and Fly Taal *loop* (e.g. "Jan *loop* soek som kataar" 'John is looking for his guitar'), which he describes as having the meaning of continuative action. The historical connection (if any) between these and Negerhollands *le* and *lo* remains unclear. However, they all appear to be closely connected to homophonous markers of habitual (§5.1.4) and irrealis (§5.1.6).

The only other progressive marker that does not seem to be etymologically connected to an expression of location is Haitian CF *ap* or Louisiana CF *(a)pé*, from the construction *je suis après chanter*, literally 'I am after singing' used in the progressive sense of 'I am singing' although Seuren (p.c.) points out a possible connection between *après* and *au près* 'near'. This construction was used in the colloquial speech of France from the sixteenth century until quite recently; it is still found in the regional but uncreolized French of both Louisiana and Canada (Hull 1979, p.c.).

It should be noted that the anterior marker can precede the progressive marker in all of the creole and African languages in table 3 (except Cape Verde CP, in which the progressive marker precedes the verb and the postverbal anterior marker *ba*), resulting in a meaning corresponding to English 'he was doing' or 'he had been doing.' It should be further noted that in many creoles progressive aspect markers can precede adjectival verbs (§5.2.2).

5.1.4 *Habitual aspect*

Many Atlantic creoles have a marker of habitual or iterative aspect, which indicates that an action occurs or recurs over an extended period of time. For example, a speaker of Miskito Coast CE used the habitual marker *doz* to stress the fact that his seventy-year-old aunt was in the habit of rowing her canoe some forty miles to Bluefields to sell produce and buy supplies: "Shi aluon *doz* guo doun to bluufiilz bai kanu" (Holm 1978). The European superstrate languages have various ways of indicating that an action is habitual; English can use the simple present tense, e.g. *she goes*, or constructions like *she often goes* or *she used to go*. The basic idea of the habitual aspect is that the action occurs not at just one point in time (punctual) but rather is spread out over a span of time (non-punctual). In this respect habitual aspect is like progressive aspect; they are both non-punctual or durative, but habitual aspect indicates greater duration.

A number of African languages use the same durative or non-punctual marker to indicate both progressive and habitual actions. In Bambara, for example, the non-punctual marker *bɛ* (discussed in §5.1.3) can have either progressive or habitual meaning, e.g. "A *bɛ* na tobi" can mean either 'He is cooking sauce (right now)' or 'He cooks sauce (regularly)' (Singler p.c.). If there is a possibility of confusion, the addition of sentence-final *la* 'at' unambiguously marks the progressive. On the other hand, Yoruba disambiguates by marking the habitual: *ń* is the non-punctual marker in "mo *ńkọ* lẹ̀tà," which can mean either 'I am writing a letter (right now)' or 'I write letters (regularly).' To make the habitual meaning clear, the marker *maa* is added: "mo *maa ńkọ* lẹ̀tà" (Rowlands 1969: 60 ff.). However, not all West African languages have a single non-punctual marker for both progressive and habitual; for example, the Fante progressive marker *re* cannot be used to indicate habitual aspect (Boretzky p.c.).

Like Bambara and Yoruba, a number of Atlantic creoles use the same non-punctual marker to indicate both the progressive and habitual, e.g. *ta* in Cape Verde CP, *lo* in Negerhollands CD (although this was much less frequent than *kan*; see below), and *ka* in Lesser Antillean CF. In fact, where creole French has influenced creole English in the Caribbean (e.g. in Grenada and Trinidad), not only the progressive but also the habitual meaning of CF *ka* has been calqued onto CE verb + -*in*, as in Grenada CE "Gud childrin go-*in* tu hevn" 'Good children go to heaven' (Le Page and Tabouret-Keller 1985: 163).

Taylor (1971, 1977) proposed that the Atlantic creoles should be grouped according to the similarity of their syntax rather than their lexicon; one of his major criteria was whether habitual aspect was indicated by the progressive marker (as in the creoles discussed above) or by the same marker as the future or irrealis (São Tomé CP *ka*, Cape Verde CP *ta*, and Negerhollands *lo*), or by no marker at all (e.g. Haitian and Louisiana CF and Jamaican CE). These differences do exist, despite Bickerton's (1980: 6) claim that in all 'true' creoles "a marker of non-punctual aspect indicates durative [i.e. progressive] or iterative [i.e. habitual] aspect for action verbs." In other words, Bickerton claims that habitual aspect is always expressed by the progressive marker, whereas Taylor claimed that some creoles express it with the future marker and others with no marker. Regarding the latter, Christie (1986) has found that Jamaican CE, which supposedly has no habitual marker and indicates this idea with the unmarked verb, does in fact sometimes use the progressive marker *a* to indicate habitual action, although apparently much more rarely than e.g. Guyanese CE. Some occurrences of the Miskito Coast CE progressive marker *de* also lend themselves to interpretation as habitual (Holm 1978: 254–260). Moreover, Bickerton (1981: 97–99) has found some occurrences of Haitian CF *ap*, supposedly only progressive, which indicate habitual aspect – an analysis with which Boretzky (p.c.) agrees. Bickerton claims that purported counterexamples to his analysis can be attributed to inadequate data, the fixation of pidgin features, or "linguistic change, internal or contact-stimulated, subsequent to creolization" (1981: 99). However, this assertion is so broad that it could "prove" almost anything and there is little evidence that any of these factors has actually intervened. While linguistic change might account for habitual uses of Haitian *ap* and Jamaican *a* as survivals of an earlier stage (see §9.5 regarding their early links), it seems inadequate as an explanation for the systematic use of the future marker to indicate habitual aspect in the Portuguese-based creoles of Africa.

There is, however, a plausible substrate explanation for the link between habitual, progressive, and future markers. As noted above, habitual and progressive meaning are both indicated by the same non-punctual marker in a number of West African languages; moreover, many such languages also use the non-punctual to indicate the immediate future, much like the English progressive in "I'm leaving tomorrow" (§5.1.6). Those creoles that Taylor indicated as using the future marker for the habitual (Negerhollands CD and the Portuguese-based creoles of Africa) do in fact use the same marker for the progressive (although preceded by *sa* in the Gulf of Guinea creoles). Thus both Taylor and Bickerton were right: the habitual marker may coincide with one, both or neither of the other two markers depending on the creole, but when there is an expressed habitual marker, it is usually the same as the progressive marker or at least related to it historically (Palenquero CS *ase* being a notable exception).

The Eastern Caribbean CE habitual marker *da* is clearly related to the progressive marker of the same form, but it has apparently been influenced by the English auxiliary *does*. Like the simple present tense in general, this auxiliary conveys the idea of habitual action (e.g. "He does drink") and in the seventeenth century it did not require emphasis as in the modern standard. Unstressed *does*, *do*, and *da* survive in England's southern and western dialects with habitual force (Le

Page 1977: 115; Mufwene 1986b). Similar forms, perhaps influenced by Gaelic, also survive in Irish English with habitual meaning, e.g. "He does write" or "He does be writing" (Barry 1982: 109). Today habitual *doz* is found in mesolectal varieties of CE throughout the Caribbean, with the notable exception of Jamaica (Rickford 1974). This habitual *doz* has the reduced forms *iz* and *z*, e.g. Bahamian CE "They *is* be in the ocean" (Holm with Shilling 1982: 111). Rickford (1980) suggests that the complete loss of these reduced forms left *be* itself with habitual force in some varieties, e.g. Bahamian "Sometime you *be* lucky" or "They just *be* playing." However, there is a good case for the convergence of multiple forces in the development of the latter forms, which are also found in American Black English. In addition to substrate influence on progressive/habitual *da* (§5.1.3) and the creole-internal innovation reducing and deleting *doz*, there is good evidence for influence from regional varieties of the superstrate. Rickford (1986) suggests that northern (i.e. Ulster) Irish English habitual *be* influenced Black English habitual *be* in North America (where the Scots–Irish predominated), whereas southern Irish English habitual *do be* influenced the development of *does be* in the Caribbean, where the southern Irish predominated in the seventeenth century.

Although Bahamian *does* can be used with anterior meaning, the more usual form is *used to*. This is generally indistinguishable from standard English except for minor differences in syntax (e.g. Bahamian "Then enter days which used to very good") and semantics (e.g. Belizean CE "Our mother used to be a Spanish"; Le Page and Tabouret-Keller 1985: 214). Miskito Coast CE *yuustu* can itself be marked for the anterior, e.g. "Shi *di yuustu* kos mi" 'She used to curse me' (Holm 1978: 260). As can be seen in table 3, habitual markers in most of the creole and both of the African languages discussed can also take an anterior marker to refer to a habit before the time in focus.

Finally, there is a widespread semantic merger between a number of creole habitual markers and verbs ranging in meaning from 'know (how to do)' to 'be able (to do).' These similarities may have resulted more from semantic universals linking these notions with habitual activity than from lexical diffusion. Portuguese *saber*, which found its way into a number of pidgins and creoles (§3.4.1), means not only 'to know (a fact)' but also 'to know (how to do something)' as in *sabe nadar* '(he) knows how to swim,' which merges in meaning with 'to be skilled at (doing)' or 'to be able to (do).' In Papiamentu CS *sa* (from P or S *saber*) means not only 'to know' but also 'to do habitually,' as in "María *sa* bende piská" 'Mary sells fish,' which can be made past by preposing *tabata*: "María *tabata sa* bende piská" 'Mary used to sell fish' (Maurer p.c.). In Sranan CE *sa* is a future marker usually derived from E *shall* or D *zal* 'shall,' but *sa* is also the short form of *sabi* 'to know how; to be able.' Eersel (p.c.) notes the habitual force of "mi *sa* e nyan" 'I usually eat.' As noted above (§5.0), *save* and *sabi* serve as habitual markers in Tok Pisin and Cameroonian PE respectively. Aitchison (forthcoming) notes how *save*, which is also a verb meaning 'to know how to,' is becoming grammaticalized as a preverbal habitual marker *sa* in creolized Tok Pisin spoken as a first language. She points out the partially parallel semantic development of *can* in English as traced by Bynon (1983) and others, from a main verb meaning 'know' in Old English ("Ne *can* ic eow" 'I do not know you'), to 'be skilled at' in early Modern English ("Yet *can* I musick too"), to the modern auxiliary meaning 'to be (physically or mentally) able.' Aitchison further points out that English *will* developed a habitual meaning alongside its more usual sense of futurity, as in "Boys will be boys." This possibly universal semantic association seems relevant not only to Sranan *sa*, but also to the habitual markers that are homophonous with future markers as discussed above, i.e. São Tomé CP *ka*, Cape Verde CP *ta*, and Negerhollands CD *lo*.

The more usual Negerhollands habitual marker is *kan*, which is also the creole and Dutch word for 'can.' The latter can merge with a habitual meaning, e.g. "Hij *kan* heel aardig zijn" 'He can be very nice.' As in English, the meaning here seems to be less one of physical or mental ability than a habitual (if interrupted) trait. Gullah CE has a similar habitual use of *kin* 'can': "In de wintertime 'e *kin* rain" 'In the winter it rains' (Stewart p.c.). Liberian CE also has this use of *kɛ̃* 'can': "hi *kɛ̃* sti" 'he steals' (Singler 1981: 46). Haitian CF *konn* (from F *connaître* 'to know') can also convey the idea of habit: "Li *konn* vin le matin" 'He sometimes comes in the morning' (Bentolila *et al.* 1976: 256). Goodman (1987) suggests that the Lesser Antillean CF habitual marker *ka* is traceable to *ka* in Haitian and Louisiana CF, a truncated variant of *kapab* 'to be able' from F *capable*. As noted above, the Lesser Antillean CF progressive/habitual marker *ka* has also been linked to the Gulf of Guinea CP habitual and future marker of the same form; Günther (1973: 73) glosses Príncipe CP *ka* not only thus but also 'to be able' ("in der Lage sein . . . kann").

If the interrelationship of the above data is insufficiently mysterious, there remains the puzzling fact that the form of the Palenquero CS habitual marker *ase* appears to come from S *hace* 'does,' just as the CE habitual marker *doz* comes from English *does*. Perhaps it would not be too far-fetched to attribute this to coincidence.

5.1.5 *Completive aspect*

The completive aspect marker indicates that an action has been completed, as in Miskito Coast CE "Ai *don* giv im a dairekshon" 'I have (already) given him an address' (Holm 1978: 261). As the English translation suggests, there is considerable semantic overlap between the creole completive and the perfect tenses in

English. Indeed, Labov *et al.* (1968) call American Black English *done* "perfective" and the latter term is often used in reference to creole completive markers. However, Singler (1984: 203 ff.) notes the distinction made by Comrie (1976) between the perfective, referring to a *complete* action as a single and unanalyzable whole, and the completive, referring to only a part of a *completed* action – i.e. its completion. After weighing the relevant Liberian data, Singler concludes that

> what evidence there is for making a distinction does favor the notion of "completive," and that is the term that will be used subsequently. Still, the overwhelming weight of the evidence is that the AUX's in question mark *both* completive and perfective; consequently the use of "completive" in describing Liberian English should be thought of as a shorthand for "completive–perfective."
>
> (Singler 1984: 210)

The same convention is adopted here.

Because the English perfect tenses convey both the idea of complete actions (corresponding to the completive) and the idea that their completion occurred prior to another event (corresponding to the anterior tense in many creoles), English speakers sometimes confuse the meaning of completive and anterior markers. However, the two are not interchangeable. For example, the anterior marker *di* could not replace the completive marker *don* in Miskito Coast CE "Wen i *don* skuor im, i salt im op" 'When he had scored him, he salted him up' (Holm 1978: 261). In fact, the two markers can co-occur as in the following sentence, where the anterior marker *di* emphasizes the fact that the completion of the action marked by *don* occurred prior to the "time-line" of the story: "Nansi *di don* gaan an lef Taiga der" 'Anansi had already gone, leaving Tiger there' (ibid.). Singler (forthcoming a) provides evidence from both Liberian and Guyanese CE that completive markers are used primarily to preserve or reinforce the time-line, not to disrupt it – an analysis supported by the Miskito Coast CE data.

Completive markers cannot combine with other aspect markers or the anterior tense marker in a number of other creoles such as Haitian CF and Jamaican CE, leading Bickerton (1981: 80 ff.) to treat completive markers as a less central element in the creole verbal system. He sees their varying status in different creoles as an indication of the stages of "a gradual process of incorporation which is well advanced in some creoles and has not begun in others." He postulates that in the initial stage, the marker can occur only clause-finally and never precedes the verb (e.g. Sranan CE and Papiamentu CS *kaba*); in the second, it can precede the verb but cannot combine with other markers (e.g. Jamaican CE *don*, which can also occur clause-finally, and Haitian CF *fin*, which cannot); in the third stage the completive marker can combine freely with other markers (e.g. Krio CE *don* and Mauritian CF *fin*). Bickerton claims that this third stage leads to a "drastic remodeling" of the verbal system, which was originally tripartite in his view (1981: 94). Boretzky (p.c.) sees no evidence to support the postverbal position as the original one. He believes that the earliest constructions followed the European word order (e.g. "I'm *done* eating," F "J'ai *fini* de manger," S "*Acabé* de comer") but that these were then made to conform with semantically similar serial verb constructions in West African languages. These generally have a verb signalling completion at the end of the clause, e.g. Yoruba *tán* 'finish' in "mo kà á *tán*," literally 'I read it finish,' i.e. 'I finished reading it' (Rowlands 1969: 134). Similarly, Bambara *ban* /bã/ 'finish' occurs with the infinitive marker *ka* after the main verb, as in "A ye na tobi *ka ban*," literally 'He PAST sauce cook to finish', i.e. 'He has already cooked the sauce' (Singler·p.c.; Bird *et al.* 1977).

The Bambara construction *ka ban* may have converged with Portuguese *acabar* 'to finish, complete' (§3.4.1) to yield the completive marker *kaba* widely found among the creoles, e.g. Príncipe CP, Papiamentu CS, Saramaccan, Ndjuka, and Sranan CE (Holm 1986), and Guyanais CF (Stolz 1986: 187) – as well as Negerhollands CD *ka* (van Diggelen 1978: 72). While CE *don* was clearly also influenced by the substrate syntactically, its lexical form was probably influenced not only by the meaning of standard English *done* 'finished,' but also by sixteenth-century Scottish English constructions like *done discus* 'discussed' (*Oxford English Dictionary*). Cape Verde CP *ja* and São Tomé CP *za* are both from P *já* 'already.' While F *finir* provided the lexical model for CF *fin(i)*, which is often of ambiguous status as a verbal marker in the Caribbean, F *déjà* 'already' (possibly influenced by P *já*) provided the model for *ja* /ža/ in the CF of Grenada and Trinidad, which can function like a preverbal marker and combine with anterior *te*, e.g. "li *te ja* vini" 'he had come' (Goodman p.c.). Palenquero CS *a* has been analyzed as a completive marker by Lewis (1970: 118), although in some respects it and Papiamentu CS *a* seem to have evolved toward past markers (§5.1.2).

Welmers (1973: 347) notes that in some Niger-Congo languages completive markers can be used with adjectival verbs that have an inceptive meaning (e.g. 'get sick') to produce what corresponds to an English present-tense meaning, e.g. Fante *ɔáfònà* 'he has become tired' or 'he is tired.' This is also found in the Atlantic creoles, e.g. Negerhollands CD "mi *ka* moe" 'I am tired' (Schuchardt 1882a: 911) or Nigerian PE "im *dɔn* sik" 'he is sick' (Rotimi and Faraclas forthcoming). In some varieties completive markers can emphasize the meaning of adjectival verbs, e.g. Lesser Antillean CF "i led *fini*" 'he is extremely ugly' (Taylor 1951: 56) or Liberian CE "hi *feni* ɔgli" idem (Singler p.c.).

5.1.6   *Irrealis*

The irrealis marker indicates that the action of the following verb is not (yet) a part of reality. Used alone, it approximates in meaning the future tense of the European superstrate languages, e.g. Guyanese CE "Fraidi awi *go* mek" 'Friday we will make [some]' (Bickerton 1975: 42). Used in combination with the anterior marker, the irrealis marker can impart the idea of European conditional or subjunctive constructions, e.g. Guyanese CE "awi *bin go* kom out seef" 'we would have come out all right' (ibid.). Irrealis has been treated not as tense but mode in a number of studies since Voorhoeve (1957: 383), thus forming one part of a tripartite system of marking verbs for tense, mode, and aspect (§5.1.7).

Like Guyanese CE *go*, the irrealis marker in a number of other creoles is also modeled on superstrate forms of words meaning 'go' which can be used to form constructions with future meaning, such as English "We are *going* to leave." In fact, part of the English *-ing* ending is preserved in Gullah CE *gwõi*. The Haitian CF irrealis marker *va* (with the alternate form *a*) is related to F *va* 'is going' used with future meaning in expressions like "Il *va* parler" 'He is going to speak.'

However, the Haitian marker *va* or *a* may also be related to the Ewe future marker *á*, from *vá* 'to come.' Future or irrealis markers are derived from verbs meaning 'to come' in a number of West African languages, such as Yoruba *á* from *wá* (Boretzky 1983: 123). As noted on table 3, Bambara *na* 'to come' is preceded by the progressive marker (and copula) *bɛ* to form the irrealis marker *bɛna*. The choice of an etymon meaning 'go' rather than 'come' for the above creole irrealis markers suggests strong superstrate influence, although some substrate languages also mark the future with a verb meaning 'go,' e.g. Ibo *gá* (Welmers 1973: 354) or Grebo *mu* (Boretzky 1983: 125). In this context it is interesting that creole irrealis markers from superstrate 'go' can be reduced to /a/ like Haitian *va* or even Belizean CE *gwoiŋ*, which has the unstressed forms /gwɛŋ ~ wɛŋ ~ wɛ̃ ~ wa ~ ã ~ a/ (Le Page p.c.).

The Jamaican CE progressive marker *a* can in addition be used with future meaning (Cassidy and Le Page 1980). While present progressive constructions can also be used with future meaning in English (e.g. "I'm leaving tomorrow"), similar usage in some West African languages suggests the converging influence of the substrate and/or universals. For example, Bini *ya* indicates progressive or habitual aspect as well as the immediate future, as does a single tonal distinction in Gã (Boretzky 1983: 125). As noted above (§5.1.4), this convergence of the progressive, habitual, and irrealis in a single marker is found in a number of Atlantic creoles, e.g. Cape Verde CP *ta*, São Tomé CP *ka* and Negerhollands CD *lo*. The Palenquero CS irrealis marker *tan* may have evolved from a nasalized form of the progressive marker *ta*, suggesting a relationship between the two markers as in

Cape Verdean. The Negerhollands CD irrealis marker *lo* appears to be related to D *lopen* 'walk, go' through its use as a progressive and habitual marker (§5.1.3) or possibly through the use of *lopen* as 'go,' although it is *gaan* 'to go' that forms an immediate future in Dutch rather than *lopen* (Stolz 1986: 165).

While *ka* marks the future in São Tomé CP, *kɛ* is the marker in Principe CP. Günther (1973: 248) derives *kɛ* from *ka* plus *wɛ́* 'go' (cf. P *vai* 'he goes'). This suggests a partial structural parallel not only to P "*vai* partir" 'he is going to leave' but also to Bambara *bɛna* (see above) and the Lesser Antillean CF irrealis marker *ke*, which Goodman (1987) suggests is a conflation of the progressive/habitual marker *ka* plus *ay*, an alternant of *ale* 'go' in Guadeloupe. This analysis is supported by the observation of Adam (1883: 44) that in Guyanais CF "*calé (ca-ale* je vais) se syncope parfois en *ké*." CF irrealis *ke* bears a resemblance in form not only to Príncipe CP irrealis *kɛ* but also to Interior Liberian English irrealis/habitual *kɛ̃* (Singler p.c.), although this may simply be coincidence.

Príncipe CP irrealis *kɛ* can also be preceded by the progressive marker *sa* to form an immediate future, e.g. "e *sa kɛ* kasá" 'he is going to hunt (right now)' (Günther 1973: 248). This is structurally parallel to Ndjuka "mi *e go* wasi" 'I am going to wash (right now)' (Huttar p.c.), although the latter connotes a certainty that might be better translated as 'I am now on my way to wash.' The use of *go* (or its alternant *o*) alone retains the idea of certainty without the immediacy conveyed by the progressive marker *e* (from *de*), e.g. "mi *o* wasi" 'I'll certainly wash (some time).' A different future marker *sa* (cf. E *shall* or D *zal*) conveys a lack of certainty, e.g. "mi *sa* wasi" 'I'll wash (as far as I know).'

Stolz (1986: 167 ff.) notes that the Negerhollands CD irrealis marker *sa* also conveys the idea of less certainty than *lo*, used for an immediate future that is certain and seldom negated. Other creoles, too, distinguish between an immediate, certain future and a distant, less certain future, such as Krio CE *go* versus *fɔ* (Jones 1971: 83–84) or Mauritian CF *pu* versus *a* (Baker 1972: 109–110). Some African languages make a similar distinction (Welmers 1973: 355, Boretzky 1983: 123–126), but further research is needed to clarify the relationship between these and creole usages.

The Papiamentu CS irrealis marker *lo* is thought to come from the Portuguese adverb *logo* 'immediately.' Like an adverb – and unlike all other creole verbal markers – it can occur outside the verb phrase, e.g. 'I will not go' is "*lo* mi no bai," "mi *lo* no bai" or even "mi no *lo* bai." Bickerton (1981: 80 ff.) speculates that its anomalous position outside the verb phrase is the remnant of an earlier pidgin stage in which *lo* still functioned as an adverb. Maurer (1985), who disagrees with much of the analysis of the Papiamentu verb phrase in Bickerton (1981), finds this interpretation plausible.

Finally, as noted above the anterior and irrealis markers can combine in most Atlantic creoles to produce a conditional meaning, e.g. Krio CE "mi *bin go* sing," Haitian CF "mwẽ *te va* chãte," and Papiamentu CS "*lo* mi *a* kanta," all 'I would have sung' (Alleyne 1980: 11). There is a similar combination of anterior *tun* and irrealis *bɛna* to produce this meaning in Bambara, e.g. "A *tun bɛna* na tobi" 'He would have cooked sauce' (Singler p.c.). However, this combination is not attested in many West African languages; it may also reflect a semantic universal as in the 'past future' construction of the conditional in English *would* (the past of *will* in indirect discourse) or Spanish *seria* '(it) would be' (future *será* plus the imperfect).

5.1.7   Other preverbal marker combinations

From the above discussion of the verbal markers in table 3, several general patterns emerge. First, the creoles indicate tense, mode, and aspect with verbal markers rather than inflections, and most of these markers occur before the verb. Secondly, there are striking semantic and syntactic similarities among the corresponding markers of each category that cannot be explained adequately by referring only to the creoles' lexical-source languages. Although these have usually provided the lexical forms of the markers (derived from European auxiliary verbs with partially similar semantic and syntactic features), the creole markers are part of a verbal system that is quite different from that of the European lexical-source language in many respects.

Regarding the ordering of the markers, at least one pattern is clear: each aspect or mode marker (including θ) can be preceded by the anterior tense marker, although there are some exceptions apparently due to decreolization – e.g. Gullah progressive [verb + -*in*] replacing [*da* + verb], or the Jamaican conditional *wuda* instead of **ben go*. Further claims about the ordering of these verbal markers have been the subject of some debate. Bickerton's (1980, 1981) analysis of the creole verbal system, based largely on Voorhoeve (1957), is that there are three basic components – tense (± anterior), mode (± irrealis), and aspect (± non-punctual) – and their markers occur in that order only (see §5.1.2 for discussion). The category of [± non-punctual] is based on the conflation of progressive and habitual into a single aspect which does not include the completive, which Bickerton claims to be a later innovation. Given these alternatives, + or − choices yield the possible combinations of markers shown in figure 1.

While not all of the combinations shown in figure 1 can be found in decreolized varieties like Hawaiian and Guyanese CE, they are all found in conservative varieties like Sranan and Saramaccan CE as well as Haitian and Lesser Antillean CF (Bickerton *et al.* 1984: 183). These include two combinations not discussed in the previous sections. The first is the combination of the future and progressive

Anterior   Irrealis   Non-punctual

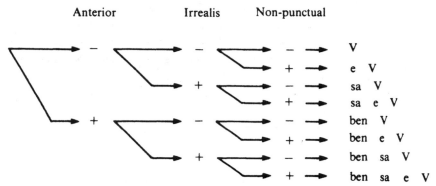

Figure 1   Possible combinations of tense, mode, and aspect markers (from Bickerton 1980:14, illustrated with Sranan markers from Voorhoeve 1957:383)

marker (Sranan *sa e*, Saramaccan *o ta*, Haitian *av ap*, Lesser Antillean CF *ke ka*) corresponding in meaning to the English future progressive, 'will be (do)ing.' The second is the sequence [+ anterior + irrealis + progressive] (Sranan *ben sa e*, Saramaccan *bi o ta*, Haitian *t'av ap*, Lesser Antillean CF *te ke ka*) corresponding in meaning to the English conditional perfect progressive, 'would have been (do)-ing.' This tripartite system is clearly different from the verbal systems of Krio CE or Mauritian CF, both of which have two distinct irrealis markers for certain versus uncertain future, as well as two distinct aspect markers for non-punctual and completive. However, Bickerton suggests that such systems developed out of the tripartite one shown in figure 1.

While Muysken (1981) objected to Bickerton's claim that the tripartite system was invariant in all creoles, he accepted the TMA (tense–mode–aspect) ordering as a principle of universal grammar for SVO languages in which AUX precedes V (and hypothesized AMT ordering in SOV languages in which AUX follows V) (1981:188). Alleyne (1980:80–82) posited MTA ordering for CE in his phrase structure rules VP→(Modal) + (Particle) + (Auxiliary) + Predicate, in which Particle→(Tense) + Aspect; Aspect→Non-perfective, Perfective; Non-perfective→ Habitual, Progressive; Tense→Past, Future; Perfective→θ (optionally rein-forced by a marker like *don*).

However, Gibson (1986:584) objects that Alleyne's structure "does not account for Guyanese durative and punctual aspects, and does not differentiate habitual and progressive aspects. Alleyne also fails to explain what he means by 'Auxiliary,' and he appears to treat 'Modal' as if it were a syntactic rather than a semantic category . . . However, his implicit MTA ordering coincides with my ordering of the notions." Gibson finds the TMA ordering that Bickerton proposed on the basis of his Guyanese CE data too simplistic to account for the data in the same creole that she collected and for her intuitions as a native speaker. Her re-analysis indicates the ordering MTA, but this is based on her redefinition of *gu/gon* (cf. *go*) as a tense marker and category 'Modal' that is very different from Bickerton's. In sum, the dissimilarity of their terminology makes a comparison of their analyses misleading.

5.1.8   *Complementizers*

Caribbean CE has several complementizers that correspond to the English infinitive marker *to*. Miskito Coast CE has *fo* ("A fried *fo* guo tek di tingz" 'I'm afraid to go take the things') and θ ("Ai niid θ tes mai ai" 'I need to have my eyes tested') in addition to *tu* ("Bai tingz *tu* iit" 'Buy things to eat') (Holm 1978:274). Bickerton (1971) argued that the variability of the Guyanese CE complementizers *tu* and *fu* was evidence in favor of the wave model of language change. He ordered by implicational ranking (§2.11) individual speakers' use of these complementizers to chart a polylectal grammar of this feature, claiming that the change progressed regularly from favored to less favored environments, first as a variable and then as a categorical rule. The most favored environment for *tu* was after modals and verbs whose meaning was "inceptive" (e.g. *staat, bigin*), then verbs whose meaning was "desiderative" (e.g. *want*), and finally "purposive" and other verbs, which favored *tu* least and *fu* most. Washabaugh (1977), using data from Providence Island CE (§10.4.1), found that complementizer scalability was 91% on the basis of simple lexical items rather than any "deep structural semantic constraints." The simplicity of his explanation of this phenomenon suggested that Bickerton's analysis had been unnecessarily complicated; Bickerton (1977a) accused him of "Putting back the clock in variation studies."

There are historical reasons why CE *fu* (with variants *fo* and *fi*) may be most firmly entrenched after purposive verbs. In regional British dialects, *for* is used as a complementizer implying purpose (e.g. "I came *for* see") in the West Country and Liverpool, while "I came *for to* see" is found in both regional (Orton *et al.* 1978: S3) and archaic English. The choice of *fu* as a complementizer in creole English might have been further reinforced by similar constructions in substrate languages, such as the Mandinka particle *fó* expressing purpose, e.g. "ṁ bàtu ngá táa *fó* íte s'iíla dòokuo nyáa sòto" 'Let me go *so that* you may have a chance to do your work' (Rowlands 1959: 82). There is syntactic evidence for such convergence in that CE *fu* introduces not only infinitives (like its regional and archaic English model) but also tensed verbs like Mandinka *fó*, e.g. Miskito Coast CE "Dem sen dem *for ai drink*" 'They sent them for me to drink' (Holm 1978: 275). This construction could be attributed to the further development of the standard

English construction in which the object of *for* is the subject of a following infinitive (and not the same as the subject of the main verb – as in the above translation), but there is evidence in creoles unrelated to English that points toward the English *for* construction converging with a creole construction influenced by the substrate. In a number of creoles not based on English there are particles that function similarly to CE *fu* which are homophonous with prepositions meaning 'for' derived from Portuguese or Spanish *para*, French *pour*, or Dutch *voor*, all meaning 'for'; it is to be noted that unlike English *for*, these can be followed by tensed verbs:

Annobón CP	"M' socu guya *pe*m cusé," literally 'I have needle *for*-I sew'	(Schuchardt 1888a: 197)
Príncipe CP	"Wadá mi, *pa* n wé kɔtá fukéta," lit. 'Wait me *for* I go cut support-beams'	(Günther 1973: 109)
Papiamentu CS	"Mi ke *pa* bo bai," lit. 'I want *for* you go'	(Goilo 1972)
Haitian CF	"M vle *pu* l vini," lit. 'I want *for* he come'	(Koopman 1986)
Negerhollands CD	"Kuj sji horn noit sal ben swar *for* him drag," lit. 'Cow's horn never will be heavy *for* she carry'	(Pontoppidan 1881: 135)

Because of the absence of case and tense marking in the structures after 'for' above, it is difficult to determine whether these are clauses with tensed verbs. However, by considering wh-extraction and the distribution of anaphors, Koopman determined that in Haitian CF "complement clauses headed by *pu* are opaque tensed clauses containing a subject marked for nominative Case" (1986: 238). The validity of this analysis for other creoles is supported by the work of Byrne (1984: 102), who found actual tense marking in such a clause in Saramaccan CE: "Mi kë tsuba kai *fu* ma *sa*-go a wosu," lit. 'I want rain fall *so-that* I-NEG *ASP*-go to house,' i.e. 'I want it to rain so I won't have to go home.' Boretzky (1983: 207–215) found no substrate models for these creole constructions but pointed out the syntactic similarity of Portuguese personal infinitives used after *para* and a subject pronoun, e.g. "Eles pediram *para eu voltar*," lit. 'They asked for I to-return,' i.e. 'They asked me to return' (Abreu and Rameh 1973: 212). Boretzky (1983: 207) considered this possible evidence for a Portuguese creole substrate for the creoles based on English and French (to which – based on the examples above – one could add those based on Spanish and Dutch). However, it should be pointed out that the Portuguese personal infinitive construction is only partially parallel to the creole 'for' constructions: while the Portuguese infinitive can take a subject and even an inflectional ending indicating agreement in person and number (e.g. "É fácil resolver*mos* este problema" 'It is easy for *us* to solve this problem') it is still an infinitive and thus – unlike the corresponding creole verbs – untensed. Moreover, Portuguese is like other Romance languages in that it uses a subjunctive construction in some of the cases in which the creoles use the 'for' complementizer, e.g. Portuguese "Quero que o faç*am*" (lit. 'I want that they do it') versus Guinea-Bissau CP "N misti *pa* e fasi-l" (lit. 'I want *for* they do it') (Kihm forthcoming). Kihm notes that the Guinea creole has three complementizers whereas Portuguese has only *que*: *ki/ku* as a complementizer and relative pronoun; *kuma* after verbs of speaking and knowing (§5.3.2) and *pa* in constructions of the type discussed above (ibid.). These follow verbs of wanting (i.e. one person wanting another to do something; cf. Bickerton's "desideratives"), verbs meaning 'begin' (e.g. "e *kumsa* kada kin *pa* i disinpeña si funson" 'they *began* each one to fulfill his function'; cf. "inceptive"), and constructions implying purpose ("lubu bai *pa* bai jubi kil si fiju" 'Hyena went *to* go see his son'). Moreover, CP *pa* marks nominal uses of verbs – much like infinitives – unlike P *para*: e.g. CP "*pa* lei i yera un tarbaju difisil" '*To read* was a hard job' (cf. P "*ler* é dificil"). Kihm identifies this usage with a construction in Manjaku (a West Atlantic language spoken in Guinea-Bissau) with the class prefix *pë*- which nominalizes verbs, e.g. "*pë*lenp" '(the fact of) working.' This *pë*- sometimes corresponds to both CP *pa* and P *para* (e.g. Manjaku "a lil *pë*re," CP "i bon *pa* kume," P "é bom *para* comer," all 'it is good *to* eat'), but sometimes CP *pa* functions unlike P *para*: 'I have *to* work' is CP "n ten *pa* tarbaja" (cf. P "tenho *que* trabalhar" but Manjaku "man ka *pë*lenp"). While recent research has begun to cast light on the origin of the creole 'for' construction, much more work remains to be done.

Connected with this question is the fact that in most of the creoles this complementizer is homophonous not only with a preposition meaning 'for' (mentioned above) but also with a modal meaning 'must' or 'should,' e.g. Saramaccan CE *fu* (Byrne 1984: 101), Haitian CF *pu* (Koopman and Lefebvre 1981: 206), Negerhollands CD *fo* (van Diggelen 1978: 86). A number of scholars have taken up the question of the possible developmental relationship between these homophonous prepositions, modals, and complementizers. Washabaugh (1980: 104) argues that the prepositional function of Providence Island CE *fi* is "prior to and more basic" than its verbal function. Koopman and Lefebvre (1981: 214) claim, on the basis of the "historical" data in Sylvain (1936) and Faine (1936), that Haitian CF *pu* changed from modal to complementizer – i.e. that the position of modal *pu* was stronger some fifty years earlier. Bickerton (1981: 118) speculates that *fi* may have originated as part of a serial verb construction. Winford (1985: 620 ff.) suggests that neither the prepositional nor the modal function necessarily had to be prior; they may have coexisted and developed together like the many homophonous verbs and prepositions found throughout the Kwa languages. Boretzky (1983: 215) came to much the same conclusion, pointing out that if complementizers (which he calls conjunctions) could have developed out of verbs in West African languages, then the two categories were probably related closely enough in the creoles for a verb to have developed out of a complementizer.

Bickerton (1981: 59 ff.) notes that in some creoles based on English and French there is a choice of complementizers that conveys a semantic distinction. In Jamaican CE "im gaan *go* bied" 'he went to wash,' *go* cannot be used if the intended action was not actually carried out, in which case *fi* must be used: "im gaan fi bied, bot im duon bied." Similarly, in Mauritian CF the complementizer *al* (cf. F *aller* 'go') can be used with an action that is carried out, e.g. "li desid *al* met posoh ladah," literally 'she decide *go* put fish in-it' (Baker 1972). However, if the action is not realized, the complementizer *pu* (also an irrealis marker) must be used. It is unclear how widespread this semantic distinction in creole complementizers is; in Belizean CE *go* can be used with an unrealized action, e.g. "i no waan *go* chap planteej" 'he did not want to (go and?) clear the scrub' (Le Page and Tabouret-Keller 1985: 104).

The preposition *fu/fi* is part of a possessive construction in some English creoles (§5.4.4). The complementizer *se* after verbs of saying etc. is discussed in section 5.3.2 as a serial verb.

5.1.9 Negation

Most Caribbean creoles negate verbs by placing a negative particle before the verb phrase:

Jamaican CE	"Jan *no* waan go" 'John *does not* want to go'
	(Bailey 1966: 55)
Haitian CF	"Li *pa*-t-konẽ," lit. 'He not ANT know,' i.e. 'He didn't know' (Goodman 1964: 92);
	cf. French "Il *ne* savait *pas*."
Negerhollands CD	"Mie *no* weet," lit. 'I not know'
	(van Diggelen 1978: 71);
	cf. Dutch "Ik weet *niet*."

Papiamentu CS   "Mi *no* ta bai," lit. 'I not PROG go,' i.e. 'I'm not
                  going'   (Goilo 1972)
                  cf. Spanish "(Yo) *no* voy.

Cape Verde CP   "El *ka* fala," lit. 'He not speak,' i.e. 'He didn't
                  speak'   (Almada 1961: 126):
                  cf. Portuguese "Ele *não* falou."

The creole syntactic pattern for negation is parallel to that of Portuguese and Spanish; this pattern is also found in many West African languages, e.g. Yoruba "a *kò* mọ," literally 'we not know,' i.e. 'we do not know' (Rowlands 1969: 16). This pattern represents a basic restructuring of negation in English, French, and Dutch. In decreolizing varieties of English-based creoles, the negator *no* is replaced by a less stigmatized form, *duon* (cf. *don't*), a single morpheme with the same distribution as *no*, e.g. Miskito Coast CE "Di wata *duon* pulin it eni muor" 'The water isn't pulling it any more' (Holm 1978: 263). Through hypercorrection, this form can also replace English *not*, as in Bahamian CE "Dancie say you better *don't* mess round with her nigger" 'Dancie said that you had better not fool around with her boyfriend' (Holm with Shilling 1982: 142).

A number of English-based creoles have the anterior negator *neva* (cf. *never*), e.g. Miskito Coast CE "ai did tayad an *neva* kom" 'I was tired and didn't come' (Holm 1978: 264). CE *neva* can negate a single possible occasion, as in British colloquial and dialect usage of *never* (R. Hudson p.c.). There is a parallel in Indo-Portuguese *nunca* (cf. P *nunca* 'never'), also used as a general past negator (Dalgado 1900: 42); the Papia Kristang CP cognate *ngka* is used to negate all tenses (Hancock 1975). Teyssier (1983) traces this usage to southern Portuguese dialects and sixteenth-century contact Portuguese (§6.1), and suggests that this *nunca* converged with substrate negators as the source of the negator *ka* in Cape Verde and Guinea-Bissau CP. Kihm (forthcoming) has identified a number of phonetically similar negators of various types in languages spoken in Guinea-Bissau, e.g. Mandinka *buka* and *kaka*, Balanta *ke*, and Mankanya *kö*.

Bickerton (1981: 65) claims that "in creoles generally, nondefinite subjects as well as nondefinite VP constituents must be negated, as well as the verb, in negative sentences." He offers only a few examples in Guyanese CE ("*Non* dag *na* bait *non* kyat" 'No dog bit any cat') and Papia Kristang CP ("*Ngka ng'*koza *nte* mersimentu," literally 'Not no-thing no-have value,' i.e. 'Nothing has any value'). This interesting claim regarding negative concord merits more substantiation. Labov (1972: 130) noted such concord in American Black English "It ai*n't no* cat can*'t* get in *no* coop," i.e. 'There isn't any cat that can get into any coop' – which leaves no nondefinite unnegated. However, Bahamian CE can extend negation to NPs as definite as proper nouns: "They ca*n't* sell that in *no* Haiti" (Holm with

Shilling 1982: 143). Liberian CE can even negate adverbial particles: "I not standing *no* up," an emphatic way of saying 'I refuse to stand up' (Singler 1981: 91). Shilling (1976) notes negative concord in the French-based creoles and underscores the parallel structure of negation in Bahamian CE with a word-for-word translation into the latter, e.g. "li *pa* repon *naye*" becoming "he *ain'* answer *nothin'*." However, it must be remembered that French itself requires the negation of the verb before a negative indefinite, e.g. "Il *n'a rien* répondu." Spanish and Portuguese have similar negative concord; although there are no studies comparing this phenomenon in creoles lexically based on them, isolated examples suggest a similar pattern, e.g. Papiamentu CS "*Nada no* ta pasa" 'Nothing is happening' (Marta Dijkhoff p.c.) – cf. Spanish "*No* pasa *nada*" idem. Negative concord can also be found in Negerhollands CD, e.g. "Sender *no* leer *niet* een Gut," literally 'They don't learn nothing' (Hesseling 1905: 170). However, double negation could also be found in seventeenth-century Dutch (Brachin 1985: 22), as in archaic and nonstandard English.

Several Atlantic creoles have discontinuous double negators, i.e. one before the verb phrase and another at the end of the clause, as in São Tomé CP "I'nê *na* ka 'tlaba na'i *fa*," literally 'They *not* ASP work here *not*,' i.e. 'They do not work here' (Ferraz 1976: 36). This feature is shared by other Portuguese-based creoles in the Gulf of Guinea: Angolar has disjunctive *na...wa* while Annobón CP has *na...-f* -*f*. Príncipe CP has a single negator *fa* at the end of the utterance, which may have originally been preceded by *na* as in São Tomé CP, to judge from the common origin (§6.3) and general structural similarity of the two creoles. Across the Atlantic Ocean, Palenquero CS has a single negator *nu* which occurs at the end of the utterance, but which can also occur before the verb for emphasis: "*Nu* ablá ma *nu*," literally 'Not say more not,' i.e. 'Don't say any more' (Bickerton and Escalante 1970: 259). This double negation is normal in imperative constructions (Friedemann and Patiño 1983: 171) and can occur in non-emphatic sentences as well (De Granda p.c.). The negator *nu* can be separated from the verb it modifies by a subordinate clause with an unnegated verb: "i sabé (si ané ba rreklamá mí ele) *nu*" 'I don't know if they're going to complain about it to me' (Friedemann and Patiño 1983: 171). This is also true of the Príncipe CP negator *fa*, which can form part of a double negative after elements like *nûka* 'never' (Boretzky 1983: 102). These similarities and others have led De Granda (1978: 435) to posit a close genetic relationship between Palenquero CS and the Gulf of Guinea creoles. Discontinuous double negators are also found in Berbice Creole Dutch, e.g. "ɛk *na* ni wat fi pam ju *ka*," literally 'I not know what to tell you not,' i.e. 'I don't know what to tell you' (Robertson 1979: 158). The preverbal negator can also take the form *nʌkʌ*; the clause-final negator *ka* has been traced to the Eastern Ijo negator -*ka* (Smith *et al.* 1987). Other African models for the creole discontinuous negators have also been proposed. Hancock (1979c: 415) points out the parallel Kongo structure in "Omuuntu *ke*-wàmmbi-*ko*" 'The man is not wicked,' in which each emphasized particle is a negator. Boretzky (1983: 102) notes that the Yoruba preverbal negator *kò* can be made emphatic by the postverbal particle *mọ́* or *rárá*, perhaps related to the verbs *mó* and *rá*, both 'vanish.' Ewe surrounds the verb with the disjunctive negators *me . . . o*, the first element of which can sometimes be omitted; the second comes at the end of the sentence, even after an intervening clause (ibid.). Boretzky points out that the discontinuous creole negators could be innovations as well as the result of substrate influence, but they could hardly have resulted from a universal creole tendency toward simplification since they represent more complex structures than the single negators in their superstrates.

Discontinuous negators are found in several language varieties that have other creole-like features. Non-standard Brazilian Portuguese (§6.7) has an optional postverbal negator not found in standard Portuguese: "*Não* quero *não*" 'I don't want to' (Marroquim 1934: 196). The first *não* can be omitted to convey emphasis (Boretzky p.c.). A variety of Spanish spoken by blacks on the Pacific coast of Colombia also has both initial and sentence-final negators (De Granda 1978: 515). Afrikaans has a postverbal negator (as does Dutch) which is followed by a second negator at the end of the sentence (not found in Dutch): "Ek kom *nie* na jou toe *nie*," literally 'I come not to you not' (Markey 1982: 198). Although this has been attributed to an apparently similar construction in dialectal Dutch, den Besten (1986) finds the parallel faulty: there is a closer parallel to a Khoekhoe structure, lending support to the theory of substrate influence on the development of Afrikaans.

5.2 Forms of 'be'

While studies of the verb phrase made clear the Atlantic creoles' structural similarity to one another and autonomy *vis-à-vis* their superstrates, it was comparative studies of the creoles' various words for 'be' that unequivocally demonstrated that the creoles were not merely simplified forms of European languages. These studies showed that the creoles were in certain respects more complex than their lexical-source languages in that they made some grammatical and semantic distinctions not made in the European languages. This can be seen in table 4, *Forms of 'be' in various creole and African languages*, which shows that these creole and African languages often use quite different words for 'be' depending on whether the following element is a noun phrase, an adjective, or an indication of location. A fourth category, the highlighter, is explained below (§5.2.4).

Table 4. *Forms of 'be' in various creole and African languages*

	– Noun phrase	– Adjective	– Locative	Highlighter
Príncipe CP	sa ~ θ	θ ~ sa	sẽ ~ tá	sé ~ ki
Guinea-Bissau CP	sedu ~ θ	θ	sta	ki
Guyanais CF	sa ~ (θ)	θ ~ (sa)	sa ~ θ ~ (fika)	sa ~ a
Haitian CF	sé ~ (θ)	θ	θ ~ (ye)	sé
Negerhollands CD	a (we:s)	mi (we:s)	be (we:s)	da ~ a
Berbice CD	da (wa)	θ (wa)	jɛndɛ (wa)	da
Sranan CE	na ~ a/de	θ	de tan	na ~ a/da
Jamaican CE	da ~ a/iz	θ	de θ	da ~ a/iz
Yoruba	ṣe ~ jẹ́	θ (rí ~ yà)	wà ~ sí	ni
Mandinka	mu	θ	be	le

Sources include: Boretzky 1983; d'Ans 1968; Goodman 1964; Günther 1973; Hall 1966; Holm 1976, 1980a, 1984; Kihm 1980; McConnell and Swan 1960; Robertson 1979; Rowlands 1959, 1969; St. Jacques-Fauquenoy 1972a; Stolz 1986; Taylor 1977; Valkhoff 1966; Voorhoeve 1962.

From the perspective of these creole and African languages, these words are not necessarily related beyond the fact that they all occur in the position of the verb, except for the highlighter. Their link here is that they all happen to be translatable by English *be* or its equivalent in the other European superstrate languages. To this category could be added one of the preverbal markers discussed above (§5.1.3): the progressive aspect marker also corresponds to a use of *be* in English ("he *is* writing"). Loosely calling all of these forms of 'be' copulas, Labov (1969) found in a quantitative study that American Black English had a definite pattern for "deleting the copula" (i.e. using θ) depending on the following syntactic environment – i.e. a low rate of deletion before nouns, a higher one elsewhere, etc. Since Labov did not believe at that time that Black English was genetically linked to the Caribbean creoles, he could offer no historical explanation for this very un-European pattern. Holm (1976, 1984) showed that the same pattern prevailed in Gullah and Jamaican CE, reflecting the structure of substrate African languages. For variationists this constituted "the first serious evidence for the Creole hypothesis" of the origin of Black English (Labov 1982: 198), although creolists had long been taking seriously other evidence as well.

5.2.1 *Equative 'be'*

Equative 'be' is a true copula in the Latin sense of a word joining two others, i.e. a subject and a complement as in "Mary *is* my sister." *Be* is equative before a noun phrase in that it means that the subject equals (i.e. is the same as) the complement – quite a different meaning from *be* before a locative ("Mary is home") or a participle ("Mary is gardening"). Equative 'be' is expressed by words that are different from those used to express other meanings of 'be' in a number of creole and African languages (table 4). While Mandinka has only one copula before noun phrases, Yoruba has two: "*jẹ́* is used when we are thinking of natural, in-born, permanent characteristics while *ṣe* is used of what is accidental, acquired or temporary" (Rowlands 1969: 152). Sranan's two equative copulas also convey this distinction; *na* and *de* have contrasting meaning in two sentences equivalent to 'I am a boatman,' i.e. "mi *na* botoman" expresses general capability or qualification, while "mi *de* botoman" expresses current occupation (Favery *et al.* 1976: 89). Jamaican CE *da* (a cognate of *na*, possibly merging with *de*) and its variant *a* express both meanings. Under English influence, basilectal *a* becomes mesolectal *iz*. All three forms are found in the closely related creole spoken on Nicaragua's Miskito Coast: "Dat *a* di fos sang" 'That's the first song'; "Mi *da* i anti" 'I am his aunt'; "Ai *iz* di straika" 'I am the harpooner' (Holm 1978: 268). Forms identical to those in the CE basilect are found in the CD equative copulas: *a* in Negerhollands and *da* in Berbice. These have alternate forms for the past or anterior, respectively *we:s* from the Dutch past participle *geweest* 'been,' and *wa* from the Dutch past form *was* 'was,' both used before adjectives and locatives as well, although the non-past forms in these three syntactic environments are distinct in each Dutch creole.

Regarding the overall pattern of the equative copula in table 4, it should be noted that in the African languages as well as in the creoles based on English and Dutch there is an expressed (i.e. not θ) form of the copula, although θ forms begin to appear in the CE mesolect as the semantic and syntactic distinctions of the basilect become blurred. In the creoles based on Portuguese and French both expressed copulas and θ occur before nouns, but in the New World varieties of CF the expressed forms predominate, as in the creoles based on English and Dutch (Valdman 1978: 233, Stein 1984: 84).

5.2.2 *Adjectival verbs*

Creole words that correspond to European adjectives semantically seem to correspond syntactically to verbs of similar meaning in a number of Niger-Congo languages. Arguments for treating these as a subcategory of verbs, at least in basilectal varieties, are discussed in §5.3.3 in connection with the comparison of such adjectives or adjectival verbs. As noted in §3.3.3, they do not follow a copula as adjectives do in the European superstrates, but rather follow the preverbal tense and aspect markers that specify verbs, as in African languages like Mandinka and

Yoruba. Thus when no such markers are needed, their absence (θ) corresponds to the position of the word for 'be' in European languages. It is misleading to speak of the "deletion of the copula" or even "θ copula" before adjectival verbs in such languages, since these terms imply that copulas occur (or should occur) in this position. While most Yoruba adjectives are verbs which take no copula, there are some phonaesthetic descriptive words unrelated to verbs which do follow a copula (*rí*), while another copula (*yà*) is followed by words "denoting a type of person of whom Yoruba society disapproves" (e.g. *ọlẹ* 'lazy') (Rowlands 1969: 122, 155). While this latter category corresponds semantically to English adjectives, it is in fact made up of nouns. This distinction is not found in the creoles.

As noted above, adjectival verbs in the Atlantic creoles can take preverbal markers of anterior tense (§3.3.3) and completive aspect (§5.1.5). In some creoles they can also take the marker of progressive aspect, indicating that the quality is coming into being or is being intensified, e.g. Sranan CE "a *e* dipi" 'it is getting deep' (Voorhoeve 1957: 377) or Haitian CF "l'*ap* malad" 'he is getting sick' (H. Gaujean, p.c.). This is also a widespread feature in African languages, e.g. Yoruba "ó ńtutù" 'it is getting cold' (Rowlands 1969: 61). Príncipe CP *sa* is also a progressive aspect marker but apparently carries no distinction in meaning when it occurs before adjectives, where it alternates with θ like Guyanais CF *sa*. Otherwise θ occurs before adjectival verbs in all creoles except Negerhollands CD, which has the expressed form *mi*. Because of this single form, Sabino (1986a) concludes that there is no "generalized Creole copula." If this means that there is no general pattern for the predominating forms of 'be' in relation to their following syntactic environment in the Atlantic creoles, the data in table 4 would not support such a conclusion.

5.2.3 *Locative 'be'*

A number of Atlantic creoles use a distinct word for 'be' when referring to location. The creole English form of this word, *de*, is derived from the adverb *there*, perhaps converging with substrate forms for locative 'be' such as Twi *dè* (Christaller 1933: xxiii). Although the semantic connection between *there* and locative 'be' is clear, the syntactic connection is less so. The link may lie in the fact that *de* can be omitted before locative phrases, e.g. Miskito Coast CE "Ai no nuo if it θ in di baibl" 'I don't know if it's in the bible' (Holm 1978: 266). This makes *de* ambiguous as 'be' or 'there' in sentences like "Di gyorl-dem aal *de* pan di veranda" 'The girls were all (there) on the veranda' (ibid.). As previously noted (§5.1.3), locative 'be' has the same form as the progressive aspect marker in a number of creole and African languages, probably due to the influence of a substrate feature that is itself the manifestation of a semantic universal. While Bambara *bɛ* has both the locative and progressive meaning, the Yoruba form for locative 'be' (*wà*, with the negative form *sí*) is less directly related to the progressive marker (Welmers 1973: 315). The semantic range of *wà* parallels CE *de* in that both can assert existence, e.g. Yoruba "Olọ́rún *wà*" 'God exists' (Rowlands 1969: 154) and CE "a *de*" 'I (still) exist' (in response to 'How are you?') (Holm with Shilling 1982: 169). It should be noted, however, that the usual creole equivalent of existential 'there is' is '(they/it) have,' e.g. Guyanese CE *get*, Haitian CF *gê*, Papiamentu CS *tin*, São Tomé CP *te* (Bickerton 1981: 66), Bahamian CE *have* (cf. *it is* idem, possibly via *it has ~ it's*), Negerhollands CD *die hab* (Hesseling 1905: 170), Ndjuka CE *a abi* (G. Huttar p.c.). The creole expressions have been traced to "Bantu languages where the existential verb is also the verb 'to have'" (Ivens Ferraz 1985: 111).

Some creoles maintain a distinction between 'to be (located); to exist' on the one hand and 'to be (a certain way)' on the other. For example, Sranan *dɛ* is locative ("Den *dɛ* na ɔndro bɛdi" 'They are under the bed'), while *tan* (from *stand*, perhaps influenced by P *estar*) has the latter meaning: "A *tá* so" 'It is like that' (Boretzky 1983: 158). The same distinction is maintained between Príncipe CP locative and existential *sɛ̃* (e.g. "E *sɛ̃* fa" 'It is not there') and *tá* ("Padasu *tá* mɔ́di pwɛ́ fa" 'A stepfather is not like a father') (ibid.). Nigerian PE has two apparently interchangeable locative copulas, *dé* and *sté* (cf. E *stay*, possibly influenced by P *estar*) (Rotimi and Faraclas forthcoming); the latter is parallel in form to locative/progressive *stay* in Hawaiian CE (Bickerton 1976).

Haitian CF normally uses θ before locative expressions (e.g. "Li θ isit" 'He is here') but it also has an expressed form (*ye*, from F *est* /e/ 'is') used only at the end of clauses, e.g. "Kote li *ye*?" 'Where is he?' (Goodman 1964: 58). Guyanais CF has the optional use of *sa*: "Nu (*sa*) ãdã lit-a" 'We (are) in bed' (St. Jacques-Fauquenoy 1972a: 227), with *fika* (cf. P *ficar* 'stay') corresponding to clause-final Haitian *ye*: "Kumã u *fika*?" 'How are you?' (Goodman 1987). (Haitian *ye* and Guyanais *fika* are both used in clause-final position after nouns and adjectives as well as locatives, although only the latter is indicated on table 4.) Like CF, American Black English cannot have the θ form of *be* in clause-final position either. Labov (1969) concluded that the Black English copula could be deleted only where the standard English copula could be contracted: cf. *"Here he's." However, clause-final forms of English *be* and French *être* must receive greater stress (cf. "Je ne sais pas où il *est*" 'I don't know where he *is*'), which seems likely to account for both the fact that the creoles retained expressed forms in this position and the fact that standard English permits no contraction here (the stressed copula can never be contracted). However, Labov's hypothesis regarding the interrelation of the standard English and Black English copulas is inadequate not only because it lacks

any historical perspective, but also because it fails to account for all the facts (see
§5.2.4).

5.2.4 Highlighter 'be'

The Atlantic creoles have a particle that highlights or emphasizes the following
word to make it the focus of discourse (Todd 1973, Holm 1980a). This emphasis
could be translated into English by simply stressing the word – "*John* lives there"
(not Jim) – or by using *it's* to introduce it: "It's John who lives there." Yoruba, like
a number of other West African languages, has a highlighter, a morpheme that
emphasizes the word it occurs next to, somewhat like English *it's* except that the
Yoruba highlighter (*ni*) occurs after the word or clause that it emphasizes, which is
brought to the front of the sentence. For example, "mo rà aṣọ" 'I bought cloth'
becomes "aṣọ *ni* mo rà" 'It was cloth I bought' (not paper). If a verb is to be
emphasized, it is fronted and prefixed by its initial consonant plus *i* and then
recopied in its original position, i.e. "nwọn *pa* á" 'They killed it' becomes "pípa ni
nwọn *pa* á" 'They *killed* it' (literally 'Killing it-was they killed it') (Rowlands
1969: 189). This process, which is called verb-fronting or predicate clefting, is
unknown in the European superstrate languages but is found throughout the
Caribbean creoles (Bynoe-Andriolo and Yillah 1975). It is discussed here since it
provides a convenient way to identify the highlighter in these creoles (italicized
below):

Sranan CE	"*Da* kom mi de kom" 'I'm *coming*'
	(Cassidy 1964: 273)
Jamaican CE	"*Iz* tiif dem tiif it" 'It was certainly stolen'
	(ibid.)
Lesser Antillean CF	"*Se* sot i sot" 'He's *stupid*'
	(Taylor 1977: 183)
Mauritian CF	"Zape *mem*, to pa kon zape?" 'Don't you even know how to *bark*?"
	(Baker 1972: 195)
Papiamentu CS	"*Ta* traha e ta traha" 'He's *working*'
	(Bynoe-Andriolo and Yillah 1975)
Negerhollands CD	"*Da* breek sender ka breek" 'They are *broken*'
	(Hesseling 1905: 155)

Verb fronting without the highlighter is found in two semi-creoles: Afrikaans
"*Kom* sal hij *kom*" 'He will certainly come' (Stolz 1986: 207) and Popular Brazilian
Portuguese "*Falar* ele *falou*" 'He certainly talked' (L. Cagliari p.c.).

The creole highlighters can introduce other elements besides verbs (and adjectival verbs, as in the Lesser Antillean CF example above), but these structures are less striking since, as in English, the element is merely fronted without being recopied in its original position. However, the creole highlighters do have another function without European parallels; this is their use before question words, which are also fronted:

Jamaican CE	"*A wa* Anti sen fi mi?" 'What has Auntie sent for me?'
	(Bailey 1966: 87)
Saramaccan CE	"*Na un-sé* a bi wáka?" 'Where (lit. 'is which side') did he go?'
	(de Groot 1981: 79)
Papiamentu CS	"*Ta kiko* Wan ta hasi?" 'What (lit. 'is what thing') is John doing?'
	(Todd-Dandare 1978: 13)
Negerhollands CD	"*Da wat gut* ja hab na ju hant?" 'What (lit. 'is what thing') do you have in your hand?'
	(Hesseling 1905: 154)

(See §3.3.4 regarding the bimorphemic structure of many creole question words.) The Yoruba highlighter *ni* must also be used with question words: "*ta* ['who?'] and *ki* ['what?'] . . . are always emphatic, i.e. followed by *ni*" (Rowlands 1969: 26). Bailey (1966: 88 ff.) treats the Jamaican CE highlighter *a* as an integral part of question words like *a-wa* 'what?,' noting that "the introductory *a* is often omitted in questions, probably as the result of the competing English forms." This use of the highlighter has not been attested in the Atlantic creoles based on Portuguese and French, but it is found in Berbice Creole Dutch, even in embedded clauses: "ɛkɛ jɛ studia *da* wa di gʊt dʌz mia," literally 'I usually wonder *is* what the thing does do,' i.e. 'I wonder what the thing does' (Robertson 1979: 147).

The creole highlighters represent a syntactic category in the substrate languages that does not correspond very closely to anything in the superstrate languages. The variety of forms that the highlighter has taken in the creoles suggests a ghost-like syntactic function rummaging through the European lexicons in search of some suitable corporeal form. Its earliest form may well have been African: *na*, the highlighter in the Surinamese creoles and Krio as well as a variant of Negerhollands *da*, was traced to the Twi highlighter *na* by Schuchardt (1914b: 132). Given the alternation of apical consonants in the creoles (§4.6.4), *na* seems likely to have given rise to *da* (possibly influenced by E *that* or D *dat*) and the reduced form *a* found in creoles based on English, Dutch, and even French (table 4). In Guyanais CF the highlighter *a* alternates with the more general copula *sa*, the latter being used before nouns and adjectives (e.g. "*sa* bõ" 'it's good') while *a* is used elsewhere (e.g. "*a* mó" 'it's me') (St. Jacques-Fauquenoy 1972a: 228). The form *sa* may be connected to the copula *sa* in the Gulf of Guinea varieties of CP (cf. P *são* 'are') and F *ça* 'it, that' – semantically connected to the possible deictic source of CE *da* (cf. also *das* below). The Haitian CF highlighter *sé* seems likely to come from F *c'est* /se/ 'it's.' It should be noted that the creoles based on French, Dutch, and English have highlighters that are nearly identical in form to equative 'be,' the link possibly being the frequency with which the highlighter also occurs before noun phrases.

Príncipe CP *sé* (of unknown origin) is again a demonstrative used to introduce a word or phrase: "ũa *sé*: a sa kũfyá na myέ fa" 'One is: one should not trust one's wife' (Boretzky 1983: 158). Günther (1973: 99) notes that there is also an emphatic use of the Príncipe CP relative pronoun *ki* (cf. P *que* idem): "éli *ki* sa káʃi aré" '*This* is the house of the king,' comparable to P "esta *que* é a casa do rei" (Boretzky 1983: 222). Chataigner (1963: 46) notes the similar use of Guinea-Bissau CP *ki* to emphasize ("Báka *ki* si pápe" 'It's the cow who is superior'), pointing out how *ki* corresponds syntactically to Mandinka *le* and Wolof *a*, both highlighters. Kihm (forthcoming) further points out the correspondence between Guinea-Bissau CP *ki/ku* and the Manjaku highlighter (*k*)*i* after focused elements like question phrases, e.g. CP "kal kasa *ku* bu na mora nel?" 'Which house do you live in?' (cf. Manjaku "kato kom *ki* m cina kon?" idem).

Finally, Mauritian CF *mem* above is clearly from French *même* as in *moi-même* '(I) myself,' at least lexically. There is a similar emphatic use of *self* in Rama Cay CE: "nat de riil biebi *self*" 'not the little *baby*' (Assadi 1983: 117). The lexical origin of the latter would seem to lie in the archaic English use of *self* for emphasis, e.g. "the Poete *selfe*" (*Oxford English Dictionary*), but the CE use of *self* to emphasize an entire clause is an innovation that suggests the influence of an African highlighter, e.g. Bahamian CE "I ain' gon stay *sef*" 'I'm not going to *stay*' (Holm with Shilling 1982: 179) or Ndjuka "mi á sabi *seefi*" 'I don't *know*' (Huttar p.c.).

In the mesolect, Jamaican CE uses *iz* as a highlighter instead of basilectal *a*, as does Miskito Coast CE: "O laad, *iz* hou orl truo mi wie laik dat?" 'Oh Lord, how is it that Earl could have rejected me like that?' (Holm 1978: 271). In both creoles *das* functions as a highlighter with somewhat more deictic force: "*Das* di smuok" 'That's the smoke' (ibid. 270). While English *that's* was clearly the model for CE *das*, it should be noted that there are no rules within the creole for contracting *iz* to *z* or *s*, suggesting that *das* functions as a single morpheme like the highlighter *da*, which is homophonous with a demonstrative pronoun meaning 'that.' This interpretation is borne out by the occurrence of *das* as 'that,' e.g. "*Das* would be de bes' place" (Cassidy and Le Page 1980: 197). Interestingly, American Black English has a parallel form /ðæs/ for 'that's,' which differs from the contraction usually used by whites, /ðæts/ (Labov 1972: 114 ff.). Moreover, sentence-initial Black English /ɪs/ 'it's' differs from white /ɪts/ in a similar way. Labov invokes phonological rules to derive /ɪs/ from /ɪt # # ɪz/, but then restricts these rules to pronouns since nouns like *Pat* cannot be thus reduced in Black English, i.e. "Pat's good" does not become */pæs gʊd/, although standard /ðæts gʊd/ corresponds to Black English /ðæs gʊd/. In other words it is not the case, as claimed by Labov (1969), that the Black English copula can be deleted wherever the standard English copula can be contracted since standard /ðæts gʊd/ corresponds to Black English /ðæs gʊd/ instead of the predicted /ðæt__ gʊd/. Labov's pronominal restriction does account for Black English *wha's* /wʌs/ 'what's,' but not *le's* /lɛs/ 'let's,' since *let* is not a pronoun. However, all of the Black English forms are found in Bahamian CE (Holm with Shilling 1982), suggesting that light might be cast on this question by using a historical approach that takes into account the possibility of phenomena known to occur in other creoles. The existence of Bahamian CE forms like *i* 'it,' *da* 'that,' *wa* 'what,' and *le* 'let' suggests that these high-frequency forms were retained from an earlier stage of the creole in which final /t/ had been lost to conform with a CV syllabic structure rule. It seems likely that under the influence of the corresponding English contractions (in which /ɪz/ became /s/ via assimilation of voicing to that of adjacent /t/), creole *i* became *is* (rather than */iz/), *da* became *das* (rather than */dats/), etc.

To conclude, table 4 reveals some clearly discernible patterns for the predominating form of 'be' in the Atlantic creoles as related to the following syntactic environment: (1) an expressed form of 'be' is required before a noun complement by both of the African languages and by the English- and Dutch-based creoles, although the expressed form can alternate with θ in the other creoles; (2) no form of 'be' is used before adjectival verbs in most of the languages; (3) a distinct form of 'be' is usually used before locatives, sometimes varying with θ; (4) all of the languages have a highlighter with specific syntactic functions to convey emphasis.

However, not all of the Atlantic creoles have copulas that fall into this general pattern. Papiamentu CS uses *ta* throughout; while *ta* has a very African function as a highlighter, its obligatory use before noun phrases, adjectives, and locatives alike may well have resulted from decreolization towards a European model, a phenomenon also suggested by other aspects of Papiamentu grammar (§§5.1.2 and 5.1.3). The brief references to forms for 'be' in Palenquero CS (Lewis 1970: 124–126; Bickerton and Escalante 1970: 260; Friedemann and Patiño 1983: 130–131) indicate a pattern with little similarity to the one discussed above.

5.3 Serial verbs

Serial verbs are frequently found in the Atlantic creoles, e.g. the two verbs in Miskito Coast CE "aal di waari *ron kom* bai mi," literally 'all the wild-boars *ran came* by me,' i.e. 'came running up to me.' As their name implies, they consist of a series of two (or more) verbs; they both have the same subject and are not joined by a conjunction ('and') or a complementizer ('to') as they would be in European languages. This working definition of serial verbs was proposed by Jansen *et al.* (1978: 125); they went on to exclude verb combinations with an auxiliary, modal or infinitive, but this part of their definition was rejected by Boretzky (1983: 164) since these categories are not always appropriate for creole and African languages. While the closest models for creole serial verb constructions are to be found in the Kwa languages (see below), European languages have some partially analogous constructions with conjunctions or complementizers that can sometimes be omitted, e.g. French "*Viens prendre* ta lettre" and its English translation "*Come take* your letter," or "*Go get* your book" (Mufwene p.c.).

Serial verbs can be treated in the context of either lexicon or syntax. Valdman (1978: 228) sees them as "ensembles lexicalisés" in that the combined meaning of the verbs is not always immediately deducible from the sum of the parts, e.g. Háitian CF *mennen vini* 'to bring' (literally 'lead come'), requiring the combination to be treated in the lexicon, as in Valdman *et al.* 1981. However, the combined meaning of the verbs can be seen as falling into several broad categories; one of these is directionality, as in the above examples in which 'come' conveys the idea of 'motion toward.' The opposite idea, 'motion away from,' can be achieved by using the word equivalent to 'go', as in the following three-verb series meaning 'run away from him' (literally 'run go leave him') from Alleyne (1980: 12):

Jamaican CE	ron	go	lef	im
Papiamentu CS	kore	bay	lagá	e
Haitian CF	kuri	ale	lese	li
Saramaccan CE	kule	go	disa	en

A similar pattern can be seen in Negerhollands CD "Džak a *kuri lo* si pat," literally 'Jack ANT *run go* along path,' i.e. 'Jack ran away . . .' (van Diggelen 1978). This parallels a structure in the Kwa languages, e.g. Ibo "ọ́ *gbàrà ọ̀sọ̀ gáa* áhyà," literally 'He *ran go* market,' i.e. 'He ran to the market' (Huttar 1974: 58). In these languages, verbs in series often serve the semantic function of European adverbs or prepositions.

Another broad semantic category that serial verbs can fall into is the instrumental, e.g. Ndjuka "a *teke* nefi *koti* a meti," literally 'he *took* knife *cut* the meat,' i.e. 'he cut the meat with a knife' (Huttar 1981). An African parallel is

Yoruba "ó *fi* ọbẹ *gé* ẹran," also literally 'he *took* knife *cut* meat' (ibid., but in conventional spelling). Jansen *et al.* (1978) note that the instrumental construction with 'take' is usually found in the Kwa languages rather than other members of the Niger-Congo family, but Boretzky (1983: 177–178) points out parallel constructions in the West Atlantic, Mande, and Gur groups. Still he concurs with their general conclusion that the presence of this feature in the Atlantic creoles points to the importance of the substrate influence of the Kwa group, where serial verb constructions are most widespread. Their apparent absence in the Guinea CP of Senegal, with its non-Kwa substratum, would support this conclusion.

The following subsections will discuss certain serial verbs that are part of some well known creole constructions. In addition to these and the serial verb constructions discussed above indicating directionality and instrumentality, there are some syntactic features taken up elsewhere in the present chapter that may have evolved from serial verb constructions either in Africa or in the New World, e.g. the complementizer/modal/preposition *fu* or *pu* (§5.1.8), the completive aspect markers *don*, *fini*, and *kaba* (§5.1.5), and perhaps the irrealis marker *go* (§5.1.6).

5.3.1 *Serial 'give' meaning 'to, for'*

Most of the Atlantic creoles have a serial verb construction in which the verb meaning 'give' occurs as the second element with the meaning of the preposition 'to' or 'for':

São Tomé CP   "Complá sapé *da* mu," lit. 'Buy hat give me,' i.e. 'Buy a hat for me'

(Schuchardt 1882a: 893)

Gullah CE   "dɛm də ca əm ʃɪ dɪ ɲɔŋ pipl," lit. 'They PROG carry it give the young people,' i.e. 'They are bringing it for the young people'

(Turner 1949: 264)

Haitian CF   "pot veso *bã*-m," lit. 'carry vessel give me,' i.e. 'bring me a vessel'

(Hall 1966: 78)

Negerhollands CD "di frou goi it de jet *gi* sinu" 'The woman throws out the food for (lit. 'give') them'

(van Diggelen 1978: 76)

Linguists sometimes make a distinction between the use of 'give' as a dative (e.g. Sranan "Kofi tjari den fisi kon *gi* mi" 'Kofi brought the fish for me') and as a benefactive (e.g. "Kofi go na Paramaribo *gi* mi" 'Kofi went to Paramaribo for me') (Jansen *et al.* 1978: 141). Boretzky (1983: 175) points out that the benefactive meaning of 'give' is quite distant from its original meaning ('giving' in the sense of an object being transferred from one person to another), which he interprets as evidence that the word is midway in a transition from verb to preposition. CF *ba* or *bay* (from archaic French *bailler* 'give') was treated by Goodman (1964: 62–63) as two separate but related words – one a verb and the other a preposition – just as *mãže* is treated as a verb 'eat' and a noun 'food,' although he was aware of the preposition's probable origin as a serial verb. It was because of their common use of *bay* that Goodman grouped together Haitian, Lesser Antillean, and Guyanais CF. However, his point seems to have been the presence of *bay* as a lexical form rather than the presence of such a serial verb, since the prepositional use of *doné* (cf. F *donner* 'give') is also found in Louisiana CF (Taylor 1977: 192). Schuchardt (1882a: 913) was the first to note that the prepositional use of 'give' is found both in West African languages and creole Portuguese, English, and French. Herskovits and Herskovits (1936: 131) pointed out specific African constructions as plausible models, such as Ashanti *ma* or Gã *ha*, both 'for' as well as 'give,' to which Goodman (1964: 63) added the parallel Ewe *na*. Yoruba *fún* 'give' can also be used serially, e.g. "rà á *fún* mi" 'buy it for me' (Rowlands 1969: 83).

5.3.2 Serial 'say' meaning 'that'

In a number of creoles and post-creoles a verb meaning 'say' can be used to introduce a quotation, and in some varieties this word can also be used after verbs whose meaning involves thinking (e.g. 'know', 'believe') to introduce a sentence complement which would begin with *that* in English:

Sranan CE	"m sab *tak* a tru" 'I know *that* it's true'
	(Voorhoeve 1962: 26)
Krio CE	"a no *se* yu bizi" 'I know *that* you're busy'
	(Jones 1971: 91)
Gullah CE	"dɛ lɔ *sɛ* wi tu ol" 'They admit *that* we're too old'
	(Turner 1949: 211)
US Black English	"They told me *say* they couldn't get it'
	(Rickford 1977: 212)
Negerhollands CD	"am nōit sa prāt *sē* a Tekoma a mata di kui" 'He will not say *that* it was Tekoma who killed the cow'
	(van Diggelen 1978: 71)
Berbice CD	"ɛkɛ pamtɛ ju *bi* fa las jer ɛk a motɛ mu kiki di dispɛnsa" 'I told you that (lit. 'say') last year I went to see the dispenser'
	(Robertson 1979: 148)

Herskovits and Herskovits (1936: 133) pointed out that this creole construction corresponded to usage in West African languages such as Ewe, in which the verb *krɔipi* 'say' is repeated to introduce quotations. Turner (1949: 201) pointed out the formal and syntactic similarity of Gullah *sɛ* and Twi *sɛ* 'that, saying' and English *say*. Cassidy (1961: 63) noted that the pronunciation of Jamaican *se* is /sɛ/ when it means 'that' rather than /sey/, leading him to support the connection with Akan *se*. Boretzky (1983: 177) finds the lexical borrowing of *se* into the creoles an inadequate explanation in light of the fact that the Surinamese creoles have completely different forms, i.e. Sranan *tak(i)* and Saramaccan *táa*, leading him to believe that the substrate influence on this construction lay in the grammar rather than the lexicon. Frajzyngier (1984) takes the opposite position, claiming that the origin of CE *se* is more likely to be English *say* since none of the French-based creoles has a lexically and syntactically parallel complementizer. Frajzyngier was apparently unaware of the parallel forms in the Dutch-based creoles; while a case might be made for Negerhollands *sē* being a borrowing from Virgin Islands CE, it could be derived from Dutch *zeggen* 'to say' via quite regular phonological rules. Den Besten (p.c.) points out that word-final Dutch /x/ was lost in the creole, so that *(ik) zeg* became Negerhollands *sē* (cf. D *weg* 'way' becoming Negerhollands *wē*, or Afrikaans *sê* 'say'). Moreover, there is no possibility of such lexical borrowing in the case of the Berbice CD complementizer *bi* from *bifi* 'say' (Robertson 1979: 147).

The evidence from creole French does not favor the lexical versus syntactic origin of *se* in CE as unambiguously as Frajzyngier assumes. The Haitian CF complementizer *si* is clearly from F *si* 'if,' as in "Je ne savais pas *si* votre père était mort" 'I didn't know *if* your father had died.' However, Haitian CF *si* is semantically more similar to CE *se*: "m pa te konnen *si* papa-ou te mouri" 'I didn't know *that* your father had died' (Valdman *et al.* 1981: 498). The semantic correspondence of Haitian CF *konnen si* to CE *know say* rather than F *savoir si* may be coincidental; while contact between CF and CE is intense on Commonwealth Antillean islands like St. Lucia and Dominica, the only known case for such contact with Haitian CF was the raiding for Jamaican slaves carried out by buccaneers from Haiti during the late seventeenth century (§9.5). Pringle (1985) notes that in Seychellois CF verbs like *tâde* 'hear' can take the complementizer *si*: "u pâkor tâde *si* i laba?" 'Haven't you heard yet *that* he is there?" (Corne 1977: 186). Moreover, verbs like *dir* 'say' and *uar* 'see' can take the complementizer *pur-dir* (cf. F *pour dire* 'to say'): "i al dir li *pur-dir* sa pa ê dimun" 'He goes to tell him *that* it's not a person' (Corne 1977). The latter suggests a calque; Sebba (1984a) notes a similar construction in the eastern Bantu languages likely to have influenced Seychellois CF.

Further evidence against the lexical borrowing of E *say* and for the influence of a substrate syntactic structure can be found in Guinea-Bissau CP. As noted above (§5.1.8), Kihm (forthcoming) found that this creole has three different complementizers corresponding to P *que* including *kuma* after verbs like 'say,' 'know,' 'tell' etc., e.g. "i fala *kuma* i na bin" 'He said that he would come' or "n sibi *kuma* bu kontra kel" 'I know that you met him.' While *kuma* has been derived etymologically from P *como* 'how,' it seems to have converged with the Mandinka verb *kuma* 'to speak, to talk.' CP *kuma* can also be used as a verb, e.g. "kolegas *kuma* pa n bin" 'My colleagues told me to come' (ibid.). Kihm further notes that tense/aspect marking restrictions on CP *kuma* exactly match those of Mandinka *kó* 'to tell,' which is used as a complementizer after verbs of saying, knowing, etc.

The case for substrate syntactic influence on serial 'say' in the Atlantic creoles seems quite convincing, but such influence by no means precludes converging influence from language universals or lexical diffusion. Evidence supporting universals can be found in Kihm's observation (forthcoming) that biblical Hebrew *lê'môr* 'saying that' corresponds directly to the CP construction with *kuma*. A case for diffusion might be seen in the "spake . . . saying" construction frequently encountered in translations of the Bible into English and Tok Pisin PE, e.g. "Em i tok *se*: Yupela kam . . ." 'He spoke saying: Come . . .' (Todd 1984: 203). Todd notes that Tok Pisin *se* and serial *i spik* belong to "mission-influenced speech . . . quite widely used by older speakers." It is also conceivable that these constructions were reinforced by German or British missionaries who had learned pidgin English in West Africa, which has the complementizer *sei* (ibid. 140). Sebba (1984a) finds support for the spread of *se* via lexical diffusion in the fact that its similarity in form to *say* makes it acceptable in varieties quite close to standard English, e.g. upper mesolectal Caribbean CE, Black London English (§10.5), and American Black English.

The syntactic status of CE *se* has been the subject of some debate. Bickerton (1981: 117) noted that Guyanese CE *se* was unlike complementizing *that* in English since *se* could not be deleted or fronted with its clause, leading him to conclude that it was not a complementizer but rather a serial verb. Boretzky, on the other hand, found some uses of *se* to be so far from any verbal function that he considered it "eine echte Konjunktion," a true [subordinating] conjunction, since – unlike a verb – it could not be fronted. Sebba (1984a) agrees that the Sranan complementizer *taki* has "the syntactic properties of a complementizer but none of the syntactic properties of a verb." The syntactic tests that demonstrate this are discussed by Sebba (1983: 305 ff.): (1) the complementizer *taki* cannot undergo predicate clefting (§5.2.4); (2) after verbs of saying, believing, seeing etc. *taki* is in complementary distribution with *dati* 'that,' an undisputed complementizer; (3)

either *taki* or *dati* can introduce a sentence-initial subject clause; (4) either one can introduce an S complement to a noun, e.g. "a bribi *taki* . . ." 'the belief that . . .' Of course the disparity between the findings of Bickerton and Sebba may lie in the fact that Sranan *taki* has evolved from a serial verb into a true complementizer under the influence of Dutch *dat* via Sranan *dati*, whereas Guyanese *se* has remained less influenced by English constructions with *that*.

Eilfort (1985) has raised an interesting theoretical question regarding the development of *se*. It has generally been assumed that African syntactic features first appeared in pidgins via native-language interference and that these structures were later nativized with the emergence of creoles. However, this would be unsatisfactory as an account of the development of *se* if it is true that pidgins have co-ordination (with or without conjunctions) rather than subordination with complementizers. This suggests several possibilities: (1) the observation that pidgins lack subordination is relevant only to early (restricted) pidgins, and *se* came into the various Atlantic creoles via extended pidgins with subordination; (2) *se* developed during creolization as the result of linguistic universals (although this kind of serialization is fairly rare among the world's languages according to Sebba [1984b]); (3) native speakers of substrate languages played a larger role in the formation of the creole than previously believed, i.e. Le Page and Tabouret-Keller (1985: 188) were right in inferring that pidgins did in fact "continue to exist alongside both the nascent creoles and the native languages of the pidgin speakers"; or (4) the distinction between pidgins and creoles is less clear-cut than has generally been assumed.

5.3.3 Serial 'pass' meaning 'than'

In a number of Atlantic creoles a verb meaning 'pass,' 'surpass,' or 'exceed' is used after adjectival verbs to indicate comparison:

Príncipe CP	"rimá mɛ mayʃ fɔrti *pasa* mi" 'My brother is stronger than I'
	(Valkhoff 1966: 102)
Lesser Antillean CF	"u grą *pase* mwę" 'You are taller than I'
	(Taylor 1951: 58)
Ndjuka CE	"a bigi *pasa* mi" 'He is taller than I'
	(Hancock 1979b: 12)
Gullah CE	"i tɒl *pas* mi" 'He is taller than I'
	(Turner 1949: 215)

Arends (1986) notes that an exact structural parallel is found in a serial-verb construction that is widespread in Kwa and other West African languages, e.g.

Ewe "so lolo *wu* tedzi," literally 'horse big exceed donkey,' i.e. 'the horse is bigger than the donkey.' As in the creoles, the first element of the serial verb is the adjectival verb (*lolo* 'be big') and the second is the verb meaning 'exceed' or 'surpass' (*wu*). Bantu languages like kiMbundu have a partly parallel construction: "iu *uatundu* una mu kuuaba," literally 'this exceeds that in beauty,' i.e. 'This one is more beautiful than that one.' This non-serial-verb construction is rare in creoles, but Arends provides an example in Sranan "a *moro* mi na koni" 'he exceeds me in cleverness,' i.e. 'he is cleverer than I am.'

Boretzky (1983: 104–107) suggests that creole constructions closest to the model 'big pass me' are probably the most conservative and are likely to be in the process of being replaced by structures more similar to those of the superstrates. The Principe CP structure "*mayf* forti pasa mi," literally 'more strong pass me,' contains the element *mayf* 'more' which is part of the corresponding superstrate structure (cf. P "*mais* forte que"). This alternates with another structure in which CP *pasa* is replaced by *di* (cf. P "mais *de* dez" 'more than ten'). Similarly, the CF construction with *pase* alone appears to be the oldest; it alternates with *pli . . . pase* and *pli . . . ki*, the last being closest to F "il est *plus* grand *que* moi."

Boretzky (1983: 105) observes that Saramaccan CE *passa* (cf. P *passar* 'pass') has merged semantically with *moro* (cf. E *more than* or archaic and regional *more nor* or *more na*). This seems likely to have occurred through the alternation of *passa* and *moro* in the comparative construction. Schuchardt (1914a: 108) noted that 'When eight months have passed' could be rendered in Saramaccan as either "teh aiti mune *passa*" or "teh aiti mune *moro*." Ndjuka has both *pasa* and *moo* in the comparative construction (Huttar p.c.) while Sranan has "a bigi *mɔrɔ* mi" (Hancock 1979b: 12). There is evidence that decreolizing forms like Gullah CE *mo'nuh* and Bahamian CE *more'n* may still function as single morphemes; Gullah *mo'nuh* alternated with *pass* in Gonzales (1924: 231): e.g. "Him strong *mo'nuh* you" (cf. *pas* above).

Whether or not Jamaican CE *muor an* once functioned as a verb, it is still used with adjectival verbs in exactly the same way as it is used with other verbs in the basilect, i.e. "Mieri *big muor an* Jan" is parallel to "Mieri *wok muor an* Jan" 'Mary works more than John' (Bailey 1966: 128). At this level of the continuum there is a good case for treating adjectives as a subcategory of stative verbs. As noted above (§5.2.4), they are fronted in predicate clefting and recopied in their original position, like verbs but unlike words in other syntactic categories. Valdman (1978: 245) notes the usefulness of this syntactic test for creole verbs. For example, Haitian CF *souèf* corresponds to the French noun *soif* 'thirst' but it can be only a verb since "Bouki *souèf*" 'Bouki is thirsty' can undergo predicate clefting to become "Sé *souèf* Bouki *souèf*" 'Bouki is really thirsty.' The verbal status of *souèf* is further verified by the fact that it can take preverbal markers such as anterior *te*: "Bouki *te* souèf" 'Bouki was thirsty.'

However, there are some valid reasons for assigning separate syntactic status to adjectives and verbs on leaving the basilect in a creole English continuum. Bailey (1966: 42) points out that only adjectives can take the mesolectal comparative ending -*a* (e.g. *biga* 'bigger') and occur before nouns; moreover, most verbs cannot follow *get* and none can follow the intensifiers *so* and *tuu*. Historically many creoles represent the continuing merger of two systems: one with strong African traits (the most conservative creoles and the basilects of continua) and the other with strong European traits (the acrolects). Whether adjectives are verbs, like many other questions in creole syntax, depends on which system predominates in the variety under discussion.

5.4   The noun phrase

The various elements that make up the noun phrase in the Atlantic creoles are so closely interrelated that none can be discussed meaningfully without reference to the others. Dealing with number, for example, requires reference to determiners and word order, and word order is a key element in indicating possession or natural gender. The following discussion has been divided up somewhat arbitrarily for the sake of convenience, however. Table 5, *Determiners in various creole languages and Yoruba*, provides an overview of several parts of this discussion, focusing on the definite article, demonstratives, and ways of indicating plurality.

5.4.1   *Determiners*

In the first two creoles examined in table 5, the definite article 'the' does not follow the word order of the superstrate language: while the article precedes the noun in Portuguese (*o* homem) and French (*l'*homme), as it does in English, it follows the noun in Príncipe CP (ómi *sé*) and Haitian CF (nõm *la*). The parallel to a number of relevant African languages such as Yoruba is especially clear when there is an intervening phrase or clause (indicated in parentheses below):

> Príncipe CP   "básta (di óru) sé," lit. 'can of gold *the*'
>
> > (Boretzky 1983: 97)
>
> Haitian CF   "istwa (wu rakõnté li) *a*," lit. 'story (you told it) *the*,' i.e. 'the story you told'
>
> > (ibid. 98)
>
> Yoruba   "owó (tí nwón fún mi) náà," lit. 'money (which they gave me) *the*'
>
> > (Rowlands 1969: 197)

Table 5. *Determiners in various creole languages and Yoruba*

	the man	*this* man	*these* men
Príncipe CP	ɔ́mi *sé*	ɔ́mi *ʃaki*	*inɛ* ɔ́mi sé
Haitian CF	nɔ̃m *la*	nɔ̃m *sa*-a	nɔ̃m sa-*yo*
Papiamentu CS	*e* hòmber	e hòmber *aki*	e hòmber-*nan* aki
Saramaccan CE	*di* ómi	di ómi *aki*	*déé* ómi aki
Sranan CE	*a* man	a man *disi*	*den* man disi
Jamaican CE	*di* man	*dis* man (*ya*)	*dem* man ya
Yoruba	ɔkùnrin *náà*	ɔkùnrin *yĭ*	*àwɔn* ɔkùnrin yĭ

Sources: Taylor 1977: 174; Günther 1973: 55; Rowlands 1969: 195–197.

In other words, it is not just that the definite articles come after the nouns to which they refer but rather that they mark the end of the entire noun phrase (note that Haitian CF *a* is an allomorph of *la*). Except for the decreolized varieties (e.g. Jamaican CE *di* 'the'), the creoles appear not to have borrowed definite articles from the superstrate languages but rather to have created them anew from demonstratives and other particles. Príncipe CP *sé* appears to come from P *êsse* 'that,' which is also the likely source (along with S *ese* idem) of Papiamentu CS *e* (note that the pronoun referring to "*e* hòmber *aki*" is "eʃaki" 'this one'). In Palenquero CS, Patiño indicates θ as the definite singular article but also notes the especially high frequency of *ese* 'that,' which sometimes has the short form *é* (Friedemann and Patiño 1983: 144, 146). Haitian CF *la* appears not to come from the French feminine definite article of the same form but rather *là* 'there,' which can add the idea of definiteness, e.g. F "cet homme-*là*" 'that man (there)' (Hull 1979: 202). However, there may have also been convergence with Ewe *la* 'the,' which not only has the same form but also occurs at the end of the noun phrase (Sylvain 1936: 60). While Sranan *a* and Saramaccan *di* are of uncertain origin, there are other creoles that have definite articles clearly derived from demonstratives, e.g. Cape Verde CP *kel* (Almada 1961: 89) and Malayo-Portuguese *akel* (cf. P *aquel* 'that [yonder]'). Hesseling considered the Afrikaans article *die* (corresponding to the Dutch demonstrative *die* 'that' rather than *de* 'the') to be a relexification of the Malayo-Portuguese article *akel* (Meijer and Muysken 1977: 36), but this may represent a universal. Singler (p.c.) notes the presumed frequent use of deixis during the early stages of pidginization, in which terms like 'that' and 'there' may have replaced more abstract notions of definiteness. Moreover, definite articles have evolved from demonstratives in a number of cases of language change, such as the transition from Latin to the Romance languages and from Proto-Germanic to German and English, and even from Polish to American Polish (Maher 1985: 122–123).

It should be noted that the use of articles in the creoles does not necessarily follow that of their lexical-source language. Bickerton (1981: 56) claims that "virtually all creoles have . . . a definite article for presupposed-specific NP; an indefinite article for asserted-specific NP; and zero for nonspecific NP." While the ambiguous status of Príncipe CP *sé* and Palenquero CS *ese* as definite articles rather than demonstratives casts some doubt on the first claim, and there is some disagreement about the status of the CE indefinite article in the second claim, the third claim seems valid: the creoles use a singular noun without an article to refer to the general category, unlike the lexical-source languages. This is found in Miskito Coast CE "θ rigl iz jos a shaat ting" 'A riddle is just a short thing' (Holm 1978: 241). A parallel is found in substrate languages like Yoruba "ewúrẹ̀ θ gọ̀ púpọ̀," literally 'goat is-stupid very,' i.e. 'a goat is very stupid' or 'goats are very stupid' (Rowlands 1969: 42). Regarding the CE indefinite article, Mufwene (1986c) claims that *wan* should be treated as a numeral, i.e. as 'one' rather than 'a.' However, this interpretation would not be suitable for cases like Miskito Coast CE "i tai im ananiit *wan* trii" 'He tied him under a tree' (Holm 1978: 277). Like *a* in English, CE *wan* asserts a specific instance of the category *tree*, which is not presupposed; its relevance is not to number, since a person could hardly be tied under more than one tree at once. Many substrate languages do not have any article in such a case, e.g. Yoruba "oun jóko ní abẹ́ igi θ," literally 'he sat under tree' (A. Oyedeji p.c.); *kan* 'a, one' would be added only for the unlikely emphasis that the person in question was sitting under *one* tree rather than more. Thus creole usage of the articles differs in some respects from both superstrate and substrate usage, but combines some aspects of each.

It can be seen in table 5 that to form the demonstrative ('*this* man'), a number of creoles add a word originally meaning 'here' to the noun and definite article (cf. P *aqui*, S *aquí*). Saramaccan uses *aki* after the noun while Sranan uses *disi* (cf. *this*). As in many other cases, Ndjuka alternates between two usages, each of which has a parallel in a neighboring creole: usually *a man ya* (parallel to Saramaccan) but sometimes *a man disi* (parallel to Sranan) (Huttar p.c.). Haitian CF *sa* appears to derive from F *ça* 'that ((one).' Valdman (1978: 366) notes that the combination of CF articles and demonstratives results in semantic nuances that can be conveyed in French only periphrastically, e.g. Haitian CF *chat-la* 'the (previously mentioned) cat' versus *chat-la-a* 'the cat (in question).' He cites this as evidence of the creoles' systematicity and complexity, which must be seen as quite independent of that of French.

5.4.2 Number

Unlike nouns in their European lexical-source languages, creole nouns are not inflected to indicate number, e.g. CE "aal di animal___" 'all the animals.' Although some creole words contain fossilized remnants of plural inflections from their lexical-source languages (e.g. CE "tuulz" 'tool' or CF "zanj" 'angel'), these no longer function as inflections (§3.5.1). However, in most of the Atlantic creoles nouns can co-occur with a free morpheme which indicates plurality and is homophonous with the third person plural pronoun 'they.' In table 5 the noun phrases in the last column (*these* men) include this morpheme, which is italicized. In this column the pluralizer co-occurs with the demonstrative, which can be omitted, e.g. Príncipe CP "*inɛ* ɔ́mi" 'the men' or Haitian CF "nõm *yo*" idem. The pluralizer is most frequently used with animate nouns, but this is not always the case, e.g. Nigerian PE "di nyám *dɛm*" 'the yams' (Rotimi and Faraclas forthcoming). The plural marker also conveys the idea of definiteness, as does the use of 'they' as a pluralizer in substrate languages like Yoruba, e.g. "àwǫn ǫkùnrin" 'the men.' This construction is so frequent in Kwa and other West African languages and so unusual among the world's languages that no serious argument has ever been put forward attributing the creole construction to the influence of language universals rather than substrate influence. Boretzky (1983:91) comments that "this means of forming the plural appears to be one of those undisputed cases in which West African influence is generally recognized." In some creoles, such as Sranan CE and Haitian CF, the plural marker also serves as a kind of plural definite article. Goodman (p.c.) points out that the Guyanais CF plural marker *ya* is historically derived from *ye* 'they' plus *a* 'the.' Van Name (1869–70: 153, 160) was the first to note this semantic property of the 'they' plural marker and how widespread it was among the creoles, including Negerhollands CD *sende*. Even certain sociolects of nonstandard Afrikaans use *hulle* 'they' to form the definite plural, as in "die skaap *hulle*" 'the sheep PLURAL' (Valkhoff 1966:226), although in standard Afrikaans *hulle* can be used only after nouns referring to persons to include associates, e.g. "Oom Sarel *hulle*" 'Uncle Charles and his people' (ibid.). While possible sources for this construction include Nama (Hottentot), Eastern Malay (via Malayo-Portuguese), and even Frisian (den Besten p.c.), it is also found in a number of West African languages, e.g. Yoruba "àwǫn Táiwò" meaning 'Taiwo and his family, schoolmates, or friends' depending on the situation (Rowlands 1969:196). This is paralleled in most Atlantic creoles, e.g. Miskito Coast CE "di sukya *dem*" 'the medicine man and his lot' (Holm 1978:240), and may be connected to nonstandard "Mary and them" with the same meaning. This use of the 'they' pluralizer is found in Lesser Antillean CF, e.g. "Mado *yo*" 'Mado and company,' but in this variety of CF the 'they' pluralizer is not used with other nouns, which are instead preceded by *se* (cf. F *ces* as in "*ces* hommes" 'these/those men') as in "*se* nõm-la" 'the men' (Taylor 1951: 52, 1977: 174).

There are also several other Atlantic creoles which have no 'they' pluralizer. One is Palenquero CS, which marks plurals with the free morpheme *ma* (cf. *ané* 'they'). Patiño notes that *ma* combines the semantic properties of definiteness and plurality, e.g. "*ma* ombre" 'the men' (Friedemann and Patiño 1983: 142, 156). Unlike 'they' pluralizers in other creoles, *ma* can co-occur with determiners to impart the meaning of plurality without necessarily that of definiteness, e.g. "*un ma* gasiosa," literally 'one PLURAL soda-pop,' i.e. 'some bottles of soda pop' (cf. S *unas* 'some'), or "*ese ma* palabra," literally 'that PLURAL word,' i.e. 'those words' (ibid. 143–144). De Granda (1978: 465) notes the similarity of the correspondence between Palenquero *ngombe* 'cow' and *ma ngombe* 'cattle' on the one hand, and Kongo *ngombe* idem and its plural *bangombe* on the other, concluding that the pluralizer *ma* was derived from the Bantu prefix. This interpretation is supported by Goodman (p.c.), who notes that while *ba* is the Bantu plural prefix for class II animate nouns, there is also a plural prefix *ma-* for class VI inanimate nouns.

In Berbice CD the plural marker *-apu* differs in form from *eni* 'they' (Robertson 1979: 74, 76). The pluralizer appears to come from the Eastern Ijo plural marker *-apu̧* for nouns that are [+ human] (Smith *et al.* 1987). Robertson (1979: 232) notes that "in the case of the noun pluralizer, some creolists, e.g. Valdman (1968) and DeCamp (1971[b]) regard the plural morpheme as a suffix." While *-apu* might be a suffix or a clitic in Berbice Dutch, the case for such an analysis is weaker in those creoles in which other elements can occur between the noun and the pluralizer, which marks the end of the noun phrase.

Cape Verde CP also lacks the 'they' pluralizer and, like Lesser Antillean CF *se*, uses pluralizers derived from plural determiners in the lexical-source languages, e.g. "*ũʃ* rapazî" '(some) boys' (cf. P "*uns* rapazinhos") or "*keʃ* rapazî" 'the boys' (cf. P *aqueles* 'those') (Almada 1961: 92). In Guinea-Bissau CP

> It is possible to form plural nouns with *-s*, e.g. ɔɔmi/ɔɔmis: 'man/men,' though usually no *-s* is used, cf. *duus* ɔɔmi: 'two men.' Creole speakers who have observed the Portuguese use of *-s* but who do not speak the language, endeavour to reproduce it when speaking formally, or when addressing a European; this leads to frequent and indiscriminate use of *-s*, with singular and plural forms being confused, while even verbs, and particles such as *awɔnti*: 'yesterday' may be heard with *-s*.
>
> (Wilson 1962: 12–13)

Such hypercorrection is found in other varieties as well, eg.. Liberian English "Hellos!" (Singler forthcoming b).

5.4.3 *Gender*

Like distinctions of number, distinctions of grammatical gender in the European lexical-source languages were not maintained by inflections on creole nouns or adjectives. For example, the gender agreement in the Spanish NP "un*a* cas*a* más bonit*a*" 'a prettier house' is not found in Palenquero CS "un__ kasa má bonit*o*" (Friedemann and Patiño 1983: 139), in which the article and adjective are derived from the masculine form in Spanish although S *casa* is feminine. Of course the very concept of grammatical gender is as irrelevant to the creole NP as it is to the English NP or the NP in most substrate languages. Although some Niger-Congo languages have noun class systems that distinguish animates from inanimates, most have nothing comparable to the system of grammatical gender in many European languages (Boretzky 1983: 85). Although Hausa does have two genders (belonging to the Chadic subgroup of the Hamito-Semitic family, rather than the Niger-Congo family), it seems less likely to have been a significant substrate language for the creoles than languages spoken nearer the coast.

Sometimes the creoles have preserved natural gender oppositions in specific nouns, but this seems to be on the level of the lexical item rather than inflection, e.g. Papiamentu CS *rei* 'king' (cf. S *rey*) versus *reina* 'queen' (S *reina*) (Mario Dijkhoff 1985). Sometimes a natural gender distinction is maintained through the juxtaposition of a noun indicating sex, e.g. Papiamentu *mucha homber* 'boy' (cf. S *muchacho* 'boy' and *hombre* 'man') versus *mucha muhe* 'girl' (cf. S *mujer* 'woman'); these appear to be calques on African idioms (§3.3.4). While most adjectives in the creoles based on European languages have been modeled on the masculine form, the feminine forms have sometimes been preserved with a distinction in meaning, e.g. Guyanais CF *gró* 'fat' (cf. F *gros* idem) versus *grós* 'pregnant' (cf. F *grosse*) (St. Jacques-Fauquenoy 1972b: 102).

Like their substrate languages, basilect varieties of the Atlantic creoles do not usually indicate gender distinctions in the third person singular pronoun (§5.4.5). However, Negerhollands CD appears to have distinguished between animate (*h*)*am* 'he, she' and inanimate *di* 'it' (Stolz 1986: 119).

5.4.4 *Possession*

Possession – and related ideas, such as association – can be expressed by a variety of structures in the Atlantic creoles as well as in their superstrate and substrate languages, several alternatives sometimes occurring within the same language.

While there is no uniformity in the creole patterns, they frequently reflect convergence and compromise between superstrate and substrate structures.

A widespread way of indicating possession is the simple juxtaposition of two nouns in the order [possessor + possessed]:

Saramaccan CE   "konu bo" 'the king's vow'

(Voorhoeve 1961: 148)

Miskito Coast CE "di uman biebi" 'the woman's baby'

(Holm 1978: 286)

US Black English "that girl shoe"

(Burling 1973: 50)

Negerhollands CD "meester kabaj" 'the master's horse'

(Hesseling 1905: 91)

Berbice CD   "mista bʊlin kuiara" 'Mr. Bullen's boat'

(Robertson 1979: 91)

The creoles with this structure are based on English and Dutch, Germanic languages that have a possessive construction similar in word order but with a genitive inflection, e.g. "Shakespeare's works" or "Vondels werken." A number of West African languages have a construction with this word order but – like the creoles – with no inflection, e.g. Mandinka "Báakari fáa" 'Bakari's father' (Rowlands 1959: 39), as well as such languages as Ewe, Ashanti, Gã, Ijo, Grebo, and Gurenne (Boretzky 1983: 92). Possessive adjectives like 'my' also precede the noun in these languages, as they do in the superstrate languages: E "*my* mother," D "*mijn* moeder," F "*ma* mère," S "*mi* madre," P "*minha* mãe." This is the order of the possessive adjective in creoles based on English (e.g. Sranan "*mi* mama") and Dutch (e.g. Negerhollands "*mi* mumã" and Berbice CD "*ɛkɛ* mama") as well as Papiamentu CS ("*mi* mama") and two varieties of New World creole French: Guyanais and Louisiana CF, both "*mo* mamã."

In addition to the genitive construction in English and Dutch, all of the superstrate languages can indicate possession with a prepositional construction of the type [possessed *of* (the) possessor]: E "the mother *of* John" (more usual with inanimate nouns), D "de moeder *van* Jan," F "la mère *de* Jean," S "la madre *de* Juan," P "a mãe *do* João." This is also found in the creoles, but the preposition can sometimes be omitted:

Guyanais CF   "ròb *di* mó mamã" or "ròb θ mamã-a" '(my) mother's dress'

(St. Jacques-Fauquenoy 1972b: 98)

Palenquero CS	"rrancho *di* tigre" 'Tiger's ranch'; "losa θ tigre" 'Tiger's clearing'
	(Friedemann and Patiño 1983:149–150)
Papiamentu CS	"historia *di* mi país" 'my country's history'
	(Goilo 1972)
Negerhollands CD	"die boek *va* Jan" 'John's book'
	(Van Name 1869–70:160)

A construction without a preposition but with similar word order [possessed + possessor] is found in a number of West African languages largely to the east of those mentioned above, e.g. the Kwa languages Yoruba, Ibo, and Bini and the Bantu language Duala (Boretzky 1983:92). An example of the Yoruba construction is "oko Aìná" 'Aina's farm' (Rowlands 1969:44). In these languages the possessive adjective also follows the noun, e.g. "oko *mi*" '*my* farm.' A number of Romance-based creoles have possessive adjectives in this position despite the word order of their lexical-source languages, e.g. Príncipe CP "myɛn *mé*" 'my wife' (Günther 1973:67), Palenquero CS "mamá *mí*" (Friedemann and Patiño 1983:147), Haitian CF "sè-*m*" 'my sister' (Valdman 1978:196). While substrate languages may have influenced this order, Goodman (1964:54) points out that it may also be "due to analogical extension that the pronominal possessive in Caribbean [French] Creole is postposed precisely as is the nominal, and is thus a linguistic innovation," or what Boretzky calls an "innerkreolische" development (1983:96). Apparently by analogy with F "c'est *à* moi" 'it's mine,' there is also another CF construction, e.g. Haitian "tab-*a*-ou" 'your table' in which the postposed possessive follows *a* (Goodman 1964:53); this may have constituted a transitional stage in the development of the postposed possessive without *a*.

Finally, there is a creole construction in which the possessive adjective occurs between two nouns in the order [possessor *his* possessed]:

Sranan CE	"konu ala *en* moni" 'all the king's money'
	(Hall 1948:107)
Krio CE	"mi dadi *im* buk" 'my father's book'
	(Alleyne 1980:13)
Mauritian CF	"mo frer *so* madam" 'my brother's wife'
	(Baker 1972:83)
Papiamentu CS	"mi tatá *su* buki" 'my father's book'
	(Alleyne 1980:13)
Indo-Portuguese	"Salvador-*su* cruz" 'the Savior's cross'
	(Dalgado 1900:37)

Afrikaans	"ma *se* hoed" 'mother's hat'
	(Valkhoff 1966: 227)
Negerhollands CD	"Jan *shi* boek" 'John's book'
	(Van Name 1869–70: 160)
Berbice CD	"Sami *fi* jɛrma" 'Sammy's wife'
	(Robertson 1979: 92)

The possibility of an English model for this construction seems remote. *His* (as well as *her* and *their*) was used after nouns (chiefly proper) instead of the genitive '*s* inflection from the fifteenth to the eighteenth century, particularly after persons' names ending in -*s*, e.g. "Purchas *his* Pilgrimage" (*Oxford English Dictionary*). Such a construction occurred only once in an extensive corpus of data on Miskito Coast CE: "di pepa staart tu bon Anansi *hiz* mout" 'The pepper started to burn Anansi's mouth' (Holm 1978: 286), and may have resulted from the speaker's attempt to produce an unfamiliar standard English construction. There is a parallel construction in colloquial Dutch: "vader *z'n* hoed" 'father's hat' (cf. *zijn* 'his') or "moeder *haar* hoed" 'mother's hat' (Valkhoff 1966: 227). The masculine form with *z'n* apparently developed into the Afrikaans possessive particle *se* (and Negerhollands CD *sji* or *shi*, and Berbice CD *fi*), which was extended to feminine nouns in standard Afrikaans and to pronouns in Griqua Afrikaans (§8.5.2), e.g. "ek *se* vriende" 'my friends' (ibid.). The fact that this possessive particle occurs in all varieties of overseas Dutch (Stolz 1986: 128) strongly suggests that it originated in the colloquial Dutch construction discussed above, although its presence in Afrikaans may have been reinforced by similar constructions in languages with which it was in contact. Den Besten (p.c.) notes that Nama (Hottentot) had a possessive particle *di* or *ti* (which could also be pronounced [si]) occurring between the possessor and the possessed. Valkhoff (1966: 196) believed that the spread of the *se* construction in Afrikaans was fostered by a parallel structure in Malayo-Portuguese, which was spoken in South Africa during the eighteenth century (§8.5). Hancock (1975) notes that the possessive particle is found throughout the Asian varieties of creole Portuguese, as well as in Bazaar Malay (§12.3.1) – but not standard Malay. A similar particle is also found in likely substrate languages of Indo-Portuguese, i.e. Marathi and Kannada (Holm 1987). This might conceivably account for its presence in the CF of Mauritius, where these and related Indian languages coexist with the creole (Baker 1972) and even Papiamentu via diffusion, although the relationship between Indo-Portuguese and the latter is tenuous at best and Holm (1987) may have overstated the case for the diffusion of this possessive particle. Stolz (1986: 129) notes that its distribution appears to coincide with the far-flung empire of the Dutch in the seventeenth century (§8.0) and attempts to trace its spread to that of the Dutch language (linking the departure of the Dutch from Mauritius in 1710 to the arrival of the French in 1715 via runaway slaves). While such a case might also be made for Sranan, the link with Krio (via Jamaican) becomes so weak that the hypothesis of diffusion as the sole explanation of the particle's distribution has to be abandoned.

The fact that this structure is found in so many different language families (Indo-European, Khoisan, Dravidian) points to its being a universal, as are the other possessive structures discussed above in all likelihood. The [possessor *his* possessed] construction is also found in Niger-Congo languages that may have reinforced its presence in the creoles through substrate influence. For example, Mandinka has not only the juxtaposition of nouns to express inalienable possession (e.g. "Báakari fáa" 'Bakari's father,' discussed above), but also the insertion of a form of *ala* 'his' to express other kinds of possession, e.g. "Báakari *la* búngo" 'Bakari's house" (Rowlands 1959: 39, Migeod 1911: 91). Twi has a parallel construction, i.e. "Ata *ne* na," literally 'Ata his mother' (Alleyne 1980: 140). A possessive particle is also found in Ewe, e.g. "alɛ̃ *fé* afɔ" 'sheep POSS foot' (Boretzky 1983: 95). In sum, the [possessor *his* possessed] construction has so many possible models in the languages of Europe, Asia, and Africa that its presence in the creoles must be attributed to the converging influence of superstrate, substrate, diffusion, and language universals.

While the above discussion covers the relationship of possession between two nouns and between a noun and a possessive adjective, there remains to be discussed the structure of possessive pronouns (e.g. *mine*) as opposed to possessive adjectives (e.g. *my*). There is some relationship between these structures, since in those varieties of CF in which the possessive adjective precedes the noun (e.g. "*mo* mamã" 'my mother') the possessive pronoun consists of the possessive adjective preceding a noun substitute, e.g. Guyanais CF *mo pa* and Louisiana CF *mo kẽ*, both 'mine' (Goodman 1964: 55–56). The first is apparently from F *ma part* 'my part'; although this does not represent any kind of pronominal structure in French, there is a parallel (possibly via substrate influence) in Liberian English "Where my part?," i.e. 'Where is mine?' (Singler p.c.). The particle *kẽ* is sometimes attributed to S *quien* or P *quem* 'who' (Goodman 1964: 56), although the semantic relation is unclear. It is conceivable that there was influence from a substrate structure like the Ibo relative pronoun *ǹkὲ*, which is similar in form and can be similar semantically and syntactically when indicating possession in the structure "úlò *ǹkὲ* ézὲ" 'house POSS king,' i.e. 'the king's house' (Boretzky 1983: 95). (As noted below, possessive pronouns can replace possessive adjectives for emphasis in both creole and African languages.) In those varieties of CF with a postposed possessive adjective, there is a corresponding structure for the possessive pronoun, e.g. Haitian CF *pa-m* 'mine,' with the northern dialectal variant *kin-a-m* (Goodman 1964: 55). In the Commonwealth Antilles the possessive pronoun is built on the French pronoun *ça* 'that (one)' (*sa-mwẽ* in Dominican and St. Lucian CF) or its full form *cela* (*sla-mwẽ* 'mine' in Trinidadian CF); in the French Antilles it is based on *ta*, of unknown origin, e.g. *ta-mwẽ* 'mine' in Martinican and Guadeloupean CF (ibid.).

In Louisiana and Guyanais CF the possessive pronoun can replace the possessive adjective for emphasis, e.g. "*mo pa* kaz" 'my own house' (ibid.). There is a parallel in Yoruba, in which a possessive adjective (e.g. *wọn* 'their') can be preceded by the preposition *ti* 'of, belonging to' to form a possessive pronoun ("*tiwọn*" 'theirs') which can then replace the possessive adjective for emphasis. For example, "oko wọn" 'their farm' becomes "oko *tiwọn*," literally 'farm theirs' i.e. '*their* farm' in the contrasting sentence "oko *tiwọn* kò tóbi tó *tiwa*" '*their* farm is not as big as *ours*' (Rowlands 1969: 47). The structure of the Yoruba possessive pronoun is parallel to that of Papiamentu CS (*di mi* 'mine'), São Tomé CP (*di mũ* idem), and Palenquero CS (*ri mi* idem) (Taylor 1977: 175, Friedemann and Patiño 1983: 149).

There appears to be a further parallel in the *fu mi* construction of the Surinamese creoles and *fi mi* in Caribbean CE, both 'mine.' The English model may have been "This is *for you*," which is nearly equivalent semantically to "This is *yours*." In Ndjuka this construction forms the possessive pronoun, e.g. "na *fu mi*" 'it's mine,' but it can also replace the possessive adjective, so that "*mi* osu" 'my house' becomes "a osu *fu mi*," literally 'the house of me' (Huttar p.c.). An alternative construction for the possessive pronoun is "*du* fu mi," literally 'that of me,' i.e. 'mine.' This can also modify a noun, but instead of following, it precedes it: "du fu mi pikin" 'my child' (or 'my child's') (ibid.). Caribbean CE has a similar construction which may have originally been emphatic, e.g. Miskito Coast CE "*fo-him* jab" 'his job' (Holm 1978: 286).

There is also a prepositional construction for the possessive pronoun in Negerhollands CD, e.g. "alle wat mie hab, bin *van jou*" 'all that I have is yours' (Hesseling 1905: 261). However, this is also Dutch: "het is *van jou*" 'it is yours.' Yet, unlike Dutch but like CE, Negerhollands can use this possessive pronoun as a possessive adjective, e.g. "*fa am* pat" 'her way' (Stolz 1986: 126). A prepositional construction is also found in Seychellois CF, e.g. "mô lakaz i vo plis ki *pur u*" 'my house is worth more than yours' (Corne 1977: 49). Again, the possessive pronoun can be used with a noun for emphasis: "u ser *pur u*" '*your* sister' (ibid.). Although the creole Dutch construction might be accounted for by reference to the superstrate, this could hardly explain the presence of this construction in creoles based on English and French, since *for you* and *pour vous* do not function as possessive pronouns in these languages. The likelihood that the model was African, such as the Yoruba construction with *ti* discussed above, seems greater, particularly since the creoles can use this possessive pronoun as an emphatic possessive adjective, unlike most European lexical-source languages.

5.4.5 *Pronouns*

The pronouns of the superstrate languages indicate number (except E *you* and the partially equivalent F *vous* and D *u*). Moreover, they frequently indicate case (*I*, *me*, *mine*) and sometimes gender (S *nosotros, nosotras* 'we'; *vosotros, vosotras* 'you [plural]'; *ellos, ellas* 'they') and degree of intimacy (P *tu* 'you [familiar]' versus *você* 'you [polite]'). Except for number, most of these distinctions are not made in the pronouns of basilectal creoles – or their substrate languages.

Bailey (1966: 22) and Valdman (1978: 205) posit parallel paradigms for personal pronouns in basilectal Jamaican CE and Lesser Antillean CF respectively. These do not make distinctions of gender or case, and also serve as possessive adjectives:

Number	Person	CE	CF
Singular	1	mi	mouen
	2	yu	ou
	3	im	i
Plural	1	wi	nou
	2	unu	zòt
	3	dem	yo

It should be noted that these paradigms do not include variant forms (e.g. third person singular CE *i* or CF *li*) that may depend on morphophonemic rules, regional dialects, or levels of the continuum. Nor are they valid for every variety of New World CE or CF, e.g. Guyanese CE includes a basilectal third person object form *am*, and in northern Haïti *zòt* means not only 'you (plural)' but also 'they' while in the rest of the country *nou* is used for both 'we' and 'you (plural)' (Valdman 1978: 205).

However, the above paradigms are suggestive of what the earliest CE and CF pronominal systems may have been like. There is certainly evidence of the radical morphological simplification that one might expect from the pidginization–creolization process. But this was not the only force involved: possible substrate languages such as Bambara and Susu also have a single set of personal pronouns, each of which serves as subject, object, and possessive (Boretzky 1983: 108). However, such a lack of morphological complexity is by no means rare among the world's languages, so this common characteristic of these creole and African languages is in itself no real proof of substrate influence. Such influence is less open to question when the features shared by creole and African languages are unusual and idiosyncratic. Among their pronouns one such feature can be found in the special use of the Príncipe CP third person singular *éli* (cf. P *ele* 'he') to connect sentences in a narration in the sense of 'and then.' Boretzky (1983:110) has uncovered a similar use of Ewe *éyè*, which is not only similar in form but also has the highly unusual combination of uses as 'he' and as a conjunction meaning 'and then.' Moreover, there is a parallel double function of Yoruba *òun* and Saramaccan CE *hén*, as both 'he' and 'and' (ibid. 111). A similar feature in unrelated languages of the world seems unlikely, and the existence of this feature on both sides of the Atlantic cannot be credibly attributed to coincidence rather than substrate influence.

There is, moreover, evidence that creolization does not necessarily lead to extreme morphological simplicity in pronominal systems. The Gulf of Guinea varieties of creole Portuguese have a more complex system of personal pronouns than the varieties of creole French and English discussed above. While this complexity does not coincide in all respects with that of the pronominal system of a Kwa language like Yoruba, it is certainly nearer to that than it is to the European complexity of the Portuguese pronouns (Schuchardt 1882a: 905–907, Günther 1973: 64–67, Boretzky 1983: 107–109). Although Príncipe CP plural pronouns have only one form, in the singular there is a distinction between (a) emphatic pronouns, which are used for a stressed subject or object, after a preposition, or in isolation; (b) unstressed subject pronouns that always precede verbs; (c) unstressed object pronouns that always follow verbs; (d) possessive pronouns:

	(Singular) person	Stressed	Unstressed subject	Unstressed object	Possessive
Príncipe CP	1	amí/mí/nã̂	n	mi/m/~	mɛ́
	2	así/sí	si	si	té
	3	éli	e	ɛ́/li	sé
Yoruba	1	èmi	mo/ng	mi	mi
	2	ìwọ	o	ọ	rẹ
	3	òun	ó	*	rẹ̀

* Yoruba unstressed object pronouns are discussed below.

The similarity of the two systems lies in the very categories of pronouns that they have as opposed to those of Portuguese, Príncipe CP's superstrate. First, Portuguese has no unstressed subject pronouns. Because of the distinctive inflections of the verb for each person, the unstressed subject pronoun is unnecessary and simply omitted, e.g. "ensinou-me tudo" '(he) taught me everything' (Cunha 1982: 296). It is not possible to omit the subject pronoun in Príncipe CP or Yoruba since neither has inflected verbs. The use of the subject pronoun in Portuguese implies emphasis: "*ele* ensinou-me tudo (não ela)" '*he* taught me everything (she didn't).' The emphasis of an object pronoun requires an additional prepositional phrase: "*a mim* ensinou-me tudo" 'he taught *me* everything (you he ignored).' The emphatic *a mim* construction is clearly the source of the Príncipe CP stressed forms such as *amí*, although there may have been some convergence with partially similar forms in Yoruba, Fante, Efik, Twi, and certain Bantu languages (Schuchardt 1882a: 906). Yet there are also differences between the Príncipe CP and Yoruba systems: Yoruba prepositions can be followed by the unstressed object pronoun as well as the stressed pronoun, and while the third person object can be the stressed pronoun, the unstressed pronoun is simply an extension of the vowel of the preceding verb, e.g. "mo ri *i*" 'I saw it,' or "mo ra *a*" 'I bought it' (Ogunbọwale 1970: 70). Still, the differences between the Príncipe CP and Yoruba pronominal systems are minor in comparison to the differences between the systems of the creole and Portuguese.

The above system is found throughout the Gulf of Guinea creoles, and the pronominal systems of the other Iberian-based creoles have some points in common with it (Taylor 1977: 172). In the Guinea-Bissau CP pronominal system, discussed in some detail by Kihm (forthcoming), there are similar categories, but those corresponding to the stressed pronouns of the Gulf of Guinea creoles are used only after prepositions. In the Papiamentu of Curaçao there are two pronouns etymologically derived from emphatic forms (*ami* 'I,' *abo* 'you') in addition to forms without initial *a-*; the Papiamentu of Aruba also retains emphatic-derived forms throughout the plural, i.e. *anos* 'we,' *aboso* 'you,' *anan* 'they' (Mario Dijkhoff 1985). Papiamentu has a distinct possessive form in the third person singular (*sù* versus subject pronoun *e*), as does Palenquero CS in the second person singular (*si* versus subject *bo*). Palenquero also distinguishes between the subject and object of the first person singular (*i* and *mí*, respectively) and sometimes in the third person singular (*ele* and *lo*) and plural (*ané* and *lo*) (Friedemann and Patiño 1983: 156).

In Berbice CD the third person singular pronoun forms retain some of the stressed versus unstressed distinctions in Eastern Ijo (Robertson 1986). Stressed *ori* 'he' has been retained for all genders as subject, object, and possessive with some "residual use ... for clarification emphasis," while unstressed *a* (with the allomorphs *ɔ* and *ə*) is used in the subject position only. It should be noted that Eastern Ijo distinguishes between 'he' (stressed *ori*, unstressed *o*) and 'she' (stressed *ara*, unstressed *a*), but this distinction has not been retained in Berbice CD.

In many of the Atlantic creoles the second person plural pronoun has a non-European form that seems likely to be of African origin. This form is *unu* in the conservative English creoles, with the variants *un* in Saramaccan, *u* in Ndjuka, *una* in Krio, *wʊnə* in Barbados, *hənə* in Gullah, and *yinə* in the Bahamas (Hancock 1987). This may be related to Haitian CF *nu* or *n*, which is used for both 'we' (cf. F *nous* idem) and 'you [plural]' (cf. Common Bantu **nu* idem and other possible African sources discussed below). Equally confusing, both Ndjuka and Sranan CE have *unu* (with the variants *un*, *u*) for both the first and second persons plural. Possibly related forms are found in the pronouns for 'you [plural]' in Palenquero CS (*enú*), São Tomé CP (*inãse*) and Negerhollands CD *yina* – although the last could come solely from West Flemish *gijnder* /yinder/ (den Besten p.c.). The first group – and possibly the second – seem to have resulted from the converging influence of similar forms for 'you [plural]' in a number of Niger-Congo languages; in addition to Common Bantu **nu* mentioned above, these include Ibo *unu*, Yoruba *nyín*, Wolof *yena*, Kongo *yeno*, and Mbundu *yenu* (Cassidy and Le Page 1980; Holm with Shilling 1982). In decreolizing varieties of CE, the distinction between singular and plural 'you' is largely maintained by replacing the *unu* form with *you-all* /yɔ(l)/, perhaps a calque on Twi *mó nyina* idem, literally 'you all' (Herskovits 1941:288). Related forms include *all you* in the Eastern Caribbean (Hancock 1987) and possibly Berbice CD *jɛndɛalma*, literally 'you all,' with the corresponding forms *enfialma* 'we' and *enialma* 'they' (Robertson 1979:76).

While the CE second person plural pronouns maintain a distinction of number lost in standard English, another creole pronoun is unusual in that it is marked for neither number nor person: São Tomé CP *a* occurs as a subject before verbs and means approximately 'someone.' A pronoun with the same form and meaning is found in Bini, a Kwa language that has influenced other areas of the creole's lexicon (Ivens Ferraz 1979:66).

Finally, a number of Atlantic creoles can convey the idea of reflexive pronouns by using a word for 'body' plus the possessive to mean 'self':

São Tomé CP	"Ê scá flá cu *ubué d'ê*," literally 'He is talking with body his,' i.e. '... to himself'
	(Schuchardt 1882a:894)
Papiamentu CS	"su curpa," lit. 'his body,' i.e. 'himself'
	(Van Name 1869–70:155)
Lesser Antillean CF	"ou ké tué *co ou*," lit. 'you FUTURE kill body your,' i.e. 'you're going to kill yourself'
	(Chaudenson 1974:733)
Nigerian PE	"ìm kɔ́m spɔ́yl *im bɔ̀di*" 'he spoiled himself'
	(Rotimi and Faraclas forthcoming)

Sylvain (1936:65) noted the Old French use of *son cors* (literally 'his body') as 'himself,' but she doubted whether it could have influenced the creoles since it had died out by the end of the fourteenth century, although Stein (1984: 46) claims it was used in written French until the seventeenth century. Hall (1966: 74) suggested that it survived in regional dialects, which Chaudenson (1974: 734) documented. Still, the presence of this idiom in creoles of other lexical bases suggests that Sylvain was right to seek an African source. Yoruba *ara* 'body' is also used as 'self' (Holm with Shilling 1982: 5), and Akan *hõ* and Gurenne *inga* each have both meanings (Boretzky 1983: 143). However, the idiom is also present in Asian creoles such as Papia Kristang CP "eu lavá *corpo*" 'I wash myself' (Coelho 1880–86: 177), suggesting that it either spread by diffusion or arose independently through the influence of other substrates that also had the idiom, which may reflect a linguistic universal. Even English uses "any*body*" in the sense of 'any person.' Another widespread feature found in unrelated languages is synecdoche, the use of a part as a symbol of the whole, as in "$10 per head" meaning '$10 per person.' In fact, the word for 'head' is also used as a quasi-reflexive pronoun in some creoles, e.g. Haitian CF "li tuyé *tèt*-li" (Sylvain 1936: 66) and Cape Verde CP "ɛl máta *kabésa*" (Meintel 1975: 232), both 'he killed himself.' Certain CE idioms also reflect this meaning, e.g. "worry your head" (Holm with Shilling 1982). Wolof, a possible substrate language, uses the same word, *bob*, to mean both 'head' and 'self' (Sylvain 1936: 66). Synecdoche is also connected to the use of the word for 'skin' to mean both 'body' and 'self' in such expressions as "bathe your skin" in Caribbean English, or "sove *po*-ou" in Haitian CF, literally 'save skin your,' i.e. 'save yourself.' Usage in Black English may have led to the phrase "save your skin" (or "save your hide") in more general English. The presence of this idiom in Dutch ("je huid redden") and German ("deine Haut retten") might be evidence for it being an Indo-European idiom – or for cowboy movies being a more important vehicle of lexical diffusion than hitherto recognized (den Besten p.c., Boretzky p.c.). Finally, synecdoche may have led to a similar use of the word for 'buttocks.' Achebe (1969: 134) noted of an Ibo speaker that "Many people laughed at his dialect and the way he used words strangely. Instead of saying 'myself' he always said 'my buttocks.' " Haitian CF *bunda* can have both meanings (W. Stewart p.c.), as can Bahamian CE *ass* as in "watch your ass" (i.e. 'watch yourself; be careful') or "carry your ass" ('get out') or even the emphatic "my ass got stuck with it" (i.e. 'I got stuck with it myself'), sometimes made more *salonfähig* as "my hip" (Holm with Shilling 1982: 5).

5.5 Other function words

Various kinds of function words have been discussed so far in connection with particular areas of grammar, e.g. preverbal tense and aspect markers, copulas, and negators in connection with the verb phrase, and determiners and pronouns in connection with the noun phrase. While a complete survey of the syntax of all the Atlantic creoles is beyond the scope of this chapter, there are several other function words of a more miscellaneous nature which should also be discussed since they reveal syntactic similarities among the creoles across lexical boundaries.

5.5.1   *Conjunctions*
The foregoing included discussion of a subordinating conjunction homophonous with the word for 'say' (§5.3.2) and a co-ordinating conjunction homophonous with the word for 'he' (§5.4.5). In a number of Atlantic creoles there is also a co-ordinating conjunction that joins two noun phrases which is homophonous with the preposition 'with':

Príncipe CP	"swá tetúga *ki* kõpwέ" 'the story of the turtle *and* (lit. "with") the godfather'
	(Günther 1973: 119)
Papiamentu CS	"papa *ku* mama a bay baila" 'father *and* (lit. "with") mother went to a dance'
	(Richardson 1977: 56)
Haitian CF	"papa-m *ak* mama-m te vini" 'my father *and* (lit. "with") my mother came'
	(Sylvain 1936: 156)
Negerhollands CD	"di a ha ēn mēnši *mi* ēn juṅ man" 'once there was a girl *and* (lit. "with") a young man'
	(de Josselin de Jong 1926: 47)
Sranan CE	"mi weifi *nanga* mi pikin ε siki ɔgri ɔgri" 'my wife *and* (lit. "with") my child are very sick'
	(Herskovits and Herskovits 1936: 150)
Miskito Coast CE	"di kaptin *wi* evibadi waz der" 'the captain *and* (lit. "with") everybody was there'
	(Holm 1978: 291)

The usage in CF was traced by Sylvain (1936: 164) to an African parallel. She noted that Haitian CF *ak* 'with; and' (cf. F *avec* 'with') was identical in form and function to Wolof *ak*. Goodman (1964: 94–95) found further functional parallels in Ewe *kple*, Fulani *be*, and Hausa *da*, and noted a remark by Homburger (1949: 116) that "In the majority of Negro African languages the conjunction 'and' and the preposition 'with' are rendered by the same particle (when 'and' joins nouns)." Boretzky (1983: 216) notes that a number of African languages (Yoruba, Ewe, Ashanti, Ibo, and Bambara) use one word to join *parts* of a sentence (corresponding to both 'with' and 'and') and a distinct word or θ to join *entire sentences* (corresponding to 'and then'). The latter would seem to correspond to Haitian CF *épi* (cf. F *et puis* 'and then'): "Pòl acheté poul-la *épi* Mari kouit li" 'Paul bought the chicken *and Mary* cooked it' (Valdman 1978: 266). On the other hand, Haitian *ak* 'with, and' appears to join sentence parts like nouns (as above) or verbs, e.g. "yo montré nou lavé *ak* pasé" 'They taught us to wash and iron' (ibid. 267). However, usage varies in the French Antilles and French Guiana, where greater contact with French may have led to a blurring of the distinction between CF *ak* for sentence parts and *épi* for entire sentences, since no such distinction is found in French, which has the single conjunction *et* 'and' for both. Goodman (1964: 94, p.c.) notes that there *épi* can function as *ak* and vice versa, e.g. "had nom la te muye *avek* i šeše asu-i" 'the man's clothes were wet *and* they dried on him.'

In Papiamentu CS *ku* (cf. S *con* or P *com* 'with') can join both nouns and verbs, e.g. "e muhé ta kanta *ku* baila" 'the woman sings and dances.' While *ku* could be replaced by *i* (cf. S *y* or P *e* 'and'), *i* would suggest a looser association than *ku*. For example, the above sentence with *ku* implies that the singing and dancing go together (as in an act), whereas *i* could imply that the woman sings on some occasions and dances on others (Richardson 1977).

5.5.2 *Prepositions*

One of the most original contributions of Boretzky (1983: 194–205) is his comparative study of prepositions in creole and African languages. Although this area of syntax had long been all but ignored by creolists, the debate between Bickerton (1980, 1981) and Washabaugh (1980) regarding the status of CE *fu* or *fi* as a preposition or verb (§5.1.8) has led to a growing number of studies in this area (e.g. Byrne 1985, Muysken 1985). The status of the second element of serial verb constructions (e.g. 'give' meaning 'to' or 'for,' §5.3.1) as a verb or preposition is still a matter of some debate. However, in those creoles most influenced by their superstrates there appears to be some evidence for evolution from verbal to prepositional status, so to some extent the answer may depend on the variety in question.

As mentioned above (§3.4.1), a number of the Atlantic creoles have a general locative preposition *na* (with related forms *ina, nã, da, a*). This can be translated as 'in, at, to,' etc. depending on context, a semantic range quite similar to that of Ibo *na* (Taylor 1971). However, Boretzky (1983: 194) has observed that its meaning is closely tied to that of accompanying verbs, some of which can give *na* the meaning of 'from':

> Príncipe CP "e šyê *na* umátu" 'he went-out of the forest'
>
> (Günther 1973: 118)

Sranan CE   "m ben-kmop *a* pranasi" 'I had come from the plantation'

(Voorhoeve 1962: 57)

Haitian CF   "paske li te-sɔti *nã* ras ak nã-fãmi David" 'because he came from the race and family of David'

(Hall *et al.* 1953: 220)

In other words, the accompanying verb specifies the meaning of *na* as 'location' or 'motion toward' or 'motion from.' While this might be seen as simply a problem of translation, it should be borne in mind that none of the possible European etyma of *na* such as P *na* 'in the (feminine)', F *dans* 'in' or D *naar* 'to' (earlier *na* 'near') has this semantic range, and one is hard put to think of any European preposition which does. However, there are parallel constructions in West African languages in which the meaning of a general locative preposition is specified as 'from' or 'out of' by a verb meaning 'exit from' or 'come out of,' e.g. Yoruba "ó jádé *nínú* ilé,' literally 'he came-out LOC house,' i.e. 'he came out of the house' (Rowlands 1969: 141) or Fante "o-fir ha *mu*," 'he came-out bush LOC,' i.e. 'he came out of the bush' (Boretzky p.c.). Of course such substrate influence by no means excludes converging influence from the superstrate prepositions discussed above.

Unlike its European etyma, creole *na* and its equivalents can often be omitted after verbs of motion, especially when used with the names of specific places:

Príncipe CP   "e vɔtá θ cyô" 'he returned (to) field'
(Günther 1973: 112)

Papiamentu CS   "bai θ skol" 'go (to) school'
(Boretzky 1983: 197)

Haitian CF   "mãmã-m al θ lavil" 'my mother went (to) town'
(Hall *et al.* 1953: 75)

Miskito Coast CE   "i gaan θ Manawa" 'he went (to) Managua'
(Holm 1978: 293)

Berbice CD   "ɛkɛ mua θ kiriki" 'I'm going (to) church'
(Robertson 1979: 157)

This follows usage in such African languages as Mandinka: "Names of countries, towns, etc . . . generally follow verbs indicating movement towards or away from a place, or rest at a place, in which case they are used without postposition" (Rowlands 1959: 117). Similarly, Welmers notes that "in Niger-Congo languages generally, it must be emphasized that such verbs have meanings like 'go to,' 'be from,' 'arrive at,' and the like, and nothing like a preposition is used with them" (1973: 454).

Welmers (1973: 453) also discusses the hypothesis that certain prepositions such as "Igbo /ná ~ nà ~ n'/ and the Yoruba /ní ~ n' ~ l'/, both referring to location in a general way, are verbal in the underlying structure, ultimately derivable from verbs meaning 'be located at.'" While both appear to constitute true prepositions in the present structure of each language, each is practically unique in this role and is used with nouns to form the ideas corresponding to many European prepositions, much as English *in the middle of* is composed of prepositions and a noun to render a more precise idea of location. For example, in Yoruba the preposition *ní* (with its allomorphs *n'* and *l'*) combines with *iwájú* 'face' to form *níwájú* 'in front of,' and with *abé* 'lower part, under side' to form *lábé* 'under,' and with *órí* 'head, top' to form *lórí* 'on, on top of' (Ogunbọwale 1970: 89–90; Abraham 1962).

Many of the most conservative creoles form phrasal prepositions in a similar manner. For example, 'under' is expressed by the general locative *na* plus a noun meaning 'under side' in Príncipe CP *na ubásu*, Sranan CE *na ɔndro*, Saramaccan CE *na basu*, and Negerhollands CD *a mole* (Boretzky 1983: 194–205). In Yoruba these phrasal prepositions act like nouns followed by possessives, e.g. "ẹiyẹ náà wà *lórí igi*," literally 'bird the is-located on-head/top of-tree,' i.e. 'the bird is on the tree' (Ogunbọwale 1970: 89). The following noun is clearly a possessive (for which the position after the thing possessed is normal in Yoruba; cf. "oko *Aìná*" 'Aina's farm,' §5.4.4) rather than an object, since it is replaced not by an object pronoun but by a possessive adjective, e.g. "lórí *rè*," literally 'on-top his,' i.e. 'on him.' This corresponds to usage in some creoles, such as Sranan "luk wan sani *na mi tapu*" 'look, something is on me' (Herskovits and Herskovits 1936: 162). Other examples of creoles using possessives rather than object pronour s with phrasal prepositions include the following:

Príncipe CP	"ubásu *sé*" 'under him'	
		(Günther 1973: 80)
Papiamentu CS	"*mi* dilanti" 'in front of me'	
		(Goilo 1972)
Saramaccan CE	"a dé a *mi* fesi" 'he is in front of me'	
		(Boretzky 1983: 199)
Haitian CF	"li rete kote-*li* tut lãnwit" 'he stayed by his side the whole night'	
		(d'Ans 1968: 139)

In general, the French-based creoles do not follow the above patterns; it could be argued that Haitian CF *kote-li* is derived from F *à côté de lui*. Moreover, all the creoles have a number of non-phrasal prepositions that can be directly derived from etyma in their lexical-source languages. However, there is convincing evidence that some creoles developed phrasal prepositions under the influence of parallel structures in substrate languages such as Yoruba, Ewe, Akan-Fante, Ibo, and Mandinka (Boretzky 1983: 201–204). It must be asked how else the phrasal prepositions could have developed in the creoles if, as claimed by Bickerton (1981, 1984), their substrates had no significant influence on their syntax. As Boretzky points out (1983: 204), European prepositions were readily available for borrowing into the creoles since they were easily isolated units corresponding to a fairly clear meaning (however idiosyncratic at times) and required no complicated syntactic analysis. The fact that more complex phrasal prepositions were favored over them in a number of cases points squarely to substrate influence.

While most of the Atlantic creoles have *pre*positions, Berbice CD has *post*positions occurring after the noun, e.g. "war *ben*" '*in* the house,' "wari *ɔndrə*" '*under* the house,' etc. (Robertson 1986). This creole has an unusually close relationship to one particular African language, Eastern Ijo (§8.2), which as an SOV language has postpositions in the form of locative suffixes. Berbice CD has retained this structure although it is an SVO language, e.g. "ɛk mua mu kop brɔt šap aŋga," literally 'I go-PROG go buy bread shop in,' i.e. 'I'm going to go buy bread in the shop' (Robertson 1986). This fact undermines Bickerton's thesis that creoles develop (rather than borrow) syntactic structures that fit their overall system: "Languages, even creoles, are systems, systems have structure, and things incompatible with that structure cannot be borrowed; SVO languages cannot borrow a set of postpositions, to take an extreme and obvious case" (1981: 50).

5.5.3   *Sentence-final -o*

A number of Atlantic creoles have a particle /o/ which usually occurs at the end of a sentence to mark increased emotion or several other meanings discussed below:

São Tomé CP	"bõ jáá-*o*" 'good day!'
	(Valkhoff 1966: 135)
Príncipe CP	"n fá fa *ó*" 'I didn't say that'
	(Günther 1973: 92)
Saramaccan CE	"mi ko *o*" 'I've come' (response of an expected visitor to a greeting)
	(Rountree and Glock 1982: 11)
Cameroonian CE	"Na palava dis *o*!" 'There'll be trouble over this!"
	(Todd 1984: 122)

Liberian CE   "a ná seti gE *o*" 'I am *not* a city girl'

                                                          (Singler 1984: 283)

Haitian CF   "moun-sa-a menm, *o!*" 'Pour ce qui est de cette
                       personne!'

                                                          (Valdman 1978: 253)

                       '*That*'s the guy!'

                                                          (H. Gaujean p.c.)

Lesser Antillean CF   "mwẽ ka viní-*o!*" 'I'm coming!'

                                            (Valkhoff 1966: 135, citing D. Taylor)

Singler (1984, 1985) characterizes *o* in Liberian English as signalling personal involvement, so that a greeting with this tag is warmer and more heart-felt. Rotimi and Faraclas (forthcoming) describe the Nigerian PE equivalent as having a "friendly, brotherly or sisterly connotation." Moreover, *-o* can imply that what has been said is of special interest and current relevance. For this reason, *-o* is used when correcting someone's mistaken assumption, as in the Príncipe CP and Liberian CE examples above.

Sentence-final *-o* is used similarly in a number of West African languages. For example, in Yoruba "mo rí i *o*" means 'I *did* see him (although you seem to think I didn't)' (Singler 1985). In Wobe, *o* added to a greeting implies that all is well between the speaker and hearer(s). Singler (1984: 289) notes that "Klao speakers say that those who would omit the *o* in leave-taking formulae . . . are either brusque to the point of rudeness or non-native speakers." Singler (1985) notes the presence of this *o* in other Kru languages besides Klao and Wobe (e.g. Bassa and Kroumen), Kwa languages (Nkonya, Twi, Yoruba), Mande languages (Mende, Kpelle, Mano), as well as in Kisi (West Atlantic) and Efik (Benue-Congo?). Beyond the Atlantic creoles mentioned above, it is also found in Krio CE, Ndjuka CE, Fernandino CE, West African PF, Seychellois CF, and Sango. Singler concludes that in Liberian English it is "an areal, hence substratal, phenomenon" (1984: 283).

5.6 Word order

As noted above (§5.0), the most frequent word order in both superstrate and substrate languages is SVO, which is also the normal order in all of the Atlantic creoles. However, SOV order is found in some Niger-Congo languages (§5.0) and can occur in some of the relevant Indo-European languages as well. In Romance languages object pronouns normally precede the verb (e.g. S "(yo) *te* hablo" 'I'm speaking to you') but they always follow the verb in Romance-based creoles (e.g. Palenquero CS "i ta ablá *bo*" idem; Bickerton and Escalante 1970: 260). However, in Spanish and Portuguese, object pronouns follow infinitives as clitics (e.g. S "quiero *verte*" 'I want to see you'). It has been suggested that Iberian colonists addressing Africans and others may have spoken exclusively in infinitives, much as modern Spanish speakers sometimes do in addressing foreigners. Whether or not this was the case, it probably bears little relation to the use of postverbal object pronouns in the creoles; those based on French certainly did not get their word order from the exclusive use of infinitives in French, since in that language object pronouns precede infinitives (e.g. 'je veux *te* voir').

Like German, Dutch has SOV in dependent clauses; although SVO is found in independent clauses with one verb, the fact that the main verb occurs at the end of the clause whenever an auxiliary is used is taken as evidence of an underlying SOV order (den Besten p.c.). Negerhollands CD, however, always follows the SVO pattern of the other Atlantic creoles, as does Berbice CD. Afrikaans is like Dutch in that past participles occur at the end of the clause in perfect tense constructions, e.g. "ek *het* die boek *gelees*," literally 'I have the book read' (cf. D "ik heb het boek gelezen" idem) (R. Lass p.c.). This is further evidence that Afrikaans is not an Atlantic creole. Similarly, the occurrence of clause-final verbs in Indo-Portuguese reflects the SOV order of its substrate Indian languages (Schuchardt 1883a: 17) and is further evidence that Indo-Portuguese is not an Atlantic creole.

In the Atlantic creoles prominence can be given to the object and other elements normally occurring after the verb by fronting them, e.g. Miskito Coast CE "an kwéschon dem di yúustu gi wi" 'And they used to ask us *questions*' (Holm 1978: 242). Such topicalization is also usual in relevant African languages such as Yoruba. As noted above (§5.2.4), the object *aṣọ* in "mo rà aṣọ" 'I bought cloth' can be fronted and followed by the highlighter *ni* to give it prominence: "aṣọ ni mo rà" 'It was cloth I bought.' Similarly, the Atlantic creoles often use a highlighter with fronted sentence elements, although the creole highlighter precedes such elements. For example, the Jamaican CE sentence "wi a taak bout Jan" can become "*a Jan* wi a taak bout" 'It's John we're talking about' (Bailey 1966: 86–89). In addition to fronting verbs, which are then recopied in their original position (§5.2.4), the creoles front question words (like their superstrate and substrate languages) and often highlight them (unlike their superstrate but like some substrate languages). For example, Jamaican CE "Boti lef ya *den*" can become "*a-wen* Boti lef ya?" 'When did Bertie leave here?' (Bailey 1966).

As in the last example, there is nothing like *do* support in the English-based creoles; the negator simply precedes the verb ("im *no* wier shuuz" 'He doesn't wear shoes') and there is no inversion of the subject and the auxiliary (or verb) to form questions ("im wier shuuz?" 'Does he wear shoes?'). Intonation alone can distinguish questions from statements in the creoles, but there are also question markers for emphasis, as in substrate languages like Yoruba, e.g. "iṣu pọ̀ lónì *bí*," literally 'yams are-plentiful today QUESTION' (Rowlands 1969: 37). Creole question markers are often indistinguishable from question tags in the superstrate language, but in the English creoles they have no syntactic relation with the main verb as in English, e.g. Miskito Coast CE "das waz a swiit stuori, *duonit*?" 'That was a nice story, wasn't it?' (Holm 1978: 244). In Príncipe CP this particle is *â*: "ci té sɛgɛdu *â*?," literally 'you keep secret QUESTION,' i.e. 'Can you keep a secret?' (Günther 1973: 93). To form a question that would have the question word *what?* in English, Príncipe begins the sentence with the word for 'thing' and ends it with the question particle, e.g. "*kwá* ci mesé *â*?," literally 'thing you want QUESTION,' i.e. 'What do you want?' (ibid.). Because of this and similar structures, creole question words often take the form 'person?' ('who?'), 'time?' ('when?'), etc. (§3.3.4).

The creoles also have sentence-initial question markers, parallel to Yoruba "*ǹjẹ́* iṣu pọ̀ lónī," literally 'QUESTION: yams are-plentiful today' (Rowlands 1969: 37). In the French creoles the question marker *èské* is clearly from F "Est-ce que . . .?," e.g. Haitian "*èské* I ap chaché kostim-yo?" 'Is he looking for their suits?' (Valdman 1978: 254). Haitian CF also has the decidedly un-French negative question marker *apa*: "*apa* ou kontan?" 'Aren't you happy?' (ibid.). In the English-based creoles the negative question marker is often derived from *ain't*, which frequently begins questions in non-standard English, e.g. Gullah "*ɛnti* rɛbəl tɔɪm kʌmɪn bak?" 'Ain't slavery coming back?' (Turner 1949: 262), or Liberian "*ɛ̃* your grandma can speak Bassa?" (Singler p.c.).

To summarize, while the creoles' lexical-source languages often require the inversion of the subject and the verb (or auxiliary) to transform a statement into a question, this is not a part of creole syntax:

Príncipe CP	"kwaitu e sa kuʃtá â?," lit. 'how-much it ASP cost QUESTION,' i.e. 'How much does it cost?'
	(Günther 1973: 94)
	cf. P "Quanto custa isso?" (QW V S)
Palenquero CS	"bo ase kume kane?," lit. 'you ASP eat meat?,' i.e. 'Do you eat meat?'
	(Bickerton and Escalante 1970: 258)
	cf. S. "¿Come Vd. carne?" (VSO)
Haitian CF	"Koté li ye?," lit. 'where he is?,' i.e. 'Where is he?'
	(H. Gaujean p.c.)
	cf. F. "Où est-il?" (QW V S) or "Où est-ce qu'il est?"
Jamaican CE	"we im de?," lit. 'where he is?,' i.e. 'Where is he?'
	(Hancock 1979b: 9)

Negerhollands CD   "am lo werək da?," lit. 'he ASP work there?,' i.e.
'Does he work there?'

(van Diggelen 1978: 91)

cf. D "Werkt hij daar?" (VSC)

It should be noted that American Black English, often considered a post-creole,
has the usual English subject–auxiliary inversion in questions that can be answered
"yes" or "no," e.g. "Can I go?" (Burling 1973: 68). However, with question words
such inversion is optional, i.e. both "Where can I go?" and "Where I can go?"
occur. In embedded questions, which have no subject–auxiliary inversion in
standard English, inversion is again optional in Black English, i.e. "I wonder
where can I go" occurs as well as "I wonder where I can go." In embedded yes/no
questions, Black English has no connecting *if* or *whether* but does have inversion:
"I wonder can I go" (ibid.). In this respect Black English is unlike English-based
creoles which have no such inversion at all and therefore happen to match
standard English word order in embedded questions, e.g. Jamaican CE "dɛm aːks
mi if a want i" 'They asked me if I wanted it' (Hancock 1979b: 14). A case might be
made for American Black English being more similar to Irish English, in which
direct questions are also embedded, e.g. "I don't know is that right or not" (Barry
1982: 108). While Irish English might well have served as a model for Black
English at an earlier period (Rickford 1986), the Black English pattern of subject–
auxiliary inversion could also be the result of decreolization. Bahamian English,
which seems to be at an earlier stage of decreolization than American Black
English, has no subject–auxiliary inversion in the basilect but frequent inversion in
the upper mesolect, even in embedded questions. Thus one finds "I can go?"
varying with "Can I go?," and "I don't know where I can go" varying with "I don't
know where can I go." This variation suggests a path of decreolization similar to
that in American Black English.

Most of the other differences in word order between the Atlantic creoles and
their lexical-source languages are discussed in connection with other syntactic
features in earlier sections of this chapter, such as those dealing with verbal
markers. The remaining differences are largely limited in scope and depend on
particular lexical items with subcategorizational rules differing from those of their
superstrate etyma. In Miskito Coast CE, for example, the adverb *bak* 'back, again'
often occurs sentence-finally after another adverb of place, e.g. "an hiz wie huom
bak" 'on his way back home.' Even at this level, though, one finds evidence
suggesting more general forces such as substrate influence. For example,
Negerhollands CE *werán* matches CE *bak* in both its semantic range and syntactic
position: "də džumbi-sini a draːi *werán*," literally 'the ghost PLURAL

ANTERIOR return back' (Stolz 1986: 218). Sranan CE *baka* also occurs in this sentence-final position (ibid.); this may in fact be connected to its semantic range, which matches that of Ewe *megbe* (Herskovits 1941: 290) and Yoruba *pada* (A. Oyedeji p.c.). Still, such lexically-related syntactic differences are so numerous and miscellaneous that they are best treated in lexical studies of each creole.

Some general remarks on the contents of this chapter are included in the following conclusion to this volume.

Conclusion

The following is a brief assessment of the theoretical implications of the linguistic data in this volume. A similar assessment of sociohistorical data can be found at the end of volume II.

The lexical data (discussed in chapter 3) reflect more readily than data from other linguistic levels the social history of the speech communities that today use the Atlantic creoles. European regionalisms preserved in the creoles suggest patterns of immigration, as do words characteristic of European social dialects. Lexical retentions and borrowings from African languages provide similar information, as do the less direct traces of African lexical influence such as creole semantic shifts, idioms, reduplications, and other effects of calquing. The creole lexicons also provide some weak evidence for the importance of Portuguese in the slave trade, but this remains rather inconclusive. The influence of adstrate languages, such as Amerindian and European languages other than the superstrate, appears to be confined solely to the level of lexicon. Morphological and semantic changes in creole words *vis-à-vis* their European etyma do not differ in kind from changes found in different stages of other languages, but the scale on which these changes occurred in the creoles – particularly morpheme boundary reanalysis – reflects the massive structural changes characteristic of pidginization and creolization.

The phonological data (discussed in chapter 4) suggest that the Atlantic creoles have what Stein (1984: 102) calls a *Doppelzugehörigkeit*, a "double belonging" to both the family of their lexical-source language and their own family, the Atlantic creoles. While some creoles – particularly the post-creoles – share so many features with their European lexical-source languages that they might well be called Romance (or Germanic) languages of the second generation (Stein 1984: 101), conservative varieties share a preponderant number of features with other conservative Atlantic creoles – of whatever lexical base – rather than with any European language. Although the balance of European versus non-European features varies considerably from creole to creole, all varieties – even post-creoles – share this double identity to some degree.

Perhaps the single most important factor shaping the phonology of many of the Atlantic creoles was the retention of substrate phonotactic rules tending to give syllables a CV structure. The seven-vowel system of many substrate languages had the effect of making the conservative creoles' vowel systems closer to one another's than to those of their lexical sources. Substrate languages also influenced other phonological patterns in the creoles, ranging from the nasalization of vowels to the palatalization of various consonants. While some aspects of the creoles' phonology may have been affected by universals, substrate influence had to be the origin of certain creole phonological features found in African but not European languages, such as co-articulated or pre-nasalized stops, or phonemic tone.

The syntactic data (discussed in chapter 5) provide further evidence of the creoles' *Doppelzugehörigkeit* but also strengthen the case for the Atlantic creoles being a typological group of languages *sui generis*. While any claim of their genetic relatedness would have to rest on the genetic relatedness of their superstrates on the one hand and their substrates on the other, there would seem to be a strong case for parallel independent development, with greater likelihood of the diffusion of features within lexical-base groups. It is hardly controversial to observe that the Atlantic creoles arose among speakers of partially similar African languages learning partially similar European languages under partially similar social conditions.

The many syntactic features common to the Atlantic creoles fall into several categories: preverbal tense and aspect markers with similar meanings that combine in similar ways; different but corresponding words for 'be' determined by the following syntactic environment; parallel serial verb constructions, the second element of which corresponds to complementizers or prepositions in European languages; similar determiners and pluralizers in the noun phrase; the substitution of possessive adjectives by possessive pronouns for emphasis; and miscellaneous parallels in function words ranging from stressed versus unstressed personal pronouns to phrasal prepositions.

While these syntactic structures are made largely of lexical building blocks from the European source languages (building blocks that carry with them syntactic and semantic elements from those languages), the model for many of these structures was clearly African. Some of these structures (e.g. serial verbs) are not rare among the world's languages and their universality may have made it easier for them to take root and develop in the creoles. Other structures, however, are indeed rare outside of Africa (e.g. the use of the pronoun 'they' as a pluralizer) and their presence in the Atlantic creoles can hardly be explained by universals. Whatever evidence there is for universals seems to be in the Greenbergian sense of general parameters on possible structures, or in the sense of universals in adult second-language acquisition that played a role in pidginization and creolization (e.g. the isolating of grammatical elements). This study has uncovered no linguistic data that could be interpreted as unambiguous evidence for neurally-based universals.

There is, however, considerable evidence that creoles function like any other languages in developing a systematicity and complexity of their own which is, in the final analysis, something quite distinct from that of either their superstrate or their substrate.

Regarding the development of theory, progress in a number of areas of research bodes well for progress in pidgin and creole linguistics in general. First and foremost, linguistic descriptions of individual varieties are being written that are more frequently of high quality and sufficient detail, reflecting native-speaker sensitivity to nuance (e.g. Bernabé 1983). Secondly, considerable progress is being made in sociohistorical studies, not only of creole speech communities but also of the trade in slaves that brought people to these communities. This improved knowledge of creole speakers' ethnolinguistic origins, coupled with more detailed and rigorous studies of the relevant African languages, promises a significant improvement in substrate studies of the Atlantic creoles. Together with broader comparative studies of universal grammar (e.g. Stassen 1985) and advances in other areas of linguistic theory, these will provide the means of uncovering the data to test and improve the theories that guide pidgin and creole linguistics.

REFERENCES

Abraham, R. C. 1962. *Dictionary of modern Yoruba*. London: Hodder and Stoughton.

Abreu, M. I. and C. Ramah. 1973. *Português contemporâneo 2*. Washington: Georgetown University Press.

Achebe, C. 1969. *Things fall apart*. New York: Fawcett Crest.

Adam, L. 1883. *Les idiomes négro-aryen et maléo-aryen: essai d'hybridologie linguistique*. Paris: Maisonneuve.

Aitchison, J. forthcoming. "Bagaraps" in Tok Pisin. Paper presented at Seminar on Pidgin and Creole Languages, University College London, February 1987.

Alexandre, P. 1967. *Langues et langage en Afrique noire*. Paris: Payot.

Alleyne, M. C. 1971. Acculturation and the cultural matrix of creolization. In Hymes (ed.) 1971:169–186.

1980. *Comparative Afro-American*. Ann Arbor: Karoma.

Allsopp, S. R. R. 1958. Pronominal forms in the dialect of English used in Georgetown (British Guiana) and its environs by people engaged in non-clerical occupations. Unpublished M.A. thesis, University of London.

1970. Critical commentary on the Dictionary of Jamaican English. *Caribbean Studies* 10 (2): 90–117.

1972. Some suprasegmental features of Caribbean English and their relevance to the classroom. Paper presented at the UWI/UNESCO Conference on Creole Language and Educational Development, University of the West Indies.

1980. How does the creole lexicon expand? In Valdman and Highfield (eds.) 1980:89–107.

Almada, M. D. de Oliveira. 1961. *Cabo Verde: contribuição para o estudo do dialecto falado no seu arquipélago*. Estudos de ciências políticas e sociais, No. 55. Lisbon: Junta de Investigações do Ultramar.

Anderson, R. (ed.) 1983. *Pidginization and creolization as language acquisition*. Rowley MA: Newbury House.

Anonymous. 1854. *Kurzgefasste Neger-Englische Grammatik*. Bautzen. (1965 reprint. Amsterdam: S. Emmering.)

Arends, J. 1986. Internal and external factors in the development of the Sranan comparative. Paper presented to the Society for Caribbean Linguistics, Trinidad.

Arens, H. 1969. *Sprachwissenschaft: der Gang ihrer Entwicklung von der Antike bis zur Gegenwart*. Frankfurt: Fischer Athenäum.

Ariza, M. M. 1980. Stress and intonation in Haitian Creole. Paper presented to the Society for Caribbean Linguistics, Aruba.

Assadi, B. 1983. Rama Cay Creole English. In Holm (ed.) 1983:115–122.

Aub-Buscher, G. 1970. A propos des influences du français dialectal sur un parler créole des Antilles. *Mélanges Straka*. Strasbourg: Centre d'Études Romances, pp. 360–369.

Bailey, B. L. 1965. Toward a new perspective in Negro English dialectology. *American Speech* 40. (Reprinted in Wolfram and Clarke (eds.) 1971: 41–50.)

1966. *Jamaican Creole syntax: a transformational approach.* Cambridge: Cambridge University Press.

Bailey, R. and M. Görlach (eds.) 1982. *English as a world language.* Ann Arbor: University of Michigan Press.

Baissac, C. 1880. *Étude sur le patois créole mauricien.* Nancy: Berger-Lerrault et Cie.

Baker, P. 1972. *Kreol: a description of Mauritian Creole.* London: Hurst.

1976a. The problem of variability with special reference to Bickerton's study of Guyanese English. Unpublished exam-option paper, University of York.

1976b. Towards a social history of Mauritian Creole. Unpublished B.Phil. dissertation, University of York.

1984. The significance of agglutinated French articles in the creole languages of the Indian Ocean and elsewhere. In Sebba and Todd (eds.) 1984: 19–29.

Baker, P. and C. Corne. 1982. *Isle de France Creole: affinities and origins.* Ann Arbor: Karoma.

Barry, M. V. 1982. The English language in Ireland. In Bailey and Görlach (eds.) 1982: 84–133.

Baudet, M. M. 1981. Identifying the African grammatical base of the Caribbean creoles: a typological approach. In Highfield and Valdman (eds.) 1981: 104–118.

Bauer, A. 1975. *Das Kanton-Englisch: ein Pidginidiom als Beispiel für ein soziolinguistisches Kulturkontaktphänomen.* Bern: Lang.

Baugh, A. C. 1957. *A history of the English language.* New York: Appleton-Century-Crofts.

Baugh, J. 1980. A reexamination of the Black English copula. In W. Labov (ed.) *Locating language in time and space.* New York: Academic Press, pp. 83–106.

Bentolila, A. *et al.* 1976. *Ti diksyonnè kreyòl-franse: dictionnaire élémentaire créole haïtien-français.* Port-au-Prince: Éditions Caraïbes.

Bernabé, J. 1983. *Fondal-natal: grammaire basilectale approchée des créoles guadeloupéen et martiniquais.* Paris: L'Harmattan. 3 vols.

Berry, J. 1959. The origins of Krio vocabulary. *Sierra Leone Studies* 12: 298–307.

1961. English loanwords and adaptations in Sierra Leone Krio. In Le Page (ed.) 1961: 1–16.

Bertrand-Bocandé, E. 1849. Notes sur la Guinée portugaise ou Sénégambie méridionale. *Bulletin de la Société de Géographie* 12: 57–93.

Bickerton, D. 1971. Inherent variability and variable rules. *Foundations of Language* 7: 457–492.

1973a. The structure of polylectal grammars. In R. W. Shuy (ed.) *Sociolinguistics: current trends and prospects.* Washington: Georgetown University Press, pp. 17–42.

1973b. On the nature of a creole continuum. *Language* 49: 640–649.

1974. Creolization, linguistic universals, natural semantax and the brain. University of Hawaii *Working Papers in Linguistics* 6 (3): 124–141. (Republished 1980.)

1975. *Dynamics of a creole system.* Cambridge: Cambridge University Press.

1976. Creole tense–aspect systems and universal grammar. Paper presented to the Society for Caribbean Linguistics, Guyana.

1977a. Putting back the clock in variation studies. *Language* 53 (2): 353–359.

1977b. Pidginization and creolization: language acquisition and language universals. In Valdman (ed.) 1977: 49–69.

1979a.   Introduction to Schuchardt (1979), pp. vi–xvii.

1979b.   The status of *bin* in the Atlantic Creoles. In Hancock *et al.* (eds.) 1979: 309–314.

1980.   Creolization, linguistic universals, natural semantax and the brain. In Day (ed.) 1980: 1–18. (Reprint of Bickerton 1974.)

1981.   *Roots of language.* Ann Arbor: Karoma.

1984.   Creoles and universal grammar: the unmarked case? Paper presented at the winter meeting of the Linguistic Society of America, Baltimore.

1986.   Beyond Roots: the five-year test. Paper presented at the Linguistic Society of America Summer Institute, City University of New York.

Bickerton, D. and A. Escalante.   1970.   Palenquero: a Spanish-based creole of northern Colombia. *Lingua* 24: 254–267.

Bickerton, D. *et al.*   1984.   The language bioprogram hypothesis. *The Behavioral and Brain Sciences* 7: 173–221.

Bilby, K. M.   1983.   How the "older heads" talk: a Jamaican Maroon spirit possession language and its relationship to the Creoles of Suriname and Sierra Leone. *New West Indian Guide* 57 (1–2): 37–88.

Bird, C., J. Hutchison, and M. Kanté.   1977.   *An ka bamanankan kalan: beginning Bambara.* Bloomington: Indiana University Linguistics Club.

Bloomfield, L.   1933.   *Language.* London: Allen and Unwin.

Boas, F.   1933.   Note on the Chinook Jargon. *Language* 9: 208–213.

Bollée, A.   1978.   Reduplikation und Iteration in den romanischen Sprachen. *Archiv für das Studium der neueren Sprachen und Literaturen* 215 (1): 318–336.

1981.   Le vocabulaire du créole haïtien et du créole seychellois: une comparaison. Paper presented at the 3e Colloque International des Études Créoles, St. Lucia.

1984.   Dictionnaire étymologique des créoles. In *Wörterbücher der deutschen Romanistik: Rundgespräche und Kolloquien.* Weinheim: Verlag Chemie GmbH, Acta humaniora.

Boretzky, N.   1983.   *Kreolsprachen, Substrate und Sprachwandel.* Wiesbaden: Harrassowitz.

1986.   Verbkategorien im Fantse und im Jamaica Creole. ms.

Bouton, J.   1640.   *Relation de l'establissement des françois depuis l'an de 1635 en l'isle de la Martinique.* Paris.

Brachin, P.   1985.   *The Dutch language: a survey.* Cheltenham: Stanley Thornes.

Bradford, W. P.   1986.   Virgin Islands Dutch Creole: a morphological description. *Amsterdam Creole Studies* 9: 73–99.

Broch, I. and E. H. Jahr.   1984.   Russenorsk: a new look at the Russo-Norwegian pidgin in northern Norway. In P. S. Ureland and I. Clarkson (eds.) *Scandinavian language contacts.* Cambridge: Cambridge University Press, pp. 21–65.

Brown, R. W. and U. Bellugi.   1964.   Three processes in the child's acquisition of syntax. *Harvard Educational Review* 34: 133–151.

Bureau Volkslectuur.   1961.   *Woordenlijst van het Sranan-Tongo/Glossary of the Suriname vernacular.* Paramaribo: Varekamp.

Burling, R.   1973.   *English in black and white.* New York: Holt, Rinehart, and Winston.

Bynoe-Andriolo, E. and M. S. Yillah.   1975.   Predicate clefting in Afro-European languages. Paper presented at the 6th Conference on African Linguistics.

Bynon, T.   1983.   Serial verbs and grammaticalisation. In U. Pieper and G. Stickel (eds.) *Studia linguistica diachronica et synchronica.* Berlin: Mouton de Gruyter, pp. 105–121.

Byrne, F.   1984.   *Fi* and *fu*: origins and functions in some Caribbean English-based creoles. *Lingua* 62: 97–120.

1985.   Some aspects of the syntax of *fu* in Saramaccan. *Amsterdam Creole Studies* 8: 1–26.

Carr, E.   1972.   *Da kine talk: from pidgin to standard English in Hawaii.* Honolulu: University Press of Hawaii.

Carrington, L., D. R. Craig, and R. Todd Dandare (eds.)   1983.   *Studies in Caribbean language.* St. Augustine: Society for Caribbean Linguistics.

Carter, H.   1979.   Evidence for the survival of African prosodies in West Indian creoles. Society for Caribbean Linguistics, occasional paper 13.

1982.   The tonal system of Jamaican English. Paper presented to the Society for Caribbean Linguistics, Suriname.

1983.   How to be a tone language. In Carrington *et al.* (eds.) 1983: 90–111.

1987.   Suprasegmentals in Jamaican: some African comparisons. In Gilbert (ed.) 1987: 213–263.

Carter, H. and J. Makoondekwa.   1976.   An introductory Kongo reader. [ms.]

Cassidy, F. G.   1961.   *Jamaica talk: three hundred years of the English language in Jamaica.* London: Macmillan.

1964.   Toward the recovery of early English-African Pidgin. In *Symposium on multilingualism (Brazzaville).* London: Conseil Scientifique pour Afrique; Commission de Coopération Technique en Afrique, publication 87.

Cassidy, F. G. and R. B. Le Page.   1980.   *Dictionary of Jamaican English.* Cambridge: Cambridge University Press (1st edn. 1967).

Chataigner, A.   1963.   Le créole portugais du Sénégal: observations et textes. *Journal of African Languages* 2 (1): 44–71.

Chaudenson, R.   1974.   *Le lexique du parler créole de la Réunion.* Paris: Champion. 2 vols.

1979.   *Les créoles français.* Évreux: Nathan.

Chévillard, A.   1659.   *Les desseins de son éminence de Richelieu pour l'Amérique.* Rennes.

Chomsky, N.   1965.   *Aspects of the theory of syntax.* Cambridge MA: MIT Press.

Christaller, Revd. J. G.   1933.   *Dictionary of the Asante and Fante language called Tshi (Twi).* Basel: Basel Evangelical Missionary Society.

Christie, P.   1986.   Evidence for an unsuspected habitual marker in Jamaican. In Görlach and Holm (eds.) 1986: 183–190.

Coelho, F. A.   1880–86.   Os dialectos românicos ou neolatinos na África, Ásia, e América. *Bolletim da Sociedade de Geografia de Lisboa.* (Republished in J. Morais-Barbosa (ed.) 1967. *Estudos linguisticos crioulos.* Lisbon: Academia Internacional de Cultura Portuguesa.)

Comhaire-Sylvain, S. and J.   1955.   Survivances africaines dans le vocabulaire religieux d'Haïti. *Études dahoméennes* 14: 5–20.

Comrie, B.   1976.   *Aspect: an introduction to the study of verbal aspect and related problems.* Cambridge: Cambridge University Press.

Corne, C.   1977.   *Seychelles Creole grammar: elements for Indian Ocean Proto-Creole reconstruction.* Tübingen: Gunter Narr.

Coromines, J.   1967.   *Breve diccionario etimológico de la lengua castellana.* Madrid: Biblioteca románica hispánica.

Crouse, N. M.   1943.   *The French struggle for the West Indies: 1665–1713.* New York: Columbia University Press.

Cruickshank, J. G. 1916. *"Black Talk": being notes on Negro dialect in British Guiana with (inevitably) a chapter on the vernacular of Barbados.* Demerara: Argosy.

Cunha, C. 1982. *Gramática da língua portuguesa.* Rio de Janeiro: Fundação Nacional de Material Escolar.

Curtin, P. D. 1969. *The Atlantic slave trade: a census.* Madison: University of Wisconsin Press.

Daeleman, J. 1972. Kongo elements in Saramacca Tongo. *Journal of African Languages* 11 (1): 1–44.

Dalgado, S. R. 1900. *Dialecto Indo-Português de Ceylão.* Lisbon: Imprensa Nacional.

Dalphinis, M. 1985. *Caribbean and African languages: social history, language, literature and education.* London: Karia Press.

    1986. French creoles in the Caribbean and Britain. In D. Sutcliffe and A. Wong (eds.) *The language of the Black experience.* Oxford, New York: Basil Blackwell, pp. 168–191.

d'Ans, A. M. 1968. *Le créole français d'Haïti.* The Hague, Paris: Mouton.

Day, R. R. (ed.) 1980. *Issues in English creoles: papers from the 1975 Hawaii conference.* Varieties of English around the World, G2. Heidelberg: Groos.

DeCamp, D. 1961. Social and geographical factors in Jamaican dialects. In Le Page (ed.) 1961: 61–84.

    1964. Creole language areas considered as multilingual communities. In *Symposium on multilingualism (Brazzaville).* London: Conseil Scientifique pour Afrique; Commission de Coopération Technique en Afrique, publication 87.

    1971a. The study of pidgin and creole languages. In Hymes (ed.) 1971: 13–42.

    1971b. Toward a generative analysis of a post-creole speech continuum. In Hymes (ed.) 1971: 349–370.

    1977. The development of pidgin and creole studies. In Valdman (ed.) 1977: 3–20.

DeCamp, D. and I. F. Hancock (eds.) 1974. *Pidgins and creoles: current trends and prospects.* Washington, DC: Georgetown University Press.

de Granda, G. 1978. *Estudios lingüísticos hispánicos, afrohispánicos y criollos.* Madrid: Editorial Gredos.

de Groot, A. 1981. *Woordregister Saramakaans–Nederlands.* Paramaribo.

    1984. *Tweedelig woordregister: Auka–Nederlands/Nederlands–Auka.* Paramaribo.

de Josselin de Jong, J. P. 1926. Het huidige Negerhollandsch (teksten en woordenlijst). *Verhandelingen der Koninklijke Akademie van Wetenschapen te Amsterdam, Afdeeling Letterkunde* 26: 1–107.

den Besten, H. 1986. Double negation and the genesis of Afrikaans. In Muysken and Smith (eds.) 1986: 185–230.

Dijkhoff, Mario. 1985. *Dikshonario/Woordenboek . . . Nederlands–Papiaments.* The Hague: De Walburg Pers.

Dijkhoff, Marta. 1985. Some observations about the passive participle in Papiamentu. Paper presented at Workshop on Universals and Substrata in Creole Genesis, University of Amsterdam.

Dillard, J. L. 1972. *Black English: its history and usage in the United States.* New York: Random House.

    1979. Creole English and creole Portuguese: the early records. In Hancock *et al.* (eds.) 1979: 261–268.

D'Offay, D. and G. Lionnet. 1982. *Diksyonner kreol–franse/Dictionnaire créole seychellois–français.* Kreolische Bibliothek, Band 3. Hamburg: Helmut Buske Verlag.

Domingue, N. Z. 1977. Middle English: another creole? *Journal of Creole Studies* 1 (1): 89–100.

Donahoe, W. A.   1946.   *A history of British Honduras.* Montreal: Provincial Publishing Co.

Donicie, A. and J. Voorhoeve.   1963.   *De Saramakaanse Woordenschat.* Amsterdam: Bureau voor Taalonderzoek in Suriname van de Universiteit van Amsterdam.

Ducoeurjoly, S. J.   1802.   *Manuel des habitans de Saint-Domingue.* Paris: Chez Lenoir.

Dwyer, D.   n.d.   An introduction to West African Pidgin English. Unpublished manuscript, Michigan State University.

Eersel, C. H.   1976.   A few remarks on some sound patterns of Sranan. Paper presented to the Society for Caribbean Linguistics, Guyana.

Eilfort, W.   1985.   On the genesis of a complementizer in creoles. Unpublished manuscript.

Elliott, D., S. Legum, and S. A. Thompson.   1969.   Syntactic variation as linguistic data. In R. Binnick *et al.* (eds.) *Papers from the 5th Regional Meeting of the Chicago Linguistic Society.* Chicago: Chicago University Press.

Ewert, A.   1933.   *The French language.* London: Faber and Faber.

Faine, J.   1936.   *Philologie créole: études historiques et etymologiques sur la langue créole d'Haïti.* Port-au-Prince: Imprimerie de l'État.

    1939.   *Le Créole dans l'univers: étude comparative des parlers français-créoles.* Tome I. Le mauricien. Port-au-Prince: Imprimerie de l'État.

Favery, M., B. Johns and F. Wouk.   1976.   The historical development of locative and existential copula constructions in Afro-Creole languages. In S. B. Steever, C. A. Walker, and S. S. Mufwene (eds.) *Papers from the Parasession on Diachronic Syntax.* Chicago: Chicago Linguistic Society, pp. 88–95.

Feist, S.   1932.   The origin of the Germanic languages and the Indo-Europeanizing of North Europe. *Language* 8: 245–254.

Ferguson, C. A.   1971.   Absence of copula and the notion of simplicity: a study of normal speech, baby talk, foreigner talk, and pidgins. In Hymes (ed.) 1971: 141–150.

Ferraz, L.   1975.   African influences on Principense Creole. In Valkhoff *et al.* (eds.) 1975: 153–164.

    1976.   The origin and development of four creoles in the Gulf of Guinea. *African Studies* 35 (1): 33–38.

Ferraz, L. and A. Traill.   1981.   The interpretation of tone in Principense Creole. *Studies in African Linguistics* 12 (2).

Focke, H. C.   1855.   *Neger-Engelsch Woordenboek.* Leiden: Van den Heuvell.

Fortier, A.   1885.   The French language of Louisiana and the Negro French dialect. *Transactions of the Modern Language Association of America* 1: 96–111.

Fought, J.   1982.   The reinvention of Hugo Schuchardt. *Language in Society* 11: 419–436.

Frajzyngier, Z.   1984.   On the origin of *say* and *se* as complementizers in Black English and English-based Creoles. *American Speech* 59 (3): 207–210.

Friedemann, N. S. and C. Patiño, R.   1983.   *Lengua y sociedad en el palenque de San Basilio.* Bogotá: Instituto Caro y Cuervo.

Fyle, C. N. and E. D. Jones.   1980.   *A Krio–English dictionary.* New York: Oxford University Press/Sierra Leone University Press.

Germain, R.   1980.   *Grammaire créole.* Paris: L'Harmattan.

Gibson, K.   1986.   The ordering of auxiliary notions in Guyanese Creole. *Language* 62 (3): 571–586.

Gilbert, G.   1980.   Introduction to Schuchardt (1980), pp. 1–13.

    1983.   Focus on creolists: Hugo Schuchardt. *Carrier Pidgin* 11 (1): 4–5.

1984.   The first systematic survey of the world's pidgins and creoles: Hugo Schuchardt, 1882–1885. In Sebba and Todd (eds.) 1984: 131–140.

1985.   Hugo Schuchardt and the Atlantic Creoles: a newly discovered manuscript "On the Negro English of West Africa." *American Speech* 60 (1): 31–63.

1986a.   The language bioprogram hypothesis: déjà vu? In Muysken and Smith (eds.) 1986: 15–24.

1986b.   Oldendorp's *History* . . . and other early creole materials in the Moravian archives in Herrnhut, East Germany. *Carrier Pidgin* 14 (1): 5–7.

(ed.)   1987.   *Pidgin and creole languages: essays in memory of John E. Reinecke.* Honolulu: University Press of Hawaii.

Gilman, C.   1979.   Cameroonian Pidgin English: a neo-African language. In Hancock *et al.* (eds.) 1979: 269–280.

Girod-Chantrans, J.   1785.   *Voyage d'un Suisse dans différentes colonies d'Amérique pendant la dernière guerre* . . . Neuchatel: Imprimerie de la Société Typographique.

Givón, T.   1979.   Prolegomena to any sane creology. In Hancock *et al.* (eds.) 1979: 3–36.

Göbl-Gáldi, L.   1933.   Problemi di sostrato nel creole-francese. *Revue de linguistique romane* 9: 336–345.

1934.   Esquisse de la structure grammaticale des patois français-créoles. *Zeitschrift für französische Sprache und Literatur* 58: 257–295.

Goilo, E. R.   1972.   *Papiamentu textbook.* Aruba.

Gonzales, A.   1924.   *With Aesop along the Black Border.* (1969 reprint. New York: Negro University Press.)

Goodman, M. F.   1964.   *A comparative study of creole French dialects.* The Hague: Mouton.

1971.   The strange case of Mbugu (Tanzania). In Hymes (ed.) 1971: 243–254.

1985.   Review of Bickerton (1981). *International Journal of American Linguistics* 51 (1): 109–137.

1987.   The Portuguese element in the American creoles. In Gilbert (ed.) 1987: 361–405.

Görlach, M. and J. Holm (eds.)   1986.   *Focus on the Caribbean.* Varieties of English around the World, G8. Amsterdam/Philadelphia: John Benjamins.

Goux, Abbé M.   1842.   *Catéchisme en langue créole, précédé d'un essai de grammaire sur l'idiome usité dans les colonies françaises.* Paris: Imprimerie de H. Vrayet de Surcy.

Grade, P.   1889.   Bemerkungen über das Negerenglisch an der West-Küste von Afrika. *Archiv für das Studium der neueren Sprachen* 83: 261–272.

Greenberg, J. H.   1966a.   *The languages of Africa.* Bloomington: Indiana University Press/The Hague: Mouton.

1966b. *Language universals.* The Hague: Mouton.

Greenfield, W.   1830.   *A defense of the Surinam Negro-English version of the New Testament* . . . London: Bagster. (Reprinted in *The Journal of Pidgin and Creole Languages* 1 (2): 259–266 ff.)

Grimes, J. E. (ed.)   1972.   *Languages of the Guianas.* Summer Institute of Linguistics, University of Oklahoma.

Grion, G.   1891.   Farmacopea e Lingua Franca del dugento. *Archivo glottologico italiano* 12: 181–186.

Günther, W.   1973.   *Das portugiesische Kreolisch der Ilha do Príncipe.* Marburg: Marburger Studien zur Afrika- und Asienkunde.

Guthrie, G. M.   1935.   *Lingala grammar and dictionary*. Léopoldville: Conseil Protestant du Congo.
1954.   Lectures on Bantu tonology. Unpublished manuscript.
Guttman, L.   1944.   A basis for scaling qualitative data. *American Sociological Review* 9: 139–150.
Hall, G.   forthcoming.   The African ingredient in the New Orleans gumbo pot. In *Slave power: the creoles of Louisiana*.
Hall, R. A., Jr.   1948.   The linguistic structure of Taki-Taki. *Language* 24: 92–116.
1950.   The African substratum in Negro English: review of Turner (1949). *American Speech* 25: 51–54.
1955.   Sostrato e lingue créole. *Archivo glottologico italiano* 40: 1–9.
1958.   Creole languages and genetic relationships. *Word* 14: 367–373.
1959.   Neo-Melanesian and glottochronology. *International Journal of American Linguistics* 25: 265–267.
1962.   The life cycle of pidgin languages. *Lingua* 11: 151–156.
1966.   *Pidgin and creole languages*. Ithaca: Cornell University Press.
1968.   Creole linguistics. In Sebeok (ed.) 1968: 361–371.
Hall, R. A., Jr., G. Bateson, and J. W. W. Whiting.   1943.   *Melanesian Pidgin phrasebook and vocabulary*. Baltimore: Linguistic Society of America, published for the United States Armed Services Institute.
Hall, R. A., Jr., S. Comhaire-Sylvain, H. O. McConnell, and A. Métraux.   1953.   *Haitian Creole: grammar, texts, vocabulary*. Memoir 74 of the American Anthropological Association, and Memoir 43 of the American Folklore Society. Philadelphia: American Folklore Society.
Hancock, I. F.   1969.   A provisional comparison of the English-based Atlantic creoles. *African Language Review* 8: 7–72.
1970.   Dictionary of Sierra Leone Krio. Unpublished manuscript.
1971.   A study of the sources and development of the lexicon of Sierra Leone Creole. Unpublished Ph.D. thesis, University of London School of Oriental and African Studies.
1975.   Malacca Creole Portuguese: Asian, African or European? *Anthropological Linguistics* 17 (5): 211–236.
1977.   Recovering pidgin genesis: approaches and problems. In Valdman (ed.) 1977: 277–294.
1979a.   On the origins of the term pidgin. In Hancock *et al.* (eds.) 1979: 81–88.
1979b.   The relationship of Black Vernacular English to the Atlantic creoles. Working paper of the African and Afro-American Studies and Research Center, University of Texas at Austin.
1979c.   Review of W. Keller Vass, *The Bantu linguistic heritage of the United States* (University of California Press, 1978). In *Research in African Literatures* 12: 412–419.
1980.   Lexical expansion in creole languages. In Valdman and Highfield (eds.) 1980: 63–88.
1984.   Romani and Anglo-Romani. In P. Trudgill (ed.) *Language in the British Isles*. Cambridge: Cambridge University Press.
1987.   A preliminary classification of the Anglophone Atlantic creoles, with syntactic data from thirty-three representative dialects. In Gilbert (ed.) 1987: 264–334.
Hancock, I. F., E. Polomé, M. Goodman, and B. Heine. (eds.)   1979.   *Readings in creole studies*. Ghent: E. Story-Scientia.
Harris, J.   forthcoming.   On doing comparative reconstruction with genetically

unrelated languages. In A. G. Ramat, O. Carruba, and G. Bernini (eds.) *Papers from the 7th International Conference on Historical Linguistics.* Amsterdam: John Benjamins.

Harrison, J. A. 1884. Negro English. *Anglia* 7: 232–279.

Heine, B. 1976. *A typology of African languages, based on the order of meaningful elements.* Berlin: Reimer.

Hellinger, M. 1985. *Englisch-orientierte Pidgin- und Kreolsprachen: Entstehung, Geschichte, und sprachlicher Wandel.* Darmstadt: Wissenschaftliche Buchgesellschaft.

Herskovits, M. 1941. *The myth of the Negro past.* New York/London: Harper and Brothers.

Herskovits, M. and F. S. 1936. *Suriname folk-lore . . .* Columbia University Contributions to Anthropology 37. New York: Columbia University Press.

Hesseling, D. C. 1897. Het Hollandsch in Zuid-Afrika. *De Gids* 60 (1): 138–162. (Reprinted in English in Hesseling 1979: 1–22.)

1899. *Het Afrikaansch: bijdrage tot de geschiedenis der nederlandse taal in Zuid-Afrika.* Leiden: Brill.

1905. *Het Negerhollands der Deense Antillen. Bijdrage tot de geschiedenis der nederlandse taal in Amerika.* Leiden: Sijthoff.

1910. Overblijfsels van de nederlandse taal op Ceylon. *Tijd* 29: 303–312. (Reprinted in English in Hesseling 1979: 23–30.)

1928. Het perfektum in het post-klassieke Grieks: overblijfsels in de taal van heden. *Mededelingen der Koninklijke Akademie van Wetenschappen, Afdeling Letterkunde* 65 A (6). Amsterdam.

1933a. Papiaments en Negerhollands. *Tijd* 52: 265–288. (Reprinted in English in Hesseling 1979: 47–61.)

1933b. Hoe ontstond de eigenaardige vorm van het Kreools? *Neophilologus* 18: 209–215. (Reprinted in English in Hesseling 1979: 62–70.)

1934. Gemengde taal, mengeltaal, kreools en kreolisering. *Nieuwe Taalgids* 28: 310–322.

1979. *On the origin and formation of creoles: a miscellany of articles.* Ann Arbor: Karoma.

Highfield, A. and A. Valdman (eds.) 1981. *Historicity and variation in creole studies.* Ann Arbor: Karoma.

Holder, M. 1982. *Accent shift in Guyanese Creole: linguistic introduction and classified word lists.* Ann Arbor: Karoma.

Holm, J. A. 1976. Copula variability on the Afro-American continuum. Paper presented to the Society for Caribbean Linguistics, Guyana.

1978. *The Creole English of Nicaragua's Miskito Coast: its sociolinguistic history and a comparative study of its lexicon and syntax.* Ph.D. thesis, University College, University of London. Ann Arbor: University Microfilms International.

1980a. The creole 'copula' that highlighted the world. In J. L. Dillard (ed.) *Perspectives on American English.* The Hague: Mouton, pp. 367–375.

1980b. African features in White Bahamian English. *English Worldwide* 1 (1): 45–65.

1981. Sociolinguistic history and the creolist. In Highfield and Valdman (eds.) 1981: 40–51.

(ed.) 1983. *Central American English.* Varieties of English around the World, T2. Heidelberg: Gross / Amsterdam: John Benjamins.

1984. Variability of the copula in Black English and its creole kin. *American Speech* 59 (4): 291–309.

1985. African substratal influence on the Atlantic creole languages. Paper

presented at the 16th Conference on African Linguistics, Yale University. To appear in P. Maurer and T. Stolz (eds.) *Kreolische Miszellen*. Bochum: Brockmeyer.
1986.   Substrate diffusion. In Muysken and Smith (eds.) 1986: 259–278.
1987.   Creole influence on Popular Brazilian Portuguese. In Gilbert (ed.) 1987: 406–430.
Holm, J. A. with A. Shilling.   1982.   *Dictionary of Bahamian English*. Cold Spring NY: Lexik House.
Homburger, L.   1949.   *The Negro-African languages*. London: Routledge.
Hudson, R. A.   1980.   *Sociolinguistics*. Cambridge: Cambridge University Press.
Hull, A.   1968.   The origins of New World French phonology. *Word* 24 (1-2-3): 255–269.
1974.   Evidence for the original unity of North American French dialects. *Revue de Louisiane* 3: 59–70.
1979.   On the origin and chronology of the French-based creoles. In Hancock *et al.* (eds.) 1979: 201–216.
Huttar, G. L.   1974.   Serial verbs in Surinam creoles. University of North Dakota, *Work Papers* 18: 55–66.
1975.   Sources of creole semantic structures. *Language* 51 (3): 684–695.
1981.   Some Kwa-like features of Djuka syntax. *Studies in African Linguistics* 12 (3): 291–323.
Huttar, G. L. and M. L. Huttar.   1972.   Notes on Djuka phonology. In Grimes (ed.) 1972: 1–11.
Hyman, L.   1975.   *Phonology: theory and analysis*. New York: Holt, Rinehart, and Winston.
Hymes, D. (ed.)   1971.   *Pidginization and creolization of languages*. Cambridge: Cambridge University Press.
Ivens Ferraz, L.   1979.   *The Creole of São Tomé*. Johannesburg: Witwatersrand University Press.
1985.   Review of Holm with Shilling (1982). *African Studies* 44 (1): 109–113.
1987.   Portuguese creoles of West Africa and Asia. In Gilbert (ed.) 1987: 337–360.
Jacobs, M.   1932.   Notes on the structure of Chinook Jargon. *Language* 8: 27–50.
Jansen, B., H. Koopman, and P. Muysken.   1978.   Serial verbs in the creole languages. *Amsterdam Creole Studies* 2: 125–159.
Jespersen, O.   1922.   *Language: its nature, development, and origin*. London: Allen and Unwin.
Jones, E.   1971.   Krio: an English-based language of Sierra Leone. In Spencer (ed.) 1971: 66–94.
Kahane, H., R. Kahane, and A. Tietze.   1958.   *The Lingua Franca in the Levant: Turkish nautical terms of Italian and Greek origin*. Urbana: University of Illinois Press.
Kay, P. and G. Sankoff.   1974.   A language-universals approach to pidgins and creoles. In DeCamp and Hancock (eds.) 1974: 61–72.
Kihm, A.   1980.   Aspects d'une syntaxe historique: études sur le créole portugais de Guiné-Bissau. Thèse de doctorat de 3e cycle. Université de Paris III, Sorbonne Nouvelle.
1984.   Les difficiles débuts des études créoles en France (1870–1920). *Langue française* 63: 42–56.
forthcoming.   Créoles et croisements. In *Mélanges offerts au Prof. Paul Teyssier*. Arquivos do Centro Cultural Português 22.

Koelle, S. 1854. *Polyglotta Africana*. (1963 reprint. Fourah Bay College, Sierra Leone.)

Koopman, H. 1986. The genesis of Haitian: implications of a comparison of some features of the syntax of Haitian, French, and West African languages. In Muysken and Smith (eds.) 1986: 231–258.

Koopman, H. and C. Lefebvre. 1981. Haitian Creole *pu*. In Muysken (ed.) 1981: 201–222.

Kramp, A. 1983. Early creole lexicography: a study of C. L. Schumann's manuscript dictionary of Sranan. Unpublished Ph.D. thesis, University of Leiden.

Krapp, G. P. 1925. *The English language in America*. New York: Century.

Labov, W. 1969. Contraction, deletion, and inherent variability of the English copula. *Language* 45 (4): 715–751.

1972. *Language in the inner city: studies in the Black English Vernacular*. Philadelphia: University of Pennsylvania Press.

1982. Objectivity and commitment in linguistic science: the case of the Black English trial in Ann Arbor. *Language in Society* 11: 165–201.

Labov, W., P. Cohen, C. Robins, and J. Lewis. 1968. *A study of the nonstandard English of Negro and Puerto Rican speakers in New York City*. Cooperative Research Project No. 3288. Washington: Office of Education.

Lalla, B. 1986. Tracing elusive phonological features of early Jamaican Creole. In Görlach and Holm (eds.) 1986: 117–132.

Lawton, D. 1963. Suprasegmental phenomena in Jamaican Creole. Unpublished Ph.D. dissertation, Michigan State University.

Le Page, R. B. 1951. A survey of dialects in the British Caribbean. *Caribbean Quarterly* 2 (3): 49–50.

1955. The language problem of the British Caribbean. *Caribbean Quarterly* 4 (1): 40–49.

1957–58. General outlines of Creole English dialects in the British Caribbean. *Orbis* 6: 373–391; 7: 54–64.

(ed.) 1961. *Creole language studies II*. Proceedings of the Conference on Creole Language Studies (University of the West Indies, Mona, 1959). London: Macmillan.

1977. Decreolization and recreolization: a preliminary report on the sociolinguistic survey of multilingual communities, stage II: St. Lucia. *York Papers in Linguistics* 7: 107–128.

Le Page, R. B. and D. DeCamp. 1960. *Jamaican Creole: Creole studies I*. London: Macmillan.

LePage, R. B. and A. Tabouret-Keller. 1985. *Acts of identity: creole-based approaches to language and ethnicity*. Cambridge: Cambridge University Press.

Lewis, A. 1970. A descriptive analysis of the Palenquero dialect (a Spanish-based creole of northern Colombia, South America). Unpublished M.A. thesis, University of the West Indies, Mona.

Lichtveld, L. 1927. Afrikaansche resten in de creolentaal van Suriname. *West-Indische Gids* 10: 391–402.

Loftman, B. I. 1953. Creole languages of the Caribbean area: a comparison of the grammar of Jamaican Creole with those of the creole languages of Haiti, the Antilles, the Guianas, the Virgin Islands, and the Dutch West Indies. Unpublished M.A. thesis. Columbia University.

McConnell, H. O. and E. Swan. 1960. *You can learn Creole*. Petit-Goâve: Imprimerie du Sauveur.

Mafeni, B. 1971. Nigerian Pidgin. In Spencer (ed.) 1971: 95–112.

Magens, J. M.   1770.   *Grammatica over det creolske sprog, som bruges paa de trende Danske Eilande, St. Croix, St. Thomas, og St. Jans i Amerika.* Copenhagen: Gerhard Giese Salikath.

Maher, J.   1985.   *Contact linguistics: the language enclave phenomenon.* Ph.D. dissertation, New York University. Ann Arbor: University Microfilms International.

Manessy, G.   1977.   Processes of pidginization in African languages. In Valdman (ed.) 1977: 129–154.

Markey, T. L.   1982.   Afrikaans: creole or non-creole? *Zeitschrift für Dialektologie und Linguistik* 49 (2): 169–207.

Marroquim, M.   1934.   *A lingua do Nordeste (Alagôas e Pernambuco).* São Paulo: Companhia Editora Nacional.

Matthews, W.   1935.   Sailors' pronunciation in the second half of the 17th century. *Anglia* 59: 192–251.

Mattoso Câmara, J.   1972.   *História e estrutura da língua portuguesa.* Rio de Janeiro: Padrão.

Maurer, P.   1985.   Le système temporel du papiamento et le système temporel proto-créole de Bickerton. *Amsterdam Creole Studies* 8: 41–66.

 1986.   Le papiamento de Curaçao: un cas de créolisation atypique? Paper presented at the 5e Colloque International des Études Créoles, La Réunion.

Megenney, W. W.   1978.   *A Bahian heritage: an ethnolinguistic study of African influences on Bahian Portuguese.* Chapel Hill: University of North Carolina Press.

 1982.   La influencia del portugués en el palenquero colombiano. *Divulgaciones etnológicos* (Universidad del Atlántico, Barranquilla, Colombia) 2: 25–42.

 1984.   Traces of Portuguese in three Caribbean creoles. *Hispanic Linguistics* 1 (2): 177–189.

Meijer, G. and P. Muysken (eds.)   1977.   On the beginnings of pidgin and creole studies: Schuchardt and Hesseling. In Valdman (ed.) 1977: 21–48.

Meillet, A.   1967.   *The comparative method in historical linguistics.* Paris: Champion.

Meintel, D.   1975.   The creole dialect of the island of Brava. In Valkhoff *et al.* (eds.) 1975: 205–257.

Mercier, A.   1880.   Étude sur la langue créole en Louisiane. *Comptes rendus de l'Athenée louisianais* 1 (5): 378–383.

Migeod, F. W. H.   1911.   *The languages of West Africa.* London: Kegan, Paul, Trench, Trubner.

Mufwene, S. S.   1984.   *Stativity and the progressive.* Bloomington: Indiana University Linguistics Club.

 1986a.   Universalist and substrate theories complement one another. In Muysken and Smith (eds.) 1986: 129–162.

 1986b.   Notes on durative constructions in Jamaican and Guyanese Creole. In Görlach and Holm (eds.) 1986: 167–182.

 1986c.   Number delimitation in Gullah. *American Speech* 61 (1): 33–60.

Mühlhäusler, P.   1979.   *Growth and structure of the lexicon of New Guinea Pidgin.* Pacific Linguistics C (52). Canberra: Research School of Pacific Studies, Australian National University.

 1982.   Tok Pisin in Papua New Guinea. In Bailey and Görlach (eds.) 1982: 439–466.

 1986.   *Pidgin and creole linguistics.* Oxford: Basil Blackwell.

Muysken, P.   1981.   Creole tense/mood/aspect systems: the unmarked case? In Muysken (ed.) 1981: 181–200.

 (ed.)   1981.   *Generative studies on creole languages.* Dordrecht: Foris.

 1985.   The syntax and morphology of *P* in the creole languages. Paper presented at the Workshop on Universals and Substrata in Creole Genesis, University of Amsterdam.

Muysken, P. and G. Meijer. 1979. Introduction to Hesseling (1979), pp. vii–xix.

Muysken, P. and N. Smith (eds.) 1986. *Substrata versus universals in creole genesis.* Amsterdam: John Benjamins.

Naro, A. J. 1978. A study on the origins of pidginization. *Language* 54 (2): 314–349.

Ogunbọwale, P. O. 1970. *The essentials of the Yoruba language.* London: Hodder and Stoughton.

Oldendorp, C. G. A. 1777. *Geschichte der Mission der evangelischen Brueder auf den caraibischen Inseln S. Thomas, S. Croix und S. Jan.* Barby: C. F. Laur.

Orton, H., S. F. Sanderson, and J. Widdowson (eds.) 1978. *The linguistic atlas of England.* London: Croom Helm.

Papen, R. 1976. La structure phonologique des parlers franco-créoles de l'Océan Indien. *Actes du Colloque des Créolistes,* Nice.

Park, J. (ed.) 1975. *Ogii sani di pasa anga Da Kelema* by Da Kelema Asekende. Paramaribo: Summer Institute of Linguistics.

Parsons, E. S. 1933–43. *Folklore of the Antilles, French and English.* New York: American Folklore Society. 3 vols.

Pelleprat, P. 1655. *Relation des missions des pp. de la Compagnie de Jesus.* Paris.

Pires, J. and J. P. Hutchison. 1983. *Disionariu preliminariu kriolu.* Boston: Anytype.

Pontoppidan, E. 1881. Einige Notizen über die Kreolensprache der dänisch-westindischen Inseln. *Zeitschrift für Ethnologie* 13: 130–138.

Poyen-Bellisle, R. 1894. Les sons et les formes du créole des Antilles. Unpub. Ph.D. dissertation, University of Chicago. Baltimore: John Murphy.

Pringle, I. 1985. More on the origin of *say* and *se* as complementizers in English-based creoles. Unpublished manuscript.

Rademeyer, J. H. 1938. *Kleurling-Afrikaans. Die taal van die Griekwas en Rehoboth-Basters.* Amsterdam: Swets en Zeitlinger.

Raidt, E. H. 1983. *Einführung in Geschichte und Struktur des Afrikaans.* Darmstadt: Wissenschaftliche Buchgesellschaft.

Rawley, J. A. 1981. *The transatlantic slave-trade: a history.* New York, London: Norton.

Reinecke, J. E. 1937. *Marginal languages: a sociological survey of the creole languages and trade jargons.* Ph.D. dissertation, Yale University. Ann Arbor: University Microfilms International.

  1969. *Language and dialect in Hawaii: a sociolinguistic history to 1935.* S. Tsuzaki (ed.). Honolulu: University Press of Hawaii.

  1977. Foreword to Valdman (ed.) 1977: vii–xi.

  1981. A selective chronology of creole studies. *Carrier Pidgin* supplement. September 1981.

  1983. William Greenfield: a neglected pioneer creolist. In Carrington *et al.* (eds.) 1983: 1–12.

Reinecke, J. E. and A. Tokimasa. 1934. The English dialect of Hawaii. *American Speech* 9: 48–58, 122–131.

Reinecke, J. E., S. M. Tsuzaki, D. DeCamp, I. F. Hancock, and R. E. Wood (eds.) 1975. *A bibliography of pidgin and creole languages.* Honolulu: University Press of Hawaii.

Rens, L. L. E. 1953. *The historical and social background of Surinam's Negro English.* Academisch proefschrift. Amsterdam: North Holland.

Révah, I. S. 1963. La question des substrats et superstrats dans le domaine linguistique brésilien: les parlers populaires brésiliens doivent-ils être considérés comme des parlers "créoles" ou "semi-créoles"? *Romania* 84: 433–450.

Richardson, L. A.   1977.   The phrasal conjunctor and the comitative marker in Papiamentu. *Amsterdam Creole Studies* 1: 55–68.

Rickford, J. R.   1974.   The insights of the mesolect. In DeCamp and Hancock (eds.) 1974: 92–117.

  1976.   *A festival of Guyanese words*. Turkeyen: University of Guyana.

  1977.   The question of prior creolization in Black English. In Valdman (ed.) 1977: 190–221.

  1980.   How does *doz* disappear? In Day (ed.) 1980: 77–96.

  1986.   Social contact and linguistic diffusion: Hiberno English and New World Black English. *Language* 62 (2): 245–289.

  1988.   *Dimensions of a creole continuum*. Stanford: Stanford University Press.

Robertson, I. E.   1979.   Berbice Dutch: a description. Unpublished Ph.D. dissertation, University of the West Indies, St. Augustine.

  1986.   Substratum influence in the grammar of Berbice Dutch. Paper presented to the Society for Caribbean Linguistics, Trinidad.

Robins, R. H.   1967.   *A short history of linguistics*. Bloomington, London: Indiana University Press.

Römer, R.   1977.   Polarization phenomena in Papiamentu. *Amsterdam Creole Studies* 1: 69–79.

Rotimi, O. and N. Faraclas.   forthcoming.   *A dictionary and grammar of Nigerian Pidgin*.

Rountree, S. C.   1972a.   The phonological structure of stems in Saramaccan. In Grimes (ed.) 1972: 22–27.

  1972b.   Saramaccan tone in relation to intonation and grammar. *Lingua* 29: 308–325.

Rountree, S. C. and N. Glock.   1982.   *Saramaccan for beginners: a pedagogical grammar of the Saramaccan language*. Paramaribo: Summer Institute of Linguistics.

Rowlands, E. C.   1959.   *A grammar of Gambian Mandinka*. London: School of Oriental and African Studies, University of London.

  1969.   *Teach yourself Yoruba*. London: English Universities Press.

Russell, T.   1868.   *The etymology of Jamaica grammar, by a young gentleman*. Kingston: DeCordova, MacDougall, and Co.

Ryan, P. A. N.   1985.   *Macafouchette: a look at the influence of French on the dialect of Trinidad and Tobago*. Port of Spain.

Sabino, R.   1986a.   An examination of copula in Negerhollands. Paper presented to the Society for Caribbean Linguistics, Trinidad.

  1986b.   Another step towards a characterization of the Negerhollands tense and aspect particles. *Amsterdam Creole Studies* 9: 47–71.

St. Jacques-Fauquenoy, M.   1972a.   Le verbe *être* dans les créoles français. In *Langues et techniques, nature et société*. Paris: Klincksieck, pp. 225–231.

  1972b.   *Analyse structurale du créole guyanais*. Paris: Klincksieck.

Saint-Quentin, A. de.   1872.   *Étude sur la grammaire créole*. Paris: Maisonneuve.

Sandoval, Padre A. de.   1627.   *De instauranda Aethiopum salute*. Seville.

Sankoff, G. and P. Brown.   1976.   The origins of syntax in discourse: a case study of Tok Pisin relatives. *Language* 52 (3): 631–666.

Sato, C. J. and A. Reinecke.   1987.   John E. Reinecke: his life and work. In Gilbert (ed.) 1987: 3–22.

Sawyerr, H. A. 1940. The Sierra Leone Patois: a study of its growth and structure, with special reference to the teaching of English in Sierra Leone. Unpublished M.Ed. thesis, University of Durham.

Scantamburlo, L. 1981. *Gramática e dicionário da língua criol da Guiné-Bissau (GCr)*. Bologna: Editrice Missionaria Italiana.

Schneider, G. D. 1960. Cameroons Creole dictionary. Unpublished manuscript, Bamenda.

—— 1966. West African Pidgin English: a descriptive linguistic analysis with texts and glossary from the Cameroon area. Unpublished Ph.D. thesis, Hartford Seminary Foundation, Athens, OH.

Schuchardt, H. 1881. Review of Coelho (1881). *Zeitschrift für romanische Philologie* 5: 580–581.

—— 1882a. Kreolische Studien. I. Ueber das Negerportugiesische von S. Thomé (Westafrika). *Sitzungsberichte der kaiserlichen Akademie der Wissenschaften zu Wien* 101 (2): 889–917.

—— 1882b. Kreolische Studien. II. Ueber das Indoportugiesische von Cochim. *Sitzungsberichte der kaiserlichen Akademie der Wissenschaften zu Wien* 102 (2): 799–816.

—— 1883a. Kreolische Studien. III. Ueber das Indoportugiesische von Diu. *Sitzungsberichte der kaiserlichen Akademie der Wissenschaften zu Wien* 103 (1): 3–18.

—— 1883b. Kreolische Studien. IV. Ueber das Malaiospanischen der Philippinen. *Sitzungsberichte der kaiserlichen Akademie der Wissenschaften zu Wien* 105 (1): 111–150.

—— 1883c. Kreolische Studien. V. Ueber das Melaneso-englische. *Sitzungsberichte der kaiserlichen Akademie der Wissenschaften zu Wien* 105 (1): 151–161. (Reprinted in English in Schuchardt 1979: 18–25; 1980: 14–23.)

—— 1885. *Ueber die Lautgesetze: gegen die Junggrammatiker*. Berlin: Oppenheim. (Reprinted and translated in T. Vennemann and T. Wilbur. 1972. Schuchardt, the neogrammarians, and the transformational theory of phonological change. *Linguistische Forschungen* 26. Frankfurt: Athenäum.)

—— 1887. Review of da Costa and Duarte. 1886. *O creôl de Cabo Verde*. In *Literaturblatt für germanische und romanische Philologie* 8: 132–141.

—— 1888a. Kreolische Studien. VII. Ueber das Negerportugiesische von Annobom. *Sitzungsberichte der kaiserlichen Akademie der Wissenschaften zu Wien* 116 (1): 193–226.

—— 1888b. Beiträge zur Kenntnis des kreolischen Romanisch II. Zum Neger-portugiesischen Senegambiens. *Zeitschrift für romanische Philologie* 12: 301–312.

—— 1888c. Beiträge zur Kenntnis des kreolischen Romanisch III. Zum Neger-portugiesischen der Kapverden. *Zeitschrift für romanische Philologie* 12: 312–322.

—— 1888d. Kreolische Studien. VIII. Ueber das Annamito-französische. *Sitzungsberichte der kaiserlichen Akademie der Wissenschaften zu Wien* 116 (1): 227–234.

—— 1889a. Beiträge zur Kenntnis des kreolischen Romanisch IV. Zum Neger-portugiesischen der Ilha do Príncipe. *Zeitschrift für romanische Philologie* 13: 463–475.

—— 1889b. Beiträge zur Kenntnis des kreolischen Romanisch V. Allgemeineres über das Indoportugiesische (Asioportugiesische). *Zeitschrift für romanische Philologie* 13: 476–516.

—— 1889c. Beiträge zur Kenntnis des kreolischen Romanisch VI. Zum Indoportugiesischen von Mahé und Cannanore. *Zeitschrift für romanische Philologie* 13: 516–524.

1889d.   Beiträge zur Kenntnis des englischen Kreolisch II. Melaneso-englisches. *Englische Studien* 13: 158–162. (Translated in Schuchardt 1979: 7–14; 1980: 23–29.)

1889e.   Beiträge zur Kenntnis des englischen Kreolisch I. *Englische Studien* 12: 470–474. (Translated in Schuchardt 1980: 30–37.)

1890.   Kreolische Studien. IX. Ueber das Malaioportugiesische von Batavia und Tugu. *Sitzungsberichte der kaiserlichen Akademie der Wissenschaften zu Wien* 122 (9): 1–256.

1891.   Continuation of Schuchardt (1890). *Literaturblatt für germanische und romanische Philologie* 12: 199–206.

1893.   Review of I. Vila. 1891. Compendio de la doctrina cristiana en castellano y fa d'Ambú . . .; Elementos de la gramática ambú ó de Annobón. *Literaturblatt für germanische und romanische Philologie* 14: 401–408.

1909.   Die Lingua Franca. *Zeitschrift für romanische Philologie* 33: 441–461. (Translated in Schuchardt 1979: 26–47; 1980: 65–88.)

1914a.   *Die Sprache der Saramakkaneger in Surinam.* Amsterdam: Johannes Müller. (Preface [pp. iii–xxxvi] translated in Schuchardt 1979: 73–108; 1980: 89–126.)

1914b.   Zum Negerholländischen von St. Thomas. *Tijdschrift voor nederlandsche taal-en leterkunde* 33: 123–135. (Translated in Schuchardt 1979: 48–58.)

1979.   *The ethnography of variation: selected writings on pidgins and creoles,* edited and translated by T. L. Markey. Ann Arbor: Karoma.

1980.   *Pidgin and creole languages: selected essays,* edited and translated by G. G. Gilbert. Cambridge: Cambridge University Press.

Schultze, E.   1933.   Sklaven- und Dienersprachen (sogen. Handelssprachen); ein Beitrag zur Sprach- und Wanderungs-Soziologie. *Sociologus* 9: 377–418.

Schumann, C. L.   1778.   Saramaccanisch Deutsches Wörter-Buch. ms. Paramaribo: Moravian Archives. (Published in Schuchardt 1914a.)

1783.   Neger-Englisches Wörterbuch. ms. Paramaribo: Moravian Archives. (Published with annotations by Kramp [1983].)

Schumann, J. H.   1978.   *The pidginization process: a model for second language acquisition.* Rowley MA: Newbury House.

Sebba, M.   1983.   The syntax of serial verbs: an investigation into serialisation in Sranan and other languages. Unpublished D.Phil. dissertation, University of York.

1984a.   Serial verb or syntactic calque: the great circuit of *say.* Paper presented to the Society for Caribbean Linguistics, Jamaica.

1984b.   Serial verbs: something new out of Africa. In Sebba and Todd (eds.) 1984: 271–278.

Sebba, M. and L. Todd (eds.)   1984.   Papers from the York Creole Conference, September 24–27 1983. *York Papers in Linguistics* 11. Department of Language, University of York.

Sebeok, T. A. (ed.)   1968.   *Current trends in linguistics. vol. 4. Ibero-American and Caribbean linguistics.* The Hague: Mouton.

Shilling, A.   1976.   Negation in Bahamian English. Paper presented to the Society for Caribbean Linguistics, Guyana.

Siegel, J.   1983.   Koineization and the development of Fiji Hindustani. ms.

Silva, B. Lopes da.   1957   *O dialecto crioulo de Cabo Verde.* Lisbon: Imprensa Nacional.

Singler, J. V.   1981.   *An introduction to Liberian English.* East Lansing: Michigan State University African Studies Center/Peace Corps.

1984.   Variation in tense–aspect–modality in Liberian English. Unpublished Ph.D. dissertation, University of California at Los Angeles.

1985.   The story of *o*. Paper presented at the 16th Conference on African Linguistics, Yale University.

1986a.   African languages and Caribbean creoles. Course at Linguistic Society of America Summer Institute, City University of New York.

1987b.   Remarks in response to Derek Bickerton's "Creoles and universal grammar: the unmarked case?" *Journal of Pidgin and Creole Languages* 1 (1): 141–145.

forthcoming a.   On the marking of temporal sequencing in Liberian English. In S. Ash (ed.) *Proceedings from the 13th NWAVE Meeting.* New York: Harcourt Brace Jovanovich.

forthcoming b.   Hypercorrection and the creole continuum: *-s* and *-d* in Liberian English. In C. Duncan-Rose *et al.* (eds.) *Rhetorica phonologica syntactica: papers presented to Robert P. Stockwell by his friends and colleagues.* Amsterdam: John Benjamins.

Smith, I.   1979a.   Convergence in South Asia: a creole example. *Lingua* 48: 193–222.

1979b.   Substrata verus universals in the foundation of Sri Lanka Portuguese. *Papers in pidgin and creole linguistics* 2, Pacific Linguistics A (57). Canberra: Australian National University, pp. 183–200.

Smith, M. G.   1972.   The plural framework of Jamaican society. In P. Baxter and B. Sansom (eds.) *Race and social difference.* Harmondsworth: Penguin, pp. 257–274.

Smith, N. S. H.   1987.   The genesis of the creole languages of Surinam. Unpublished Ph.D. dissertation, University of Amsterdam.

Smith, N. S. H., I. Robertson, and K. Williamson.   1987.   The Ijo element in Berbice Dutch. *Language in Society.*

Spencer, J. (ed.)   1971.   *The English language in West Africa.* London: Longman.

Stassen, L.   1985.   *Comparison and universal grammar.* Oxford: Oxford University Press.

Stein, P.   1984.   *Kreolisch und Französisch.* Tübingen: Niemeyer.

1986a.   Les premiers créolistes: les frères moraves à St. Thomas au 18e siècle. *Amsterdam Creole Studies* 9: 3–17.

1986b.   The documents concerning the Negro Dutch language of the Danish Virgin Islands, St. Thomas, St. Croix and St. John – Negerhollands – in the Unitäts-Archiv (Archives of the Moravian Brethren) at Herrnhut. A commented bibliography. *Amsterdam Creole Studies* 9: 19–31.

Stein, P. and H. Beck.   forthcoming.   *Kommentierte Ausgabe der Sklavenbriefe aus St. Thomas, 1737–1768.* Hamburg: Buske Verlag.

Stewart, W. A.   1962.   Creole languages in the Caribbean. In F. A. Rice (ed.) *Study of the role of second languages in Asia, Africa and Latin America.* Washington: Center for Applied Linguistics, pp. 34–53.

1965.   Urban Negro speech: sociolinguistic factors affecting English teaching. In R. W. Shuy (ed.) *Social dialects and language learning.* Champaign IL: National Council of Teachers of English, pp. 10–18.

1967.   Sociolinguistic factors in the history of American Negro dialects. *Florida FL Reporter* 5. Reprinted in Wolfram and Clarke (eds.) 1971: 74–89.

Stolz, T.   1986.   *Gibt es das kreolische Sprachwandelmodell? Vergleichende Grammatik des Negerholländischen.* Frankfurt, Bern, New York: Peter Lang. Europäische Hochschulschriften 21 (46).

Sylvain, S.   1936.   *Le créole haïtien: morphologie et syntaxe.* Port-au-Prince, Wetteren: Imprimerie de Meester.

Taylor, D. R.   1947.   Phonemes of Caribbean Creole. *Word* 3: 173–179.
    1951.   Structural outline of Caribbean Creole. *Word* 7: 43–59.
    1953.   Review of Hall *et al.* (1953). *Word* 9: 292–296; 10: 91–92.
    1956.   Language contacts in the West Indies. *Word* 13: 399–414.
    1959.   On function words versus form in "non-traditional" languages. *Word* 15: 485–589.
    1960.   Language shift or changing relationship? *International Journal of American Linguistics* 26: 155–161.
    1963.   The origin of West Indian creole languages: evidence from grammatical categories. *American Anthropologist* 65: 800–814.
    1971.   Grammatical and lexical affinities of creoles. In Hymes (ed.) 1971: 293–296.
    1977.   *Languages of the West Indies.* Baltimore: Johns Hopkins University Press.
Teyssier, P.   1959.   *La langue de Gil Vicente.* Paris: Klincksieck.
    1983.   La négation dans les créoles portugais. Paper presented at the 17e Congrès International de Linguistique et Philologie Romanes, Aix-en-Provence.
Thomas, G.   1698.   *An historical description of the province and country of West-New-Jersey.* London.
Thomas, J. J.   1869.   *The theory and practice of creole grammar.* (1969 reprint. London: New Beacon Books.)
Thomason, S. G.   1980.   On interpreting "The Indian interpreter." *Language in Society* 9: 167–193.
    1983.   Genetic relationship and the case of Ma'a (Mbugu). *Studies in African Linguistics* 14 (2): 195–231.
    1984.   Is Michif unique? Unpublished manuscript.
Thomason, S. G. and A. Elgibali.   1986.   Before the Lingua Franca: pidginized Arabic in the eleventh century AD. *Lingua* 68: 407–439.
Thomason, S. G. and T. Kaufman.   forthcoming.   *Language contact, creolization, and genetic linguistics.* Berkeley: University of California Press.
Thompson, R. W.   1961.   A note on some possible affinities between the creole dialects of the Old World and those of the New. In Le Page (ed.) 1961: 107–113.
Tinelli, H.   1981.   *Creole phonology.* The Hague, Paris, New York: Mouton.
Todd, L.   1973.   To be or not to be? What would Hamlet have said in Cameroon Pidgin? An analysis of Cameroon Pidgin's "be" verb. *Archivum Linguisticum* 4: 1–15.
    1974.   *Pidgins and creoles.* London, Boston: Routledge and Kegan Paul.
    1984.   *Modern Englishes: pidgins and creoles.* Oxford: Basil Blackwell.
Todd Dandare, R.   1978.   Negation and interrogation in Papiamento. Paper presented to the Society for Caribbean Linguistics, Barbados.
Trudgill, P. (ed.)   1984.   *Language in the British Isles.* Cambridge: Cambridge University Press.
Turner, L. D.   1949.   *Africanisms in the Gullah dialect.* (1974 reprint. Ann Arbor: University of Michigan Press.)
Valdman, A.   1968.   Language standardization in a diglossia situation: Haiti. In J. Fishman (ed.) *Readings in the sociology of language.* Paris, The Hague: Mouton, pp. 313–326.
    1970.   *Basic course in Haitian Creole.* Bloomington: Indiana University Press.
    (ed.)   1977.   *Pidgin and creole linguistics.* Bloomington: Indiana University Press.
    1978.   *Le créole: structure, statut et origine.* Paris: Klincksieck.
    1983.   Creolization and second language acquisition. In Anderson (ed.) 1983: 212–234.
Valdman, A. and A. Highfield (eds.)   1980.   *Theoretical orientations in Creole studies.* New York: Academic Press.

Valdman, A., S. Yoder, C. Roberts, and Y. Joseph. 1981. *Haitian Creole–English–French dictionary*. Bloomington: Indiana University Creole Institute.

Valkhoff, M. 1966. *Studies in Portuguese and creole with special reference to South Africa*. Johannesburg: Witwatersrand University Press.

1972. *New light on Afrikaans and 'Malayo-Portuguese.'* Louvain: Peeters.

Valkhoff, M. et al. (eds.) 1975. *Miscelânea Luso-Africana: colectânea de estudos coligidos*. Lisbon: Junta de Investigações Científicas de Ultramar.

Valls, L. 1981. *What a pistarckle! A dictionary of Virgin Islands English Creole*. St. John, US Virgin Islands.

van Diggelen, M. 1978. Negro-Dutch. *Amsterdam Creole Studies* 2: 69–100.

van Dyk, P. 1778. *Nieuwe en nooit bevoorens geziene onderwijzinge in het Bastert Engels . . .* Amsterdam: Jacobus van Egmont.

van Ewijk, P. A. H. 1875. *Nederlandsch–Papiamentsch–Spaansch woordenboekje*. Arnhem.

van Ginneken, J. 1913. *Handboek der nederlandsche taal . . . Deel I. De sociologische structuur der nederlandsche taal*. Nijmegen: Malmberg.

Van Name, A. 1869–70. Contributions to creole grammar. *Transactions of the American Philological Association* 1: 123–167.

Vendryes, J. 1921. *Le langage: introduction linguistique à l'histoire*. Paris: Renaissance du Livre.

Voorhoeve, J. 1953. *Voorstudies tot een beschrijving van het Sranan Tongo (Negerengels van Suriname)*. Amsterdam: Noord-Hollandsche UM.

1957. The verbal system of Sranan. *Lingua* 6: 374–396.

1961. Le ton et la grammaire dans le saramaccan. *Word* 17: 146–163.

1962. *Sranan syntax*. Amsterdam: North Holland.

1970. The regularity of sound correspondences in a creole language (Sranan). *Journal of African Languages* 9: 51–69.

1971. Church creole and pagan cult languages. In Hymes (ed.) 1971: 305–316.

1973. Historical and linguistic evidence in favor of the relexification theory in the formation of creoles. *Language in Society* 2: 133–145.

Warantz, E. 1983. The Bay Islands English of Honduras. In Holm (ed.) 1983: 71–94.

Warner, M. 1971. Trinidad Yoruba: notes on survivals. *Caribbean Quarterly* 17 (2): 40–49.

Washabaugh, W. 1977. Constraining variation in decreolization. *Language* 53 (2): 329–352.

1980. From preposition to complementizer in Caribbean English creole. In Day (ed.) 1980: 97–110.

1983. The off-shore island creoles: Providencia, San Andrés, and the Caymans. In Holm (ed.) 1983: 157–179.

Weinreich, U. 1953. *Languages in contact: findings and problems*. The Hague: Mouton.

Welmers, W. E. 1973. *African language structures*. Berkeley: University of California Press.

Westermann, D. and M. Bryan. 1952. *Languages of West Africa*. Handbook of African languages, vol. 2. Oxford: Oxford University Press.

Whinnom, K. 1956. *Spanish contact vernaculars in the Philippine Islands*. Hong Kong: Hong Kong University Press.

1965. Contacts de langues et emprunts lexicaux: the origin of the European-based creoles and pidgins. *Orbis* 14: 509–527.

1977. Lingua Franca: historical problems. In Valdman (ed.) 1977: 295–312.

Williamson, K. 1965. *A grammar of the Kolokuma dialect of Ijo*. Ibadan.

Wilson, W. A. A.   1962.   *The Crioulo of Guiné.* Johannesburg: Witwatersrand. University Press.

Winford, D.   1985   The syntax of *fi* complements in Caribbean English Creole. *Language* 61 (3): 588–624.

Wolfram, W. and N. Clarke (eds.)   1971.   *Black–White speech relationships.* Washington: Center for Applied Linguistics.

Wood, R. E.   1972.   The hispanization of a creole language: Papiamentu. *Hispania* 55 (4): 857–864.

Wullschlägel, H. R.   1856.   *Deutsch–Negerenglisches Wörterbuch.* (1965 reprint, Amsterdam: S. Emmering.)

Wurm, S. A.   1977.   The nature of New Guinea Pidgin. In Wurm (ed.) 1977: 511–532.

(ed.)   1977.   *New Guinea area languages and language study.* vol. 3. Language, culture, society and the modern world, Pacific Linguistics series C 40. Canberra: Australian National University.

Yansen, C. A.   1975.   *Random remarks on Creolese.* Margate: Thanet Press.

Zinzendorf, N. von.   1742.   *Büdingische Sammlung einiger in die Kirchen-Historie einschlagender Schrifften.* vol. 1. Büdingen: Stöhr. (1965 reprint. Hildesheim: Olms.)

Zyhlarz, E.   1932–33.   Ursprung und Sprachcharakter des Altägyptischen. *Zeitschrift für Eingeborenen-Sprachen* 23: 25–45, 81–110, 161–194, 241–254.

INDEX

Page numbers in *italics* refer to maps or tables; headings in **bold** are languages (or varieties). The following abbreviations are used: def., defined; P/C, pidgin and/or creole; see also key to maps 1 and 2.

Abaco, 76
abbreviations, xv, 72
Abe, 88
abolition of slavery, 22, 54
abrupt creolization, 8(def.), 64, 66
acrolect, 9(def.), 54, 108
Adam, L., 15, 28–31
adjectival verbs, 64, 85–6, 100, 189–90
  and 'be', 176–7
  comparison of, 189–90
  and preverbal markers, 177
adjectives, 85–6
  comparison of, 32, 189–90
adstrate, 11(def.), 89, 92–6, 105, 216
adult second-language acquisition, *see*
  second-language acquisition
affinities among Atlantic creoles
  lexical, 24, 28, 71–104
  phonological, 31–2, 71, 105–43
  syntactic, 11, 24, 32, 61, 64, 71, 144–215
African languages, 11, 22, 44, 50, 61, 68,
  74, 218
  influence on creoles, 19, 26, 28–9, 31–2,
  38, 106
  lexical influence, 74, 79–89; calques, 86–
  8; lexical items, 80–2; reduplication,
  88–9; semantic influence, 82–4;
  syntactic influence on creole lexicons,
  85–6
  P/Cs based on, *xvii*, 47
  phonological influence of, 105–43 *passim*
  retention in New World, 79–80
  semantic influence of, 82–4
  syntactic influence of, 144–215 *passim*

Africanists, 68, 138
Afrikaans, *xvi*, 10, 35, 53, 69, 73, 174, 179,
  191, 198, 212
  nonstandard, 157, 193, 198
agglutination, 98
  of articles, 97
Akan languages, 67, 135, 186, 205, 210
al-Bakrī, A., 14
Alleyne, M., 37, 42, 50, 54, 66
allomorphs, 96, 135–6, 191
allophones, 107, 135, 137
Allsopp, R., 45
Alsatian German, 44
American Black English, *see* **Black English,**
  American
American Indian English, 30
Amerindian languages, 92–3, 95
  P/Cs based on, *xvii*, 39, 47
anaphors, 169
Anglo-Romani, 10
Angola, 145
Angolar CP, *xvi*
Anguila, *xix*
animate/inanimate, 193, 195
Annobón CP, *xvi*, 30, 41
anterior tense, 28, 46, 85–6, *149*, 151(def.),
  152–4, 156–7, 166–7, 176
  versus completive aspect, 162
  with future, 164
anthropologists, 36–7
Antigua, *xix*
aphasics, 2
aphesis, 109(def.)
apicals, 135(def.), 136, 180

CONTENTS OF VOLUME II